March of America Facsimile Series

Number 37

A Journal of the
Proceedings in Georgia

VOLUME II

William Stephens

—

A Journal of the Proceedings in Georgia

VOLUME II

by William Stephens

ANN ARBOR

UNIVERSITY MICROFILMS, INC.

A Subsidiary of Xerox Corporation

A Journal of the
Proceedings in Georgia
VOLUME II

A

JOURNAL

OF THE

PROCEEDINGS

IN

GEORGIA,

BEGINNING

OCTOBER 20, 1737.

By *WILLIAM STEPHENS*, Esq;

To which is added,

A STATE of that PROVINCE,

As attested upon OATH

IN THE

COURT of SAVANNAH,

November 10, 1740.

VOL. II.

LONDON:

Printed for W. MEADOWS, at the *Angel* in *Cornhill.*
MDCCXLII.

JOURNAL

CONTINUED.

EDNESDAY. Wrote fome 1739. Letters to the South, and fent them, together with what came Yefterday, to *Frederica*, St. *Simon's* Camp, &c. by Mr. *Mace*, who took fpecial Charge of what related in a more particular Manner to the General; and promifed a fafe Delivery of the reft. Mr. *Horton*, on his Return from *Matthews's*, acquainted me (with equal Satisfaction to us both) that he and his Wife had promifed him to go forthwith, and wait on the General in the Camp, with Intent to fhew

May 2.

1739. their Readineſs, in whatever he required of

May them concerning the late Movement of the *Indians*; and that old *Tomo Chichi* would go alſo, and lay what Reſtraint on them he could, from proceeding any farther in what they purpoſed. In theſe three Days that Mr. *Horton* had been in Town, I could plainly diſcover what Sort of Sentiments he began to entertain of the Place, from ſuch Talk as we had together: And indeed a Man of much leſs Diſcernment, could not well miſs in that Space of Time, to find Demonſtration ſufficient to convince him what Miſchief an intemperate, ſelf-ſufficient Conduct, cloathed with Power, is capable of creating in the Publick.

3.   *Thurſday.* In the Morning, Mr. *Horton* calling on me, it was thought a fit Time to enquire into another Affair, that he was charged with from the General, to learn the Truth of; relating to an Information made (as noted 23 *ult.)* wherein the General's own Safety ſeemed to be in Danger: In Order whereto, Meſſ. *Parker* and *Gilbert* (two Magiſtrates) aſſembled at my Houſe, Mr. *Chriſtie* the Recorder being out of Town; and the Informant *Green* being ſent for, together with his Boy *Cundal*, Mr. *Robert Williams* the Owner of the Sloop, and —— the Maſter of her, were alſo called: Then *Green* being aſked if he

was

was sure he knew the Men again when
he saw them, with whom he had that
Talk on *Saturday* Night was Se'nnight, on
board the Sloop; and both he and his
Boy affirming, that they should know
them upon Sight; they were sent with a
Constable on board the Sloop to find them;
as they readily did, and came all together
before the Magiftrates; where, upon a ftrict
and careful Examination, the Informants
Green and his Boy did feverally make Affidavit to this Effect, *viz.* That upon their
going aboard the Sloop on the *Saturday*
Night, as aforefaid, and afking what News
from the South; the two Men now prefent,
whofe Names were *Nelfon* and *Conn*, the
one Mate, and the other a Sailor belonging to the faid Sloop, anfwered him in
thefe or the like Words: " The Soldiers at
" the Camp told us they heard the Gene-
" ral was laid hold on at *Charles-Town*;
" which they faid they were glad to hear;
" for if ever he came among them at the
" Camp again, fome of them would give
" him a Pill; and if one did not fhoot
" him, another would; after which they
" would go off to the *Spaniards*, &c."
To which the two Sailors now prefent
anfwered, That they utterly denied their
having ever faid fo much: They acknowledged the firft Part of it, that the Soldiers

talked

talked of the General's being in Cuſtody at
Charles-Town; but farther than that, they
never heard, nor did they ſay they had,
which they offered to ſwear, if they might
be allowed ſo to do; but that not being
admitted, they objected againſt the Credit
of *Green* the Informer, who they heard
had a bad Character, and indeed he had
not a good one; he having been formerly
convicted of bad Crimes, and his Teſtimo-
ny on ſome Occaſions in our Court being
regarded but very little by our Juries : Neverthelefs, on ſuch poſitive Evidence, nothing could be done leſs than ſending them
down to the General at *Frederica*, or con-
fining them here till the General's Pleaſure
ſhould be farther known : Whereupon they
rather choſe to be ſent thither inſtantly, to
make their Defence, left by delaying it,
they might loſe the proceeding on their
Voyage ; and therefore making it a Requeſt of their own, the Magiſtrates allowed it, and Lieutenant *Horton* undertook to
carry them down with him when he went.

4.   *Friday.* Among other Things ſent from
the Truſt by the Ship *America* lately arrived, was a Parcel of Vine-Cuttings, which
with proper Care in packing would have
been extreamly valuable, and are much
coveted : But unhappily they came naked,
without any Covering, and only bound up
like

like a common Faggot; so that being in 1739.
that Manner exposed, and possibly thrown
carelesly up and down in the Voyage, they May
had the Appearance of no other than a 4.
Bundle of dry Sticks; adding to all which,
the uncommon Length of Time in their
Passage, being several Months; I was very
sorry to see little or no Hopes left, of any
Good to be expected from what was so
truly desirable : Nevertheless, that nothing
might be omitted which could be done, I
called *De Lyon* the *Jew* to my Assistance,
who has the most Skill of any among us,
and has planted some Hundreds of the
Portugal Grape this Year, out in his Plantation, which he reared last Year from
Cuttings and otherwise : And when I had
ordered a Spot of fresh Ground, in the
Swamp of the Garden belonging to the
Trust, to be cleansed and dressed, I left it
to him to put some of them into the Earth,
that we might at least try if any of them
would haply make Shoot. *N. B.* He told
me, that the Time they were cut in *(viz.
December)* was a right Season, and had
they been rightly packt too, notwithstanding so long a Passage, he believed most of
them might have been saved : Wherefore
for future Instruction, I learnt of him,
that the proper Way of preserving the Cuttings, is to fill a Cask half full of good

1739.
May

Earth, wherein the Cuttings are to ſtand
half their own Depth, and the Tops of
them only bound with Straw, without any
other Covering, by which the Air may
come to them ſo much as is proper; but
no Sprey of the Sea; wherefore they ſhould
not be expoſed upon Deck. I found nothing elſe all Day, which I thought ſo
much worth my regarding as this.

5.
Saturday. Mr. *Horton* went off this
Morning, on his Return to the General at
Frederica, taking with him thoſe he deſigned. Mr. *Bradley,* I was informed,
killed another Steer, which he called his
own; but other People were of a different
Opinion, and thought him making the
moſt of what was in his keeping, before
he ſurrendered all up.

6.
Sunday. Mr. *Haberſham* read the Prayers
of the Church, as before, in Mr. *Norris's*
Abſence; and two Sermons on the Working of God's Holy Spirit within us.

7.
, Monday. What I had to obſerve now
principally was, the Diſlike which the Magiſtrates and Mr. *Jones* had conceived a-
gainſt each other, and which was every
Day (as I thought) increaſing, notwithſtanding all the Endeavours I had a good
while uſed to reconcile ſuch Differences,
and to bring them into better Temper;
that by uniting heartily, the publick Good
might be the ſooner promoted: But all I
could

could fay began to be but little regarded on
either Side; fo keen was their Refentment
grown of late. What feemed to be the
Ground-Work of all this was, that Mr.
Jones thought he had not Deference enough
paid him; and they thought what they had
paid him was too much. He by Virtue of
Power fuperior to any (which he had, or
appeared to have) expected the ready Attendance of the Magiftrates whenever he
pleafed to fend for them; and they complained of being treated in the Manner of
ordinary Servants, to come wherefoever he
pleafed to call them; and moreover when
met, they faid they were looked on as
Cyphers, and hardly allowed to examine
into Facts, but required to act in every
Thing as Mr. *Jones* dictated, &c. This
they had often expreffed great Uneafinefs
at to me, thinking themfelves made contemptible to the common People; and I
had frequently on fuch Occafions, when I
faw Matters of Confequence like to pafs
too lightly over, made Ufe of an Expedient to bring them together, without Di-
minution of either of their Authority (fo
highly rated) by engaging them all to meet
at my Houfe; which fucceeded well, and
I hoped a little Time would wear out
thefe pernicious Jealoufies; till *Monday* the
23 *ult.* all fuch Hopes began utterly to va-
nifh; and from that Time they are grown

more

more and more exafperated on both Sides
(vide the Notes of that Day.) Mr. *Chriſtie,*
as I apprehend, was a little too dilatory
then, in coming on that Occaſion ſo long
after the Time appointed; in which to
vindicate himſelf, he alledged afterwards,
that he did not know it was a Matter of
ſuch Importance, and believed it would
make no Difference whether he came in a
Quarter of an Hour, or ſtaid a whole one:
But to have the Door ſhut againſt him in
that ſcandalous Manner, was uſing him ſo
as he could not bear: From whence aroſe
that ſmart Tongue-Fight betwixt him and
Mr. *Jones* at *Jenkins's* ſoon after (as noted.)
The ſame Afternoon, the Magiſtrates aſ-
ſembling all three at my Houſe, without ſo
much as my knowing it, ſent a Meſſenger to
find me, and very well pleaſed I was to be
ſo ſent for, that the Truth might be enquired into of that Morning's Outrage:
And I wiſh that Mr. *Jones,* who was in the
ſame Manner ſent to, had gone as readily:
But upon his returning that rough Anſwer,
they all cried out immediately, "Now you
"ſee how we are uſed;" and ſo breaking
up, went their Way. The next Day
Mr. *Jones* purſued his Deſign of going to
wait on the General at *Frederica*; and
there being two Steers killed before he went,
for the neceſſary Support of ſuch as had
any Dependance on the Stores; when the
Meat

Meat was given out in small Pieces the Day
after, and every Body that had any Pretence, was defirous of getting a Bit of frefh
Meat (none falt at the fame Time in the
Store) Meff. *Parker* and *Chriftie* each fent
to afk for a little; but were anfwered, that
Mr. *Jones* had left Orders there was none
for *them*. This put them both into very
ill Mood, and made them exclaim heavily
to be fo fingled out. *Chriftie* declared publickly his pofitive Refolution of going foon
for *England,* &c. &c. *Parker* grew fullen,
and faid, it could not be poffible for him
to act the Part of an honeft Man, if he
muft be in Dread of the Store being fhut
againft him, whenever in the Execution of
his Office he differed in Opinion with Mr.
Jones; and came to me this Day purpofe-
ly to acquaint me, that he would be ready
at any Time to come to me, or meet me
when fent for, on any Thing relating to
the Publick, provided it was not to attend
Mr. *Jones*; but whatever were the Confequence, he never would wait on him
again as a Magiftrate, who fhould expect
Mr. *Jones* to come to him, if he had any
Thing to fay to him as fuch. Which Declaration of his, was the Occafion of this
long Paragraph, reciting fome Occurrences
previous thereunto.

Tuefday. Divers Servants being lately 8.
run away from their Mafters, which there
was

was Reaſon to believe were got the Length of *Charles-Town*, where they found Shelter, as Experience had too often ſhewn: At the ſame Time having full Information by Mr. *Shenton*, who had apprehended him, that *Iſaac Bradford*, that notorious Thief, who lately had committed ſo many Villanies here, was, at the Inſtance of the Perſon that took him, committed to Goal there by the civil Magiſtrate; it was thought proper to ſend a Boat with proper Inſtructions, as well to demand the Criminal, in order to his being brought to Juſtice, as alſo to diſcover and retake (if poſſible) ſome, if not all of thoſe Deſerters. Taking an Opportunity to talk with Mr. *Jones* on the Subject-Matter of the Magiſtrates Uneaſineſs; and letting him know what it was that they ſeemed moſt to ſtick at: He ſhewed no Concern about it; but told me, he ſaw what they would be at, was an unlimited Credit in the Stores: Which effectually ſtopt me from going farther; for as he had the Cuſtody of all, and muſt account for what he did, as well as others; he certainly ought to obſerve ſuch Rules as were given him, and it was not my Buſineſs to perſuade him to deviate from them, not knowing what Lengths they went: So I left it to him to do as he thought fit; but ſaw plainly, from many Inſtances,

Inftances, he had fet himfelf againft them both.

Wednefday. Mr. *Jones* being required to call on Mr. *Bradley*, to furrender up all Things in his Cuftody belonging to the Truft, purfuant to his Agreement with the General lately at *Charles-Town*; and defiring me to be prefent at his demanding it, I was fo: When Mr. *Bradley* made Shew, by his Words, of his Readinefs to do it; but at the fame Time made Ufe of a little Chicanry (as I thought) to put it off for a while, by faying, that he ought firft to have the General's Orders in Writing before he could be juftified in fo doing: And fo we parted; Mr. *Bradley* appearing pleafed at the Anfwer he had given to that Demand.

Thurfday. Lieutenant *Dunbar* arriving this Morning from the South in one of the Scout-Boats, he fpent fome Time with Mr. *Jones* in private; but as he was not pleafed to fee me, going on the fame Day for *Palachocolas*, all that I could come at the Knowledge of was, that he was to take fome Horfes there for the General's Service, which he was to convey over Land from thence Southward. Mr. *Jones*, in the Afternoon, calling on me, faid, he was quite empty of Meat in the Stores, having none to feed even the Truft's Servants; and wifhed to have two or three Steers killed for that

that Purpofe: Whereupon knowing that
Mr. *Parker*, who had the Care of thofe
Steers, had alfo Orders from the General
to deliver at any Time to Mr. *Jones* what
he needed of them; I told him, that he
had no more to do, but to fend Directions
to Mr. *Parker* about it, who without Doubt
would take Care they fhould be brought
up: But was furprized at his faying, whatever the Want was, he would neither afk
him, nor fend him any Directions about it:
However, that the publick Service might
not thereby fuffer, Mr. *Mercer* being prefent, I defired him to acquaint Mr. *Parker*
with it, who I was confident would readily fee it done; and Mr. *Mercer* promifed
me to let him know it.——To fuch a
Height was Mr. *Jones*'s Refentment grown
fince the 23d paft.

11.   *Friday.* Upon the Notice that Mr. *Mercer* gave, Mr. *Parker* took Care to fee three
Steers brought in this Day for the Ufe of
the Stores; in which Service he got a fevere Fall with his Horfe upon him, that
had well nigh fpoiled him. Moft of my
Time and Thoughts this Day were employed in promoting what was needful to
be done about the Corn, &c. which I had
planted this Spring; for unlefs continual
Attendance was given, in houghing the
Ground, and keeping down the Weeds,
that grew apace, all our paft Labour would
come

come to Nought; and the villanous Falf-
hood of thofe Servants I had, without frequent Infpection, would not allow me to
hope for any Good ; neither with all the
Care that my Son and I could ufe, was it
in our Power to attain that Perfection we
propofed to ourfelves, almoft in any Work:
But if we could come up to, *cæteris pari-
bus*, in keeping clean what Ground we
had planted, we muft not look for more.

Saturday. Finding myfelf under a little
Indifpofition, I kept home, and began pre-
paring neceffary Papers to make up another
Packet for *England*. 12.

Sunday. Mr. *Norris* being yet in the
South, Mr. *Haberfham*, as before, went on
with the proper Service of the Day, in
reading the Common Prayer, and after it
fome of Archbifhop *Tillotfon*'s Doctrine,
which is fo univerfally admired. 13.

Monday, ⎱ Thefe two Days I fpent 14.
Tuefday. ⎰ wholly at the Mouth of *Ver-* 15.
non River, having Mr. *Mercer* with me,
whofe Judgment in many Things relating
to Improvements, I approved of very well,
and therefore confulted him fometimes:
Moreover, he had lately obtained from the
General a Promife of a Grant of three
hundred Acres upon Leafe, under the fame
Covenants with feveral others ; and as he
had a View of being near the fame Place,
I was willing to promote it, and get him
fixed

fixed my next Neighbour, being affured in myfelf, that he would not be idle upon it: Our Bufinefs now was to look narrowly into, and make fuch Obfervations, that we might, at our Leifure, be contriving betwixt ourfelves at home, what was proper to be done as foon as it was furveyed, and Poffeffion given us. At my Return home on *Tuefday* Evening, what I met with for News was, that Captain *Shubrick*, in the *Mary Ann*, was newly arrived at *Charles-Town*; by whom Mr. *Verelft*, in his laft Letter, promifed me I fhould hear fully from the Truft; but was now forry to hear it reported by fome who came lately from *Charles-Town*, that Captain *Shubrick* was bound to *Frederica*, as foon as he had delivered what Merchants Goods he had aboard him for *Carolina*; and that he would deliver no Letters for *Georgia* till he came to *Frederica*, where he would deliver them himfelf: But when that would be, who could tell? Which gave me a little Uneafinefs, being what I could not underftand the Meaning of.

16.　　*Wednefday. Samuel Lacy* arrived this Morning from *Charles-Town*, and brought with him four Letters from *England*, that were put under Cover for the General, and fent to me by the Attorney-General; which Cover, when I had opened, I found three of the faid Letters came by Captain *Shubrick*,

Shubrick, and one of them by Captain *Gerald*; by whom alfo came other Letters, which I received (as noted) the 1ft Inftant; fo that it appeared to me, that all thefe Letters came over from *England* in the common Bag, and were taken up by the Attorney-General at the Poft-Office; which made me give the more Credit to what was faid laft Night, of Captain *Shubrick*'s having with him a Packet from the Truft not yet delivered : In the Afternoon Mr. *Purry* arrived from *Charles-Town*, and brought with him a Packet of more Letters for the General, and others at St. *Simon*'s, which came under Cover to Lieutenant Governor *Bull*, from whom Mr. *Purry* received them, and delivered them to my Care. Mr. *Jones* told me, that he had a Letter or two alfo for the General from *Charles-Town*; but did not acquaint me who it was that fent it to him. By all thefe fcattered Letters thus collected, and none from the Truftees Office ; it appeared now paft all Doubt, that *Shubrick* had the Truft's Packet with him, which he would not deliver till he arrived himfelf at *Frederica*, or fome other Port in *Georgia*; which might be a great while yet to come.

   Thurfday. Mr. *Hird*, a Freeholder, and one of the Conftables at *Frederica*, after two or three Days fpent here on his own Affairs, intending to return thither this

     17

2   Day;

Day; I delivered into his Care all the Letters that came to my Hands Yesterday, making them up in one Packet for the General; to whom also I wrote myself in Answer to one which I had through Mr. *Jones*'s Hands from him. Captain *Wood* from *Frederica*, in his Way to *Charles-Town*, came ashore here last Night, and called on me this Morning; but brought no Letters. Very heavy Rain came on in the Morning, and held all Day; which prevented both Captain *Wood* and Mr. *Hird* from setting out on their Passages North and South till another Day.

18. *Friday.* Little happening worth Notice abroad, stuck mostly at home to my Pen and Ink. Captain *Wood* and Mr. *Hird* went off their several Ways. In the Evening I was informed, that Bailiff *Parker* had received a Letter from the General, signifying his being informed by Mr. *Jones* of an Intention some Persons had to make Waste of certain Stores belonging to the Trust, and requiring him to look into it, and take Care that the Trust might not be injured in their Property : Wherein my Son apprehending, that Mr. *Jones* had again been doing him some ill Office with the General, relating to some Wines bought of Colonel *Cockran*; he now expected and wished that Affair might be thoroughly canvassed, so that it might appear with

what

what Juftice fuch an Accufation was brought 1739.
againft him: The Particulars of which ought
not to be paffed over, without a full and May
explicit Relation of the Whole, when Mr.
Jones fets forth before the Magiftrates what
he has to alledge.

Saturday. Got forward with what Pa- 19.
pers and Letters I had to fend to *England*;
and loft as little Time as I could to make
another Packet ready, not knowing how
long it might be, ere we heard from Captain *Shubrick*, whether he had any Letters
for us, or what they were; which I wifhed
to have learnt. My Son expected to have
been called before the Magiftrate, purfuant
to what we were informed Yefterday; but
Mr. *Jones* had yet made no Step about it,
and what he had to fay, as well as when,
was wholly in himfelf. Towards Evening
Captain *Defbraffie*, and Enfign *Maxwell*,
arrived from the South, by whom I had a
Letter from the General, and one under
the fame Cover for Mr. *Jones*, which I delivered to him inftantly; he accompanying
thofe Gentlemen to my Houfe.

Sunday. This Morning two Letters 20.
were brought me by a Servant of Mr.
Cuthbert, which his Mafter fent him with,
from his Plantation at *Jofeph's Town*, where
they came to his Hands from Lieutenant
Willy in the *Indian* Nations; the Contents
of one of which would require my laying

1739. it before the General. Mr. *Haberfham*,
May during Mr. *Norris's* yet continuing in the
South, performed the Duty of the Day in
the fame Manner he before had done.

21.   *Monday*. Bailiff *Parker*, in Obedience
to the General's Letter (as mentioned the
18th) calling the other Magiftrates together; Mr. *Jones* at the fame Time appearing, together with all Parties fuppofed to
be concerned, *viz.* my Son and I, and Mr.
Bradley; Mr. *Parker* read Extract out of
the faid Letter from the General to him,
in thefe Words: " Mr. *Jones* acquaints me,
" that fome Perfons have refufed to deliver
" to the Truftees their Wines by them
" bought, and the Poffeffion of their own
" Cellar. I hope you will fee Juftice done
" to the Truftees, and that they are not
" ftript of their Properties with Impuni-
" ty." Which Words, importing a grievous
Charge, that without Doubt pointed particularly at my Son; it will be needful to
look back, and trace this Matter from the
Beginning, that the whole Truth may be
underftood. ———— When Colonel *Cockran*
came hither with Part of the Regiment
in *May* laft Year, and brought a large Parcel of Wines with him, Part for the Regiment, and Part for his own Account; he
found no Place in the Town fo capable
and fit to put them in, as a Cellar under
the great Houfe that Mr. *Bradley* lived in,
and

and was vulgarly called Mr. *Bradley*'s Houſe:
Whereupon Colonel *Cockran* applied himſelf to Mr. *Bradley* for the Uſe of it on
that Occaſion; who readily granted it;
and when the Wine was all ſecured there;
the Colonel knowing my Son, gave him
the Cuſtody of the Wine, with the Key of
the Cellar, &c. (for farther Information,
vide 10th of *March* laſt.) After a whole
Year paſt, and all the Wine diſpoſed of;
the Cellar was now cleared of the Whole,
excepting only two Pipes of Wine, which
had been bought for the Uſe of the Truſtees Stores, and yet remained there: On
which Account Mr. *Jones* demanded of
my Son the Keys of the Cellar, intending
to make Uſe of it for the Truſt; but
Mr. *Bradley* had cautioned him ſome Time
before not to deliver the Keys to any one
but himſelf; from whom he ſhould expect
them; for though he had lent the Uſe of
the Cellar for a Seaſon, to anſwer a certain Purpoſe; yet he would not give up
his Property in it: Which put my Son
under ſome Doubt what Courſe he muſt
take to be ſafe; often telling Mr. *Jones*,
that he might ſend for the Wines when
he pleaſed; but was deſirous to avoid having any Contention with Mr. *Bradley*, and
only wiſhed to have Directions that were
proper from one that would ſupport him.
Matters thus depending, and my Son
dreaming

dreaming no Harm; Mr. *Jones* gave him
this Wound in the Dark, fetting forth
thefe Tranfactions in fuch a Manner, as
fhewed plainly the General was irritated,
by what he had wrote to Bailiff *Parker*.
But now on Enquiry before all the Magiftrates (for I refolved to have it difcuffed as
publickly as might be) it appeared on full
Proof, that my Son was perfectly blame-
lefs; that he had never refufed delivering
the Truft's Wine; that there was not the
leaft Shadow of his being concerned in fo
vile an Act, as ftripping the Truft of their
Property; and that the only Thing he
boggled at, was whether he was legally
cautioned or not by *Bradley* about furren-
dering the Keys: Which the Magiftrates
now gave their Judgment in, and made
an Order, that the Keys fhould be delivered
up for the Ufe of the Truft: This my Son
was very glad of, being thereby freed from
any farther Care about it: And this might
have been done much fooner, had Mr.
Jones applied himfelf to the Magiftrates,
who would readily, at any Time, make
Enquiry into Abufes of fuch Kind, if any
there are, and rectify them: But that he
feems to think is condefcending too much,
and wherever he apprehends his Will is
obftructed, he makes no Scruple of heaping Abundance on the General for Advice;
a great deal more (as fome think) than
the

the General cares to be troubled with, unlefs where Matters of Difficulty and Importance require it. My Son could not
help thinking this Act of Mr. *Jones*'s
favoured of much Ill-will towards him,
and muft be reprefented in a very bad Light
to the General, that it produced fo fharp
an Anfwer; when he was confcious of no
Crime he had committed: And bringing
frefh to his Remembrance the Difpleafure
of the General, which he unhappily (tho'
innocently) fell under in a former Affair
(March 10.) it affected him deeply, and fo
difcouraged him, that it became a Matter
of great Concern to myfelf. Lieutenant
Delegal arrived in the Evening, on his Way
to St. *Simon*'s from *Port-Royal*.

Tuefday. This Morning my Son delivered up the Keys of the Cellar for Mr.
Jones's Ufe; taking one of his Men with
him, to fee that the two Pipes of Wine
there for the Truft were perfectly full, and
in good Condition. Captain *Defbraffie*,
and Enfign *Maxwell*, who arrived here on
Saturday from the South, taking a Tour
up the River to vifit fome Friends, and being not yet returned; and Lieutenant *Delegal* arriving here fince, in his Way from
Port-Royal Southward; he thought fit to
wait their coming, not knowing what Orders he might meet with by them from the
General.

Wednef-

Wednesday. The General in a late Letter recommending it to me to settle the Matter amicably, between those who hunt Cattle for themselves, and the Pindar appointed by him, great Variance already arising among them; I got the Pindar, and two or three of the principal among the others, to my House; where with a little cool Reasoning, and soft Words, shewing them how much it was all their Interest to agree, and be assisting to one another; I soon brought them to good Temper, and at length to (I hope) a perfect Unity. On which Occasion I cannot help reflecting on the like Success I have often met, in healing Discord among some that have been at Strife, by the like Means; and it is most certain these People pay more Regard to gentle Treatment, than to Menaces; which generally sit sour upon them, and often do more Harm than Good.

24. *Thursday.* Expected to have sent several Letters (some of which were from myself, and some from others) to the South by Lieutenant *Delegal,* who was going to wait on the General, but I was disappointed; for he no sooner saw Captain *Desbraffie* and Ensign *Maxwell,* but he met with such Orders as obliged him to return to *Port-Royal* with them, on some particular Business of the Regiment; so that I knew no more when or how I should
have

have Opportunity of fending them, than I
did thofe I had prepared to go to *England*.

Friday, } The long continued Series
Saturday. } of perfect Health, which
had been fo remarkable ever fince the laft
Fall, throughout the Colony, began a little
to alter with us: The great Viciffitude of
Weather, betwixt Thunder, Rain, and fultry Heats (all violent in their Turns for a
few Days paft) catched many People una-
wares, and taught them to be more cautious hereafter, not to expofe themfelves to
fuch Inclemencies more than Neceffity required; from whence Fevers began again
to grow rife among us all on a fudden;
and though I had been but little abroad of
late at fuch Seafons, yet feveral ugly Symp-
toms began to tell me it was Time to take
Care of myfelf; wherefore I thought it
not amifs to confine myfelf thefe two Days,
when by Abftinence, and a little Self-De-
fence, I began to hope the worft was
over. Mr. *Bradley* called on me on *Saturday,* to let me know that he was going
again to make a fhort Trip to *Charles-Town,*
if I had any Service that Way; and that
he intended not to ftay there above three
or four Days; how far he meant as he
faid, he beft knew himfelf; the common
Talk of the People was, that fome of his
beft and choiceft Goods were fent before;
fuch as Scrutores, fine Tables and Chairs,

with

with other fashionable Furniture, which
was moftly the Operation of an ingenious
Workman, whom either the Truft or Mr.
Bradley paid (I know not which) and was
employed many Months on fuch Curiofi-
ties; and as he had now but a fmall Remainder of his Family left here, which I
knew not when he meant fhould follow the
reft, I had no great Inclination to commit
my Packet to his Care, that I defigned for
England; but would rather take another
Chance.

27.   *Sunday.* Mr. *Haberfham*, as before, continued to read the Prayers and a Sermon;
whilft the Return of Mr. *Norris* began now
to be thought long. In the Evening by a
trading Boat arriving, bound up the River,
I had Opportunity of fending inclofed, under Cover, to Lieutenant *Kent* at *Augufta*, a
Letter from the General to Mr. *Willy* in the
Creek Nation.

28.   *Monday.* Nothing ftirring that was worth
Obfervation; only a Difference happening
betwixt Captain *Davis*, Owner of a Snow
laden with Lumber for the *Weft-Indies*,
which now lay at *Tybee* ready for failing,
and the Mafter which he had put in her;
it produced great Controverfy before the
Magiftrates, where many People had the
Curiofity to attend; and both of them
pleaded their Parts fo well, that there was
great Difficulty in fo uncommon a Cafe to
decide

decide it to general Satisfaction; neither

was it ended the whole Day.

Tuesday. The Contention yet continuing as Yesterday betwixt Captain *Davis* and the Master, whose Name was *Pope*; it may not be improper to take some Notice of the Cause whence it arose; which from what I could collect, was thus: *Davis* had newly built this Snow at *Port-Royal*, where *Pope*, who was a good Carpenter, as well as a good Seaman, had a good Hand in hastening the Work, and getting her out to Sea; when by Promise before made from *Davis*, he took to her as Master, and brought her to *Savannah*, where *Davis* had made his Abode for some Time, and now was settling in good Earnest, having lately the Favour of one of the best Lots on the Strand granted him by the General, whereon he was intending to build a Dwelling-House and Store-House, &c. being a Man who in all Appearance traded with the most Money of any that used the Place, and had generally three or four Sloops, Snows, or such like Vessels, going and coming betwixt these Parts and *Augustin*, the *West-Indies*, or elsewhere, that he found most to his Advantage: In which Capacity he was looked on, and regarded, by all who wished well to the Colony, as an useful Man to promote Traffick. But his most visible Foible, was keeping a Mulatto

latto Servant (or Slave) who in Reality was his Miſtreſs: For he had in former Years, by trading much in the hotteſt Parts of *America*, contracted ſuch Diſtempers, as well nigh bereft him of the Uſe of both his Legs and Arms: And this Girl (who was of an exceeding fine Shape, and ſetting aſide her ſwarthy Countenance, might compare with an *European)* was of much Uſe to him; not only as an Helper to put on his Cloaths, dreſs him, and look after his Linen, *&c.* which ſhe did to great Perfection; but having very good natural Parts alſo, and by Length of Time having obtained good Knowledge of his Buſineſs, and learnt to look into Accounts; he ſuffered almoſt every Thing to paſs through her Hands, having ſuch Confidence in her, that ſhe had the Cuſtody of all his Caſh, as well as Books; and whenever he ordered any Parcel of Silver to be weighed out for any Uſe, whether it were two or three hundred Ounces, more or leſs, in Dollars, ſhe had the doing of it: And as this had been the Courſe of ſeveral Years paſt, wherein he had found her very faithful, and of great Service to him; it may eaſily be ſuppoſed the Life of ſuch Slavery was not a heavy Burden upon her, and that ſhe had Art enough to ſhew, all Perſons who had any Buſineſs with Captain *Davis*, were expected not to treat her with Contempt.

Contempt. It so happened, that *Pope*, who is a rough Tar, and naturally surly, upon some Difference with this Damsel, made Use of some Words she did not like; and she wanted not to return in softer Terms what was not a Jot less provoking; whereupon he gave her a Stripe cross the Face with her own Fan; and having raised such a Flame in the House, left it. The Snow was now at *Tybee* ready for sailing, and Mr. *Robert Williams*, who had a good Share with *Davis* in the Loading, was intending, together with his Brother, to go Passengers to St. *Kit*'s, where, upon their Arrival, it was agreed, that *Williams* should have the Direction of all Things, and to freight her from thence as he saw good, to what Port he thought most likely to turn to Account. This (it seems) was what *Pope* neither expected or liked, depending on it, that on the Delivery of the present Cargo at St. *Kit*'s, the whole Direction of all was to devolve to him, and that he was to be both Master and Supercargo; on which Occasion some Words falling from him, which *Davis* could not well relish, and the Abuse of Madam being also fresh in Memory, *Davis* told him he discharged him from being Master of the Snow; and that he was ready, upon making up his Accounts, to clear with him, and pay him what was owing for Wages: To which the other

replied,

replied, it was not in his Power to difcharge him from the Ship in fuch a Manner, neither would he fubmit to it; and
thereupon went haftily to his Boat, in order to go immediately on board, and keep
Poffeffion: To prevent which *Davis* and
Williams with fome others, went to the
Guard, and defired them to ftop the Boat
as fhe was paffing by; for that *Pope* was
running away with the Boat, and afterwards with the Ship, in a piratical Manner. And the Guard finding upon hailing the Boat, that they refolved to keep
on their Way, did their Duty, and fired a
Gun to bring them to; whereat they
came afhore. This was on *Sunday* Night
laft about Eleven a Clock; and the next
Day Complaint on all Sides was made to
the Magiftrates, when the Complainants
inveighed heavily againft each other; but
it was too knotty a Point for them to
determine upon hafte, being doubtful of
their own Knowledge; and informed moreover, that it ought regularly to be brought
before the Admiralty; wherefore they proceeded no farther, than to direct *Pope* to
make up his Accounts with *Davis* as faft
as he could; in order to which, his Cheft
was to be fent for afhore with his Papers;
but he was not permitted to go aboard
himfelf, without *Davis*'s Knowledge, fearing the Confequence might be his going to
Sea

Sea as foon as he fat his Foot upon the
Deck. So ended this Affair on *Monday:*
And this Day divers Meetings were had
again about it; when all Expectance of ac-
commodating Matters were given over on
both Sides; and hard Speeches, with
Threats, fucceeded. By this Time it began to be the Opinion of moft Folk, that
forafmuch as Mr. *Robert Williams*'s Brother was to go a Paffenger, who was a
good Seaman, and had been Mafter of feveral Ships; it was thought expedient by
them, that it would be well, as one of
them had the Difpofal of the Cargo, the
other alfo might have the Direction of the
Ship as Mafter; in order to which Captain
Davis had been perfuaded to lay hold of
this Quarrel, and put *James Williams* in
Mafter, in the Room of *Pope*, at fo fhort
Warning.

Wednefday. The fame Controverfy ftill 30.
increafing, drew the Attention of many
People, efpecially fuch as made themfelves
Partifans in the Difpute; but I did not
want Employment any Day fufficient to
take up my Time, about my own proper
Bufinefs, without meddling of what did
not belong to me. *Pope* was now ready
to make up his Accounts; but having the
Regifter of the Ship in his Poffeffion, could
not be perfuaded to give up that, alledging,
that there were feveral Bonds out againft
him,

him, which he had entered into as Master; beside, that the Sailors, who were all shipped by him, might come upon him for Wages for the Time he had been Master, in case they had not a Mind to re-ship themselves under a new Master: Whereupon our naval Officer, Mr. *Fallowfield*, being out of Town, was sent for in order to get a new Register; and Mr. *Williams*, impatient at these Delays, brought an Action against *Pope* of several hundred Pounds Damages, for detaining Vessel and Cargo; to answer which, *Pope* not readily finding Bail, Mr. *Parker* withdrew, not apprehending how such Damages could ensue, by a Vessel delayed a few Days, that was only loaden with Lumber; and Mr. *Gilbert* being likewise away, Mr. *Christie* took the farther Proceedings on himself; and, at the Instance of the Complainants, committed *Pope* to Prison, for not offering Bail.

31.   *Thursday.* All pretty quiet this Day: *Pope* shut up fast, made an open Field for his Adversaries to triumph in; and Mr. *Fallowfield* provided them with a new Register, to Content. Very near a Fortnight was now past, since I had prepared a Packet for the Trustees, to go by the Way of *Charles-Town*, or any other, if I could find it; but no Opportunity offered in all that Time, to my Sorrow, which I had too often experienced.

Friday.

Friday. Very early this Morning Mr. *Williams* and his Brother went for *Tybee,* in order to bring the Snow to fail, which they feemed more than ordinary hurried in, upon fome Intelligence they had got, that the Admiralty, at the Inftance of *Pope,* were intending to ftop the Veffel. *Pope* was now out of Prifon, upon offering Bail; and refolved not to fit quiet without carrying Matters as far as he could: Wherefore he in his Turn alfo brought an Action of Damages to the Value of   *l.* againft *Davis,* which he likewife was to find Bail to; and fo for the prefent this Difpute ceafed. Mr. *Parker* with me this Morning, complaining of Mr. *Jones's* dealing fo intolerably with him, that he could not bear it, and that his Servants whom the Truft had ordered to be provided for, would be obliged to leave him, and get their Bread where they could, Mr. *Jones* refufing to allow any Thing farther towards their Support; I told him, that as I knew nothing of the Rules Mr. *Jones* went by, nor what Orders he might be under about the Delivery of Stores; it would not become me to be too officioufly meddling; but his proper Way, was to apply to the General, who was now in the Province, and was the only Perfon to judge what was proper in this Cafe, as well as all others that required immediate Determination; and therefore I advifed

1739.
June

advifed to put what he had to fay in Writing, and fend it to him, not doubting but
he would take it into Confideration.

2.

Saturday. All People moft worth regarding, looked peaceably after their own
Affairs, and attended what would conduce
to their Benefit; efpecially the Planters,
whofe prefent Care was to fubdue the
Weeds from annoying the Corn, &c. in its
Growth; which my good Folk would have
been well content to have allowed, unlefs
quickened by frequent Infpection.

3.

Sunday. That notorious Rogue *Ifaac
Bradford*, who was lately taken at *Charles-
Town*, and brought back to Prifon here,
that he might anfwer for his Crimes at our
Seffions (which were on his Account adjourned a while, till the principal Evidence
againft him returned, who at prefent was
in the South) this Morning early found
Means to break out of Prifon; which gave
Caufe of Uneafinefs to many People, who
knowing him to be fo dextrous and accom-
plifhed a Villain, expected more Mifchief
would be done, unlefs he could foon be taken; which there were but little Hopes of.
It was moft probable, that his Efcape was
owing to the Negligence of his Keeper,
who had fuffered feveral to get off in the
fame Manner; particularly the Ring-leader
of thofe three Deferters from the Regiment,
as formerly noted, who could never fince
be

be recovered. Mr. *Norris*'s Abode in the 1739.
South yet, fhewed that he was welcome
there; and though he found fome Marks June
of a cold Reception here at his firft Arrival, from Caufes that having been formerly
taken Notice of, need not be again repeated *(vide October* 22.) yet his Abfence now
was generally regretted to that Degree, that
moft People wifhed apparently for his Continuance among us, and no more Changes.
Mr. *Haberfham* in the mean while read the
appointed Service of the Day, &c. as before.

Monday. Bailiff *Parker* called on me in   4.
the Forenoon again, and now told me,
that his Cafe was become fo defperate, as
not to admit of any farther Delay, for that
his Servants were upon leaving him, which
muft end in his own Deftruction; for that
his Plantation now to be neglected, muft
occafion his irreparable Lofs, it being the
principal Dependance he had for the next
Year's Support of himfelf and Family;
wherefore he was feeking to get a Boat and
two or three Hands, which fhould carry
him to wait on the General wherever he
could find him. My Son, who was daily
more intent on his intended Voyage to
England, but had yet taken no Step towards
it; upon hearing this, concluded it a lucky
Conjuncture for him; forafmuch as he
would by no Means ftir in it, till he had

firſt paid his Duty to the General, and thought he now had the faireſt Opportunity he could wiſh: Wherefore he preſently laid hold of it; and Mr. *Parker* and he agreeing upon it together, whilſt I ſat ſtill and ſaid nothing; in the Cool of the Evening they both ſet out for *Frederica*.

5. *Tueſday.* Nothing particularly worth remembring happened this whole Day, that came to my Knowledge.

6. *Wedneſday.* *Peter Emery* arrived with his Boat from *Charles-Town*, and brought two ſmall Packets, which the Attorney-General ſent me, that he had by two Ships newly arrived; and wrote a ſhort Letter with them, adviſing me, that one of thoſe Ships came by Way of *Madera*, and the other in ſix Weeks from *London*; by which he found he might expect ſome more Letters by another Ship which ſailed ſome Days before *him*. In theſe Packets were Letters for the General, &c. and one for me from Mr. *Verelſt* of the 15th of *February*; incloſing Copy of the Minutes on Mr. *Cookſey*'s Petition, and referring ſeveral Reſolutions taken thereon by the Common-Council, for me to enquire into Facts, and report them to the honourable Truſtees. Mr. *Verelſt* was pleaſed alſo to ſignify to me, the favourable Diſpoſition of thoſe Gentlemen, to gratify my Requeſt formerly made, concerning *Joſeph Watſon*'s

five

five hundred Acre-Lot; which I had wrote them he never had a Grant of, nor shewed any Regard to; and at that Time I had a great Inclination to fix upon, for Reasons then given; wherefore they were now pleased to direct, that I should state the Case with respect to *Watson*'s Pretensions to it, or the Value of any Improvements made upon it. Mr. *Verelst* farther added, that my Journals and Letters to *November* 21, were come to Hand, and would be answered by the *Mary Ann*, Captain *Shubrick*, who has been arrived at *Carolina* several Weeks since, and is now at *Frederica* (as I hear) but no News of any Letters by him for me yet.

Thursday. Understanding early in the Morning, that a Boat was setting out South by Order of Mr. *Jones*, who (it was said) intended to go as far as *Skeedoway*, expecting there to find Captain *Desbrassie*, &c. on their Return to St. *Simon*'s from *Port-Royal*; and Information coming Yesterday, that the Scout-Boat those Gentlemen went in, was seen to turn in at *Augustin Creek*, making their Way South: Thereupon I would not let so fair an Opportunity slip, of sending those Letters to the General, &c. which I received Yesterday; but putting them all under one Cover, directed to the General at St. *Simon*'s, I sent my Packet to Mr. *Jones*'s Care; writing also therewith,

1739.
June

a few Lines to the General from myself. Afterwards I went to make my People a Visit, and see how well they followed their Work, in fulfilling the last Directions given them; and here I employed good Part of my Time this Day.

Friday. Mr. *Jones* returned this Morning from *Skeedoway*, where he missed Captain *Desbrassie*, who continued yet at *Port-Royal*; but found Lieutenant *Delegal*, who was going South with the Boat; to whom he told me he had given Charge of my Packet to the General, together with others Letters. What the Occasion of this secret Expedition was, I could not learn. Mr. *Habersham*, the School-Master, having received a large Packet of Letters from Mr. *Whitfield*, by the same Ship that brought those I received on *Wednesday* last, directed to many People in the Town; among whom I was one; he went with particular Delight to deliver them, and rejoice at the good News of Mr. *Whitfield*'s being appointed to return again to his former Charge at *Savannah*, which those Letters from him imported. As to myself, I must own, that it was a Matter of more Indifference; for as I thought Mr. *Whitfield*, when among us, took great Pains in preaching God's Word, and doing his Duty; so I cannot say Mr. *Norris* was defective in his; and as he was particularly recommended by the

honourable

honourable Truftees, for being a Perfon of
very good Qualifications, fo I found him;
and in Obedience to their Orders, gladly
did what lay in my Power to promote a
good Opinion of him among the People at
his firft coming; which by his good Conduct he had now well eftablifhed.

Saturday. Captain *Hunt*, Mafter of a   9.
Brigantine that traded to thefe Parts from
New-York, arrived from St. *Simon*'s again,
where he had been once before, offering
his Cargo to Sale; but having (it feems)
fome Rum on board him, which he faid
he was bound to *Providence* with; the General was fo offended at his daring Prefumption to bring it into Harbour, that he
would not allow him to difpofe of any
other Goods among them; wherefore after having been and difpofed of his Rum
elfewhere, he made this fecond Offer to fell
the reft of his Cargo; but in that, he did
not yet fucceed, the late Offence given being too frefh in Memory: Neverthelefs, it
was manifeft (as I thought) that moft of
the Loading was difpofed of fome how or
another, by the Veffel's appearing fo much
lighter in the Water, than fhe formerly
did. He brought no Letters, except one
for Mr. *Jones*; nor any particular Advices,
only that our Minifter, Mr. *Norris*, was
foon coming to us again, in order to take
Leave of his Friends.

    Sunday.

Sunday. Mr. *Haberſham* continued the publick Service of the Church, Morning and Afternoon; and took Occaſion to read an Epiſtle he had received from Mr. *Whitfield*, who had directed him to do it publickly to the Congregation; wherein he acquainted them with his being appointed their Miniſter, that he was returning to them ſoon, and exhorted them to bear in Mind the Doctrine he had formerly preached among them, *&c.* In the Evening arrived *Dondonald Stewart*, with his ſmall Sloop from *Frederica*; where he had been ſome Time to attend Mr. *Brownfield*, carrying divers Goods thither to diſpoſe of; and now Mr. *Norris*, our Miniſter, returned with him; who reported, that he had been exceeding kindly treated by the People there, in every Reſpect; and that the General had been pleaſed to give him great Countenance and Marks of Eſteem. He acquainted me, that Captain *Shubrick* had been there ſeveral Days, delivering what was committed to his Charge from the Truſt; and brought me a Packet from them, which was given to the Captain's Care; wherein I found divers Letters for ſeveral People, and one from Mr. *Vereſſt* of *March* 3, which contained ſome weighty Matters that would require due Conſideration and Obedience, *&c.* But it was not in my Power to write any Thing immediately

diately about it to the Truſt, having delivered to *Peter Emery* a Packet, which he was to proceed with to-morrow Morning early for *Charles-Town* (on various Buſineſs of other People) and glad I was at laſt, after three Weeks Waiting, to catch this Opportunity; ſo uncertain and rare does any happen, to keep a due Correſpondence with *England.* The Packet that I now ſent, was directed (by a Letter I ſent with it) to the Care of Mr. *Hopton,* whom always I found very punctual in diſpatching whatever came to his Hand; and the laſt which I ſent, he had the good Luck to forward the ſame Day he received it, by Captain *Watts* in the *Greyhound,* dated *April* 21, as this was *May* 19.

Whit-Monday. High Holy-Day among   11. moſt of our common People in Town; but ſuch as were concerned in planting, could ſpare no Time from cloſe Attendance in dreſſing their Land, to preſerve the Fruit of the Ground from being over-run with Weeds.

Tueſday. Captain *Wood* of *Frederica* ha-   12. ving been ſome Time at *Charles-Town* on Account of Traffick; on his Return, ſtopt here ſince *Sunday* laſt; by whom I took Occaſion to write to the General, and ſend ſeveral other Letters, which I gave him before his Departure. *Duchee* the Potter, who I formerly took Notice had agreed

D 4   with

with the General, to build a Wharf under our Bluff, for the better Landing of Goods, having framed moſt of it, began to ſet it up; but for many Days paſt, finding many Difficulties in fixing a certain Foundation in the looſe Sand, without Piles; and often altering his Purpoſe, now ſeemed determined how to proceed, in the Manner we ſaw; which from what I could judge, as well as many others of better Experience in ſuch Works, did not promiſe any long Duration, for divers Reaſons which I thought were apparent.

13.

Wedneſday. Several *Indian* Traders began now to apply for Licences; ſome to obtain new, and ſome to renew their old ones : Wherein it was my Duty to acquaint the General with the Circumſtances as I found them, and take his Orders. I learnt by moſt of them, that divers of the Nations began to ſeek Occaſion of falling out with one another: Better ſo, than by too long Peace among themſelves, to differ with us, whoſe Buſineſs it is to avoid taking Part with one or the other, or meddling in their Quarrels (at leaſt openly.)

14.

Thurſday. Devoted this Day almoſt wholly to my little Plantation; wherein falling ſo far ſhort of the Number of Acres I had laſt Year, through the Defect of bad Servants, that inſtead of fifteen, I could not reckon fully ten; I made it my Care,
that

that what I had, fhould be at leaft as well
dreffed and cultivated as any of my Neighbours: And the Crop this Year generally
promifing very well, I concluded I fhould
have as great a Produce, at leaft, as laft
Year, out of a larger Piece of Ground,
when a dry Seafon and bad Seed was a
great Baulk to moft People: And from
hence alfo I concluded a pretty juft Efti-
mate might be made hereafter, of what
might be expected by a diligent Planter, if
the Land were reafonably good, to pay him
for his Labour.

Friday. Little in Town worth Notice.
In fome Converfation with Mr. *Norris*, I
found he was fomewhat uneafy at his Appointment here being fuperfeded by the honourable Truftees, to make Way for Mr.
Whitfield, who (he faid) had found Means
to fupplant him; which he thought little
agreed with that open Simplicity which was
made fo diftinguifhing a Part of his Character, by his Intimates at this Place; who
with the like Candour had done what in
them lay, to leffen *him* in the good Opinion of the People, though not with that
Succefs they expected; for he muft do
them the Juftice to acknowledge, he had
found a kind Reception from the Generality, and a Readinefs to attend the publick Service; wherefore he was forry to
leave them: Neverthelefs he fhould continue

1739.
June

nue doing his Duty, till Mr. *Whitfield* showed him his Authority to take his Place; and then (he seemed determined) upon quitting it, to quit *America* with it. I told him I was very sorry to hear that; for indeed I thought him a valuable Man, of good Endowments, constant in his Duty, exceeding affable and courteous, and wholly inoffensive in his Behaviour throughout: Wherefore I would persuade him not to resolve too hastily in it, since I was confident the Trustees meant it as no Disfavour towards him, and without Doubt would have an equal kind Regard to him whatever Part of the Province he resided in: Which he said little to at present, and so we parted.

16.

Saturday. Arrived a Pettyagua from *Frederica*, mostly laden with Corn; which surely was the first Instance of that Kind; and it would have been indeed worth noting, had it been the Produce of the South; but that Time is not yet come, nor (it is to be hoped) will *Savannah* suffer her younger Sister to contribute more to her Support, than she has done for herself, or will do hereafter. This Corn (as the Master reported) came from the Northern Settlements in *Carolina*; and the Stores being pretty well provided in the South, it was ordered, without landing there, to come to the Aid of those who stood in Need of

it

it in *Savannah*; where (be it as it would) it was exceeding welcome, to People who at that Time were in Want of Bread.

Sunday. Mr. *Norris* officiated regularly at Church, and administred the Sacrament; which he was prevented from doing the *Sunday* before, by a long Passage from *Frederica* by Water.

Monday. Spent some Time again with my People abroad, giving what Directions were needful. The late Rains we had, which were so seasonable and refreshing, began now to come on in so great Abundance, having continued daily, more or less, for three Weeks past, that several of our Plantations in the low Lands were overflowed, and the Corn (we feared) was in Danger of suffering Damage. Mr. *Bradley* returned home from his late Expedition to *Charles-Town*, where his Business was known to himself only. In the Evening my Son also, and Mr. *Parker*, returned from the South; where I before took Notice of the Occasion of their going *(vide* 4th Instant.) Mr. *Parker* found his Ends in some Measure answer'd, by some present kind Relief from the General, who promised him to take it into farther Consideration, as soon as he came to *Savannah*, which he designed the Beginning of next Month; from whence he intended to take a farther Progress into some of the *Indian* Nations,

Nations, where we heard he was earneſtly expected, and his Preſence would be of great Uſe, at this Time eſpecially, when the *French* and *Spaniards* were buſy infuſing what Miſchief they could, by endeavouring to alienate their Affections from us. My Son, I found, had little Satisfaction from his Journey; the General, he ſaid, retained yet a ſtrong Suſpicion of his being an Accomplice in ſome intended Fraud, about thoſe Wines of the Truſtees, remaining in *Bradley*'s Cellar; notwithſtanding that full and open Examination made into it, as related on 21 *ult.* when there appeared not the leaſt Room for any Suſpicion of ſuch a vile Practice; from whence my Son concluded his Character was ſo deeply ſtained by Mr. *Jones*, that he deſpaired of ever ſetting it right again with the General, which ſat very heavy upon him; and indeed affected me alſo now pretty much, to ſee a young Man (my Son) whom I knew to be endued with a virtuous Diſpoſition, and ſcorn'd to be guilty of baſe Acts, and uſing little mean Arts to conceal them; but was always open and honeſt, and dared be ſo, whomſoever he might give Offence to, through Want of Caution perhaps in his Words: To ſee him ſo ill treated by a Perſon whom he neither deſerved, nor expected it from (I mean Mr. *Jones)* it put me upon a little Reflexion

Reflexion on divers former Passages betwixt him and me; where he had too plainly discovered (as I thought) what an Opinion he had conceived of my Abilities, so far short of his own, whose Vanity led him to imagine he saw clearly to the Bottom of other Peoples Capacities, whilst his was unfathomable; which Conceit of his, he was welcome to enjoy; but when those boasted Talents, in Contempt of all others, are employed to the Injury of such as have done no Ill, but perhaps stand suspected by him, that they may possibly in Time be looked on too favourably; to get rid of such, may, for ought I know, require the Skill of a Man of deep Reach (an Expression he is very fond of) but I fear it will in Justice require another Name. In short, I began to think it was Time for me no longer to look on Mr. *Jones* a Friend to me, or mine; which would have been no Ways incompatible, as I apprehend, with either of our Duties to the Trust, whom we served.

Tuesday. Mr. *Obrien*, a Keeper of Stores at *New-Windsor*, coming to Town last Night, called on me, and brought with him several Licences from some of our *Indian* Traders, to be renewed in this Province; which I would lay before the General, together with some others of the like Sort for his Direction; to whom I
wrote

19.

wrote in the Evening, and sent it by Mr. *Phelps*, a Keeper of Stores with us, who was to set out early for the South, glad of such an Opportunity, which I would not miss, not knowing when I might find another. Mr. *Parker* came and told me, that he had been with Mr. *Jones*, to confer with him on what the General had said at *Frederica*; when Mr. *Jones* took out some sola Bills; (Part of them which the Trustees wrote were to be issued by Mr. *Jones*, Mr. *Parker*, and myself, or any two of us) desiring he would sign them; which Mr. *Parker* said he demurred at, asking him if he had offered any of them to me for that Purpose; by whom he was informed of the Trustees Orders; which were, that the Bills to be issued by any two of us three, were likewise to be accounted for by them that issued them, who were to certify what Uses the Produce of said Bills had been applied to; which he did not conceive was possible to be done, when the Bills so signed, were no longer within his Cognizance how disposed of. Though I heard, that Mr. *Jones* had a considerable Quantity of those Bills by him for some Days past, I was no Ways disturbed at not being taken any Notice of about them, so far was I from coveting to meddle with Matters that were not well understood at

2

present,

prefent, and might fubject me to great Inconveniencies hereafter, in accounting for.

Wednefday. This Morning I underftood that Mr. *Jones* went off very early for *Frederica*, to wait on the General; that he went out of Town on Horfeback, in Company with two or three others, among whom Mr. *Phelps* was one, to whom I had given my Letters laft Night, knowing no better; that they intended to ride fo far as Mr. *Fallowfield*'s Plantation, to which Place they had fent a Boat round to meet them. About Noon Mr. *Upton* arrived from the South, who brought no Advice of any Kind for me; but had a Letter for Mr. *Jones*, whom he miffed meeting by the Way: He had the Pleafure to tell me, that the General had been very kind to him, in taking the Land off his Hands, which had been granted him near *Frederica*, and made him a new Grant on the Ifland called *Allhony*, lying a little beyond *Skeedoway* Southward: That what he had done on his other Plantation, he was to be paid for as fhould be valued, which the General would convert to pious Ufes, *&c.* More *Indian* Traders were now frequently coming, this being the ufual Seafon of the Year for granting Licences: Two fuch were with me this Day, who were told by me, the General intending to be here very foon himfelf, it would be needlefs to write

to

to him any more about thofe Matters, which he would give his Directions about when he came.

21.　　*Thurfday.* Heavy Rains continued to fall daily, which would admit of very little Attendance from any at their Plantations, and began to raife fearful Apprehenfions of much Damage. Time paft fince the Date of my laft Packet to the Truft, put me in Mind that another might be now expected; wherefore I began to prepare what was needful, and ftirred but little from home, nor did I hear any Thing worth regarding abroad.

22.　　*Friday.* Bufy good Part of the Day in finifhing my Difpatches for *England.* It was currently reported about Town, that we might have had a little Money circulating among us, had not I been the Occafion of the contrary, by refufing to fign the iffuing of a great many fola Bills, which had been offered me by Mr. *Jones:* Whereat I was the lefs furprized, expecting fome fuch malicious Turn might be given to what paffed betwixt Meffieurs *Parker* and *Jones* on the 19th, wherein I was no Party, nor had any Bills been offered me; but *Parker's* refufing was conftrued by Mr. *Jones* my Advice; though in Truth I had not any Way confulted *Parker,* nor knew any Thing that paffed, till Mr. *Parker* informed me of it; when I muft confefs I told

told him that I thought the Anfwer he had given Mr. *Jones* was right. From hence I
had Reafon to imagine, that Mr. *Jones*'s fudden Expedition South arofe from thefe Grounds.

Saturday. Nothing obfervable happened this Day; but late in the Evening arrived a Pettyagua, fent by the Attorney-General, with two Men and five Women from *Saltzburgh*, together with fundry Goods, which he wrote me were lately arrived *per* Captain *Harramond*, and configned to him by the Truft, with their Direction to forward them to Mr. *Jones*; whereof he was to give me Notice, *viz.* eighty Barrels of Flour, thirty Cafks of Butter, fourteen of Cheefe, and a Box of Books for Mr. *Norris:* With thefe came alfo a large Packet from the Truft to me, wherein I found great Store of Letters; fome for thefe Parts, and many more for the South; efpecially divers for the General: What concerned me particularly was a Letter from Mr. *Verelft* of the 2d of *April,* fignifying the Pleafure of the honourable Truftees in divers Matters of Importance; wherein they required me to act in Conjunction with Mr. *Parker,* *Jones,* &c. *invicem,* as Occafion required: And withal had fent a Commiffion, empowering us three to examine and ftate the Truth of fundry Accounts, certified by Mr. *Caufton* to be owing from the Truft: More-

over to examine and state the several Debts owing by the Store in *Georgia* the 10th of *October* last; with which Commission came also Instructions for executing it, and for examining and stating the Accounts of Messieurs *Causton* and *Bradley*: These were Matters of so great Moment, that I had not Confidence sufficient in my own Abilities, to acquit myself, as I wished to do; but resolved to shew my Good-will towards it as well as I could, in not declining to act as far as my Understanding would admit. By several Passages in this Letter, I was now fully convinced, that I had not misconstrued the former Directions sent to Mr. *Parker* and me, relating to our joint issuing, together with Mr. *Jones*, divers sola Bills; as *per* Mr. *Verelst*'s Letter of the 3d of *March*; which Mr. *Jones* told Mr. *Parker*, we had no more to do with, than only to sign our Names *(vide* 19th Instant;) for now we were plainly appointed to cheque the Delivery of not only those Stores now sent, but also the Remains of all others. As Mr. *Jones* was now in the South attending the General, and we should probably (I thought) see upon his Return, what the General's Instructions to him were, relating to those Bills, &c. and his Excellence being also expected very soon himself, I most heartily wished to find the Way made plain wherein I was to walk, that I
might

might not be subject to stumble so frequently, and in Danger of falling into Displeasure, do what I could.

Sunday. Mr. *Norris* did his Duty at
Church as became a good Man; and after
the publick Service was over, I thought it
no Breach of the Sabbath, to divulge the
welcome News I had received of the honourable Trustees being about preparing an
Act, to enable the Possessors of Land in
Georgia, in case of Want of Issue Male, to
dispose of it by Deed or Will to their
Daughters, or for Want of such, to their
other Relations, and their Issue Male, &c.
Such Tidings soon spread thro' the Town;
nor would it be unknown long in all Parts
of the Province, to the great Joy of many People: And (if I may venture to speak
so plain, without giving Offence) I am fully persuaded in myself, that the same Act
of Grace a few Months ago, would have
produced a hundred Acres at least of Corn
more than we can now find is planted in
this Part of the Colony this Year; and I
am very confident a visible good Effect will
arise from it in another.

Monday. This being the Grand Anniversary of the Free Masons every where
(as it is said) the Brethren with us would
not let it pass without due Observance:
Mr. *Norris* accordingly was asked to give
them a Sermon, which had been customary

1739. mary with his Predeceſſors; and he made
June them an ingenious Diſcourſe, with a decent and proper Application: From Church
they marched in ſolemn Order to Dinner
at a publick Houſe, the Warden Dr. *Tailfer*
(who likes Pre-eminence as well as any
Man) attended by four or five with Wands,
and red Ribbands in their Boſoms, as Badges
of their ſeveral Offices, took Place fore-
moſt; but the Train that followed in white
Gloves and Aprons, amounted only to a-
bout Half a Dozen more; which ſome,
who are apt to burleſque the Order, turned into Ridicule. My principal Affair this
Day was, to ſend off thoſe Packets and
Letters to the General which I received on
Saturday; wherein I met with no ſmall
Trouble: None that I could apply to,
would go without ready Money; till at laſt
I prevailed with one to undertake it, upon
my perſonal Engagement to be his Pay-
Maſter, and then he went.

26.   *Tueſday*. Meſſieurs *Samuel Brown* and
Mc Bane, two *Indian* Traders, came to
Town from *Auguſta* laſt, and brought me
a Letter from Lieutenant *Kent* there; together with one *Wright*, whom Mr. *Kent*
wrote he had ſent a Priſoner; having lately taken him, and was the ſame who was
taken up laſt Summer, committed to Priſon here, and broke out of Goal on the
25th of *July* with *Hetherington, Biſhop*, &c.
But

But in their Way down the River now, a
fatal Accident happened to one *Evans*, who
was one of the two fent to guard the Prifoner; his Gun by fome Means unknown
going off, killed him outright; which was
the more to be lamented, for that he was a
fober, diligent young Man, well looked on
by all that knew him, was lately out of
his Servitude, and gave more promifing
Hopes of future Good to be expected
from him, than too many do. A great
Misfortune of another Kind, came to our
Knowledge alfo; which was, that very
much Damage was done to the Goods
which came by the Pettyagua on *Saturday*,
and which was now unloading: The Flour
and Cheefe efpecially appeared fo damni-
fied, that it was feared little or none of
it could be faved, the Wet having gone to
the very Heart of the Cafks; from whence
it was the Opinion of the moft knowing
People here, that the Damage was done at
Sea; for it is univerfally agreed, that a Cafk
of Flour well packed, though it ftand feveral Days in the Rain (as this did in an
open Pettyagua) yet will not take wet more
than an Inch in; but this in general appeared mufty and ftinking to the Centre of
it, where they bored to try; from whence
it is judged it muft have lain in Water in
the Ship's Hold. I advifed, that two or
three Men of honeft Characters, and good

Under-

Underſtanding, àmong whom one to be a Baker, ſhould take a Survey of it all upon Oath: Such being found, and looking into ſeveral Caſks before they were ſworn, they reported to me, that the whole Cargo of Flour and Cheeſe was loſt; which I was not ſo ſatisfied in, but to tell them, that till they had ſtripped the Caſks off, and gone to the Heart of it, and reported then upon Oath as they found it, I thought it was of no Significance: Whereupon, as Mr. *Jones* was expected ſoon, who was not yet returned from *Frederica*, they were of Opinion it would be beſt to wait his coming; which I had no Objection to, the Goods being all carried into the Store, and a Receipt given to the Maſter of the Pettyagua for the whole Cargo much damaged, by —— *Harris*, who acts under Mr. *Jones*; as he told me himſelf. I fear no Care was taken at *Charles-Town*, upon taking the Goods out of the Ship, to ſee whether or not they came in good Order and well conditioned, as in the Bill of Lading: And if ſo, it is farther to be doubted if Satisfaction for the Damage will with great Difficulty be come at.

27.   *Wedneſday*. Little to be done in Town; wherefore I took Occaſion to look again into what my few Hands were doing at my Plantation; which I found drenched with Water by the heavy Rains, which

had

had fallen for fo long a while paft, and
did not yet ceafe in frequent Showers;
but we hoped yet upon Change of Weather, to find the Corn recover. Fevers began now to grow rife, occafioned by a
thick, unwholfome Air, and fultry Heat;
but they did not yet prove very mortal:
Only Mr. *Bradley* lay dangeroufly ill, in
one that he brought home with him.

Thurfday. Not the leaft Appearance
this whole Day of any Thing worth taking any Notice of.

28.

Friday. The fame. Mr. *Jones* ftaying
fo long from home, gave Occafion to many
of thinking that he would return when
the General came, and not before; and as
I had good Reafon to believe, that the Difpatches from the Truft, &c. which I fent
off on *Monday* laft, were now before the
General; I hoped he would fo well confider of thofe Directions I had received from
the Truft, that I might be under no Miftake in the Conftruction of them, nor become liable to any Blame for not executing
them.

29.

Saturday. All Things feemed at a Stand,
and fcarcely any Body ftirring. The Stores
had no Flefh Provifion of any Kind to give
out to the *German* Truft Servants, who
were ill fatisfied to live upon Bread Kind
alone, till better could be; tho' it was too
evident, that the Bread they eat, was more

30.

than

than they earned; and many poor People in Town (that I knew) were hard put to it to provide *that* for themfelves. Some proper Courfe, without Doubt, would be taken by the General when he came, to make fuch Provifion for the future, as he fhould think neceffary. This proving a fine Day, and the only one without Rain for a long while paft, we hoped good Summer Weather was coming feafonably, to ripen the Fruits of the Earth.

Sunday. The publick Service was performed by Mr. *Norris* with due Decency: About Noon happened a moft violent Tornado, with fuch a Guft of Wind and Rain, as we had fcarcely feen the like, holding for about Half an Hour; in which Time feveral of the Huts and weaker Buildings about Town were blown down, and even the ftrongeft fhook, fo that we were apprehenfive of much Mifchief; and there was Reafon to fear, that we fhould find a great deal of the ftrongeft Corn blown down.

Monday. People upon a Review of what Damages the Storm Yefterday might occafion, had the Satisfaction to find it much fhort of their Fear; fo that the old Adage of being more afraid than hurt, was literally verified: And the Weather again promifing fair in Appearance, we hoped the foul had taken its Leave in this laft Effort.

Effort. Many *Indian* Traders were now in Town, in order to get Licences; for which End they waited the General's Arrival, whom, together with Mr. *Jones*, we looked for every Day. Several printed Papers (being Extracts of the *Weekly Miscellany* in *London*, Nº 320.) were sent from *Charles-Town* by some Persons there, to their Acquaintance here; in which Mr. *Whitfield* particularly, as well as the whole Sect of Methodists, were so animadverted on, that it was like to be the Entertainment of most publick Conversation, for some Time; and appeared to be an odd Preparative for Mr. *Whitfield*'s Reception, whenever he came. It is said, that Mr. *Cooksey* brought over a Number with him when he came to *Charles-Town* lately; where I am informed he has taken up his Residence, and bid Adieu to *Georgia*, for some Time at least.

Tuesday. *John Penrose*, whom I hired to go with his Boat on the 25th *ult.* for *Frederica*, and carry that Packet to the General, now returned, and brought me a short Letter from Mr. *Jones*, signifying, that the General intended to set out from *Frederica* as Yesterday, or this Day at farthest, in his Way hither, and thence up into some of the Nations; so that we looked for him now every Day. Hearing that one Mr. *Cattle* was in Town, who is a Merchant in *Charles-Town*, I found him, and afked the Favour of him to carry a fmall Packet, which I had for Mr. *Verelft*, defiring he would deliver it to Mr. *Hopton*'s Care, whom I alfo wrote to with it; and he readily promifed me to do it, intending to be going very early to-morrow Morning. *N. B.* This was the Packet which I inclofed on the 22d *ult.* and this was the firft Opportunity I could find fince of fending it.

4.　　*Wednefday.* Rain ceafing now for two or three Days, and hot Weather fucceeding, as in this Part of the Year might be expected, the Waters began to fink away, which had overflowed the low Lands, and done much Damage in fome Places; but there remained ftill an Appearance of a plentiful Crop in general, though fome few might fuffer Lofs. The printed Paper mentioned two Days fince to have been made publick among us, began to fhew the Effect that I expected it would produce; People of all Ranks engaging fiercely in Difputes (as is too common in religious Matters) and it was pretty difficult for any one to avoid difcovering his Sentiments therein, howfoever cautious he might be, not to meddle in Controverfy: Whilft it afforded Sport, not only to *Jews* and *Deifts*, but many of our Proteftant Diffenters from the Church of *England*, could not but

but fneer at fuch Divifions. It ought neverthelefs to be obferved, that Mr. *Norris*
manifefted a meek Difpofition, and Defire
to promote Peace, without offering to ble-
mifh the Character of his Succeffor, whom
(he faid) he was ready to furrender to, as
foon as he fhewed his Authority from the
Truftees. This was what only I thought
worth Notice this Day, and wifhed it lefs,
for I feared great Difcord enfuing.

Thurfday. An uncertain Report going 5.
about for two Days paft, of a Man being
drowned, or fome how loft, out of a Sloop
lying at Anchor here; whereof Captain
Davis had two now, which he intended to
fend abroad on fome Trade or other; Providence fo ordered it, that the Corpfe float-
ed this Morning, and was brought afhore,
and left by the Tide very near us on the
Strand: Whereupon the Recorder, who
acted as Coroner, fummoned a Jury, who
upon Infpection of the Body, with the Affiftance of two experienced Surgeons that
probed feveral Wounds given, brought in
their Verdict *Wilful Murder*, by Perfons
yet unknown to them. It appeared, that a
certain Perfon who was faid to have had
fome Contention with the Deceafed on
board, fome Days ago, was now miffing,
and gone out of the Way, fuppofed to be
fled; and there were fome Circumftances
by which divers were apt to imagine, that
the

the Master of the Sloop himself (one *Brixy*) was not wholly guiltless, but at least knew of what was done, and never discovered it: No positive Evidence yet however appeared, sufficient to found a Charge against him; but it was to be hoped by some Means or other so base a Murder would ere long come to Light, and the Authors meet with due Justice: In the Interim the Master of the Sloop, and two of his Men, who were under the strongest Suspicion, from what the Mate deposed, (*viz.* that they had been all quarrelling) were confined, till it could be seen what farther Evidence might appear; and due Course was also taken, that such Evidence as could be come at, should be forth coming when required.

6.   *Friday.* To-morrow being the Anniversary of the Day, when the first Court was holden at *Savannah*, proper Care was taken to summon a Grand Jury, and to open it as customary at the stated Time. Nothing fell within my Knowledge, that I thought deserved any Remark; and I resolved not to meddle in any Contention touching our future spiritual Welfare, which at present was the Employment of more Tongues, than would be of any good Use, as I thought.

7.   *Saturday.* The Court sat, the Grand Jury was sworn, received a proper Charge, and

and had divers Matters committed to their Confideration: After which the Court adjourned till next *Thurfday*; before which Time we hoped to fee the General, who was looked for with fome Appearance of Certainty this Day; but in vain.

Sunday. Mr. *Norris* officiated, and the publick Service was performed with due Decency. Information being made, late in the Evening Yefterday, againft a Perfon now in Town, for uttering fome Words among the Soldiers (where he had been lately) magnifying the good Living of the *Spanifh* Troops at *Auguftin*, in Comparifon of the fhort Allowance of ours here, &c. tending to their Difcouragement; he was ordered into the Cuftody of our Guard, where he was detained, in order to make a full Examination into it to-morrow.

Monday. The firft News I met with this Morning was, that the Fellow who was taken into Cuftody Yefterday (whofe Name was *Kipp)* was gone off, and not to be found. Upon Enquiry I underftood, that the Foundation of committing him, appearing doubtful, forafmuch as it arofe only from the Report of a Perfon in Town, newly returned from *Frederica*, and no Information given upon Oath; Mr. *Chriftie* thought proper to give him the Liberty of walking about Town, upon one of the Freeholders engaging for his Appearance:

But

But now his going off in such a Manner, carried in it such a Shew of Guilt, that a Hue and Cry was sent out, to take him if they could. Our Expectations of seeing the General this Day were again baulked; but in the Evening Mr. *Jones* came, whom we looked on at this Time as his Forerunner; and told us he believed he would be with us to-morrow.

10. *Tuesday*. The Court sat, and received from the Grand Jury such Indictments and Presentments as they had prepared; among which were three Indictments they had found against some of the Persons concerned in the late Murder, whereof one was against *Brixy* the Master of the Sloop. In the Evening the General arrived from the South, and was received under a Discharge of the Cannon, and about forty of the Freeholders under Arms; which he was pleased to say, was more than he expected not run away.

11. *Wednesday*. Upon my acquainting the General (among other Things) with what Circumstances Matters appeared relating to the Murder, which were very strong, but no positive Evidence of Fact; he was of Opinion not to proceed too hastily on the Trial, but postpone it for a while, in Hopes of making the Proof clear; and I acquainted the Magistrates with it, who thereupon adjourned the Court to *Monday* next.

next. My Duty requiring clofe Attendance

on his Excellence, to learn his Pleafure,
moft Part of the Day was fo taken up;
when he was pleafed to difcourfe freely,
and lay open his Sentiments on divers Matters of great Importance.

Thurfday. The General's Stay among
us being very likely to be fhort, many People fucceffively fought Audience of him,
on various Occafions; whom he difpatched
in fuch Manner as he faw good: But as he
called on me pretty frequently, either to
give Direction, or enquire into fuch Matters as he thought proper; it behoved me
to be near at Hand, fo that I faw little of
what paffed elfewhere in Town. Upon a
Survey of the Flour lately imported, it was
found totally bad, and ftinking; infomuch
that it was believed to be old caft Goods
when fhipped, that were impofed villanouf-
ly on the Truft: The Cheefe efcaped with
fome fmall Damage, and the Butter with
lefs.

Friday. Several of the *Indian* Traders
now in Town applying for Licences, and
Mr. *Charles Wefley* having taken all the
Books and Rules with him to *England*, relating to that Affair, which was his Care
when here; I had the General's Orders to
difpatch four of them, by writing only
fhort Permits, inftead of the regular Form
to be obferved at a proper Time; till
when,

when, this Method would fufficiently anfwer their Purpofe, which limited their
Power, and kept them under the fame Regulations as their former Licences, where-
unto Relation was had. I did fo, and delivered fuch a Permit to each of them. In
the Evening, waiting on the General, when
Meffieurs *Jones* and *Parker* were alfo prefent, he was pleafed very generoufly to call
on Mr. *Jones*, to fay *that* now to my Face,
relating to my refufing to iffue thofe fola
Bills of 500*l.* which he had told him at
Frederica; from whence I made no Doubt
of his fetting forth that Affair without that
Candour which I thought myfelf entitled
to; and thereupon, taking Mr. *Verelft's*
Letter out of my Pocket, of *March* 3,
wherein the Truftees Orders were fully and
clearly delivered (as I thought) relating to
that Matter; I read them as I had formerly done to Mr. *Jones*; when I told
him, that I found myfelf therein farther
concerned, than barely to write my Name,
for the Reafons fo apparent; wherefore it
behoved me to take Caution in what I did,
and therefore was willing, before I took
any farther Step in it, to be advifed how
to act by the General himfelf, who was
expected foon: Which he called a Refufal,
(and had fuggefted it fo to the General)
and now upon referring to that Letter, the
General readily faid, he could not blame
me:

me: But as for thofe Bills, he had taken it on
himfelf to iffue them; and as for that Part
of the 710 *l*. which was to be applied in
cloathing and maintaining the Truftees Servants, whofe Service was to anfwer the Expence thereof, as far as 400 *l*. towards
building a Church at *Savannah*, &c. he
had fent thofe Bills home again, with his
Reafons for fo doing. Wherefore upon the
Whole, I looked on myfelf, and fo did Mr.
Parker on himfelf, excufed of any farther
Trouble about iffuing, or accounting for,
any of the Bills that were fent, as mentioned in Mr. *Verelft*'s Letter aforefaid.

Saturday. The Evidence to prove the
late Murder, not yet appearing fo full and
plain, as to leave no Doubt of Conviction;
by Reafon that moft of the Perfons who
belonged to the Sloop, were fuppofed to
be concerned in the Fray that happened a-
mong them, when they had been drinking;
and therefore, a Man being loft, unlefs
the particular Perfon who gave the mortal
Wound could be diftinguifhed, they were
all equally guilty; they ftuck together,
and the Truth was hard to come at: I
had the General's Order to call upon the
Magiftrates, and together with them, to
take a Re-examination of the Whole, as
well thofe who were in Cuftody, as thofe
others who yet appeared lefs fufpected:
Which took up the whole Day; neither

1739.

July

14.

could

could we, after all our utmoſt Care, come at the Point we wanted: The Queſtion being, whether the Deceaſed voluntarily leaped out of the Veſſel, reſolving to go a-ſhore, againſt the Maſter's Will; and it being dark, miſſed the Boat, and ſo was drowned (which was what they all alledged) or whether he had received his Death among them, and then was thrown over-board; which there was great Reaſon to believe, from ſeveral Wounds that appeared on the Body, ſuppoſed to be done with a Fleſh-Fork, or a Pair of Compaſſes, which were found near the Place where they had been drinking; each of which anſwered to the Form of the Wounds, and appeared ruſty at the End, near about the Depth of the Surgeon's probing when the Coroner's Inqueſt ſat, whoſe Verdict was *Wilful Murder.* From ſo many concurring Cir-cumſtances, every Body was perſuaded to believe the worſt; and the General, for the better Diſcovery of the Truth, ordered Publication to be made, that any Perſon concerned in that Fray, who would appear and give Evidence who it was that was the Author of this Man's Death, ſo far as that he might be convicted, except the Per-ſon himſelf who did it, ſhould not only have the General's Intereſt to be pardoned, but alſo receive a Reward of 40 *l.* to be

paid

paid him in Sterling Money at the Stores
upon such Conviction.

Sunday. The ordinary Service of the
Day was duly performed, with a full Congregation, where the General was one; and
Mr. *Norris* afterwards administred the Sacrament to such as were so well disposed.

Monday. Great Crouding and Hurry of
Business this Day; when it was expected
the General would have set off in the
Evening on his *Indian* Expedition; but
such Variety of Matters with-held him,
that he was constrained to defer it till tomorrow.

Tuesday. The General left us in the
Forenoon, and proceeded up the River in
his Cutter, with Lieutenant *Dunbar*, Ensign *Leman*, and Mr. *Eyre* (a Cadet) his
Attendants, besides Domesticks and menial
Servants: At the *Euchie* Town, about twenty-five Miles above *Ebenezer*, he purposed
to quit the Water, having appointed some
of our principal *Indian* Traders to wait his
coming there, with a Number of Horses,
as well for Sumpture as Riding; and also
some of our Rangers to assist; intending
from thence to travel on to the *Creek* Nations, &c. The Court at *Savannah* now
sat, as *per* Adjournment, thinking themselves fully prepared to enter on the Trials of the three Persons under Commitment
for Murder. Accordingly *Brixy* the Master

was

was firſt brought to the Bar. The Trial laſted ſeveral Hours, though the Priſoner made but a poor Defence; but the Proof againſt him conſiſting of ſundry Circumſtances, which when put together left not the leaſt Room to doubt of his being a Principal in the Murder, the Court omitted not to produce all that appeared worth regarding; and the Jury were ſo fully convinced of the Fact, that they conſidered but a very little while, after being withdrawn, before they brought in their Verdict *Guilty*.

18. *Wedneſday*. The other two Sailors, —— *Cozens*, and *Levett*, came on their Trials ſeparately; and after a full Hearing of the ſame Evidence, and ſtrong Circumſtances which appeared Yeſterday againſt *Brixey*; and it being proved, that they were all together in Company at the Time of the Fact committed (as alſo one *Jones* who fled the next Morning) the Jury found them alſo *Guilty*. Two of our *Indian* Traders, coming for *Savannah*, and meeting the General on the Water, brought me a Note from him, with his Orders to continue their Licences, and ſome ſhort Directions in what Manner to diſtinguiſh ſuch others, as applied for Licences in his Abſence.

19. *Thurſday*. The Court proceeded to try other Indictments, for Miſdemeanours and other petty Offences; which being of no great
Import,

Import, I could ill spare Time to attend till
the Evening; when having gone through
all Matters before them, relating to the
Crown, I went again to hear Judgment given; and Sentence of Death was pronoun-
ced against the three Murderers; which
they seemed little affected with, but appeared more and more hardened; as it was
evident they had stuck closely together all
along, from a Presumption (as it was supposed) that the Evidence given was not
sufficient to take away their Lives: But
they were advised not to flatter themselves
with Hopes of Mercy. *Wright*, who was
sent down a Prisoner from *Augusta (vide
June* 26.) and one or two more committed
for Crimes of a high Nature, were allowed
to find Bail (if they could) for their Appearance the next Session, the Court not
having yet sufficient Evidence to try them.
Adjourned to *Monday* next.

Friday. Very little or nothing to be
observed. Towards Evening Captains *Norbury* and *Desbrassie* arrived in a Scout-Boat
from *Port-Royal*, intending to stop two or
three Days with us in their Way South.

Saturday. Early in the Morning a Messenger from the General, whom he left at
the *Euchie* Town, and brought Letters to
me and Bailiff *Parker* from him; requiring to be informed concerning the late
Trials for Murder; that so in case the

20.

21.

Prisoners

Prifoners were convicted, and Sentence was given according to Law, he might bring it to Effect. About the fame Time an Ex-prefs-Boat arrived from Mr. *Fallowfield* at *Tybee*, who was ordered by the General, as Naval Officer, to keep a good Look-out there for the Return of a *Spanish* Launch, which he was lately informed, came all the Way from *Auguftin* within Land, and was gone for *Charles-Town*; which at this critical Juncture gave Occafion to People to fay, that his principal Bufinefs was, to found the Depths of the feveral Inlets of the Sea on this Coaft; and which was not improbable. Hereupon the two Captains, with Mr. *Jones*, Captain *Davis*, and fome others, took a Boat with a few Hands armed, and went to give Mr. *Fallowfield* Affiftance; who had wrote, that the Launch was now returned thither, which he had prevailed with to ftay there till fhe was fpoke with farther: On which Occafion, I would gladly have made one; but my immediate Tafk was to fulfil the General's Orders, in giving him a full Relation of the late Trials, and the Proceedings of the Court thereupon; which would take up moft of the fhort Time allowed for the Meffenger to ftay. In the Evening the Gentlemen came back from *Tybee*, after fpeaking with the commanding Officer of the Launch, who told them he had been

at

at *Charles-Town*, to deliver to the Governor there a Packet, from the Government of *Auguſtin*; and that he had another to deliver to the General (which by
the Bye he might as well have delivered as
he went, had he not imagined that he
ſhould have been well watched) and that
Packet he now gave to theſe Gentlemen,
together with a Preſent of Sweetmeats for
him: His whole Talk being of the Pacifi-
cation agreed on between the two Crowns
lately (though not ſo perfectly, we apprehended, as to put all Breach of it out of
Doubt.) He ſeemed to be offended at his
Reception at *Charles-Town*; where he ſaid
he was only permitted to go aſhore alone,
but none of his Men; wherefore he made
but a ſhort Stay there. He was very
earneſt to take the Inland Paſſage in his
Way home, but was told it could not be
allowed him. The two Captains wrote
each a Letter to the General, to give him
an Account of their Proceedings, and gave
them to the ſame Meſſenger very oppor-
tunely that carried mine, and one alſo from
Mr. *Parker*, the head Bailiff, incloſed in
mine; with all which he ſet off about
Midnight, with Deſign to make all poſſible
Haſte, the General intending to wait his
Return at the Place where he left him.

Sunday. The publick Service of the
Church was obſerved as uſual. Captain

Norbury

1739. *Norbury* and *Desbrassie*, who had both been
lately ill in Fevers, were each of them taken with the same again, and forced to
submit to proper Means used for their Recovery.

July

23. *Monday.* Received a Letter this Morning from Lieutenant *Kent* at Fort *Augusta*,
brought me by one *Morrison*, who intended a very short Stay, and was returning into the *Creek* Nation: And the Letter he
gave me, containing some particular Relations of the Talk of the neighbouring *Indians*, as if the *Cherokees* were ready to fall
out with the white Men among them
(which I did not find any certain Foundation for giving too hasty Credit to) I
thought it not so trivial, but that the General should be acquainted with it: Wherefore I resolved to write to him of it, and
inclose the Letter I had received; which
I did, by the same Person; who returned
in the Evening with Design (if possible) to
overtake the General in his Progress. The
Court met again, in order to go on upon civil Actions, which multiplied too fast; and
the Recorder being not well, the Magistrates made Use of it as a good Cause to
adjourn farther to *Monday* next.

24. *Tuesday.* Most of my Employment
this Day was in preparing Letters, and divers Papers for *England*. One of Captain
Davis's Sloops, which had lain here a long
while,

while, fell down the River to *Tybee*, bound (as it was said) for *Auguſtin*; but what her Cargo was, I did not learn; it was ſuppoſed moſt of it to be Proviſions, chiefly the Produce of *Carolina*, together with ſome Bale Goods for Cloathing; alſo Hats, Shoes, &c.

Wedneſday. Followed the ſame Employ as Yeſterday, and made up my Packet; but left it yet unſealed, by which Means I had Opportunity remaining, to add any Poſtſcript I ſaw proper: And it well ſo happened, for late in the Evening arrived *Peter Emery* from *Charles-Town* (who with his Boat of late kept pretty conſtant going betwixt this Town and that, as often as he found ſufficient Freight) by whom I received a Packet from the Truſt, with divers Letters incloſed, and ſome looſe, for the General, and divers private Perſons, ſent me by the Attorney-General, who alſo wrote what Ship they came by from *England*, &c. *viz.* the *Prince Galley*, Captain *Bowles*. Mr. *Verelſt* was ſo kind to write me by the ſame Conveyance two Letters, one of the 27th of *April*, and the other of the 10th of *May*; in both which acquainting me with the favourable and kind Determination of the honourable Truſtees, in relation to me and my future Support; which was Matter of great Comfort to me, not doubting but it would be equivalent

lent to my Need; though the Particulars I was not yet acquainted with.

Thursday. By the Return of the Boat which carried the General up the River, Letters came to Messieurs *Parker*, *Jones*, and myself, in Answer to what had been wrote him on the 21st Instant, advising us in what he thought proper, relating to the Execution of the Criminals: Upon which we met, and went to the Prison; where we took *Levett* aside, who was weak and sickly, and had been so some Time before the Murder was committed; but it appearing at the Trial, that he was one among them when the Fact was done, and consequently that he must be privy to it, though possibly he might not actually give any Wounds to the Deceased; whereby he was in Law equally guilty with the others; we let him know, that we had Leave to reprieve him, if he would ingenuously confess which of them gave those mortal Wounds; which would give the greater Satisfaction to the Publick; and in so doing he would discharge his own Conscience, and leave Room for Mercy to be shewn to himself: All that we could get from him was, that without Doubt the two Persons under Sentence with him, together with *Lewis Jones*, who fled the next Morning, must be the Persons who did it; but which of them particularly,

he

he could not tell; for that he was ill him-self, and laid down to sleep on the Deck: But that was not credited by the Jury, who thought it impossible for such an Act to be done, wherein so many were concerned, all which must be in so small a Vessel, with-in the Space of a few Feet before the Mast; and that any Man could, in the Midst of all such Confusion, lie down quietly to sleep, and not know what was done: As this was all the Defence he made at his Trial, so he yet persisted in the same; whereupon we left him, and spoke to Mr. *Norris*, who visited them, to use his En-deavours in trying what he could prevail with him to say farther.

Friday. Heavy Rains returning upon us again for some Days past, on this more especially there was little or no stirring a-broad: Fevers and Agues increased apace, and our two Captains could not yet get free of them, so as to proceed South: Nevertheless these Distempers hitherto were so far from proving mortal, that I scarce ever knew fewer People die here, than of late: Mr. *West*, late Smith to the Trust, died this Afternoon of a Consumption, wherewith he had been wasting for near a Year past: Besides this Occasion, I hardly remember a Grave opened for any other, for some Months past; and it is generally remarked, that the catching these intermitting Fevers,

27.

is

1739. is moftly owing to Peoples Unwarinefs in
taking cold when they are hot.

July 28.

Saturday. The Magiftrates convened at my Houfe this Morning, to confider of what was needful to be done about the Execution, which was agreed to be on *Friday* next the 3d of *Auguft*; accordingly a Warrant was given out to the Conftables for that Purpofe, and Orders given for a fufficient and proper Guard to attend it: It was alfo ordered, that a Gallows fhould be erected on the Bluff, towards the Extremity of it, near the Water, as near as we could judge oppofite to the Place where the Sloop lay, when this Murder was committed; which was agreeable to what we underftood to be the General's Inftructions: And if there was Room given by *Levett*, betwixt this and the Time of Execution, for him to find Mercy on the Terms advifed by the General, he might yet obtain a Reprieve.

29. *Sunday.* The ordinary Service of the Day was regularly obferved. In the Evening, upon Intelligence, that a Perfon had been fkulking in Town, under the Character of a *Jew* practifing Surgery and Phyfick, ever fince *Friday*; and giving out, that he came from *North-Carolina*, intending to go for *Frederica*, and hoped to get Leave to fettle there; it was thought proper to have him taken up, and examined

ned before the Magiftrates; which was
done: And it appeared by the Teftimony
of our principal *Jews* here, that he was not
of that Religion: Then, upon afking him
what Country he was of, he faid, of *Germany*: But his Complexion not agreeing
with that Climate, we could not prefently
give Credit to it: And moreover it appearing he had his Pockets well ftored, and
that finding he began to be fufpected, he
had agreed with fome Hands to row him
up the River in the Night to fome convenient Place, from whence he might travel
by Land as far South as *Darien*; we were
more and more confirmed in our Opinions,
that he was a dangerous Perfon; whereupon it was thought needful to have his
Pockets well fearched, where he had A-
bundance of Papers, *&c.* among which,
though we could not make a plain Difcovery of his Defigns, yet many Tokens appeared of his deferving to be taken good
Care of: When he found that it was in
vain for him to deny, what we fhould
quickly prove, he confeffed himfelf born
in *Old Spain*; that he had been rambling
for a few Years paft, farther Northward,
in the Practice of his Profeffion, particularly in *Virginia* and *North-Carolina*, &c.
but had made no Abode in *South-Carolina*,
nor feen *Charles-Town* for a long while
paft: But upon looking into his Papers, it
was

was evident he was in *Charles-Town* about a Fortnight or three Weeks since; which, as near as we could guess, was much about the Time that the *Spanish* Launch was lately there: It was plain, that he had gone by several Names; and in short there was sufficient Reason for suspecting strongly that he was no better than a Spy: Whereupon he was committed to the Guard, to be there secured till the next convenient Opportunity of enquiring farther, after having made as strict an Examination as we could till Midnight.

30.

Monday. The Court sat again this Morning; and after determining some petty Causes, adjourned till to-morrow. In the Afternoon we made a farther Examination into the Affair of the *Spaniard*, who was brought before the Magistrates Yesterday; and it was found needful to continue his Confinement till the General's Return. Arrived at *Tybee* a Brigantine belonging to the *Assiento*, Captain *Fennell* Commander; who, together with two other Gentlemen that were Passengers on board him, came up to Town in a Boat, out of Curiosity (as they said) to see the Place: And as soon as they were housed, I had the like Curiosity, to make them a Visit of Compliment, hearing they came from the *Havannah*, to learn what News I could from thence: Mr. *Jones* accompanied me; and we soon found,

found, that Captain *Fennell* was a Man
well known on this Coaft; and though he
had never feen this Town before, he had
often been at *Charles-Town* and *Port-Royal*,
near which laft he had an Eftate of his
own. He reported, that he left *Havannah* twelve Days fince, where all Things
continued in their ufual Pofture; and as to
Peace or War, they were under the fame
Uncertainty as we: So that the Captain
faid he was not without Apprehenfions of
being ftopt; nor did he think himfelf fafe,
till he was out of Gun-fhot from the Forts:
That he was now bound for *England*, after having difpatched fome Bufinefs in *Carolina*, where he fhould put afhore a pretty
many Men, who had been detained Prifoners at *Havannah*, and were making their
Way now home, in fuch Ships as they
fhould like: That the two Gentlemen with
him were *Creolians* at *Jamaica* (one of
whom had been a Writer in the *South-Sea*
Company's Service) and were defigning to
take Paffage home thither from *Carolina*.
This Brig was fuppofed to have a rich Cargo, and carried twenty Hands or more:
The Captain was a Man of courteous Behaviour, and agreeable Converfation: After
paffing away Part of the Evening with
them, I took my Leave.

Tuefday. The Court fat again great   31.
Part of the Day, difpatching fuch Affairs

as

1739.

July
31.

as were indispensable, and postponing such as well might be; importing rather Strife betwixt the Parties, than Benefit to either Plaintiff or Defendant; which ought to be discouraged: Nevertheless the Day was not sufficient for what they had to do; but somewhat yet remained to take up Part of to-morrow. Nothing occurred to me worth Notice; but heavy Rains fell almost daily, insomuch that it was much to be feared the Corn which was now in Ear, would suffer greatly, and rot, instead of growing hard, and ripening.

August
1.

Wednesday. This Forenoon the Court made an End of what they thought needful at present, and adjourned to the 22d Instant. My Son, who had waited a pretty while for a convenient Opportunity of making a Voyage to *England*, now thought that a better could never offer, than to go in this Brig commanded by Captain *Fennell*, now lying at *Tybee*, and bound directly for *Portsmouth*: Wherefore, applying to the Captain, he readily admitted him as a Passenger, intending the Ship should sail to-morrow, or next Day; which short Warning must unavoidably create some Inconvenience to my Son and me both, by parting in such a Hurry: And, as many Things were to be looked into, and well considered, before his Departure, it found us full Employment this Day, as it must

at

at least another, so to adjust Matters, that 1739.
no Defect therein might occasion any Detriment to the Publick. The two Captains August
(though weak yet) went this Day South for
St. *Simon's*.

Thursday. This whole Day was found 2,
short enough, for what Work my Son and
I had to do, pursuing what we were upon
Yesterday; and I heard of nothing abroad,
that required my Avocation from what I
thought needful at home.

Friday. This was the fatal Day, which 3,
called those wretched Criminals for Murder, out of Prison to Execution (which
was appointed on the 28th *ult.)* and Gallows now were prepared, at the Place
were Orders had been given about it. The
Freeholders were called to Arms by Beat of
Drum, and in an Hour's Time more than
seventy appeared, well accoutred; which,
considering the Absence of some, who
were occasionally out of the Way, and
others not well able to attend, being not in
perfect Health, besides Orphans, &c. &c.
shewed that *Savannah* was not yet quite so
much deserted, as by some reported. Before the Hour of Execution came, the Magistrates met, to consider farther of *Levett's*
Case; whose Sickness and Weakness at the
Time when the Murder was committed,
inclined Abundance of People to believe,
that he was not one who actually gave any

Vol. II.   G   of

of the Wounds to the Deceafed; from whence he feemed to be an Object of Pity, though by the Law he was undoubtedly guilty, being privy to it, and not difcovering it; for the Jury could not believe what he alledged in his own Defence, that he was afleep all the while it was doing *(ut antea:)* All thofe Circumftances being now again debated, Pity prevailed; believing if it was an Error to fhew Mercy, it was an Error on the beft Side of the Queftion: Wherefore it was refolved to reprieve him for two Months, in which Time we might expect the General again, who would direct what farther he faw proper about it: It was fo ordered neverthelefs, that the Reprieve fhould not be known, till the very Minute he was to fuffer; whereby we thought it poffible that he might make a fuller Confeffion, than he had yet done, as before recited. At the Gallows, *Brixy*, the Mafter, behaved very refolutely, confeffed nothing, nor abfolutely denied any Thing: He had been of different Sects of Religion, conformable to the Country he was in; a Prefbyterian in the Northern Provinces, and at *Auguftin* a Papift, as it was generally thought he died; though he received the Sacrament at the Hands of a Divine of the Church of *England*, who attended them fince their Condemnation, and at the Place of Execution: He went up

the

the Ladder more nimbly than the Hang-
man, and faſtened the Rope to the Beam
himſelf: Then turning about to the Spec-
tators, told them he was ſatisfied to die
(which was interpreted variouſly by ſeveral)
and after a ſhort Prayer, he was turned off.
Cozens owned himſelf to have been a very
wicked Man; for which, he ſaid, God's
Vengeance had overtaken him: He behaved with Penitence in Priſon, and now
alſo; but made no Confeſſion of the Guilt
for which he ſuffered, nor ſaid any Thing
in particular of it. *Levett* was conducted
to the Foot of the Ladder, after the other
two were turned off, before his Reprieve
was declared: He made great Lamentation
for his former Courſe of Life, and appeared under much Terror; but continued to
deny that he ſaw the Wounds given; and
was ſo affected with his unexpected Reprieve, that he was very near loſing his Life
by an exceſſive Return and Flow of Spirits; after which he was returned in ſafe
Cuſtody to the Priſon from whence he
came. Theſe Things being over, I had a
few Hours left to ſpend with my Son before his Departure; which was at Six in
the Evening, when we took Leave of each
other (for a ſhort Seaſon, it was hoped) and
he went, in Company with a few others,
for *Tybee*, where he was to embark immediately on board the St. *Francis* Brig, com-

G 2   manded

1739.

Auguſt

manded thus far by Captain *Fennell:* But now the Captain had determined to ſend her for *England* under the Conduct of his Mate; intending, after a ſhort Stay in *Carolina*, to return to *Jamaica*, together with the other two Gentlemen that came with him: Wherefore he would only ſtay at *Tybee*, to ſee her under Sail over the Bar; which was intended early in the Morning, and then he would quit her, and make the beſt of his Way to *Port-Royal.* Sent my Packet of the 25th *ult.* by my Son.

4.

Saturday. My Son being now gone, Mr. *Jones*, who had been a great while a Stranger at my Houſe, came and made me a neighbourly Viſit, ſitting an Hour with me in familiar Converſe on divers Matters relating to the Publick; which I was very glad of, and determined with myſelf, that I would not be behind him in all Kinds of Courteſy, to promote the Service, as far as in me lay; but could not avoid reflecting on his implacable Diſpoſition towards my Son; which had carried him ſuch a Length as to avoid my Houſe, during his Abode with me; and which I could no otherwiſe account for, than becauſe he would not tamely ſubmit to thoſe ſevere Imputations that came upon him through his Means; but thinking himſelf injuriouſly treated (as indeed I apprehend he was) uſed all proper Means to vindicate his Innocence;

nocence; and that was conftrued by an angry Man of a haughty Temper, to be an Oppofition of his Authority. Thefe Things I concluded would now blow over, and the Remembrance of them be extinct, by the Time of my Son's Return again.

Sunday. The publick Service of the Church was duly obferved. In the Evening I received Intelligence by a Letter from my Son on board the Ship at *Tybee*, that they were at the Time of his writing, weighing Anchor, in order to put to Sea with a fair Wind : Which Letter was brought me by the Pilot, who lives there; and after conducting the Ship over the Bar this Morning, left them about a League off Land.

5.

Monday. This Morning, at the Requeft of *John Lyndall* (appointed Pindar) there was a voluntary Convention of the Freeholders, who had any Property in Cattle in thefe Parts; when the Orders and Inftructions lately given to the Pindar, by the General, were read; and the Pindar requiring in Confequence of thofe Orders, that fome other little Regulations fhould be agreed on among themfelves, for the better enabling him to do his Duty; they readily agreed to them, and figned a Paper fignifying their Confent, &c. It was now thought high Time, to begin the Execution of the Commiffion lately fent by the

6.

Truft

Truft to Meſſieurs *Parker, Jones*, and me; and we met accordingly in the Afternoon at Three a Clock, when we began with the Account of Meſſieurs *Montaigut* and *Purry* firſt, where we were apprehenſive of meeting with ſome Intricacy; eſpecially from what Mr. *Verelſt* had lately wrote in his Letter of *April* 22; and was likely to prove ſo; for after inſpecting it cloſely ſome Time, we adjourned the farther Conſideration of it till to-morrow Morning.

Tueſday. The Commiſſioners met again, and ſpent both the Forenoon and Afternoon in cloſe Application to the Matters before them, taking proper Minutes of what was thought worth Notice: Among ſome other Things, obſerving that Mr. *Williamſon* had Credit given, in the Account of Mr. *Purry* and Company, for about 13 *l.* which was now made Part of the Debt owing to him as Claimant from the Truſtees, and which was certified by Mr. *Cauſton:* Upon looking into Mr. *Purry*'s Books, it appeared Mr. *Williamſon* was made Debtor there for ſundry Goods bought of that Value: Upon which we examined Mr. *Purry* upon Oath, to know how he came to transfer that as a Debt in the Account of the Truſtees; and he ſaid he did it at Mr. *Williamſon*'s Requeſt, and by the Conſent of Mr. *Cauſton:* Mr. *Cauſton* alſo appeared Debtor in his own Name in Mr. *Purry*'s Books, for

for divers Goods fold and delivered to him
for his own private Ufe, in the Sum of a-
bout 70*l.* which he had likewife transferred
to the Truftees Account, and made Part
of what was certified by him, as the Debt
which Mr. *Purry* claimed, to the 29th of
September laft: Since which Time Mr.
Caufton appears Debtor to Mr. *Purry*, in
his Books, for fundry Articles, in the fame
Form and Manner as the foregoing Account fhewed till *September* 29. How far
Mr. *Caufton* can exonerate himfelf of this
Charge, is yet unknown, but looked for.

Wednefday. Continued our Examination: **8.**
And Captain *McPherfon's* Account, together with his Rangers, being before us; we
could not but obferve the exceeding great
Difference we therein found, of what he
claimed for the laft half Year, from *Lady-
Day* to *Michaelmas* 1738, from any preceding Account for the fame Time; but
having Recourfe to my Journal of *March*
24, and *April* 1, 2, 3, 1738, I perfectly
recollected what I there found, and withal
feveral other Particulars, not fully noted
there: The Captain at that Time, when
we could not be too much on our Guard
againft the *Spaniards*, took that Advantage,
and in a great Meafure extorted fuch a
Compliance with his Demands, as he
thought we durft not refufe: Wherefore
after exhorting him to be very watch-

ful,

ful, and more than ordinary diligent in keeping a good Look-out; he was promised, that, as far as it was in our Power, he and his People should have all their Demands fulfilled, which they then insisted on — which now is humbly submitted to the Judgment of the honourable Trustees. In the Course of this Enquiry, *William Elbert*, who at that Time, or very little before, was one of Captain *McPherson*'s Rangers, was found to have sold a Mare to Mr. *Causton* on his own Account, as he believed, together with two or three other small Articles, which in the Whole came to 6*l.* 15*s.* 6*d.* for which the Trustees are made Debtors in the said *Elbert*'s Account certified to Mr. *Jones*.

9.   *Thursday.* In the certified Account of *Nunes Henriquez*, the Trust is made Debtor for 5*l.* 15*s.* 7*d.* which we apprehended, from what we could discover, properly belonged to Mr. *Causton*, as also to ten Shillings charged to their Account, and owing by Mr. *Williamson*: And in a subsequent Account with the said *Nunes Henriquez*, he charges 2*l.* 14*s.* 6*d.* ½ to the Trust for Table-Cloths and some Pewter, delivered to Mr. *Causton*'s Wife; and 1*l.* 14*s.* 2*d.* ½ to the Trust for Pewter, which was delivered to Mr. *Thomas Upton*. Mr. *David Provost*'s Account, certified for one thousand and eighty-five Pounds, was found unexceptionable; and so was Mr. *Thomas Ware*'s
for

for 221*l.* *Thomas Trip*, a Joiner, charging the Truft, in a Bill delivered, with
the Sum of 5*l.* 14*s.* 11*d.* was content to
take 4*l.* 12*s.* 5*d.* of Mr. *Jones*; the remaining 1*l.* 2*s.* 6*d.* being for Work done
for Mr. *Caufton*. Upon finding that a continual, daily Attendance on this Work,
would render each of us incapable of a
due Regard to any other, we agreed una-
nimoufly, that for the future one Half of
the Day, either Forenoon or Afternoon
only, fhould be alotted for that Purpofe;
and to appoint at parting, which would
beft fuit our Purpofe for the Day following, from Time to Time.

1739.

Auguft

Friday. Went through four Accounts
more, *viz. William Woodrooffe*, *John Lloyd*,
Samuel Mercer, and *Benjamin Adams*, wherein fuch Errors as we found were moftly to
the Injury of the Claimants; efpecially the
latter of them; where it appeared fo defective in due Entries of Credit given, that
we poftponed it for a Review fome other
Time. Meffieurs *Jennys*'s and *Eveleigh*'s
Accounts we much wifhed to get over;
but it was thought proper, that fomebody
fhould appear in their Behalf when we
went upon them; and therefore we muft
wait a little till we had Advice about it
from *Charles-Town*.

10.

Saturday. Spent the whole Forenoon in
examining Mr. *Brownfield*'s Accounts, relating to the Claims of Meffieurs *Pyt* and
Tuckwell;

11.

Tuckwell; wherein many Difficulties occurred, from divers Articles charged to that
Debt of the Truſt, which we apprehended
they had nothing to do with; but upon farther Enquiry it appeared more and more
intricate; and we found Mr. *Cauſton*'s Account in divers Places ſo blended with the
Truſt's, that it was not an eaſy Taſk to
ſeparate them: But Mr. *Brownfield* ſhewed a ready Diſpoſition to explain it fully,
in a Manner more intelligible; wherefore
we deferred the Conſideration of it to another Day. By a Boat arrived from Fort
Auguſta, I received a Letter from Lieutenant *Kent*, informing me, that from
ſome Intelligence they had lately received,
there were ſome Reaſons to doubt the *Creek
Indians* not to be ſo much our Friends as
we took them to be: But the General
being now himſelf among them, we did
not doubt but he would beſt judge of their
Sincerity, and take proper Meaſures to
ſtrengthen their Fidelity. By the ſame
Boat came a Priſoner, whoſe Name is
Shannon, ſent down by the General, and
committed by him to ſafe Cuſtody in our
Priſon, for treaſonable Practices: He had
been of the General's own Regiment, liſted and brought over from *England*; but
was diſcovered to be a Villain, in endeavouring to ſeduce ſome of his Fellow Soldiers, &c. for which he was whipped,
and

and drummed out of the Regiment; moreover, upon searching, he was found to belong to *Berwick*'s Regiment, and had a
Furlow in his Pocket from the said Regiment: After which he went up among the
Indian Nations, and was now found to
have been practiſing his former Work, endeavouring to perſuade them into the Intereſt of the *French*; for which it was to
be hoped he would meet with his Demerits. Spent the Afternoon at my little Plantation.

Sunday. The Duty of the Day was ob-   **12.**
ſerved as uſual, and the Sacrament admi-
niſtred by Mr. *Norris*, to ſuch as were ſo
well diſpoſed. Mr. *Francis Moor*, who
went South not long ſince, returned to us
again, intending now to continue his Abode
here till the Return of the General.

Monday. The Commiſſioners met again,   **13.**
and proceeded in a farther Examination of
the Accounts of Mr. *Brownfield*; which
we found true in all its Parts of Credit
claimed; but there were ſundry Articles,
wherein we apprehended the honourable
Truſt would not readily own themſelves
Debtors, being ſuch as were placed to their
Account by Mr. *Cauſton*'s Orders, as Mr.
Brownfield very readily acknowledged; and
withal, that it was no more than what
he had divers Times done before, not
doubting but it would be approved of,
as

as it had been, and that Mr. *Cauſton* gave
the Truſt Credit for it in his Accounts:
Which, together with others of the
like Sort, poſſibly might be better explained to us, before we made an abſolute
Charge of them on Mr. *Cauſton*, whom it
behoved to look to it. In the Afternoon
the Magiſtrates aſſembled at my Houſe, to
enquire into a Riot committed laſt Night
(Sunday) by ſome drunken People, who
had inſulted one of the Tything-men, a
Peace-Officer then upon Duty, who required them to go peaceably home, and
whom they had ill treated; wherefore he
had confined them upon Guard: And the
Matter appearing very heinous againſt
them, they were three of them bound o-
ver under ſufficient Bail, to anſwer it at
the next Seſſions: Which perceiving them
much terrified at, I propoſed it to them to
confeſs where it was they bought the Rum
which had occaſioned it, and I would in-
tercede with the Magiſtrates to be the milder
in their Puniſhment, upon Conviction of
the Offence which they had been guilty
of; and they promiſed they would another Day; but why not now, I could not
tell: Wherefore I doubted their Sincerity.
N. B. Theſe three Men were not long ſince
out of their Servitude, had each of them
behaved well in their Services, as was acknowledged by their ſeveral Maſters; were
all

all promising to be useful Men in the Colony, and one of them lately married, at whose House they had thus debauched themselves. From whence it is an obvious Reflexion, how fatal this Excess of Rum-drinking is likely to prove among the common People; and how ineffectual all Means have hitherto been found, for suppressing the Sale of it by unlicens'd Persons, in all the bye Corners of the Town. Mr. *Bradley*, who yet continued very weak since his late Sickness, no sooner began to recover, but he returned to his former Practice, of making Havock among the Cattle which had been under his Charge; and notwithstanding his being absolutely discharged from meddling any more with any of the Trust's Goods or Effects (as they were pleased to write me lately, and which I made no Doubt but they had signified to him in those Letters which I had delivered to him from them) I had Intelligence of his having killed a Calf last *Saturday* Evening, and selling three Fourths of it; moreover, that he had fixed upon a fat Heifer, which he purposed the same Way to convert to his own Use the Beginning of this Week: Wherefore upon my taking Notice of it to those who were now with me of the Magistracy, and Mr. *Jones* being also one with us; I proposed it to them, to go all of us in a Body to him, to

ask

afk his Meaning, and when he intended to furrender all that appertained to the Truft, into fuch Hands as were appointed to receive it: Which we did; and he entertained us in his ufual rambling Way of Talk, very little to the Purpofe, and not coming to any fixed Point, partly feeking by evafive Anfwers to blind us, and chiefly preffing our Forbearance till the General returned, who he would have perfuaded us to believe, would allow of what he had done, though we were convinced of the contrary; and moreover we could not expect him among us again yet awhile; in which Space of Time it was unknown what Mifchief might be done: We therefore were obliged to charge him at his Peril, not to touch a Hoof more, or offer to difpofe of any; which if he did, he might expect to be proceeded againft as a Felon: So we left him.

14.

Tuefday. Mr. *Jones* having received a Bruife by an accidental Fall over a Log in the Dark, could not well attend the Bufinefs this Day, which we were purfuing, in looking into what we were directed: Wherefore Mr. *Parker* and I fpent fome Hours upon it without him, comparing divers Accounts, &c. but we thought it beft not to make Minute of any determinate Opinion relating to it, till we were all together, and agreed in the fame. The Afternoon

I

ternoon I took to myself at home, where I never wanted Matter sufficient to keep me employed; and heard of nothing abroad that I thought worth Notice.

Wednesday. Mr. *Jones* continuing yet 15. unable to act in the Examination of what we were upon, it was thought proper to respite it for a Day or two longer, in Hopes of his Attendance to assist, as he now grew better: And I took this Opportunity of paying some Regard to my Plantation Affairs, where we might hope soon to reap some Fruit of what Labour had been bestowed; especially as the Season was grown more favourable for bringing on Harvest; and the Heats which this Month began with, made an agreeable Alteration in ripening the Corn: But I was not a little chagrined to think, that the Number of Acres planted near the Town I feared would fall short of what the last Year produced; which indeed should be imputed in a great Measure to the Distress which divers of the Inhabitants were driven to last Winter; which put them on the Necessity of earning their Bread by any honest Means they could use, at such Time as their Labour might well have been bestowed on their Lots, could the Stores have afforded them a few Months Credit: For I must again repeat (what I have elsewhere taken Notice of) that the major Part of the Freeholders

remaining

1739. remaining in *Savannah*, shew a good Disposition to Work, and endeavour to maintain their Families: And the Alteration lately made in the Tenure of Lands by the honourable Trustees, in their Favour, has had already such an Influence, that several, even at this Time of the Year, have begun to give a Specimen of what may be expected from them when the Planting Season returns. As for the out-lying Plantations that are distant from the Town, I have Reason to expect such an Account may be returned of them, that I need not be ashamed of; several of which are occupied by some of our Freeholders, who hold those Lands upon Lease (they tell me) and where, by Reason of a convenient Situation, they are enabled to raise a live Stock of Cattle, and Hogs, &c. whereby their Substance increasing, they will soon attain to a comfortable Way of living, and become downright Farmers. —— But these are such as have a little Stock to begin with.

August

16. *Thursday.* This Day passed over with very little or no Variation from the preceding.

17. *Friday.* The Commissioners met again early, and followed their Employment till past Noon; in which Time Captain *William Thompson*'s certified Account came under Consideration, which divers Exceptions

were

1739.</br>Auguſt

were made to, having in it ſundry Articles, where Credits were given by him to particular Perſons, whoſe Accounts we thought ought to be charged with the ſame, as being accountable to him properly, and not inſerted in the ſaid Certificate: Several other Charges we thought unwarrantable, which we yet could find no Original of in the poſting Books belonging to the Stores, and muſt leave it to Mr. *Cauſton* to give a Reaſon for. Then we reconſidered the Accounts of Meſſieurs *Montaigut* and *Purry*, where ſeveral Exceptions were alſo made; among which we found the Sum of 26*l*. 13*s*. 4*d*. taken Notice of particularly in Mr. *Verelſt*'s late Letter, to ſtand thus: Mr. *Cauſton* had taken *(i. e.* borrowed) of Mr. *Purry* that Sum, for which he gave him a Bill on Mr. *Jenny's*, and therewith debeted the Truſt; but upon that Bill being returned unpaid, we could no where find, that the Truſt had again any Credit given them; for which no Reaſon yet is given, why the Truſt ſhould find it ſo ſtated.

Saturday. Stuck cloſe to the ſame Employment, and went through *Recompence Stenbury*'s Account, without any Objections that we could ſee Cauſe for; as well as one or two more of no great Moment: But looking into the Account of Meſſieurs *Pyt* and *Tuckwell*, which was ſaid in Mr. *Ve-*

18.

relst's Letter not to be yet offered; we there found divers Articles to ftick at, Mr. *Caufton*'s Certification and Mr. *Brownfield*'s Books not agreeing in the Sums which the Truft was made Debtor for: Which put us to a Nonplus for the prefent, and obliged us to defer a farther Enquiry till the Beginning of the Week, when we might hear what Mr. *Brownfield* could fay to it, and how it came to pafs that the Account certified to be due, was in any Place more than he had charged in his Books; which we obferved were very regular; and hitherto he had not (as far as we perceived) ufed any evafive Anfwers, to whatever we queftioned: He happened, at this Juncture, to be rode a few Miles out of Town. In the Evening arrived *Peter Emery* with his Boat from *Charles-Town*; but brought no Letters from *England*, no Ship being arrived thence fince the *Prince Galley*, Captain *Bowles*. *(Vide July* 25.)

19.   *Sunday.* The publick Service was regularly obferved, as ufual. In the Afternoon two Sloops belonging to *New-York*, —— *Tingley* and —— *Ware* Mafters, laft from *Frederica*, arrived at our Port; having difpofed of the greateft Part of their Cargoes in the South; with whom came Monfieur *Thomas*, chief Engineer there, together with his Family: By whom we underftood a Stop was put to the carrying on

any

any Fortification for the preſent: He ſaid
he was going to *Charles-Town*, to view the
Fortifications there; and from thence probably he ſhould go for *England*.

Monday, } Theſe two Days were whol-
Tueſday. } ly taken up in purſuing our
Examination into ſome of thoſe Accounts
which were expected from us: And in ſeveral of them we found Errors of the like
Nature with ſuch as we had before obſerved, *viz.* making the Truſt Debtor for divers' Sums which did not appear to us to
belong to them, but properly ſhould have
been charged to the right Owners; ſome
to Mr. *Cauſton,* and ſome to others: Whereof though ſundry of them poſſibly might
not be thought very groſs, yet in an aggre-
gate Sum, probably would, in the End, be
looked on otherwiſe. We began now to
think of a proper Account being prepared,
to be laid before the Truſtees, of our Proceedings, ſo far as we had gone, with our
Obſervations thereupon, as we went on:
To which we ſhould give Mr. *Cauſton* (as
due to him in Juſtice) an Opportunity of
exculpating, as far as he is able, ſuch
Charges as now ſtand againſt him. This
being the ſtated Time of the Court ſitting,
the Magiſtrates met in Form, and adjourned to *Monday* next. Finding it impoſſible
to ſit *de Die in Diem* on the publick Accounts, without great Detriment to other

H 2 Affairs;

Affairs; we reſolved to dedicate to-morrow to our own private Uſes, and appointed to meet again on *Thurſday* Morning.

Wedneſday. Plantation - Work required ſome looking into, which employed Part of my Time. An heavy Complaint being exhibited againſt the *Moravian* Brethren, by Mr. *Gilbert* (one of the Magiſtrates;) foraſmuch as the honourable Truſtees had ſeveral Times adviſed, that thoſe People ſhould be dealt tenderly with; it was thought proper to aſk Mr. *Jones*, Mr. *Francis Moor*, and me, to be preſent when it was enquired into: And it may not be improper to take Notice, how that Affair truly appeared. One *Robert How*, a Freeholder here, the ſame who had his Houſe burnt, and was ſo kindly holpen by the Truſtees to rebuild it again, though he never did; and moreover, being a Favourite of Mr. *Weſley*'s, had conſiderable charitable Collections made for him; by both which Means, his Gains abundantly overpaid his Loſs; from that Time laid aſide all Thought of Improvement of Land, but ſeemed rather deſirous of appearing an Adept in the Improvement of Grace: And being made Choice of by Mr. *Weſley* as a Clerk to ſet the Pſalms, and do other little Offices about the Church, he became a cloſe Attender on the Miniſter, and was looked on by many weak Folk, as a Perſon

ſon of extraordinary Piety; ſuch as divers
in thoſe Days ſought to be diſtinguiſhed
by, and ſome others ſince have copied after. This *How* married a Daughter of Mr.
Gilbert, that died, leaving two Children
(Girls) behind her, whom their Grandmother ſhewed a kind Affection for; but
their Father purpoſing to go for *England*,
(ſince Mr. *Weſley* was no more expected,
and Mr. *Whitfield*'s Return was impatiently
waited for) he diſpoſed of his two Children (moſt unnaturally, as I conceive) and
againſt the Will of their Grand Parents,
to the Family of *Moravian* Brethren, under a Shew of their being brought up in a
ſtricter Courſe of Religion, than the eſta-
bliſhed Church afforded, unleſs it were
more purified; though what Kind of Religion theſe *Moravians* profeſs, nobody here
knows, except themſelves: And to make
Payment for the breeding up theſe two
Children, of the Age of about ſeven or
eight Years, their Father contracts for their
Servitude in all Kinds of Work implicitly,
till their attaining the Age of Twenty-four,
and ſo leaves them. It pleaſed God to
take away one of them a while ſince, by
Sickneſs; which no great Notice was taken of, every Body ſuppoſing that due
Care was taken of her in her Illneſs; tho'
now, from what has happened to the other,
many ſuſpect otherwiſe: For upon the

Grand-

Grandmother's hearing accidentally of this Child's being not well, ſhe went to ſee her; but was denied that Satisfaction, which made her the more importunate; and taking one of her Neighbours with her, by ſome Means or other they got Admittance; when they found the poor Child in a moſt miſerable Condition, with cruel Uſage, and uncommon Severity; which occaſioned this Complaint, and the preſent Enquiry into the Matter. The Child was produced, and upon taking off her Cloaths, ſhe appeared to be ſcourged in a moſt terrible Manner, from her Neck down to her Heels, with Stripes laid on by a maſculine Hand, moſt piteous to look at, and her Fleſh torn, after the Manner of what a Criminal uſes to have, at the Hands of a common Executioner. Three of the *Moravians* owned it to be of the Brotherhood's doing, who appeared; that they held a Conſultation among themſelves (which is their ordinary Way in moſt Caſes) and that this was the Reſult of it; foraſmuch as the Child had fouled her Bed: In Conſequence of which Sentence, ſhe was thus inhumanly mangled; and that too not done by a Woman, but a Man of a cruel Diſpoſition. We ſent for a Surgeon to give his Opinion of it; who ſaid, he could not apprehend any Danger from the Stripes, farther, than if the Anguiſh ſhould throw her into

a Fever, he knew not what might happen; 1739.
and the Child appeared very weak, with
her Arms much emaciated. Upon the Auguſt
Whole, the Magiſtrates thought, that the
leaſt they could do, was to require good
Bail for the Perſon's Appearance at the next
Seſſions, who had been the Inſtrument of
inflicting ſuch Cruelty; and that the other
two alſo ſhould be obliged, on their own
Recognizances, to appear at the ſame
Time. In the mean while, the Child was
delivered to the Grandmother, to take
Care of it, till it ſhould be farther conſidered at the Court.——From ſuch Marks
of Sanctification, *libera nos:* And whether
ſuch a Father, or ſuch Guardians, have
the beſt Title to it, is not my Taſk to enquire.

Thurſday,⎫ Theſe two Days were whol- 23.
Friday. ⎬ ly taken up in the ſame 24.
Manner as *Monday* and *Tueſday* laſt; when
we found many abſtruſe Points to get thro'
in divers Accounts before us, more eſpecially thoſe of *Abram Minis* the *Jew,* and
Patrick Graham Surgeon; which we gave
each of them Time till *Monday* next to
unfold; to which Day we deferred the
farther Conſideration of them. Meſſieurs
Jones, Parker, and I, being together, took
Occaſion to call again on Mr. *Bradley,* to
know what he purpoſed about delivering up
the Truſt's Goods and Effects in his Hands,

purſuant

purfuant to Order. We found him and his Son both indeed weak, which was admitted as fome Excufe for their not having yet wrote out an Inventory of all Particulars; but the live Stock (we told him) might be brought together, by his principal Director under him, without any Trouble to himfelf: Which he now promifed fhould no longer be delayed; and to make a Beginning, four Horfe Beafts were delivered into Mr. *Jones*'s Cuftody on *Friday*, which he faid was all he had, and they had been fadly battered, and near worn out; but having lately found a little Refpite, they appeared to be fomewhat thriving. As for the other Cattle, we thought it beft to commit the Care of them to the Pindar, who was firft to take fuch an Account of them in Writing as he could get, and then to fee in the feveral Droves which fhould be made, how well it agreed with what he found. Hard Rains came on again, fince the Change of the Moon.

25.   *Saturday.* Having by Agreement between ourfelves, adjourned our farther Confideration of the Matter of Accounts from laft Night to *Monday* Morning, we took each of us this Day to fuch Ufes as we faw beft: Wherein an Affair happened, which, though unwillingly, I cannot avoid taking fome Notice of, not knowing what may be faid more of it another Time, when

possibly

possibly I might be called on to testify what I observed, *viz.* Mr. *Jones* sitting an Hour with me in the Afternoon in Conference, upon several Points of the Service; it so fell out that Bailiff *Parker* called on me at the same Time; which would have been not in the least amiss, had he not brought Mr. *Causton* with him, who possibly might have it in his Intention to say something to me, relating to his own Affairs at the Office; and it was a long while since he had been within my Doors, though I had never treated him but with Civility: Mr. *Jones* and he indeed had such personal Animosity one against the other, that such a Convention (I feared) could forebode no Good: And as Mr. *Parker* was known to be so much a Friend of Mr. *Causton*'s, as to wish he might clear himself of all foul Practices; Mr. *Jones* always looked upon him in that Light, and sometimes gave shrewd Tokens of his Disesteem; which the other was ready enough to remember: And in that Manner they both carried a mutual Ill-will, which sooner or later would be smothered no longer, but must inevitably break out, as it sometimes had done, and now again did. Mr. *Parker* and he soon fell into some Talk, about delivering of Stores to *Parker*'s Family; wherein he alledged, that he was used unkindly, his Wife lying in,

and

and one of the *German* Servants with him (by Order from the Truſt) had at the ſame Time a ſick Wife, for whom her Huſband, by his Maſter's Order, went to the Stores to beg a Bottle of Wine; but was told it would not be delivered without Money; which, Mr. *Parker* ſaid, was a ready Way to make Servants Thieves, and pilfer their Maſters Goods, to make Money: This Mr. *Jones* grew warm at; and *Parker* not a Jot leſs ſo; when throwing his Arm to and fro (as is common with him to do in any Vehemence of Expreſſion) Mr. *Jones* ſtarted from his Seat, and dared him to ſtrike; both then ſhaking their Fiſts at each other, but Care was taken to prevent Blows, and it ended in ſcurrilous Language on both Sides, each looking on himſelf as the beſt Man, and throwing out Ribaldry in Abundance, with ſcurvy Reflexions on one another's former Courſes of Life, before they came here: During this Hurly-burly *Cauſton* vaniſhed; and at length the Diſputants growing cooler, and coming in Appearance to better Temper, Mr. *Parker* alſo took his Leave, and left us as he found us: When Mr. *Jones* told me he could not but believe, that *Cauſton* had blown up *Parker* into that Heat before he came, aggravating his being denied a Bottle of Wine for ſuch Uſes, to be what the Truſtees would not well approve of; and that he brought him

purpoſely

purposely to affront him: So at present it
ended.

Sunday. The uſual Service was performed at Church. Monſieur *d'Beauſaine* brought
me a Letter in the Afternoon, together with
a ſmall Packet incloſing others, which Mr.
Montaigut had received at his Plantation
up the River in *Carolina,* near *Puryſburgh,*
and now ſent it to Mr. *d'Beauſaine* (at preſent in Town) to deliver to me. It came
per Expreſs from Lieutenant Governor *Bull,*
who wrote me of what Intelligence he
lately had received from Lieutenant Governor *Clarke* of *New-York,* concerning the
French marching from *Mont Reall* near
Quebec, with a Body of about two hundred *French* regular Troops, and five hundred *Indians,* who are to be inforced by
French and *Indians* in their Journey: That
this Army was deſigned againſt *Indians*
who are now in Friendſhip with his *Bri-
tannick* Majeſty's Subjects of *Carolina* and
Georgia, and who are ſituated near ſome
Branches of the *Meſſaſippi* River: That a
Frenchman, who was redeemed by General
Oglethorpe (having been taken by thoſe *Indians)* and furniſhed with a Paſs, and Money, to go back to *Canada,* is with this
Army: The Governor added, that he
ſhould immediately diſpatch an Expreſs to
the *Creek* Nations, to adviſe General *Oglethorpe* of the Contents of his Letters:
Then

Then he added — " The Confequence and " Event of this Undertaking cannot be " forefeen, yet it may be neceffary for us " to think of our Prefervation, and be " upon our Guard : And in a Poftfcript " he wrote, that he fuppofed the Defign " to be againft the *Chickafaw Indians*." — Thus far Colonel *Bull*.——— As to myfelf, I could not but think it a very lucky Incident, that the General was now up in the Nations himfelf, where he, upon receiving the Intelligence fent him by Colonel *Bull*, would undoubtedly leave thofe *Indians* who are in Amity or Alliance with us, confirmed without wavering, in their true Friendfhip and Fidelity : Which well effected, we fhould have little Caufe to be apprehenfive of Danger from the *French* ; though moft undoubtedly they were very bufy in fomenting Difcord betwixt us and the *Indians* our Friends : And if the prefent Defign of the *French* was againft the *Chickafaws*, whofe Valour they had formerly experienced to their Coft ; on Condition the *Creeks* prove true to thofe People, in an Alliance fince made ; the *Creeks* being a great Nation, it may be reafonably hoped, that betwixt them they will make Monfieur once again pay dear for his Attempt.

27.   *Monday.* The Commiffioners met again, and Mr. *Graham* the Surgeon's Account took us up the whole Morning, to get

thro' what we had left undone on *Friday* laft, fo much Incricacy was found ftill remaining in it, Debtor and Creditor often jumbled, and wrong placed, which occafioned many Exceptions, and will not pafs without due Obfervation. Having a Piece of roaft Meat for my Dinner, I engaged my two Affociates to take Part with me, hoping, by bringing them together again, they might grow better tempered: We fat an Hour after eating, and nothing was offered by either that could give any Offence: And I declined touching upon what was paft, hoping it might die away, and be no farther talked of; for it would not bear being revived, without Mifchief enfuing; which I well knew. The Court, which ftood adjourned to this Day, was now again farther put off, and adjourned to the 7th of *October*, before which Time we expected the General's Return again; and there were fome Prifoners in Goal, whom it would not be advifable to try, before fuch a Charge was exhibited againft them, as he thought proper.

Tuefday. Another Day's Intermiffion from meddling in Accounts, by Confent. Mr. *d'Beaufaine* returning up the River to his Plantation, I wrote a Letter by him to Mr. *Montaigut*, acknowledging the Receipt of what Letters he had fent me from the Lieutenant Governor, and alfo inclofed one

28.

to Colonel *Bull,* which I wrote in Return
to his; and thought I could not chuſe a
fitter Canoille, than the ſame which he
had made Uſe of, more eſpecially as Opportunities of writing to *Charles-Town* were
very rare with us. Mr. *Norris* coming to
ſit an Hour with me, whom I had obſerved for a while paſt to be more reſerved
and dumpiſh than uſual (as I thought, tho'
not particularly ſo to me) ſeemed to wiſh
for Captain *Thompſon*'s Arrival, by whom
Mr. *Whitfield* was expected; ſaying, that
he was determined to take the firſt Opportunity of returning for *England*; which I
was ſorry to hear, and offered ſome ſuch
Reaſons as occurred to me, why he ſhould
lay aſide ſuch Thoughts; for that I was
very confident he ſtood well in the Opinion of the Truſtees, and I did not doubt
but all future Matters would be rendered
eaſy to him: He replied, that he had met
with many Diſcouragements, even from
the Day of his firſt Landing, ſuch as none
of his Predeceſſors had ever found, and
ſuch as he truly believed the Truſtees never
meant he ſhould; but they were far off,
and it was not his Temper to be complaining often about little Things, which often
repeated, were grown ſuch, as now he
could not, with any Comfort of Life, bear
any longer, *&c.* I obſerved, that one great
Grievance (as he termed it) was, that he
thought

thought himself ill treated at the Stores, where he said he scarce ever met with civil Usage: If he sent for the Boys and Servants Allowance, who lived under the same Roof with him, they were worse served than any others: If at any Time he sent for a few Bottles of Wine for his own Use, he had often such brought him, as was not fit to drink; when at the same Time he knew, and had taken Part of what was given out to other Favourites, that was good. I told him, that possibly it might happen through the Carelessness or ill Judgment of Servants, and therefore I would advise him to speak with Mr. *Jones* himself of it, who I hoped would rectify any Mistakes that might have happened: But he told me he had so often done that in vain, that he was absolutely resolved not to have any more to do with him, having found whatever he said, always disregarded, and plainly perceived he was to fare the worse with him for his Function Sake, whose Aversion to the established Church was too apparent; whilst others were in a particular Manner caressed: To which I offered in Reply, that I hoped he was mistaken, and though he was a Dissenter from our Church, yet surely he knew better than openly to throw any Obstacles in the Way of promoting the publick Worship: Whereat, with more Marks of Resentment

1739.

August 28.

Reſentment than any I had before obſerved, he aſked me what I thought of his
not allowing Candles (as always had been)
for the daily Evening Service? Probably
(ſaid I) there might be none in Store at the
Time they were aſked: Then (ſaid he)
they might have been provided ſince; for
unleſs I had got ſome by ſeeking after them
myſelf, there would have been no Evening
Prayer for ſeveral Months paſt. I was
willing to put an End to this Talk, which
I found I could not turn to any Good;
and after diverting it a little while to ſome
other Point, he took his Leave with his
uſual Complaiſance and Civility, which he
had always ſhewn remarkably in his general Carriage to every Body; and I was
concerned now to ſee what Impreſſion of
Mind he was under.

29.
Wedneſday. A Veſſel from *Philadelphia*,
having a ſmall Quantity of Proviſions to
diſpoſe of, ſuch as Mr. *Jones* thought neceſſary for preſent Uſe; Mr. *Jones* was in
Treaty for them with the Maſter, whoſe
Sloop lay at *Tybee:* And afterwards, Mr.
Purry (whoſe Partnerſhip with *Montaigut*
was ended, and he going to live elſewhere)
having divers Remnants of Iron-work left
on his Hands; among which were ſeveral
uſeful Tools, often wanted, which Mr.
Jones ſaid he could buy a great Penny-
worth, &c. he dealt alſo for that: Mr.
Parker

Parker at the same Time was gone up the River, by Invitation, out of Curiosity to see a Sloop launched at Mr. *Williams*'s Plantation; which was building by his Order before he went hence, and was the first ever known to be built on this River: So that no immediate Progress could be made on the Commission of Accounts. Mr. *Cadogan*, in his Way from *Carolina* Southward, calling here, I took the Opportunity by him of writing to the Major (at present the Commander in Chief over the King's Troops in this Province) and transmitting to him those Papers and Advices which I had received on *Sunday* last from Colonel *Bull*. By this Opportunity we had News from *Charles-Town*, that *Lewis Jones* was taken there, and committed to safe Custody; being the Person who made his Escape by Flight the next Morning after that Murder was committed, which he was deeply a Party in, and for which two of them had been hanged. Spent the Afternoon at my Plantation.

Thursday. The frequent heavy Rains which had fallen this Summer, gave me sometimes fearful Apprehensions of great Damage ensuing: And the ill News we now received, shewed those Apprehensions not to be vain; for by a Letter from one *Tyrrel,* appointed Director of the Saw-Mill Work at *Old Ebenezer,* to Mr. *Jones*

30.

laſt Night, we were informed in few Words, that a great and uncommon Flood came down upon them, and had blown up the Mill; and therefore deſiring ſome Direction as ſoon as poſſible might be ſent, or given, what they muſt do. This was judged impoſſible without ſeeing it; wherefore it was propoſed, that ſome of us ſhould go up thither, and upon viewing it, give ſuch Directions as we then found neceſſary: Mr. *Jones* wiſhed that he and I might both go, as he had never ſeen the Place; which I readily conſented to, and withal, Mr. *Francis Moor* being at preſent (in Appearance) not overcharged with Buſineſs, it was aſked him alſo to go with us, that ſo our Enquiry into the Damage, and our joint Opinion thereon, might have the greater Weight with the General, when we ſaw him again. It being ſo reſolved, we ſet out in a Boat with five Hands, and one to ſteer, about Nine or Ten at Night, taking the Benefit of the firſt of the Flood, to carry us as far as it would help; which uſually is as far as *Puryſburgh*, and that is reckoned twenty-ſix Miles: But now by Reaſon of the great Stream that came down and overpowered the Tide, we had the Benefit of it no farther than about *Joſeph's Town*, which is ten Miles; and with very hard Labour againſt the Current, we made

it

it paſt Eight the next Morning before we reached *Puryſburgh*.

Friday. After two or three Hours Reſt and Refreſhment, about Eleven we ſet out again, having only fifteen Miles to *Ebenezer*; but now the Stream was grown ſo rapid, that after long Toil, we made it paſt Ten at Night ere we could reach it: From whence (having the Benefit of the Moon) we ſent away a Meſſenger immediately, to *Barker* the Cow-Pen Keeper by the Saw-Mill, to furniſh us with each a Horſe before Sun-riſing: After which we were kindly received by Mr. *Bolzius* the Miniſter, who has lately built a very good Houſe, where he lives; and Mr. *Groneau* another near him, of ſomewhat leſs Size. We lodged very commodiouſly with Bedding laid on the Floor, and ſlept comfortably.

Saturday. Horſes coming according to Appointment, we mounted very early, and got to the Mill about Seven, where we ſaw indeed a melancholy Wreck, and the Mill ſunk away and fallen all to one Side, but ſtill held entire, though impoſſible to be ſet ſo to right again: From whence it appeared, that the Work was of ſufficient Strength, as the Artificer had put it together; ſo was likewiſe the fore Bay, and the main Hatch-way, through which the ſpare Water was to be carried off, no Part

I 2   of

of it that we could difcover, giving Way, or taking any Damage: But the Flood was fo ftrong, and fpread fo wide, that when it came, it covered the whole Ground near it, overflowing the whole Work, which was perfectly buried under Water, and thofe Waters worked their Way from the Outfide of the Work underneath the Mill, which occafioned its Ruin: For after it had once found Vent, thro' ever fo fmall a Cranny, it foon made it larger, the Ground wafhing away apace, being of a loofe, fandy Nature, fo that Cavities were quickly made almoft every where round it; the Frame of the Whole yet holding together, after the greateft Part of the Foundation wafhed away and gone. Wherefore we thought the only Expedient at prefent neceffary was, that the Frame of the Mill fhould be taken to Pieces as foon as poffible, whilft it remained whole, before it received any farther Damage; and that the feveral Parts of it fhould be forted, and carefully laid together, as well as the Iron Work, and Tools, &c. in a Place of Safety, till the General's Pleafure could be known; for which we gave Orders: And after fpending what Time we had to fpare there, in other Enquiries, we returned to *Ebenezer*, were kindly entertained there for an Hour or two, and taking Boat about One a Clock, we came to *Savannah* betwixt Eight and Nine,

Nine, performing that in fo fhort a Time
with the Stream, which took up more
than three Times as much againft it.

Sunday. Another exceeding heavy Rain   2.
began about Four in the Morning, which
held till Afternoon; and many People began to expect fo much foul Weather would
end in a Hurricane at laft. The publick
Service of the Day was not neglected.

Monday. We met again, to proceed on   3.
the Commiffion of Enquiry into Accounts,
and took Mr. *Minis*'s in Hand again, whereon we had fpent fome Time on a former
Day, and was the more difficult to get
through, from the loofe Way of Book-
Keeping ufed by his late Partner *Colman
Salamons*, who difcovered himfelf guilty
of divers Frauds in his Partnerfhip; which
therefore was put an End to, and *Minis*
was fuing him; but he was fled and gone:
Minis himfelf not being capable of keeping his own Books (which had been the
principal Inducement of his taking *Salamons* into Partnerfhip with him) and fince
the Breach betwixt them, he hired an able
Clerk to do his Bufinefs; by whofe Readinefs we got fuch Light as was neceffary,
and proceeding very warily, we made fhift
to get over the Whole: Wherein we found
many fmall Errors of little Moment, and
no vifible Marks of any defigned Fraud;
unlefs it be charged to him as fuch, that

Mr.

1739. Mr. *Caufton*'s private Account was blended
with the Truſtees in ſome Articles, to the
Septemb. Value of about 40*l*. Sterling, in the ſame
Manner as we had found it with ſeveral
others. Confined myſelf at home the latter Part of the Day, and began to think
it Time to prepare another Packet for the
Truſt.

4. *Tueſday*. Spent good Part of my Time
in copying my own Journal, *&c. Paſquin*
began to appear again, in like Manner as
laſt Year, and was very free with all Sorts
of People, which was good Entertainment
to many: But whether it was genuine *Savannah* Wit, or the Produce of ſome other
Country, was not eaſy to diſcover. Mr.
Jennys not appearing yet, or any one from
him, we were at a little Stand in going on
with our Examination of Accounts; but
reſolved at our next Meeting, to try how
far we could penetrate of ourſelves, into
that of Mr. *Jennys's*, which carried the
Face, ſo far as we yet ſaw, of much Perplexity.

Wedneſday. After a few Hours employed, looking into Mr. *Jennys's* Accounts,
which through Length of Time, and other
Ways, required a cloſe Examination; upon
finding myſelf under a little more than ordinary Indiſpoſition, I retired home, to
compoſe my Diſorder, and laid aſide Buſineſs the reſt of the Day.

Thurſday,

Thurſday. Finding myſelf better, I re- 1739.
turned to what we were doing Yeſterday;
the ſame Account which then employed Septemb.
us, yet holding out to puzzle; neither 6.
could we get to an End of it, after a long
Morning's Work. Copying Work at home
was my Afternoon's Employment; and I
found nothing of the Day more worth
Notice, than the general Complaint which
every Body made of the uncommon Heat
they felt, which was attributed to a black,
heavy Sky, without Thunder to clear it,
as it commonly does, and without it is almoſt ſuffocating.

Friday. By Appointment with Mr. 7.
Jones, we were to have gone to the Truſt's
Farm this Morning, which was under Mr.
Bradley's Management, to take an Inventory of what we ſhould find: But by
Means of ſuch a Glut of Rain as had fallen
of late (and particularly the Night paſt)
ſome Swamp Lands in our Way were rendered unpaſſable at preſent; wherefore we
deferred it for a few Days, and betook ourſelves again to what we were looking after
in the Account of Mr. *Jennys,* freſh Matter ſtill appearing to ſtumble at: But we
got through it, as well as we could, at
laſt, making ſuch Obſervations in our going on, as will be beſt determined when
laid before the Truſtees: And we purpoſed to ſtop our farther Enquiry for the

I 4 preſent

1739.
Septemt.

present here, that we might methodize what we had done since we began, in order to send it away as soon as might be. In the Afternoon, by the Help of a Horse that I borrowed, I made a Visit to my litle Plantation, which I found grievously drenched with the Wet; and I feared it might have a bad Effect upon our Potatoes and Roots under Ground; but the Corn being generally ripe in most Places, and the Stalks bent down (as the Practice of the Country is) thereby to defend itself, we hoped it would be safe till a proper Time offered to gather it; it being common among many old Planters, after their Corn is so bent down, to let it hang till the rest of their Crop, whether Pease, Rice, &c. are all housed.

8. *Saturday.* Very sudden and unexpected News, of open War being declared with *Spain*, was brought us by a Sloop that arrived here this Day, with some Provisions to sell, from *Rhode-Island:* The Master of which reported, that the *Tartar* Pink sailed out of *England* the 17th of *June*, by Order of the Government, being sent Express, to inform the Provinces in the Northern *America* of it, &c. That she arrived first at *New-England*; from whence Packets, which she brought, were immediately dispatched by a Messenger over Land to *Connecticut, Rhode-Island, New-York, &c.* That

That the Meſſenger made no Stay, but went on in great Haſte: And that ſoon af- ter, the Governor of *Rhode-Iſland*, toge- ther with his Council, went into the Bal- cony of a publick Houſe; from whence his Secretary read to the People, who aſ- ſembled by Beat of Drum, what Orders he had received; whereby he was empower- ed to grant Commiſſions to all ſuch as were fitly qualified, to ſet out Privateers, and to take, burn, or deſtroy, any *Spa- niſh* Ships that they could: That before he left *Rhode-Iſland*, there were accord- ingly three Sloops got ready, with eighty Men each, and preparing immediately to put to Sea, and three or four more were preparing to follow them: That he under- ſtood the *Tartar* Pink was deſigned to ſail, with as little Loſs of Time as might be, from *Boſton*, for *Carolina* and *Georgia*, with Packets from the Government for thoſe two Provinces; and that he expected ſhe was here before him. It was thought proper to require the Maſter's Affidavit to the Truth of this Report; which he readily complied with: And thereupon, Mr. *Fran- cis Moor* being in Town, he went South in few Hours after, to acquaint the Major, who at preſent is Commander in Chief there, with theſe Things, taking a Copy of the Affidavit with him.

Sunday,

Sunday. The publick Divine Service was duly obferved at Church, and the Sacrament adminiftred. In the Afternoon an Exprefs was difpatched to the General (if haply he could be found, up in the Nations) to whom I wrote fully what occurred relating to the Affidavit, which I alfo fent Copy of: And whereas in the laft Packet that I received from the Truft on the 25th of *July*, there were feveral Letters for the General, which at that Inftant I delivered into his Secretary, Mr. *Moor's* Hands; he now recommending the Care of thofe Letters to fuch as fent the Exprefs, I made one Packet of the Whole: After which, I wrote alfo to the Lieutenant Governor of *Carolina*, inclofing Copy of the Mafter's Affidavit, as before; and alfo to the commanding Officer of the Company in the Barracks at *Port-Royal*, fending it to the Care of Meffieurs *Woodward* and *Flower* at *Port-Royal*, to whom likewife I wrote: All which I did, upon Advice newly received, by a Boat arrived from *Charles-Town*, that they had none of this News there at his coming away, and poffibly might not have any certain Account of it, till the *Tartar* Pink brought it: Moreover, in cafe they had authentick Advice, before mine reached them, it would appear a Token of our Readinefs to impart any Intelligence we received, that either Province

were

were interested in. In the Evening a trading Boat from *New-Windfor*, arrived in her Way to *Charles-Town*; the Patroon of which reported, that the General in his Travels, finding himself not well, was returning this Way, being not far from *Augufta*, where it might be expected he was arrived before this Time; but how far this Patroon might be credited, I cannot say.

Monday. Captain *Davis* having a Sloop laying here for some Time past, which was publickly known to be bound for *Auguftin*, with the same Trade that he sent hence by another not long ago; she now fell down the River to *Tybee*, intending thence to pursue her Voyage: But as Affairs stood at present with the *Spaniards*, we were a little alarmed at it, and of Opinion, that no Vessel ought to be permitted to sail thither from hence, whereby they were to be served in any Thing; and moreover we believed, that at *Auguftin* they had yet no Intelligence of this Rupture, which could only be from the *Havannah*; and probably no Advice of it was yet arrived there from *Spain*: Wherefore we thought it would be wrong to allow this Sloop to sail thither on any Account: And after a little Conference with Captain *Davis* thereon (who at first seemed to dare us to stop his Vessel, at our Peril, but afterwards finding we were determined to do it) he wrote an

10.

Order

Order himſelf to the Man whom he had appointed to command her, to bring her up again, and come to an Anchor where ſhe lay before; which Order Mr. *Fallowfield*, our Naval Officer, was to carry down, and ſee executed; waiting farther the General's Pleaſure when he would be here.

11. *Tueſday.* Mr. *Fallowfield* returned from *Tybee*, and Captain *Davis*'s Sloop anchored again at her old Birth. What elſe happened worth Notice, was a malicious, wicked Act done by ſome Perſon yet unknown, either Yeſterday, or in the Night, upon Mr. *Parker*'s Cattle; two whereof, *viz.* a Milch Cow that had a Calf ſucking, and a young Heifer, were both cruelly maimed, and mortally wounded, by a Stroke with an Axe, or ſome heavy Weapon, croſs the Chine, which cut through the Back-Bone of each alike: For the Diſcovery of which vile Act, it was thought fit to publiſh a Reward of 5 *l.* Sterling to any who ſhould bring the Perſon to Juſtice that did it; which Mr. *Jones* has promiſed to pay upon Conviction of the Offender. This was the more remarkable, becauſe Mr. *Parker* had ſuffered divers Loſſes of late in his Cattle, and therefore it was pretty evident the Spite was at him particularly, and probably might ariſe from ſome Villain whom the Magiſtrate had found ſufficient Cauſe to deal ſomewhat ſharply with,

with, when he was in the Execution of his Office.

Wednefday. Notwithftanding what Precaution was taken on *Monday* laft with Captain *Davis,* to hinder any Intelligence going to *Auguftin,* we had now Notice, that he was preparing to elude it all, and determined, by fome Means or other, to carry on his Defign; which gave great Apprehenfions to many People of the Confequence: Whereupon the Magiftrates met again, and refolved to demand fufficient Security of him, by entering into a Bond of 500 *l.* Sterling Penalty for himfelf, and his two Sureties in 250 *l.* each, that he would not proceed farther in that Affair, till the General came: In Purfuance of which, the Recorder (Mr. *Chriftie)* was to fee it done; and in the mean while Mr. *Parker* and I meeting the Captain, he feemed readily to agree to it: But the Recorder afterwards (either through Miftake, or rather defignedly, as we had Reafon to believe from what Temper he difcovered) made the Condition of the Bond to be only for the Veffel's not failing, and no Reftraint on the Captain himfelf, who might go where he pleafed: The Confequence of which was —

Thurfday. About One a Clock in the Morning, we were alarmed again, at a frefh and unexpected Movement of the Captain's, who with feveral Hands was

carrying

carrying divers Parcels of Baggage to the Water-Side; among whom was one *Foster* a Tything-man, at whose House the Captain lodged, and who was privy to the whole Intrigue (as we found afterwards) in Breach of his Duty to the Colony, and was to be one, among others, that should accompany the Captain in his Expedition: Another Tything-man that happened accidentally to be strolling about the Bluff at that Time of Night (on what Occasion we know not) seeing what was about, went immediately and knocked up Mr. *Parker*, who in like Manner calling on me, I rose, and called Mr. *Mercer* the Constable, and thence in our Way we also took Mr. *Jones* with us, making what Haste we could to the Water-Side; where we found *Foster* and the other Tything-man (whose Name is *Salter*) skuffling about putting the Baggage into a Boat: Whereupon the Guard was called, which we were at a good Distance from; and on their coming all was secured. Here it is to be noted, that a Skooner lay at Anchor hard by, which came with some petty Cargo for Sale, a long while since, the Master whereof was an idle, drunken Fellow, and had but newly taken out his Clearance to return to some Northern Plantation: It was so concerted now (as afterwards appeared) that upon the Captain's Sloop being stopt, he had hired, or

(as

(as some believed) bought this Skooner, to supply the Place of his Sloop, on board of which these Parcels were shipping, at this unseasonable Time in the Night; and the Captain, with his Followers, were also going in her; which the Captain himself acknowledged, but denied his Intention of going to Sea in her, telling us, that he was only going to *Tybee* for the Benefit of Change of Air, by the Advice of Dr. *Tailfer*, where he purposed to stay waiting the General's Arrival: Which we thought was not probable, *Tybee* being a Place so exceedingly pestered with Musketas, by Reason of the adjacent Marshes, that no Person would ever be fond of taking his Abode ashore there, as he pretended he meant to do in a Hut; where the Skooner, he said, was to leave him. After looking into the Baggage at the Guard, where we then came, and finding that most of it consisted of Bedding, and some other Things useful, whether on board or ashore, we dismissed the Company, leaving with the Guard a strict Charge, that they should suffer no Vessel or Boat to go off without a Permit from the Magistrates. Captain *Davis* growing very warm at these Disappointments, and directing his Discourse to me, told me I might expect a Protest, for Damages, &c. which I told him in Return, I valued not, and bade him do his worst.

Soon

Soon after, we fent for the Mafter of the Skooner out of his Bed where he lodged; and upon Examination, found him grofsly prevaricating; but could not deny that Captain *Davis*, with other Company, was to go in his Veffel to *Tybee*, whilft he lay afhore, and moft of the Sailors were the Captain's own, which belonged to his Sloop that was ftopt. Upon the Whole, therefore, it was pretty manifeft what was intended; and it was judged neceffary to ftop the Skooner alfo in the River, as well as all other fmall Craft: After which we all returned to our Reft. Towards Noon an Exprefs arrived, with Letters of the 10th, from the Government at *Charles-Town*; and of Yefterday's Date from the Magiftrates in and near *Port-Royal*, confirming the War being actually declared, which they had Advice of by a Sloop alfo from *Rhode-Ifland*, that arrived fince the other which brought the firft News of it: But the *Tartar* Pink was not yet heard of. By thefe Letters we were farther informed, that at the coming away of the Exprefs, feveral Guns were fired, and Signals made at *Johnfon*'s Fort, in the Mouth of that Harbour; by which they underftood feveral Ships were feen over the Bar, which they hoped came from *Europe*. But in the Midft of thefe Hoftilities from abroad, it was now their great Unhappinefs to have

a

a more dangerous Enemy in the Heart of
their Country to deal with: For their Negroes had made an Infurrection, which began firft at *Stonoe* (Midway betwixt *Charles-
Town* and *Port-Royal)* where they had forced
a large Store, furnifhed themfelves with Arms
and Ammunition, killed all the Family on
that Plantation, and divers other white
People, burning and deftroying all that
came in their Way; fo that the Meffenger
who came, told us the Country thereabout was full of Flames: Our Letters
alfo informed us, that they were fearful
left it fhould prove general; and that the
Militia was raifed upon them throughout
the whole Province; a Party of whom, of
about twenty, had met and engaged ninety
of them in one Body, of whom they had
taken four Prifoners, and killed ten, &c.
They farther wrote us, they had Reafon
to believe, that many of them would bend
their Courfe to the South, and endeavour
to crofs the *Savannah* River; from whence
they intended to go on for *Auguftin* to the
Spaniards: Wherefore they hoped we would
do what we could, in fecuring the Paffes
on that River, promifing a Reward of 50 *l.*
Currency for every Negro taken alive, and
delivered at *Charles-Town*; and 25 *l.* ditto
for every one killed. Upon thefe Advices,
we difpatched Intelligence of it to the
Major, commanding in the South, who

possibly might, by small Parties, intercept some of them, if they escaped in crossing the River *Savannah*, and pursued their March to the Southward by Land: And as we could ill spare any of the few Men we had, that were fit to bear Arms, and by so doing leave ourselves more and more defenceless, we sent immediately Notice of it to Mr. *Montaigut*, whose Plantation with Negroes is not many Miles distant, and who is also a military Officer himself; recommending it to him, to have a Guard at those Passes beyond him, and to send proper Caution to the Fort at *Palachocolas*, farther than which would be needless: And we would do the best we could below, to the Mouth of the River.——Now it fully appeared, that the securing that *Spaniard* some Time ago *(vide July 29.)* was not upon a groundless Suspicion (as some People then termed it, who are rarely pleased with whatever is done, because they have not the doing it) for it is more than probable, that he had been employed a pretty while, in corrupting the Negroes of *Carolina*; and was certainly with *Don Pedro* at *Charles-Town*, at the Time when he lately came thither with his Launch.

14.   *Friday*. All appeared quiet, without any farther Disturbance at present: And I was very glad to see the Storm composed also, which lately happened betwixt our

first

firſt Magiſtrate and Store-Keeper; who
both ſeemed deſirous, that what was paſt
might be forgot; and they converſed with
mutual Tokens of Friendſhip. Late in the
Evening arrived Captain *Norbury*, and with
him Enſign *Cadogan*, from St. *Simon*'s, being alarmed at the News of War, which
we had ſent them from hence; the Captain now making his Way to his Poſt at
Port-Royal, and *Cadogan* going for *Carolina*
on Buſineſs of the Regiment, which was
ordered him by the Major.

Saturday. Mr. *Francis Moor*, who came
with thoſe Officers Yeſterday as far as Mr.
Fallowfield's Plantation by Water, and lay
there; rode thence this Morning, and returned to Town. Captain *Norbury* had an
Expectation of taking a Sum of Money
now with him that belonged to his Company, and was left, it ſeems, (on what Occaſion not known) in the Hands of Mr.
Upton, by Lieutenant *Delegal*, when he
went for *England*: This Money Mr. *Upton*
had been trading with at *Charles-Town*, and
was going to diſpoſe of the Goods in the
South after his having ſtaid here two or
three Days; and Captain *Norbury* thereupon ſent to ſpeak with him about it, underſtanding he intended to proceed next
Day: But Mr. *Upton*, inſtead of ſeeing
him, went off in the Morning very early
with his Boat and Cargo; which the Cap-

tain

tain was so enraged at when he rose, that
he got a Warrant from Mr. *Parker* to stop
him at *Thunderbolt*; which was done by
Mr. *Mercer* the Constable: And Mr. *Upton*
came to such Terms with the Captain, by
Assurance of the Money being paid into an
Officer's Hands at St. *Simon*'s, as soon as
the Goods were disposed of ; that at length
he permitted him to go on, after a great
Hurly-burly, and warm Controversy, which
the Captain had with Mr. *Jones* ; who he
thought took upon him to justify Mr. *Upton*
farther than was right.

16.   *Sunday*.   The ordinary Duty of the
Day was regularly observed.

17.   *Monday*.   Early this Morning died the
Reverend Mr. *Edward Dyson*, Chaplain to
General *Oglethorpe*'s Regiment: He had
been absent upon Furlow some Time ; most
Part of which he passed away in this Town,
where he sickened a while since, and a
Pleuretick Fever carried him off at last.
Captain *Norbury*, with Mr. *Cadogan*, purposed to have gone off this Afternoon;
and I took this Opportunity by them, of
sending my Packet of the 10th Instant to
Mr. *Verelst* ; which they promised to take
Care of, together with my Letter to Mr.
Hopton, recommending it to him to send it
off by the first fitting Occasion : But being
invited to Mr. *Dyson*'s Funeral this Evening, where they attended, and did the
                                                Corpse

Corpſe the Honour of firing ſome ſmall
Arms in Token of his being one of the
Regiment, they put off their Deſign till
to-morrow.

Tueſday. Mr. *Parker* acquainted me this
Morning, that after Mr. *Fallowfield* (as
Conſtable on Duty) had looked curſorily
into Mr. *Dyſon's* Cheſts, Scrutore, *&c.*
wherein many Writings of various Kinds,
and Accounts, were found; at which Inſpection we had deſired Mr. *Francis Moor* to be
preſent, and alſo Mr. *Jones*; and they had
locked and ſealed all up, to prevent any
Embezzlement, till a proper Adminiſtrator
was appointed: Mr. *Chriſtie*, the Recorder,
had now applied to him *(Parker)* to join
in putting the Seal to an Adminiſtration
which he had prepared, wherein Mr. *Fallowfield* was appointed of Right (as he
deemed it) to take that Office upon him:
But Mr. *Parker* (knowing better than to
commit the Truſt of ſuch Effects, that
were ſuppoſed to be very conſiderable, to
thoſe two) had refuſed him: And indeed
it was well provided, that the Seal was never to be come at, without more Keys than
one; otherwiſe it is to be doubted our Recorder might have gone ſometimes unwarrantable Lengths; and the Chagrin which
ſat cloſe upon him for a while paſt, was
generally imputed to the Defeats and Diſ-
appointments he had met with in his Attempts.

tempts. I told Mr. *Parker* what I thought, that he was much to be commended; and my Advice was, that every Thing being safe, under Locks and Seals, it would be beft, for farther Security, to remove all into the publick Stores, and Mr. *Fallowfield* might keep the Keys till the General came, and a proper Person or Persons were appointed by him to adminifter. About Noon arrived *Peter Emery*, with his Boat from *Charles-Town*, after feveral Days Expectation; but brought no News of any Ship come from *England*, or any Letters thence: But I had one from Lieutenant Governor *Bull*, informing us, that what I had wrote him of the 9th, and the Affidavit inclofed, was verified in all its Parts; and that Captain *Warren* in the *Squirrel* was lately come in, who acquainted him of his having been at *Bofton*, and that he parted with Captain *Townfhend* in the *Tartar* Pink three Days before, who was ftationed at *Carolina*, and was to follow him to the South after Delivery of the Orders he had brought; where he defigned, with Captain *Laws* in the *Spence*, to vifit the Gulph of *Florida*, and the *Spanifh* Coafts: Moreover, Captain *Warren* affured the Lieutenant Governor (as he writes me) that he, with all his Majefty's Ships on this Northern Station, have particular Orders, upon the firft Notice or Sufpicion of the *Spaniards* intending

tending to invade either of thefe Provinces, to come to their Affiftance immediately; and that he, as the fenior Commander, upon due and full Information, would fend for all his Majefty's Ships aforementioned. This was good News indeed : But it occafioned a little Obfervation to be made, that whilft all the Northern Provinces had each of them one, two, or three ftationed Ships always ready to protect them, poor *Georgia* had never any but the *Hawk* Sloop yet. Colonel *Bull*, after touching upon a few other Particulars, in Conclufion tells me, that all Matters which may concern the Safety and Advantage of either Province, fhould from Time to Time be communicated to me : And he informed me likewife, that their Militia had attacked the rebellious Negroes, with that Vigour and Succefs, killing fo many of them, that they had put an End to their Defigns; which was alfo happy News. But by fome other Letters which came thence, a very terrible Calamity of Sicknefs had befallen them at *Charles-Town*, which proved exceeding mortal, great Numbers dying weekly, and it is termed a contagious, malignant Fever : Which among a Multitude of others, had carried off alfo fome of our Freeholders, who preferred living there to this Place; namely, *Coates*, *Muer*, *Delgrafs*, and *Holmes*; whether any others of them or not, we are yet to learn. From several Inftances it appearing, that Captain *Davis* was ftill carrying on his Defign, of getting fecretly away, and to go to *Auguftin*, in Spite of all Caution ufed to prevent it; which might be of moft dangerous Confequence to this Colony: And alfo receiving Information, that his Sloop which he fent thither about two Months fince, was returned, and coming up our River; but upon fecret Advice fent her, fhe turned back, and was failed to fome other Port, which we imagined was done to prevent any Examination being taken of her by the Magiftrates here: It was now thought high Time to be no longer trifling, when we knew not but our All was at Stake; wherefore the Magiftrates took him into fafe Cuftody: But in Confideration of his being an infirm Man, would not commit him to the common Prifon; but at his own Requeft, ordered him to be confined to his own Lodgings, with two Centuries over him. *N. B.* Mr. *Chriftie* was not prefent, either at this, or any of the former Proceedings concerning *Davis*, though fent to; but joined with the Cabal, which ftill fubfifted at *Jenkins*'s, cenfuring and oppofing every Thing, as far as they could, that was done, calling it arbitrary and tyrannical, againft Law, *&c.* Nay, fo far was he poffeffed with that Spirit of Contra-

diction,

diction, that in my Hearing he declared it an unjuſt Act, to do what was before done, only on a groundleſs Suſpicion: Which I could not without ſome Indignation reply to, and aſk him, whether or not Captain *Davis's* own Words of Defiance, which he uſed, and daring any one to ſtop him at their Peril, for to *Auguſtin* he was going, and thither he would go: Whether or not after ſuch a Declaration and Attempt to go off ſecretly in the Night, the Magiſtrates proceeded on *groundleſs Suſpicion*: For if he propagated ſuch Doctrine, there would be more than a groundleſs Suſpicion, that he himſelf was not ſo well affected as he ought. It was too remarkable, that for ſome Time paſt, he was become a cloſe Diſciple under our famous Demagogue, whoſe continual Practice for a long while had been to inſtruct his Hearers in being very circumſpect, leſt their Liberties ſhould be infringed; and that it was their Duty always to ſtand in Defence of them: So that from this Nurſery moſt of thoſe Evils have ſprung that have formerly been taken Notice of; and this poor, weak Man, having his Vanity tickled, and being perſuaded that his Knowledge in the Law was ſuperior to the others his Aſſociates in the Magiſtracy, which they ought to pay an implicit Regard to, but did not; he became peeviſh, and inſtead of giving any

Aſſiſtance

1739.
Septemb.

Affiftance to the publick Affairs carrying on, he advifed with none but thofe, who never approved of any Thing which they had not the Direction of, or at leaft were confulted in: So that by his thus withdrawing himfelf, the greateft Weight of civil Power to fecure the Peace, fell to Mr. *Parker*'s Share almoft totally for the prefent, Mr. *Gilbert* being incapable in many Things to take a Share abftractedly to himfelf, though always ready to join in doing his Duty *fans Reproche :* By which Means *Parker* has fhewn fully a good natural Underftanding, and clear Difcernment of Juftice, with a fuitable Courage, not foon to be terrified from purfuing what he thinks fo, like a right honeft Man : And fo Mr. *Jones* efteems him, notwithftanding their late Difcord, which I hope is pretty well forgotten between them, and they will be better cemented hereafter : It would be pretty hard to determine which of them was in the right at that Time ; I thought them both wrong.

19.

Wednefday. Our two Officers bound to *Port-Royal*, and not liking the Weather to crofs *Delfufka Sound* Yefterday, they went off this Morning : And this proving a Day of more Leifure, every Body followed quietly their own Bufinefs ; which among fuch as had any Plantation, was to get in fome of their Harveft.

Thurfday.

Thursday. This Morning I was knocked up about One a Clock by an Exprefs from the General, who wrote me of Yesterday's Date from *Palachocolas,* that he was come thither; that his Health was pretty much recovered; that he fhould ftay there till this Day, to receive Advices of what was doing by the revolted Negroes; and that if nothing happened extraordinary, he intended to proceed to *Ebenezer* this Evening; then call at Mr. *d'Beaufain's,* and fo make all the Hafte he could down. By which we found the Report of his Sicknefs was too true; and all who had a due Value for him, when I publifhed the News, as the Day came on, were very joyful to hear it. Towards Evening I received a large Packet, fent by the Attorney-General from *Charles-Town,* which he wrote me of the 15th he received the Day before, by the *Tartar* Pink arrived juft then, which had been earneftly expected, and brought Orders from *England* to the Governor what he was to do, upon this War breaking out: On opening it, I found the Bulk of what was enclofed, was a diftinct Packet to the General, and one of a fmaller Size directed to me; both which had been put under one Cover by the Attorney-General, and came both to him from the Truft: In that for me, were a few Letters for private Perfons, and one to myfelf from

Mr.

Mr. *Verelst*, who wrote me of the 22d of *June* a short Letter, but a very kind one, relating to my own Affairs, and the Trust's Benevolence towards me; which gave me more and more Vigour: What else he had to say, he told me (being in a Hurry) I might expect by Captain *Thompson*, who was ready to sail, but a general Embargo at present stopt him, which it was expected the Trustees would soon get a Licence from the Government to free him from, and then he would sail. These Packets were sent from *Charles-Town* by the Way of *Puryburgh*, under the Care of one Major *Bryan* who was going that Way, who had the Charge of another Packet, that came also by the *Tartar*, not from the Trust, but supposed to be from some of the publick Offices of State, directed to the General; and by the same Conveyance likewise came another Letter of the 15th from Colonel *Bull* to me, signifying his having received Orders to grant Letters of Marque, &c. and to act offensively against the *Spaniards*; and referring me farther to his Letter of the 13th, which I had received. All these Dispatches coming to the Hands of Mr. *Montaigut* in the Neighbourhood of *Puryburgh*, he sent his Boat away with them immediately hither, where we also looked wishfully to see the General to-morrow.

Friday.

Friday. Took a Walk very early this Morning, and catched the Opportunity of a few Hours to fpend with my Crew, and fee what Advances they had made in the Work appointed them laft. We were getting in Corn now, which *Jones* thought would have been exceeded by nobody in Goodnefs, on the like Quantity of Ground: But the long, heavy Rains that fell this Summer (more than common) and often covered the low Lands with Water, bred fuch an Excefs of Worms and Infects, as did very great Damage, more than Half not efcaping; which muft reduce our Meafure to the fame Proportion: But the higheft and dry Lands have produced fuch a Crop for thofe who have taken proper Care in Cultivation, as ought to encourage them. Thefe Accidents are not uncommon in all Countries; and in my Native of *England,* the Farmers in the up-land Parts feldom or never grieve, when they fee their Neighbours in Vale almoft drowned. I returned in Expectation of feeing the General fome Time to Day; but upon his not coming, we concluded that he fpent the Night enfuing with Meffieurs *Montaigut* and *Beaufain,* agreeable to what he had wrote. Nothing ftirring worth Note.

Saturday. Little Attention given to any Thing, befides the earneft Expectation that almoft every Body fhewed of the General's Arrival,

Arrival, which drew many People to the Water-fide, to wait his Coming; but it proved in vain yet. Captain *Davis*, with fome of his principal Affiftants of the Club, we underftood was fully employed for two or three Days paft in drawing up a Remonftrance of the ill Ufage he had met with, to be prefented to the General as foon as he came; wherein it would appear fo unexampled (as they gave out) that the Authors of it would have Caufe to repent of what they had done: All which we were to fee, and how far our Actions would be approved of by the General, or cenfured.

Sunday. The Service of the Church had due Obfervance. About Five in the Afternoon the Boat was efpied coming down the River, wherein was the General, who landed foon after, under the ufual Compliment of our Cannon, and as many of our Freeholders, as could get under Arms in little more than a Quarter of an Hour, which was about fifty, to receive him; all glad to fee him fo well, and healthy, as he appeared, after fo dangerous a Sicknefs as he had gone lately through. He was attended to his Lodging by the principal Officers and Magiftrates of the Town; who after paying their Refpects, and hearing what he was pleafed to acquaint them with (briefly at prefent) all took their Leave, and withdrew. I delivered

vered him the Packet from the Truſt, 1739.
which came to my Hands the 20th; and
after he had opened it and read ſome of Septemb.
thoſe Advices he ſeemed to think of moſt
Moment, I retired, and left him to his
Reſt, which I thought he wanted.

Monday. My Duty prompted me to a 24.
pretty cloſe Attendance on the General,
which I gladly paid; and in Converſation
he was pleaſed moſt agreeably to inform us,
how unqueſtionably he had the Friendſhip
of the Lower and Upper *Creek Indians* ſecured to us, which at this Time more eſpecially was of ſo great Value, when we
were apprehenſive, thro' the ſecret Working
of our Enemies, their former Amity began
to wax cold: But as they were a very numerous and bold Nation, and lay immediately on the Back of this Province, we
now looked on them as a Wall of Defence. After imparting to us what he
thought proper, relating to his Travels, the
next Thing deſirable was his Approbation
of the publick Proceedings here ſince he
left us; which he let us underſtand he
was very well pleaſed with, particularly in
bringing the Authors of that late Murder
to Juſtice, for which two of them had ſuffered; and next, for being ſo watchful in
guarding againſt any dangerous Correſpondence at this Seaſon with the *Spaniards,*
commending the Spirit which appeared
among

among us on that Occafion, and confirming what was done relating to Captain *Davis*, as what the Exigence of Time required; whom he moreover fent for in the
Evening, and after a private Conference
with him for a little while, he remanded
him to his former Confinement, till he
fhould confider farther of it another Day
with the Magiftrates. This was the more
acceptable, becaufe it was a fufficient Token to our Gentry of the Cabal, how vain
and impotent their little Craft, mixed with
much Malice, would appear, in Oppofition
to thofe who purfued fuch Steps as condu-
ced to the Welfare of the Colony.

25.	*Tuefday,*	The great Variety of Mat-
26.	*Wednefday,*	ter, which the General had
27.	*Thurfday,*	under his Confideration, du-
28.	*Friday,*	ring his Abode among us,
29.	*Saturday.*	at this important Juncture,

made it impracticable for me fo to keep Pace,
as to make an exact Diary of all that paffed:
Wherefore it was only in my Power to
note fome of the moft remarkable Tranfactions that happened during thefe five
Days paft, without fpecifying particular
Times. Captain *Davis*, by the General's
Order to the Magiftrates, was difcharged
from his Confinement, upon his entering
into a Bond of 100 *l.* Penalty not to go to
Auguftin, or any *Spanifh* Port, and to be
of the good Behaviour: And afterwards he
found

found Means of obtaining the General's Opinion of his Sincerity so far, that he undertook to turn his Sloop, which was intended for *Augustin*, into a Privateer, and the General would grant him a Com- mission for that Purpose: So that he now appeared as earnest to plunder the *Spani-* *ards*, as before he was to succour them: And it was well known, that through the long Intercourse he had with them, and the Knowledge of all their Coasts, he was capable of annoying them very much: Wherefore we were now to expect some Performances of those Exploits which he proposed, and due Diligence at present was used, to fit out this Privateer, and get her well manned. Frequent Dispatches were sent to divers Places, with Orders, as the General saw needful: And Lieutenant *Dun-bar* being sent on this Occasion to *Charles-Town*, I wrote by him to Mr. *Verelst* (to be forwarded by my Correspondent Mr. *Hopton*) a Letter of the 25th; wherein I enclosed, by Order from the General, Co-pies I had taken of three Affidavits, made in the *Indian* Nation, by *Brown* and *Gar-dener*; setting forth the fatal Consequence of Rum in such Abundance, sent from *Carolina* among the *Cherokee Indians*, &c. and it was not improbable but that this Letter might overtake at *Charles-Town* the former which I wrote of the 10th. Every

1739.
Septemb.
25.
26.
27.
28.
29.

Body that we faw from *Carolina* confirmed the deplorable State they were in at *Charles-Town* (as before noted on the 18th) and the frefheft News thence informed us, that *Saturday* and *Sunday* laft they buried nineteen and twenty on a Day; fo that it is deemed next to a Peftilence; moft of thofe who are taken with it, dying in lefs than forty-eight Hours; and by a careful Computation among themfelves, they reckon the Small-Pox among them a little while fince, and this dreadful Mortality now, have taken away at leaft one Fourth of the white People of that Town: One or two more of our deferting Freeholders are faid to be among the Deceafed, namely, *Defborow* the Carpenter, and his two Sons, both grown to Man's Eftate; Mr. *Amiens*, Clerk of the Affembly; Mr. *Lewis*, a Lawyer, and Judge of the Admiralty; and old Monfieur *Thomas*, a noted Engineer, who left St. *Simon*'s lately, upon a Stop being put to any farther Fortifications there at that Time. Mr. *Eyre*, a Cadet in the Regiment, who with others attended the General in his Progrefs among the *Indians*, was now fent back thither, with Inftructions, and a Commiffion, to one Mr. *Samuel Brown*, a noted and well efteemed Trader among the *Cherokees*, to bring down a confiderable Body of that Nation, and to march at the Head of them, expecting

they

they would be feveral Hundreds, whom it
is prefumed his Excellence purpofes to make
ufe of, as a Diverfion with the *Spanifh In-*
dians in the Neighbourhood of *Auguftin:*
And he depends on a ftrong Detachment
from the *Creeks*, purfuant to their late A-
greement; whom he will not keep idle.
During thefe Preparations againft the Enemy, which were carried on and directed by
him alone, who beft knew how, and in
whom proper Powers were invefted, our
Juntillo, who fought all Occafions to dif-
tinguifh themfelves at all Times, now projected to form themfelves into a Body, under the Title of Volunteers, who defired
to be regulated a Company for Defence
of the Country, &c. but exclufive of any
Commands from the ftanding Militia of
the Town where they lived: For which
End, they believed it the wifeft Courfe to
name their own Officers; and accordingly
they chofe their Captain, Lieutenant, and
Enfign among themfelves; who, all together, did not exceed fix or feven in Number; but were looked on as Men qualified
to conduct any Enterprize they took in
Hand (though miferably defeated hitherto
in all their political Schemes) and having fo
laid this Ground-Work, they made no
Queftion but Gentlemen Volunteers would
flock together, under the imaginary Command of Captain *Tailfer*, &c. till after two

1739.

Septemb.
25.
26.
27.
28.
29.

or

or three Days Waiting, and feeing no Recruits come in, they then betook themfelves to follicit fuch as they could prevail with, to be enrolled in a Piece of Paper; where at length they picked up about a Dozen more to be added to the former; and thefe were generally loofe Fellows, moftly *Scotch* Servants lately out of their Time, or the like. Thus provided, they next addreffed the General, by Petition, that he would authorize them to act conformable to what they conceived would render them ufeful to the Colony: But his Excellence not happening to think as they did, that an Independant Command in fuch Hands would contribute to the Safety of the Colony, which required Unity, and due Obedience in all Things for our Prefervation; he received it with Contempt, and not without fome Refentment (it may be imagined) at their Infolence, in conftituting Officers of their own, in Expectation that he would give them Commiffions, exalting them above all others. —— And fo the Week ended.

30.   *Sunday.* Due Obfervance was paid to the Day; and the General was pleafed to attend Divine Service both before Noon and after.

October
1.
    Monday. The General ceafed not from a continual Application to regulate every Thing that he thought expedient for us to

govern

govern ourfelves by, in his Abfence, when
he fhould go for the Southern Frontier,
which we now expected would be in few
Days more. Towards Evening arrived
Captain *Davis*'s Snow, under the Command of Captain *James Williams*, who
failed hence with Lumber for the *Weſt-
Indies* fome Months fince (*vide May* 28,
29, 30, and *June* 1.) and leaving the Snow
at *Tybee*, he came up in his Boat, when he
waited on the General, and made his Report, *&c.* His Loading was principally
Molaffes and Sugar; which unlefs he found
a Market for here, he intended to look
farther: His Brother *Robert*, who failed
with him from hence, ftaid at St. *Kitt*'s;
and it was fuppofed was gone ere now for
England.

Tuefday. Nothing worth Note, unlefs a
violent Rain may be thought fo, which began with the Sun-rifing, and held all Day
in an uncommon Manner; fo that the
Ground was covered with Water, even on
the high Land where the Town ftands; and
there was no ftirring out of Doors, neither
did it entirely ceafe at Bed-Time: But
fuch Rains being always looked for in other
hot Countries, at this Seafon of the Year,
puts an End to any Admiration here. To-
morrow being the Day when the Reprieve
would expire, which was granted to *Levett* (one of thofe condemned for Murder)

and

1739.

October

2.

and he writing a Petition to the General for Mercy; wherein, inftead of owning himfelf guilty of any Crime, he infifted on his Innocence, lamenting his Misfortune that he lay under *Sufpicion* of Murder; the General was much offended at it, and conftrued it to be arraigning the Juftice of the Place, and particularly of the Jury, who had found him *Guilty:* For how was it poffible for them to believe what he alledged in his own Defence, *viz.* that he was not well, and laid down to fleep, fo that he heard nothing of it; when it was confeffed by himfelf, and known, that the Place where he faid he lay, was upon the Deck, and within very few Yards of where the Fact was committed; which in the barbarous Manner it was carried on, muft take up much Time, and could not be without Strife and Noife? The General farther obferved, that he now fell fhort even of that Confeffion which he had made before, and found him prevaricating: Wherefore, to vindicate the Juftice of the Court and Jury, and not to leave it in his Power, by a Pardon, to throw Reproaches on both hereafter, he refolved he fhould die; and ordered that he fhould have Notice to prepare himfelf for it in four Days more.

3. *Wednefday.* The General intending to publifh the War with *Spain,* in due Manner

ner and Form; he gave Orders for all the Freeholders to be under Arms at Beat of Drum, and that the Magiftrates, in their Gowns, fhould be on the Bench at Noon in the Court-Houfe; whilft in the mean Time he directed a proper Declaration to be wrote, fetting forth the Orders he received from his Majefty's Secretary of State, relating thereto; and alfo another Paper, cautioning all Perfons in this Province, to have a watchful Eye upon any Negroes, who might attempt to fet a Foot in it; forafmuch as many of them, at the Inftigation of the *Spaniards*, had run lately away from their Mafters in *Carolina*, and found kind Reception at *Auguftin*: And moreover, the late Infurrection of them in that Province, which was but newly fuppreffed, gave Reafon to apprehend, that fome of fuch as had yet efcaped, might be lurking about in *Georgia*, in hopes to make their Way to the Enemy; and in paffing on, might do great Mifchief among our Settlers; promifing, as a Reward for taking them, what the Act here directs, and withal, what the Government at *Carolina* promifes to pay, for every fuch runaway Negroe, delivered at *Charles-Town*, alive or dead. When the General came to the Court-Houfe, where he found the Magiftrates on the Bench, he took his Seat by them; and the Militia, who being drawn

L 4   up

up before the Court-Houſe, had grounded
their Arms, and were all come within the
Doors; his Excellence then made a Speech
to them all, ſuitable to the Occaſion, commending that Chearfulneſs which he obſerved to be in all Ranks of People, aſſuring
them, that effectual Care had been taken by
him to prevent any Enemy coming on our
Backs from the Weſt and South; and as
we lay open only to the Sea, we had already ſome Frigates cruiſing on the Coaſt to
protect us; and he had Aſſurance from the
Government of more Strength at Sea; as
alſo ſome Expectation of an additional
Force by Land, to be ſent him in a little
while. Then he put thoſe Papers into my
Hands, which were prepared, directing me
to read them to the People; which I did,
as audibly as I could; afterwards the Conſtables read them again to the Men, on
taking up their Arms; and next, they were
affixed to the Doors of the Court-Houſe.
Upon the General's Return to his Lodgings
five Cannon were fired, and the Militia
gave three handſome Vollies with their
ſmall Arms, as it were in Defiance, without the Appearance of any Dread of the
Spaniards.

4.   *Thurſday,* ⎫ So little Intermiſſion was
5.   *Friday,*   ⎬ found theſe few Days
6.   *Saturday.* ⎭ from attending the General's Commands, which rather multiplied
than

than abated, through his inceſſant Application, that the moſt material Thing which happened abroad, and I thought worth noting, was the Death of the old *Mico Thomo Chichi*, ſaid to be upwards of ninety Years of Age: And as the General always eſteemed him a Friend of the Colony, and therefore ſhewed him particular Marks of his Eſteem, when living; ſo he diſtinguiſhed him at his Death, ordering his Corpſe to be brought down; and it was buried in the Centre of one of the principal Squares, the General being pleaſed to make himſelf one of his Pall-Bearers, with five others, among whom he laid his Commands on me to be one, and the other four were military Officers: At the Depoſiting of the Corpſe, ſeven Minute Guns were fired, and about forty Men in Arms (as many as could inſtantly be found) gave three Vollies over the Grave; which the General ſays he intends to dignify with ſome Obeliſk, or the like, over it, as an Ornament to the Town, and a Memorial to the *Indians*, how great Regard the *Engliſh* would pay to all their Nations, who maintain true Friendſhip with us.

Sunday. Divine Service was performed in the uſual Manner. A Boat arrived from Captain *Thompſon*, juſt come to an Anchor without the Bar at *Tybee*: In the Boat was Captain *Hugh McKay*, who went as ſoon

as

as afhore to wait on the General, to whom he carried a Packet: And at the fame Time the Cockfwain of the Boat brought me a Bag fealed, wherein I found alfo a Packet directed to me, and many Letters loofe in the Bag for divers People; befides one from the Captain of the Ship to me, defiring me to make hafte down to him, or to fend a Reafon why not: And moreover I received a Letter from Mr. *Verelft* of the 16th of *July*, fignifying the Orders the Truft had given Captain *Thompfon*; as alfo importing the Truftees Orders to me, to go forthwith on board the Ship, on her Arrival, and receive the Packet directed to me; in which Packet I fhould find a Direction to a covered Box directed to me, N⁰ I. wherein were Bills General *Oglethorpe* would fign and deliver to me, purfuant to the Truftees Requeft to him. With Leave of the General, about Ten at Night, I fet off (the Tide then ferving) together with Captain *McKay*, in the Ship's Yawl, which returned; and we had provided a fmall Veffel to follow us (a Skooner) fufficient to bring away what Paffengers were for this Place; likewife fome few Goods that we were in great Need of, fuch as could be readily come at, and by which I myfelf might be fure of getting home again, with what Speed I could poffibly; the General fending his Orders by

us

us to Captain *Thompſon*, to make Sail for
St. *Simon*'s without Loſs of Time, apprehending that the Ship might lie in Danger where ſhe was, either from bad Weather ſuddenly riſing on the Coaſt, or poſſibly from the Enemy, by ſome of their
Launches, or ſmall Craft well armed: So
that there could be no Expectation of the
Bulk of thoſe Goods conſigned to me,
being delivered at *Savannah*, till the Ship
returned thither; which probably could
not be in leſs than four or five Weeks. The
General granted a farther Reprieve to *Levett*, who otherwiſe muſt have ſuffered
Death to-morrow.

Monday. About Three in the Morning
we got aboard, the Ship lying far out at
Sea, where with great Impatience I waited
the Skooner's Coming, all the fore Part of
the Day, which gave Room for a little
Chat what was doing in *England*, &c. And
by Reaſon of an eaſterly Breeze, it was
long ere the Skooner got out; ſo that ſhe
came up to us late in the Day, and then
we uſed all poſſible Diſpatch to put on
board her four Pipes of *Madera* Wine
(there being not a Drop to be had in
Town) and ſeventeen Caſks of Flour, Part
of the forty ſent; which alſo there was
great Need of: And then putting the Paſſengers aboard, I took my Leave; but not
without remembring to carry the Box N° 1.
with

with me, and immediately both Veffels made Sail, about Seven in the Evening, fine Moon-Light, with a fmall Breeze at Eaft, which anfwered equally our Purpofes; but a ftrong Tide with-held us from getting in

9. at *Tybee*; fo that we were forced to come to an Anchor near the Bar till towards Morning; and then the Wind fhifting to the North-Weft, we made it a whole Tide's Work to reach *Cockfpur* Road, about two Miles within the Light-Houfe; and there (feeing Matters fo crofs to my De-figns) I got a fmall Canoe, and rowing up againft Tide, I came to *Savannah*, *Tuefday* Evening, juft at fhutting in of Day-Light; when I waited on the General, and made Report of what I knew.

10.   *Wednefday*, ⎫ The greateft Part of my
11.   *Thurfday*, ⎪ Time being taken up, as
12.   *Friday*, ⎬ for a while paft, moft a-
13.   *Saturday*. ⎭ greeably in attending the General's Commands, and executing fuch as were required; I had only the Power of making a few fhort Obfervations thefe four Days on the Temper of the People (as I could eafily difcover) fince Captain *Thomp-fon's* Arrival, and the great Alterations which came by the Letters he brought, that were to be made in the Magiftracy of this Place: And I faw plainly, that they were in a good Difpofition to be well pleaf-ed, and pay all due Obedience to whatever
the

the honourable Truſtees thought proper, for the good Government which they were to live under: But the Advancement of Mr. *Chriſtie* to the Place of firſt Bailiff, was a little ſhocking to almoſt every Body, even the beſt of the Inhabitants; that a Man, who for ſome Time paſt was grown ſo obnoxious among them, for his bare-faced Partiality, for his ſcandalous living in open Adultery with a Man's Wife *(Richard Turner)* who run away hence to the *Weſt-Indies* a while ago; and his cloſe Adherence to that miſchievous Aſſembly at *Jenkins's*, who had been continually ſtirring up Strife and Sedition, inſomuch that, not without good Reaſon, they were apprehenſive his future Behaviour on the Bench, would ſhew manifeſtly under what Influence he acted; and it began already to appear, how far that Rump of an almoſt worn-out Party, were again elated, and pricked up their Ears at this News; for when it was underſtood by them, that Mr. *Chriſtie* was to take that Office upon him, as ſoon as he had made out Copies of the Proceedings of the Town-Court to the Time Mr. *Williamſon*, who was to ſucceed him, was ſworn in; when I was to deliver to Mr. *Chriſtie* his Conſtitution as firſt Bailiff, and not before; and likewiſe that I was to deliver Mr. *Williamſon's* Conſtitution for the Place of Recorder, as ſoon

as

1739.

October
10.
11.
12.
13.

as Mr. *Chriſtie* had perfected his Copy of the Proceedings of the Court, to the Time of Mr. *Williamſon*'s taking upon him that Office, and not before; (the former of which was ſuch a Taſk, as was well known would employ him a long Time, if ever it could be perfected; in ſuch Confuſion and Diſorder were the Court Proceedings kept; and the latter no Man could foreſee when it would happen, Mr. *Williamſon* having left this Place, and being gone to *Charles-Town* to practiſe there as an Attorney, uncertain when, or whether ever, to return hither:) This ſo galled them, that they could not contain themſelves; but they gave a full Looſe to their Paſſions: And thereupon, after a Day or two whiſpering their Sentiments about Town, endeavouring to inveigle unwary People into an Opinion, that ſome Craft was at the Bottom to deſtroy their Liberties; it became an open Talk in the Streets, that it was determined, as ſoon as the Court opened, which would be next *Monday*, to ſet Mr. *Chriſtie* on the Bench, which was his Right, forcibly, if it could not be done otherwiſe. All this I took Care to inform the General of; who ordered me to put it into Writing by Way of Letter to him, and to give Notice to the Freeholders to make a full Appearance at the Time of opening the Court: I did ſo, and well knew

knew that the Orders the General gave, were sufficient to defeat the Purposes of such pigmy Enterprizers, should they attempt any Violence: For how faulty soever we may have been at *Savannah*, I am very confident more than nine Parts in ten, would on such, or any other Occasion, oppose and defeat all Contrivances to annoy the Civil Power.—— But the Peace is best preserved without such Experiments.

Sunday. Mr. *Norris* officiated at Church, in the publick Service, as usual; and the General was pleased to attend it. 14.

Monday. The General having well considered the present Circumstances of Affairs, was pleased to direct, that I should deliver to Mr. *Fallowfield*, and Mr. *Jones*, their several Constitutions, appointing them to be second and third Bailiffs; and also to Mr. *Christie* his Constitution, appointing him to supersede Mr. *Henry Parker* in the Commission for examining Accounts, &c. But as to the Place of first Bailiff, he thought it not advisable to invest him with that Authority immediately, without either of the Conditions performed on his Part: Wherefore he farther ordered, that Mr. *Parker* might very properly keep his Seat, as before, on the Bench, till the Pleasure of the Trustees was farther known. Pursuant to this, I gave to each of them the several Constitutions for the Uses beforementioned: 15.

mentioned: After which the two new Bailiffs were sworn duly before the General; and then the Court sat, when they took their Places; Mess. *Parker* and *Christie* yet continuing in their former, till farther Orders, in a full Court, without any Interruption or Disorder; the Abettors of all Disturbance finding themselves sufficiently over-awed. A Grand Jury was called and sworn, and proper Matters laid before them to consider of; and then the Court adjourned till to-morrow.

16. *Tuesday.* Several Presentments were delivered into Court by the Grand Jury, and Indictments for Misdemeanours, *&c.* after which they were discharged: Then the Court proceeded to determine some little Matters; but there being some Actions of considerable Moment and Value commenced, carried on, and multiplied, by some Persons in Trade, against each other, with the Appearance of much Rancour; it was the Opinion of the Court to postpone those Trials a little, that some Means might be sought, if possible, to bring them into better Temper, and see if they would be persuaded to refer their Differences to Arbitration, especially as they consisted chiefly of Matters in Accounts: Wherefore the Court adjourned to *Friday* Morning.

Wednesday.

Wednesday. The General obferving, that fince the Land of the Common being clear- ed of Trees, Abundance of Shrub-Wood was daily growing up, which filled the Ground; and that the publick Squares, and moft open Parts of the Town, were filled with an offenfive Weed, near as high as a Man's Shoulders; both which were a great Annoyance, and befides hindering Grafs from growing up, harboured and in-creafed many troublefome Infects and Ver-min; and moreover if fet on Fire when dry, might endanger the Burning of the Town: For thefe Reafons, he was pleafed over Night to fend out Orders, that upon Beat of Drum, this Morning, all Perfons inhabiting the Town, whether Freeholders, or Inmates, and Boys of a competent Age, fhould appear at Sun-rifing this Morning, and go to Work in clearing this great Nufance: Which accordingly they readily did; and all falling to Work heartily, be-fore Night they had (fome with one In-ftrument, and fome with another) laid fmooth fome Hundreds of Acres: The General was pleafed to be among them himfelf; and every Body, without Diftinc-tion, took Pains to do what he could; which gave his Excellence a double Plea-fure, it being not only a Trial of the Peo-ples Difpofition to obey, but hereby he faw plainly, under his own View, the Number of People within this Town; which (allowing fome Boys of good Stature and Strength, and reckoning Servants, and Inmates of all Sorts, living in Town) appeared to be very near two hundred Men, able, on Occafion, to bear Arms. He ordered a Cafk of Bread, and another of Beer for them at Breakfaft-Time in the Morning, and at leaving off Work in the Evening, another fuch Refrefhment; highly delighted to fee how large a Tract of Land they had cleanfed: And as there remained another Day's Work, but much lefs than this of the Day, which would compleat the Whole; the General ordered that fhould be on the 5th of *November*; when at their finifhing it, they were to be fo again treated, and they might make a Bonfire of the Rubbifh they had now under Foot.

18.   *Thurfday*. The Affair of fettling the Militia of the Town under proper Officers, was one Bufinefs of this Day, which took up great Part of it, in the General's enquiring after the Caufes of many little Squabbles, which he found growing among the Tything-men, and the Conftables alfo: As Things now ftood with us, he was of Opinion, that inftead of eighteen Tythingmen, which we had, ten good ones would be fufficient, and two Conftables only: Wherefore he made Choice of ten fuch Tything-

Tything-men as he liked, and appointed 1739.
Robert Potter Conftable (in the Room of
John Fallowfield, now made fecond Bailiff) October
to act in Conjunction with *Samuel Mercer*,
the other Conftable, formerly appointed.——
But he refolved to confider of thefe Things
a little farther.

Friday, } The publick Affairs now   19.
Saturday. } urgently calling the General   20.
Southward, thefe two Days required clofe
Attendance, from fuch as waited for his
Orders and Directions in many Cafes du-
ring his Abfence: So that I had little to re-
mark elfewhere.

Sunday. The Divine Service was duly   21.
obferved; and the General, as before, failed not to give a good Example in attending it. In the Evening, having obferved
that in Times paft Difputes had frequently
arifen among the Conftables and other Officers, concerning their feveral Commands
in the Militia, which in the prefent Situation of Affairs might prove to be of very
dangerous Confequence; and being of Opinion, that the beft Way to prevent it,
would be to lodge the principal Command
in one Perfon, whofe Orders all were to
obey; he was pleafed to entertain fo good
an Opinion of my Behaviour, as to make
Choice of me for that Purpofe; and accordingly delivered me his Commiffion,
appointing me to train, inftruct, exercife,

and

and govern, the Militia of the Northern Part of the Province, for the special Defence and Safety of the said Province: To assemble in martial Array, put in warlike Posture, the Inhabitants of the said Northern Division; and to lead and conduct them, and with them to encounter, expulse, repel, resist, and pursue, by Force of Arms; and to kill, slay, destroy, and conquer, by all fitting Ways, Enterprizes, and Means whatsoever, all and every such Person or Persons, as shall at any Time hereafter in an hostile Manner, attempt, or enterprize the Destruction, Invasion, Detriment, or Annoyance of the said Province, &c. Which Commission (how unworthy soever I thought myself of it) it behoved me not to scruple the Acceptance of, lest an Imputation should follow, either of my setting little Value on the Honour conferred, or of such a Sort of Bashfulness, as at this Time would be very unseasonable, and might be construed something else, which I avoid naming: For which Reasons I threw aside any Marks of Reluctance, resolving in all Things, as far as I was capable, to exert myself in promoting the publick Welfare.

22. *Monday.* This Day the General purposed to have left us; but upon Intelligence received, that a Body of *Indians,* partly *Chicasaws,* and partly *Euchies,* had joined,

to the Number of a hundred Men, and
were coming down voluntarily, to attend,
and ferve againſt the *Spaniards*, and would
be here in few Days; he thought it worth
his while to wait their Coming, knowing
of what Uſe they might be, and therefore
would take them with him. *N. B.* Theſe
Indians were no Part of thoſe much greater
Numbers he expected from the populous
Nations of the *Creeks*, and *Cherokees*, that
he had ſent for, and ſhould expect to march
to him at St. *Simon*'s directly.

Tueſday. The Court having diſpatched 23.
what Buſineſs they thought neceſſary to be
done this Seſſions, adjourned to the next
orderly Time of their meeting again towards the latter End of *November*. The
General granted a farther Reprieve for *Levett*, upon his altering the Stile of his Petition, and owning that he was juſtly condemned by the Law, for being privy to the
Uproar which happened on board, when
the Murder was committed, and not re-
vealing it; for which he begged Mercy,
perſiſting ſtill in ſaying he had no Hand in
it, nor knew of his Death till he was over-
board: And it was now expected theſe repeated Reprieves would end in a Pardon at
laſt.

Wedneſday. Finding a little Vacancy, 24.
from Buſineſs growing leſs urgent than hitherto, with the General; I devoted this
Day

Day almoſt wholly to look into what my People were doing abroad, and what Product was to be ſeen off the Land that I had planted this Year, which now was pretty near got together: And what I before had obſerved, relating to the uncommon wet Summer we had, *(vide Sept.* 21.) appeared now too well verified; for all the low Lands had ſuffered extreamly; among which, thoſe Lots happened which I occupied, and Abundance of the Corn was utterly ſpoiled, partly by the Stalks rotting ere it came to Maturity; and moſt of that which ripened, was infeſted with the Worm, that did great Damage; whilſt the dry Lands threw out a plentiful Crop: Nevertheleſs, *communibus annis*, the Summer Heats here are ſuch, that I would, in my own Judgment, always prefer the low Lands to the high; and though it happened that they failed this Year, through ſuch exceſſive Wet, yet moſt undoubtedly they are leſs apt to do ſo than the other. The General having lately confirmed the Grant of five hundred Acres, which he partly put me in Poſſeſſion of on the 19th of *April* laſt, at the Mouth of *Vernon* River *(ut antea)* it was now my Deſire, with all convenient Speed, to ſet ſome Hands at Work there, and make what Improvements I could, as the Seaſon was proper; taking Care at the ſame Time,

that

that thofe Lots I had been cultivating for
two Years paft, fhould be occupied; fo
that what Labour had been beftowed,
fhould not be thrown away, till the right
Owner came to poffefs it.

Thurfday. Enfign *Cadogan* arrived this
Morning from *Carolina*, whom I was very
glad to enquire of, what came of the Packet which I delivered to his Care, together
with Captain *Norbury*, on the 17th of *September* laft, which I had for fome Time
fince been very uneafy about, not hearing a
Word of any fuch Packet coming to the
Hands of my Correfpondent Mr. *Hopton*,
who always had been very exact and punctual, and to whom (as ufual) I had wrote
a Letter with it: Moreover he had advifed
me of the Receipt of another Letter of
mine, to Mr. *Verelft*, dated *December* 25,
and what Ship he had fent it by; but ftill
not a Word of my former, dated the 10th
Ditto; till now that Mr. *Cadogan* brought
me a Letter from him, informing me,
that that former Packet was at laft come to
Hand, and juft timely enough to fend it
away by a Ship bound for *Topfham*, which
failed the fame Day (*viz.* the 21ft Inftant)
Captain *Ward* in the *Mary* Brig. Mr. *Cadogan* in Excufe faid, that both he and
Captain *Norbury* were taken very ill at
Port-Royal, which continued a long while
upon them, before he was able to proceed

to

to *Charles-Town*; and he was not willing to put it out of his own Hands to the Care of another: By which Means it may be expected, that my Letter of the 25th of *September*, will find its Way some Time sooner than that of the 10th. The reducing the Number of Tything-men, which the General had several Times under Consideration, so as to leave a competent Strength for carrying on the Duties of that Office, and yet not to establish an Expence more than could be answered, since no Provision was made in the Estimate for that Service; he now settled that Affair to his Liking, appointing only ten for it, *viz.* two for each of the old Wards, instead of four; and one for each of the new; and dividing the Town through *Broughton-Street*, from East to West; he appointed two Constables only, one over the Northern Division, consisting of three Wards; and the other over the Southern, consisting of the like Number; pursuant to which, he gave out the Tything-mens Warrants for me to deliver to them, and the Constables he delivered to them himself.

26.   *Friday.* An Express from the South, with Letters, &c. to the General; which brought ill News from the Camp, that they were grown very sickly, and that they had not Officers sufficient to do the common Duty; but the Sickness did not prove mortal,

tal, being a Sort of Ague and Fever with
regular Intermiffion, which pulled many
down, both Officers and Soldiers, to a very
weak State; fuch as is pretty common in
thefe Parts, at certain Seafons, efpecially a-
mong frefh People from *Europe*, and is
ufually termed a Seafoning. On this Occafion the General immediately fent off
two or three Subalterns who attended him
here, and began to grow impatient till he
could go himfelf; but was very unwilling
to leave the hundred *Indians* behind him,
whom he looked earneftly for every Day,
as noted on *Monday* laft. In the Afternoon
I convened all the Officers, Conftables and
Tything-men, to whom I firft read my
own Commiffion, and afterwards theirs;
from whence I took Occafion to exhort
them all to lay afide all little Picques and
Animofities among themfelves, and to unite
heartily in promoting the publick Peace,
and difcouraging all Attempts to fow Difcord among them, efpecially at this Time,
when it behoved us to be on our Guard
againft all Enemies, whether open, or fecret, the worft of the two. I affured them
of my ready Difpofition to confult with
them, and advife, upon all Emergencies;
and in Cafe of any dangerous Attempt upon our Safety, my Command fhould not
expofe them to fuch Service as I would de-
cline myfelf; And withal openly told them,

that

that I muſt (in Juſtice to the Commiſſion I had the Honour to bear) expect due Obedience to be paid to ſuch Orders, as at any Time I ſhould iſſue, whether my Superiors or my own; and as I ſhould be a vigilant Obſerver of their ſeveral Deportments, ſo they might be aſſured of my repreſenting it without Partiality, to thoſe whoſe Favour was well worth deſerving. They expreſſed themſelves well pleaſed with my being at their Head, and ſeemed to be truly of Opinion, that all Occaſion of Diſputes about Priority was now removed, much to their Satisfaction (as they ſaid:) Mutual Aſſurances were given on all Sides, of an hearty Good-will towards one another; which I obſerved ſome of them were of Opinion would be beſt confirmed over a Bottle; wherefore taking the Hint, I willingly agreed to what they termed wetting my Commiſſion; and took a chearful Glaſs with them for an Hour or two in the Evening, to drink the King's Health, and the Royal Family, the honourable Truſtees, Succeſs to his Majeſty's Arms, and General *Oglethorpe* at the Head of them in theſe Provinces, &c. every Body, when we parted, going home in good Order, and good Humour.

27. The General now *(Saturday)* finding himſelf a little more at Leiſure than for a while paſt, diverted his Care about other

Matters,

Matters, to look into the State of the great
Lots of five hundred Acres; and some Doubts having arisen about the Certainty of those Lands, whether run out true or not, by the late Surveyor *Jones*; the General went himself to see the first original Lines, as they had been marked out; from whence, if due Observance was had, in running the traverse Lines, it must unavoidably prove the Truth of the Whole: And this it was incumbent on the former Surveyor to demonstrate, that so the Person whom the General should think fit to appoint for the future ascertaining those Lands, to whom they belonged, might be well instructed by the present Plan how to proceed; which took up this whole Day, and was likely to be Work enough for another. During which Intermission, I had Matter sufficient to employ my Pen at home, and which I stuck closely to, to get forward what my Duty required, being unavoidably fallen much in Arrear, and it would cost me some Pains to fetch up again.

Sunday. The Divine Service was what 28. called all People to the Performance of, and which it was to be wished every one was alike careful to observe, as the proper Business of the Day: And nothing of any Moment happened to divert their Thoughts from it.

Monday.

Monday. The General, waiting only for his *Indians* coming now, before he left us, was intent upon looking carefully into the Plat of Lands formerly run out, to prevent any Miſtakes; and I was not leſs ſo in reducing my looſe Papers into right Order, tranſcribing what was needful, &c. which required ſome Time. Mr. *Bradley*, after too long trifling, and ſeeking many Shifts and Evaſions, not to quit the great Houſe belonging to the Truſt, which he had taken Poſſeſſion of; finding himſelf driven to the Neceſſity of it, now moved his Goods to another in Town that was vacant, at a moderate Rent, intending it for his Habitation no longer (as he gave out) than till he had provided a Place to be in, upon the five hundred Acres allotted him; which he had a long while raiſed many Objections to, and ſhewed himſelf diſſatiſfied about; but now thoſe imaginary Obſtacles being diſſipated by the General, it would appear ere long, how far he was in earneſt to cultivate that Farm.

30.

Tueſday. Mr. *Norris* taking Breakfaſt with me this Morning, began again to complain very heavily of the unkind Uſage which he met with; and which for a pretty while paſt, he refrained from ſpeaking of to me (probably from his obſerving, that I ſhewed not an Over-readineſs to liſten to ſuch diſagreeable Controverſy, as far as I could

could well avoid it) but now, he said, he could with-hold no longer, since it was God's Cause, and his Service was impugned; insomuch, that for Want of Candles, the Evening Prayers now ceased; as they must have done a long while since, had not he himself, at his own Expence, bought Candles where he could get them, but now he could find none in Town to be sold; and knowing Mr. *Jones* had some in the Stores, he sent thither to buy, with Money to pay, but was refused: From hence he took Occasion to expatiate largely on the Treatment he had met with, so different from any of his Predecessors, ever since his being here; particularly at the Stores, as he had divers Times before made known, and which he little expected, from those Assurances he had, of kinder Regard being shewn him, before he left *England*: But as for the little malicious Stories spread of him, and the frequent Reproaches so basely whispered about, by a Set of Men, who (he believes) think the Lessening of his Character will conduce to aggrandize that of him who succeeds him; he prays God to forgive them, and they create him not the least Uneasiness: At the same Time he was so just to acknowledge the Readiness I had always shewn to do him any Service I could, and looked upon me as his true Friend. To all this I had little to say: The

The Want of Candles, and thereby the Want of Evening Prayers, I know was too true: But as Mr. *Jones* and I were (I hoped) in a mutual good Underſtanding with each other, in all Things that our Duties required us to act jointly together, I was not fond of entering into any Arguments with him, knowing his teſty Temper: Wherefore I told Mr. *Norris*, that as the General was now here, the beſt Way undoubtedly for him, would be to lay open any Grievances there, where it was moſt likely to find a Remedy: But at the ſame Time, underſtanding the General had engaged him to go with him to *Frederica*, where for Want of a Miniſter, the moſt neceſſary Parts of a Prieſt's Office were wanting, more eſpecially Baptiſm and the Lord's Supper; I hoped with myſelf, that finding Things more agreeable to him where he was going, would make him forget what he took amiſs here, from very few; for the Generality of the People ſhewed him the Reſpect which his truly unblameable Behaviour among us deſerved : And it was probable, that Mr. *Whitfield*'s coming ſoon hither (whom we now looked for) might prevent any future Cauſe of Complaint from him hence.   After he left me, I betook myſelf to my own Work, the ſame as Yeſterday.

Wedneſday.

Wednesday. The General doing me the Favour of asking me to dine with him, was pleased afterwards to engage my Stay there the remaining Part of the Day; when, free from all other Company, most Part of the Time, I had the Pleasure of a long Conversation with him, and of knowing his Sentiments in many Things, which might be of Use to me in my future Conduct: Divers Matters he gave me a particular Charge in, which he seemed to think of great Consequence; and among others, he required me not to fail laying before the honourable Trustees, a true State of the whole Affair relating to the late Change of Magistrates, and the Reasons why their Orders concerning *Parker* and *Christie* had not yet been entirely fulfilled: I told him, that I never missed noting in my Journal every Thing of Moment that came to my Knowledge, and there it would be found; but he said, he did not think that sufficient, without a Letter; for Journals might, or might not, be read; but Letters to be sure always were: And tho' he was more and more confirmed in Opinion, that what Orders he had given in that Affair were needful, till the Pleasure of the Trustees could be farther known; yet it would be necessary, for his Honour's Defence, to have that Business laid open, as clear as possible: Which I promised to

do

1739. do as well as my Capacity would allow; and then took my Leave.

Novemb. 1. 2.

Thurſday, } Being ſeized with ſome
Friday. } ſharp Pains in my Breaſt,
and divers other Parts, I was bound to keep
in, hoping by Warmth, and good Kitchen
Phyſick, to get the better of it: As I
did; for in twenty-four Hours it began to
wear off, and plainly ſhewed me it was no
more than a Cold; which might reaſonably
be expected from the ſudden Change of
Weather in very few Days paſt; in which
ſhort Time, the great Warmth we had, by
Means of a Southerly Wind and clear Sky,
was changed into a North-Weſt Wind and
thick Clouds, which made as great a Difference in the Temper of the Air, as is
uſually found in *England* between the
Months of *June* and *December:* And theſe
ſurprizing Alterations ſome Times happen
at any Seaſon of the Year. All that I could
learn worth noting in theſe two Days was,
that Captain *Fennel,* whom I gave ſome
Account of, in my former Notes of the
30th of *July* and the 1ſt and 3d of *Auguſt,*
was now come in from *Carolina* to *Cockſpur,* with a new Sloop of his own, carrying ten Guns and twenty Men, and
bound for *Jamaica;* where he ſhould alſo
have another Sloop; and with thoſe (being now diſingaged from the *South-Sea*
Company and *Spaniſh* Trade) he purpoſed

i

to carry on a private Trade of his own, 1739.
betwixt the *West-Indies* and the Northern
Provinces, being well armed, and provided Novemb.
for Attack or Defence, as he should see
needful. With him came Mr. *George Saxby*,
and Mr. *William Williamson*, as Passengers
from *Charles-Town*; the first on his Pleasure, more than any Business; and the other
we supposed might come on Account of the
Recordership of this Place, which he understood was his Appointment, and which
now would soon be considered of by the
General, &c. —— By whom they were all
courteously received.

Saturday. Finding myself pretty well at 3.
Ease, I went abroad again and waited on
the General, where I found the Strangers at
Breakfast with him: And Captain *Fennel*
being a sensible, genteel Man, beyond the
common Level of some unpolished Tars;
he seemed pleased with the Opportunity of
such a Conference, with such an intelligent
Person, who could satisfy his Curiosity in
divers Things which he thought fit to enquire into: Wherefore on their withdrawing, he engaged them both to dine with
him, as he did afterwards Mr. *Williamson*
also. Nothing could fall out more oppor-
tunely for me, than such a Conjuncture;
for having a Bill sent me from the Trust,
drawn by Mr. *Hammerton*, for 200 *l.* Sterling on this same Gentleman (Mr. *Saxby*)

for Value received of the Truftees, for his Majefty's Service; and Mr. *Saxby* being Deputy-Receiver of the King's Quit-Rents in *Carolina*, I now prefented the fame to him, together with Mr. *Hammerton*'s Letter of Advice; but was a little furprized at his telling me he could not accept it, for that he had not half fo much of the King's Money in his Hands; which was all that paffed betwixt us then : But in the Evening I thought it proper to take Mr. *Jones* with me to *Jenkins*'s, where thofe Gentlemen quartered; and there in a civil Manner, over a Glafs of Wine, I again prefented the Bill for Acceptance, before proper Witnefs, acquainting him, upon his Refufal again, that I fhould be obliged to proteft and return it; which he faid he was forry for, but could not help it.

4. *Sunday.* Young Mr. *Vernon*, who had failed under Captain *Gafcoigne* in the *Hawk* (which was gone for *England*, as was alfo Captain *Gafcoigne* in another Ship) having been fome Time at *Charles-Town*, waiting in Expectation when his Uncle the Admiral would come to the *Weft-Indies*, now took the Opportunity of a Paffage with Captain *Fennel* to *Jamaica*; and coming up to Town this Morning from *Cockfpur*, firft waited on the General, and afterwards did me the Favour of a Vifit; which I took very kindly, and wifhed any little Civilities

vilities I could shew him here, might be rated as a Respect due from me to his Father. The Church Service was orderly observed, which the General was pleased to attend, as did also the two Strangers. In the Evening Mr. *Saxby* discovered a little Uneasiness at my Intention of returning that Bill, knowing how great Cost must attend it; wherefore he said he should take it as a Favour, after my protesting it, if I would defer returning it a little while, till he got home to *Charles-Town*, from whence he would write me positively, whether he could pay it or not; for that he wished to do it if he could: Wherefore, presuming no Damage could ensue, by a short Delay, I agreed so to do. Soon after, I attended the General, together with Mr. *Jones*, where we met Mr. *Williamson*; and the Affair of the Recordership was the Subject Matter to be considered; which Mr. *Williamson* said he was ready to accept of, and was what brought him hither at this Time from *Charles-Town*: But in his Conversation and Discourse elsewhere, he discovered different Sentiments; and talking with me of it in particular Yesterday, he said plainly it was a Thing of great Indifference to him, whether he had it or not; for that the Business which he was falling into at *Charles-Town*, was likely to be of much greater Value to him; and indeed the

N 2 principal

principal Motive which induced him to came now after it, was his knowing that his Uncle *Taylor* had obtained it from the Truſtees; and now for him not to accept of it, would be giving Offence to his Uncle, to whom he had lately wrote to procure him either the Place of Judge of the Admiralty (if he could) void by the Death of Mr. *Maurice Lewis*; or that of Clerk of the Aſſembly, void by the Death of Mr. *Amiens*; either of which would be of abundant greater Value to him than this; but his Uncle having procured him this, before he had heard from him about the other; he would not be thought to make light of it: I then ſaid it looked to me as if he meant to make this a Sort of *Sinecure*, which he might execute by a Deputy; but I preſumed the Truſt would not allow of any ſuch Appointments, nor ſuffer their Favours to be undervalued: To which he told me in plain Words, that when he was once poſſeſſed of the Place, he would ſee who could hinder him, or to that Effect: And now in this Conference with the General, the chief Topick of the Whole ſeemed to favour much of the Reſtrictions, which it was expected a Perſon occupying that Place muſt ſubmit to; and to lay aſide all Imagination, that the ſame Power which created him ſuch an Officer, could not in the ſame Manner take it away

way from him again at Pleafure, without
Regard to *quamdiu fe bene geferit:* Then
it was fhewn to Mr. *Williamfon,* what the
Truftees had been pleafed to direct me, relating to the feveral new Conftitutions lately fent; and therein particularly, what I
was to do in this prefent Affair now before
us, and what was required to be done by
Mr. *Chriftie* before a Succeffor could take
Place; which Mr. *Williamfon* finding little
Room to fay any Thing to, he then afked
me peremptorily, whether I would deliver
him his Conftitution or not; and upon my
faying that I fhould do it as foon as Mr.
Chriftie enabled me, by performing his
Part, and not fooner, unlefs I had new
Commands from my Superiors; he appeared not difappointed in the leaft; and
fo that Difcourfe ended.

Monday. Upon my feeing Mr. *Williamfon* this Morning, I afked him how he re-
lifhed the Anfwer he preffed me (againft
my Inclination) to give him laft Night;
and he told me frankly, that had he been
in my Place, he did not fee how any other
could be given; which he faid he was very
eafy at, telling me, at the fame Time, that
he faw no Likelihood of the prefent Recorder's quitting that Place in hafte; for he
had fworn deeply to him, that he would
never deliver up any Copy of his Records
to me, nor to any one elfe, but the Truf-

5.

tees

tees only; which I only smiled at, and wished he had it in his Power to do *that* compleat, as it was expected; but I feared it was not: At parting soon after, he told me, that he had wrote, and sent in to the General, a Letter, wherein he begged he would please to remember, that he had been to offer his Acceptance of the Recorder's Office, &c. intimating, to preserve his Uncle's good Opinion: But the General conceived something farther meant in it, and ordered his Secretary to take particular Care, and keep it safe. And now the Time was come, when the General would not stay longer waiting for his *Indians*, who must come after: For having received a Letter from Captain *Warren* (the oldest Sea Commander of all in these Northerly Stations) that he was upon sailing to St. *Simon's*, to confer with him for the better Protection of this Province; he left us about Three in the Afternoon, having spent six Weeks here in doing what he thought needful; and going off in the Scout-Boat, with three or four *Indians* that he had a special Value for, Mr. *Norris*, and his Secretary Mr. *Moor*, went in another Boat that attended, making the best of their Way South. The only Matter in Town that I had to observe, was, that the Inhabitants at Beat of Drum early in the Morning assembled, and went on vigorously with
the

the Work of clearing the Common of all *1739.*
that ſhrubby Matter which it was over-run
with; and what they could not accom- Novemb.
pliſh at their laſt Meeting (the 17th of
October) they put an End to now, under
the Direction of the Town-Officers, *&c.*

Tueſday. All now in Appearance huſht and 6.
quiet. The General was gone, and every Body at Leiſure to mind their own proper Buſineſs; which I made as good Uſe of as I
could, that another Packet might be ready
ſoon to ſend to the Truſt. Mr. *Williamſon*
(I was informed) diſcovered what Diſpoſition he was in plainly, by joining in cloſe
Council with the Committee, which continued to ſit at *Jenkins*'s (Dr. *Tailfer* in the
Chair) to enquire into Grievances, in order
to get them redreſſed, by ſuch Means as
their Wiſdom ſhould deviſe: Thither re-
ſorted at all Times, as to an Oracle for
Advice, every Malecontent, who believed
himſelf more deſerving than his Neighbours; and this knotty Point how to get
over, of ſettling the Recorderſhip and Magiſtracy, immediately to their better Liking,
was now thought worth their Conſideration; from whence I did not doubt I ſhould
ſoon hear ſomewhat more about it: And,
as I expected,

Wedneſday, in the Morning, Mr. *Wil-* 7.
liamſon came again, bringing Mr. *Fallow-*
field with him as Witneſs (I underſtood it)

of

of what paffed betwixt us: And then Mr. *Williamfon* again renewed his Demand of being put in Poffeffion of the Place of Recorder, *&c.* To which I anfwered (as I had before done) that when Mr. *Chriftie* had fulfilled the Truftees Orders, of making out Copy of the Court Proceedings to this Time, I fhould be then ready to obferve on my Part, their Orders likewife of delivering their Conftitution to him (Mr. *Williamfon)* and not fooner, without frefh Orders: He then told me, that Mr. *Chriftie* had informed him he was ready with his Copy of the Court Proceedings; but fwore he would deliver them neither to me, nor to any one, except the Truftees themfelves (the fame he had fo folemnly fworn before) with this Addition now, that I was an old Fool to expect it: Such dirty Compliments gave me not the leaft Difturbance; but I then replied, that if he thought me not worthy the Sight of them, though upon this Occafion I apprehended, by the Office I had the Honour to execute under the Truft, I might infift upon feeing them; yet I was very ready to wave that Point, to facilitate the Affair as much as I could: But I hoped, and expected, that he would fhew his Work to the Magiftrates at leaft, who furely had a Right to it; and upon their certifying the Truth of it, I would be fatisfied; But to fpeak plainly, he was grown

a

a Man of so little Veracity, that whatever
he said, found little Credit with almost any
Body: And as I well knew, that the Books
he had made out the last Year, and sent
to the Trust then with my Packet, was
the Work of Mr. *Causton* and him together at *Ockstead*, where they sat close a-
bout it some Weeks, Mr. *Christie* having
then Notice from me, that it was expected from him; and if he had not found
that Help, it is most probable he had been
nonplus'd: For these, and divers other
good Reasons, I was fully persuaded to believe him as much and more at a Loss
now, unless he had the Skill of collecting
Sybils Leaves. It so happened, that Mr.
Jones, calling at my House, was present at
this Conference; which I was very glad
of, to be as well prepared as the Com-
plainer, with Evidence of what was said
and done. After some little Wrangling,
which I gave no great Heed to, they walked
away; and Mr. *Williamson*, in few Hours
more, took Boat to return to *Charles-Town*;
but not till he had first paid his Respects to
Dr. *Tailfer* (as Care was taken to observe)
at his own House, where no Doubt but
he made Report of what he had been
doing, in Pursuance of that Resolution
which Yesterday brought forth: And their
farther Operations we are next to wait for.
Thursday.

Thursday. Ill News came to Town this Morning of Mr. *Montaigut*'s Death, who sickened in a Fever of the worst Kind, about eight Days since, at his Plantation up the River in *Carolina*, whereof he died Yesterday in the Evening. Mr. *Christie* not thinking it convenient (I suppose) to be observed going out, and coming in, so frequently to his Doxy Mrs. *Turner*, at her House here, thought it best to remove to his Hut on the Lot, about two Miles off: So he sent her with Bed and Bedding, *&c.* before, following her soon after.

9.

Friday. Little worth observing till the Afternoon, when Mr. *Montaigut*'s Corpse was brought down and decently buried, the *French* Minister of *Puryburgh* performing the Funeral Rites, in the Absence of Mr. *Norris*, who was now gone to the South: Most of the principal Inhabitants (who were particularly invited) attended him to the Grave; and in Regard to the military Command, which he had in *Carolina*, thinking it a Respect due, I ordered twelve Minute Cannon to be fired, during the Time of his Interment; to answer which Purpose, having not Powder sufficient in Store, Monsieur *d'Beausain* ordered some to be provided. It is to be hoped we shall ere long be furnished with what is necessary of that Kind, when Captain *Thompson* arrives from the South, where he

yet

yet continues; and without it indeed, we
seem among some Folks to be a Subject of
Ridicule. *N. B.* This I wrote upon what
Information the Gunner gave me: But
Mr. *Jones* has since told me, that he got
some Powder for that Use from Mr. *Brown-field.*

Saturday. This Day I converted to my
own peculiar Use, and spent most Part of
it at my little Plantations, forming to myself new Schemes of what I proposed next
Year, which according to the Planters
Way of reckoning, began about this
Time. At my Return home, hearing accidentally of a Boat going South, I wrote
to the General, acquainting him with
what I apprehended he ought to be informed of from hence since he left us. Mr.
Christie, I understood, had been exposing
to publick Sale a few of his own old Goods
of little Value; such as two or three ordinary Chairs and Stools, a Table, one
Pewter Dish, a few common *Dutch* printed Pictures coloured upon Paper, and the
like; by which it was intended to be understood, that he purposed soon to leave
the Colony; but most People were of a
different Opinion, and took it rather to be
an Experiment made by his trusty Advisers,
to see whether or not we would suffer so
valuable a Man to quit the Place, through
the ill Treatment he found, in not meeting

with

with the Promotion intended him, so readily as he expected. As to myself, I gave little Heed to it, having, to the best of my Understanding, and not without proper Advice, acted in that Affair, as I have now done; neither could I readily believe his real Design to be leaving the Colony, from what was said; having ever since I knew the Place, been frequently giving it out, that he was determined to go soon for *England*, for that he found not Encouragement to continue in that Office; though it is well known, that *he only* took Fees in many Cases, when the other Magistrates never pretended to make any Demand; and I myself have heard him in the Height of his Vanity boast, that he made a hundred Pounds a Year of it.

11.   *Sunday.* In the Absence of Mr. *Norris*, Mr. *Habersham* read the Prayers of the Church.

12.   *Monday.* Early this Morning arrived an *Indian* trading Boat, bound for *Charles-Town*, by which came *John Rea* (a Freeholder here) from Fort *Augusta*, with divers Letters for the General, importing (among other Things) that the *Chicasaw Indians*, our good Friends, whom the *French* had attempted several Times to destroy, had lately, by a small Party in Ambuscade, attacked a large *French* Boat, in her Way on the *Messasippi* to *Moville*, from the
Mouth

Mouth of that River, laden with many very valuable Goods, and Letters to the French Governor at that Place: That they had killed feveral of them, and taken fome Prifoners; then plundered the Boat of what they thought moft valuable, namely, fine Woollen, Linen, Plate and Ammunition, which by them is moft prized; and (what we apprehend to be of more Value to us) a Packet of Letters for that Governor, which they fent as a Prefent to our General, whereby probably fome Difcovery might be made of the *French* Defigns; and after taking with them what they could carry off, they funk the Boat with the Remainder. Which Packet and Letters to be fure we loft no Time in fending forward to the General.

Tuefday. The Seafon now requiring every one to be bufy on his Lands, who had any Defign of improving them; and my chief View the enfuing Year, being towards my five hundred Acres (as before noted *October* 24.) I employed what Hands I could poffibly, to fet about that Work; and it being a confiderable Diftance from Town, which would not admit of my Eyes being over them frequently, I chofe, on that Occafion, to allow myfelf the whole Day. At my Return in the Evening, Mr. *Jones* informed me, that the Report of Mr. *Chriftie*'s Intention to quit the Colony,

Colony, began to find a little more Credit than hitherto; and some People were inclined to believe it; as also that he would take his Beloved with him.—A little Time probably might bring to Light what his Purposes were. He farther told me, that Mr. *Bradley* having applied for a Permit to go in a Boat for *Carolina* (as no Boat, now for some Time past, was allowed by the Guard to put off hence, without such Leave under one of the Magistrates Hands) which was denied him upon divers Applications from Persons he was indebted to, or had Disputes with; who apprehended that he designed never to return: He privately took Horse, and rode up the River, with Design to pass it at the first convenient Place he could come at, leaving Part of his Family at the House he had lately taken in Town, when he went out of that great one belonging to the Trust. His real Intention also, as well as the other's, will require a little more Time to unfold.

14.   *Wednesday.* Upon Enquiry after what became of the Effects of *Wise*, *Clarke*, and others, after their Decease; in Pursuance of the Orders I received from the Trust; I learnt, that there had formerly been some Care taken in it by the Court, who had directed the Jury to make Inquisition strictly into that Affair; and they found, that there was publick Sale made of *Wise*'s Goods,

Goods, an Account whereof was returned
to the Recorder Mr. *Chriſtie*: Since which
Time I could not find that any farther Notice was taken of it; nor could I get any
Information, whether the Money ariſing
by that Sale, or any Part of it, was paid
to Mr. *Chriſtie*, or any other: Wherefore I
applied to the Magiſtrates, and told them,
that as there was a Box in Mr. *Chriſtie*'s
Cuſtody with two Locks upon it, whereof
he kept one Key, and one of the Magiſtrates another; it would be very needful
for them all together to look into that Box,
and ſee what Papers were in it that might
be of Value, &c. and they appointed ſo to
do to-morrow; and in the mean while to
give Notice to Mr. *Chriſtie* to be there with
them. In the Evening Enſign *Maxwell*,
and Quarter-Maſter *Wanſell*, arrived from
St. *Simon*'s; by whom I received a Letter
from the General of the 11th Inſtant, relating to Mr. *Douglaſs*'s having Leave to
ſell his great Houſe which he had built
here: The former in his Way to *Frederick*
Fort at *Port-Royal*, from whence he was to
detach ten Men to go with him to the
South; and the other came to look into
the Goods and Stores that had been lodged
in this Town by Colonel *Cockran* at his
firſt Coming, and lay here ever ſince: But
now the General had ordered them all to
be taken hence, and carried to the South.

2 *Thurſday.*

Thursday. The Magiſtrates met, and together with Mr. *Chriſtie* opened the Box, wherein were found divers Papers, giving an Account of the Effects of ſeveral Perſons deceaſed; and among others, thoſe of *William Wiſe*, which had been moſt of them ſold, as before-mentioned; and the Particulars charged to ſundry People; whereof a Return had been made to Mr. *Chriſtie* by the Jury that was directed to make Enquiry into it; and the Sum amounted to 20*l.* and odd; but how to come at the Knowledge of what had been paid, and to whom, was not to be eaſily diſcovered; Mr. *Chriſtie* pleading Ignorance of it, and denying that he had ever received any Money on that Account: Wherefore that Nut was a little too hard for us to crack yet, and required our farther Endeavour to come at what we wanted. After ſo wet a Summer, the Air was ſo thin and purified, that our Winter began earlier than common, with ſharp Froſts for ſome Days paſt; which made it very delightful, and probably would conduce much to the Health of the People: But it behoved ſuch as were nurſing up Vines, and Oranges, *&c.* to take good Care of thoſe eſpecially which were young and tender: And it was now evident from Experience, that all ſuch Kind of Plants thrived the better, the nearer
they

they grew to the Sea, where the Froſt is
leſs ſevere.

Friday. This Day paſſed over without
any Thing notable: But late in the Evening we received the ill News of the Death
of Captain *John Cuthbert*, by the Arrival
of *Scroggs* from *Carolina*. The State of
War which we were now in, occaſioned
the General to revive the Company of Rangers, which Captain *McPherſon* before had
the Command of, till broke: And now
they were to conſiſt of thirty Men, well
horſed, and armed, whom this Gentleman
was to command; and he was lately ſent
into *Carolina*, together with his Lieutenant
Scroggs, by the General's Order, to buy
Horſes, &c. being furniſhed with Money
for that Purpoſe; but he unhappily ſick-
ened and died in that Country: Whereupon Mr. *Scroggs*, after ſecuring his Papers, Money, and Effects, and ſeeing him
buried, now returned; and the News of
his Death occaſioned Grief to many People, being a good-natured, ſprightly Man,
generally beloved; and it was believed by
all, that he would have acquitted himſelf
well in that Poſt. He had made conſiderable Improvements upon his five hundred
Acres up the River *Savannah*, and was
judged to have one of the beſt Plantations
yet in the Colony: He died unmarried,
leaving a Siſter (who took Care of his

House) dangerously ill here, insomuch that her Death was feared, when we little expected to hear of his; and whether she will survive him long or not, none can tell.

17.   *Saturday.* All that I found material to be observed, was, that some of our wise Reformers (who would in all Things be meddling) thought it worth their peculiar Care, to be providing such an Administrator, to the Effects of our deceased Friend, as *they* judged fit for that Purpose, and in the same Manner as was attempted when Mr. *Dyson* died *(vide Sept.* 17 and 18.) all was to be done in a Hurry: But it happened, that every Body did not agree with them in that Opinion; for which Reason it was thought proper to defer the farther Consideration of it to another Day.

18.   *Sunday.* Mr. *Habersham* read the Service of the Day, and a Sermon after it, setting forth the Operation of the Spirit upon a new Birth, *&c.* (out of what Author I know not) which was a Subject some of the Audience were pretty well tired with heretofore.

19.   *Monday.* The Affair of an Administrator was renewed by such as began it the other Day; and Mr. *Jones* being applied to on that Occasion, he sent to Mr. *Parker* and me to be present at the Time it was debated: When in Answer to what was urged in Behalf of the Creditors (of whom Dr.

Dr. *Tailfer* and Mr. *Jenkins* alledged they
were the chief, one a Victualler, and the
other a Difpenfer of Phyfick) they were
told, that the Truft alfo were Creditors,
and muft be looked on as fuch; but it appeared very ftrange to us, that they fhould
offer at it, when they knew the Deceafed
had a Sifter yet living, who undoubtedly
claimed a Priority; and if fhe fhould fail,
poffibly fome other near Relation might be
found, who had a Right of Preference to
either of *them*; moreover, that it was the
univerfal Practice of the Civil Law Courts,
to allow a certain limited Time in fuch
Cafes, for any Perfon concerned to offer a
Claim, if they had any to make in their
own Behalf, or to enter a Caveat againft
any other. For the Satisfaction of all then
prefent, it was thought not amifs, that a
Lift and fhort Inventory fhould be taken of
the ready Money, Notes, Bills, or the like,
found upon him at the Time of his De-
ceafe, and now in Cuftody of Mr. *Scroggs*:
Which appearing to be no inconfiderable
Sum, and being well known to be Part of
what the General had advanced for the
Purpofes aforefaid; it was thought proper
to commit it to the Care of Mr. *Scroggs* a-
gain, to carry to the General where he
was to go: And in the Evening I wrote
what I thought needful to the General; as
Mr. *Jones* alfo did, to be ready for the

1739.

Novemb.
19.

fame

same Bearer, who was to set off in the Morning.

Tuesday. Mr. *Scroggs* went off early for St. *Simon*'s. In the Afternoon arrived Lieutenant *Dunbar*, and Captain *Æneas Mackintosh*, whom the General had sent to Fort *Augusta*, to enquire after some *Chicasaw Indians*, that lived in that Neighbourhood remote from their own Nation, in a vagrant Manner; but were looked on by all as a daring, bold People: And some of these the General had expected before he went hence. These Gentlemen now told us they were coming, and we might expect them to-morrow or next Day; that they were but few (under thirty) but were pickt Men, all Warriors, led by experienced Chiefs, and might be esteemed more than equal to a hundred common Men.

21. *Wednesday.* Nothing occurred to my Knowledge this whole Day, that I thought deserved any Notice here.

22. *Thursday.* What happened most remarkable this Day, was the Receipt of a Packet from the General, brought me by Mr. *Upton*, who came from *Frederica* last *Sunday:* Enclosed in it I found a small Packet directed to the Trust from his Excellence, together with one to Lieutenant Governor *Bull*; one to Mr. *Pinkney*, Speaker of the Assembly; one to Captain *Warren*, commanding his Majesty's Ships at

at *Charles-Town*; and one to Colonel *Palmer*, at his Plantation in *Carolina*: All which I was to send forward by the first Opportunity. The Letter to Colonel *Palmer*, I guess, might be in Return to an handsome Offer which I heard the Colonel had made to his Excellency; that in Case he had any Design upon *Augustin*, he (the Colonel) would attend him with an hundred and fifty good Men, and himself at the Head of them, under the General's Command, on that Enterprize. Such a seasonable Complement (if punctually performed) might be a good Example to others in that Province to do the like: But from the Behaviour of too many of them towards this Colony, I doubt we have little Reason to expect much Assistance from them; though it is evident, that whatever good Success may attend our General's Toil in Arms, they will be sure to find the Benefit of it in *Carolina*. The first Blood spilt, that we heard of in these Parts, since the War broke out, unhappily fell to our Lot: The General acquainting me, in a Letter he was pleased to write me by this Packet, that the Enemy had attacked and murdered two Highland Men in *Amelia*; and from Mr. *Upton* I gather some particular Circumstances thereto relating: But first it is to be understood in what Posture we were there, when this happened. *Amelia Island*

O 3

Iſland is the fartheſt Look-out we have
againſt the *Spaniards*, where a Scout-Boat
was ſtationed with ſixteen Men belonging
to her, who were to relieve one another as
the Service might require; they who ſtaid
aſhore employing themſelves in cultivating
Land, whilſt the reſt were upon Duty:
To theſe the General added a Serjeant's
Guard of twelve Men; and as ſome of
each Sort had Wives and Children, they
might be computed at near forty in all;
who were fortified with a Paliſade, *&c.*
and two or three ſmall Pieces of Cannon,
to command any Boat paſſing that Way.
It happened (as I am told) that three of
the Scout-Men, ſtraggling unwarily into
the Woods, were attacked in the Manner
aforeſaid, when two of them were thus
ſlain; and the third being miſſing, it is believed he is carried off Priſoner: One of
thoſe killed being ſcalped, and the other's
Head taken off, it is not doubted but the
Authors of it were *Spaniſh Indians*, who
landed unſeen at the Back of the Iſland,
and ſtole their Way thus privately to do it.
At the Hearing of ten or eleven Guns fired
(which diſcovered them to be at leaſt that
Number) our People were alarmed, and
made all the Haſte they could to come up
with them; but they fled in ſuch Haſte,
that they got off unſeen, before we could
intercept them. The General, on the firſt
Hearing

Hearing of it, got what Boats he could find, and went in Pursuit, with about fifty Men, hoping some where or other to repay them: And it is supposed he went for the River St. *John*'s, where there is a *Spanish* Settlement: But as this is known to himself alone, it is only guessing his Designs at Random.

Friday. As the greatest Danger we imagine ourselves exposed to in this Colony, may be from such *Indians* as are in the *Spanish* Interest; whom it is pretty hard to distinguish from our Friends, in Case they straggle far Northward; though our neighbouring *Indians* know them well: The General's Orders to me in Yesterday's Packet, were to give out in Orders here, that no Person should presume to go into the Woods in these Parts without Arms, at their own Peril; which I took Care to publish accordingly.

Saturday. The *Indians* (partly *Chicassaws*, and partly *Euchies*) who Messieurs *Mackintosh* and *Dunbar* told us, were coming to us on *Tuesday* last, arrived here this Day; and we received them with all Demonstration of Friendship: They appeared highly pleased to hear of Action began by the *Spaniards*, and seemed to thirst for some of their Blood in Requital.

Sunday.

Sunday. The Prayers of the Church continued to be read by Mr. *Haberſham.* It was with great Uneaſineſs I waited to ſend off the General's Packet to the Truſt, with other Letters, which had been ever ſince *Thurſday* laſt in my Cuſtody; and not doubting but they were of the greateſt Importance, I feared the Blame would fall on me for ſuch a Delay; for which Reaſon I had ſeveral Times applied to Mr. *Jones* (who had all Boats and Servants at his Command here) to aſſiſt me in ſending away that Packet; but he ſtill put me off, in telling me there was no Boat or Hands to ſpare; for that they were all employed in the Service, ſome one Way, and ſome another: But had the General ſent his Packet to *him*, I well knew he would have ſhewn his Diligence, and loſt no Time in it; though he was in no Care what Reflexions might fall on me.

26.

Monday. Mr. *Bradley* having abſented himſelf ever ſince the 13th, when he went off in the Manner then ſet forth; and having a little before bought a ſmall Skooner, under Pretence of trading with it to the Northward; but ſince his Departure, it being obſerved, that divers of his beſt houſhold Goods were privately put on board by his Son, from the Houſe he was removed to, near the Water-ſide; his Creditors grew alarmed at it; and two of them

having

having before got Judgment for their Debts, now made hafte to take out Execution (which hitherto they had delayed) and ftopt the Veffel from proceeding, intending to make Sale of Effects fufficient to pay what was owing to them. No Token yet appeared how, or when, I might difcharge my Duty, in fending off the General's Packet to the Truft, with other of his Letters; which threw me into the utmoft Impatience, and I could not forbear remonftrating it to Mr. *Jones* in fuch a Manner, that he muft perceive I was determined to acquit myfelf of whatever ill Confequence might attend it.

Tuefday. Mr. *Jones*, with Mr. *Upton*, 27. acquainted me, that a Boat would be provided this Evening, wherein Mr. *Upton* was going to *Charles-Town*; and if I thought proper, it would be a good Convenience for me to fend what I had in my Care: I thought fo too, fince I could come at none fooner, and refolved fo to do: But as Mr. *Upton* told me, when he brought me that Packet laft *Thurfday*, that he defigned foon to go to *Charles-Town* on Bufinefs of his own; I could not avoid furmifing, that either this Delay was contrived to accommodate Mr. *Upton* when he was ready; or elfe that Mr. *Jones* had Letters to write by him which were not fooner perfected: Whereas I had not allowed myfelf to write

more

more than a few Lines to Mr. *Verelft*, dated the 25th; every Day and Hour expecting to be called on in hafte, for what I had
ready at a Moment's Notice; and now delivered into Mr. *Upton*'s Hands immediately
the General's Packet, together with one
from myfelf; writing to my Correfpondent
Mr. *Hopton*, at the fame Time, to take
fpecial Care (as indeed he had always
done) to forward them by the firft Ship
for *England*.

28.　　*Wednefday*. Mr. *Upton* went off for
Charles-Town very early in the Morning;
and in an Hour or two after, the *Indians*
under the Conduct of Lieutenant *Dunbar*,
accompanied by the Quarter-Mafter *Wan-
fel*, after refrefhing themfelves here a few
Days, made the beft of their Way to the
General in the South. The late Accounts
we had from *Charles-Town* acquainted us,
that that Place was growing pretty healthy
again; but the Numbers fwept away by
Death in fome Months paft, during that
grievous Sicknefs, occafioned a melancholy
Appearance of the Inhabitants, who were
much thinned; and that it was hardly
known, when fo few Ships were there, as
at prefent; but that probably might be
owing to the prefent State of War we
are in, it being fuppofed that few *Englifh* Ships would put to Sea, but as they
found

found Opportunity of Convoy, the firſt
Part of their Voyage.

Thurſday. The Court now ſat again,
according to the ordinary Courſe; when a
Grand Jury was ſworn; and leaving them
to preſent what was properly cognizable
when the Court met again, they adjourned till to-morrow. More ill News of People wrecked and loſt at Sea, came to Town
by a Boat which arrived this Day from
Charles-Town; who reported, that in his
Way hither, he ſaw the Wreck of a Boat
upon a ſmall Iſland, with her Stern beat
out, but her Maſt and Sail ſtanding, the
People that were in her being ſuppoſed to
be drowned; for that it appeared ſhe had
ſtruck on the North-Breakers off St. *Helena
Sound*, in attempting to go without all:
From whence it was feared it could be no
other than a Boat of Mr. *Upton*'s, which
was laden at *Charles-Town* by his Order,
and which he had impatiently expected
here for ſome Time, wondering why ſhe
ſtaid ſo long; and it was moſt likely, that
good Part of the Buſineſs which he went
hence about Yeſterday Morning, was to
enquire after her: And in few Hours after
this, we were more confirmed in the Belief
that this Report was true: For as it was
known the Cargo was of conſiderable Value, being partly Butter, Soap, Candles, *&c*
for his own retailing (which were all much
wanted

wanted in this Town) and partly feveral Coils of Rope and Cordage, belonging to the General, for rigging fmall Veffels in the South, together with fome Cafks of Pitch and Tar, and a Parcel of Saddles for equipping the Troop of Rangers; we had it now certified to us, that what Goods remained yet in the Wreck, were fome Cafks of Butter, and fome of the Coils of Rope; being fuch as were not liable fo immediately to be loft, as the other Part of the Loading; and the Owner of the Ifland was taking an honeft Care, to fave what could be faved; but the Perfons in her, nobody doubted their being loft; which were four Hands, whereof *Andrew Barber*, as Patroon, had the Direction, who was looked on as a pretty good Pilot within Land; and I fear his attempting to go without, at this Time of the Year with a Boat loaden, hardly can be juftified.

30.   *Friday.* There remained now no farther Queftion of the Truth of Yefterday's News, which came confirmed from all Hands, and withal, that two of thofe Men loft were faid to be Soldiers belonging to Captain *Norbury's* Company at *Port-Royal*; which we wifhed might not prove as true as the reft. The Court fat again; but the Recorder being taken fo ill, that he faid he could not avoid going home, they broke up, after doing little Bufinefs,

and

and adjourned till to-morrow. This being
St. *Andrew*'s Day, which the *Scotch* never
fail to celebrate annually, and look on it as
a friendly Act in such as join them; I went
in the Evening to shew the Regard I had
to their Society; as Mr. *Jones* also did, and
several others; when we passed it away
inoffensively, with Chearfulness, without
entering into any political Arguments,
which could not well take Place at this
Time; the usual Committee at *Jenkins*'s
well knowing, that divers of their own
Countrymen were possessed of Sentiments
very different from theirs; as also were several others then present.

Saturday. Once again the Court sat to
little Purpose; for the Recorder did not appear, by Reason of his Indisposition, who
had the most material Papers relating to
what was to come before them at this
Court: Wherefore the Grand Jury was
discharged, after delivering into Court what
Presentments they had to offer; and then
the Court adjourned farther to *Monday* the
10th Instant, in Expectation they might by
that Time find all Things ready to proceed
on. The Magistrates, as well as Mr. *Bradley*'s Creditors, having Reason, from good
Information, to believe that he was actually buying some Sows, and other Stock
in *Carolina*, with Design to return hither;
that no Discouragement might be given
him

1739.
Novemb.
30.

Decemb.
1.

1739.
Decemb.

him in it, they took off the Attachment that was on the Skooner, allowing her to proceed, and his Son in her, to his Affiſtance; taking Care at the ſame Time, that no ill Uſe was made of this Indulgence, by carrying off hence any of his beſt Goods and Effects. *(Vide Nov. 26.)*

2.

Sunday. Mr. *Haberſham* read the Prayers of the Church, as he uſed to do, during Mr. *Norris*'s Abſence in the South.

3.

Monday. Mrs. *Matthews* calling here on her Way to the General at St. *Simon*'s, and ſeeing Mr. *Jones*, he had the Opportunity of writing Letters thither; which I miſſed, for want of timely Notice: However, Mr. *Eyre* coming to Town ſoon after, in Company with one Mr. *Holmes*, an *Indian* Trader from the *Cherokee* Nation, whither he was ſent ſo long ſince by the General, as the 29th of *September* laſt (ſee the Notes of that Day) and was now on his Return to the General; I could make good that Defect. He was ſo kind to call upon me immediately on his Arrival, when I delivered him the Packet that was committed to my Care, which came with the other Letters by Captain *Thompſon*, and which I received about a Week after Mr. *Eyre* was gone, from his Kinſman, one of the honourable Truſtees; and it was Matter of great Joy to him, as therefore it was a Pleaſure to me: For he was eſteemed

2   by

by every Body as a good-natured Gentleman, very active in his Duty, and wanted
not Resolution and Spirit sufficient to carry
him through all Parts of it with Bravery.
He had not the good Fortune to meet with
that Success immediately which he expected, in Execution of the Commission
he carried; which was occasioned partly
through the great Mortality among them,
which had swept away great Numbers of
their best Men; whereof the Cause was set
forth in some Affidavits I sent by the General's Order in my Letter of the 25th of
September to Mr. *Verelst*, as it is also noted
in my Journal of that Date; and their
chief Warriors now happened to be all abroad upon their Hunt, which is carefully and duly observed by all *Indians*, and
generally holds two or three Months at a
Time, when perhaps they wander on that
Employment some Hundreds of Miles:
But Mr. *Eyre* had now with him one of
their principal Leaders, who would attend
the General with him, and give his Excellence Assurances of a great Body of chosen
Men, that would certainly join him early
in the Spring: But as for the common
Run, Mr. *Eyre* wisely chose to meddle
with none of them: For such as stay at
home, on these appointed Seasons of being
abroad, are looked on by their own People, as good for nothing; and he rightly
judged,

judged, that the General wanted none such as must be fed and cloathed, without any good Service to be expected from them.

4. *Tuesday.* This Day I laid hold of, to make another Visit to my People, and provide for their intended Movement to my other Plantation near *Vernon* River. At my Return my Ears were presently filled with the Talk which almost every Body had at their Tongue End, of Mr. *Scroggs's* being defrauded of a great Sum of Money, which it was supposed was done by picking his Pocket of a Letter-Case, wherein were Notes to the Value of about 70 *l.* Sterling, and was Part of that Money which the General had advanced to Captain *Cuthbert,* to buy Horses, Mr. *Scroggs* having waited on the General, from whom he was newly returned with this Sum for the Purpose aforesaid *(vide* 16 and 20 of *November* ;*)* but now in all Appearance was thus cheated : Which occasioned various Conjectures, but all at Random : It was certain that the Letter-Case, with the Notes in it, was seen in his Hands, in an honest Man's House in Town ; where he was also seen to put it up again, about an Hour or less before it was lost : The next Question then was, what Company he had been in since ; and it did not appear that he had sat down any where, nor could he remember that he had associated himself
with

with any one, only as he might accidentally, in common with others; three Perfons
he particularly remembered he had talked
with, in that cafual Way : But as they
were all well known in Town, and lay
under no fufpicious Character, there could
be no Accufation againft them : Mr. *Jones*
(who had good Experience in detecting
Roguery) told me he had made ufe of the
beft Skill he had, in his Enquiry; but it
was paft his finding out yet : And fo it
remained till fome lucky Accident or other
poffibly might give us more Light another
Time.

Wednefday. What I had feveral Times
before heard as a flying Report only, I had
fuch farther Information of, that I now
took it for Truth, *viz.* that Meffieurs *Sterling, Baylie, Grant* and *Douglafs*, feeing
no Hopes left of obtaining Negroes, or
Profpect of fettling in *Georgia* to their own
Liking, were determined, and preparing,
to try their Fortune on the Banks of the
River *Savannah*, in *Carolina*, about fifty
or fixty Miles by Water fhort of *New-
Windfor.* This by fome few, very few,
was looked on and talked of as a confiderable Lofs to the Colony; but People of
more Difcernment could not think fo; for
what Lofs can it be to any Place, if fuch
leave it, who will put their helping Hands
to no Good in it? Which thefe Perfons

have evidently fhewn they had no Intention of: The Committee at *Jenkins*'s will indeed hereby lofe fo many trufty Members, who never failed conftant Attendance; and I conceive the total Diffolution of that mutinous Affembly is approaching, Difcord of late being crept in among them, and fome of them now thinking themfelves pretty good Adepts in the political Way, fometimes differ in their Sentiments, about what they have been fo long forming Schemes in vain. for, and refufe paying implicit Obedience to the Dictator any longer; who, if Fame is to be credited, or he himfelf believed, is alfo threatning to leave us to ourfelves, and remove to fome Ifland or another in the *Weft-Indies*. —— May *Georgia* fuffer no greater Lofs, and all will be well.

6.　　*Thurfday*. Meffieurs *Eyre* and *Holmes*, lately arrived from the *Cherokee* Nation, preparing to fet off for the South this Day, and attend the General there; I wrote by them to his Excellency, inclofing divers Letters and Papers that came to my Hands, defigned to be fent him. I had no fooner finifhed what I had to do, and delivered it to Mr. *Eyre* juft taking Boat, when a Packet was brought me from the Truft, forwarded by the Attorney-General at *Charles-Town*; who fent me a Letter with it, dated *November* 5, wherein he wrote me, that

he

he had juſt then received it by Captain *Nicholſon*, newly arrived in the *Minerva* from *London*, who had a tedious Paſſage of twelve Weeks: And the Paſſage which this Packet had from *Charles-Town*, was much after the ſame Rate; the Fellow who had the Charge of it, though a Freeholder here, loitering at *Port-Royal* by the Way, on Buſineſs of his own; ſo that it was a full Month in coming from *Charles-Town*. I luckily ſtopped the Gentlemen a few Minutes, and the Tide preſſing them away, I had juſt Time to deliver to them for the General, what I received for him from *England*, together with other Letters that came with it from *Charles-Town*; but had no Time to write him any more than that I had before done. Afterwards I had Leiſure to peruſe Mr. *Verelſt*'s Letter to me, dated the 10th of *Auguſt*; which was ſo near after the Date of the former *per* Capt. *Thompſon*, that the Purport of it chiefly was, to inform me of the Subſtance of the Act, which the honourable Truſtees had prepared for his Majeſty's Approval, and which, when printed, would be ſent hither.

Friday. Enſign *Maxwell* having finiſhed what he had to do in *Carolina* by Order, returned with the ten Soldiers detached from the Gariſon at *Port-Royal*: And in the Evening Mr. *Upton* alſo came back from *Charles-Town*; who found all that

7

had

had been reported here, too true, concerning the Loſs of his Boat and Cargo; but was of Opinion there was Roguery in it, and that the Men were not drowned, but run away, after plundering the Boat of what was moſt valuable and portable; which they might do eaſily, he ſaid, and go to ſome remote Place on the Coaſt, by the Help of a Canoe they had with them: And what induced him the more to ſuſpect it was, that ſome Trunks, which had the moſt valuable Things in them, were found broke open, and ſtript: The Truth of which might in Time be diſcovered. He brought me a Letter from Mr. *Hopton*, informing, that he had received the Packets which I committed to Mr. *Upton*'s Care the 27th *ult.* and that they came in very good Time to go for *England*, in the Ship *Endeavour*, Captain *Alexander Hope*, who was juſt upon ſailing, and to whoſe Care he had committed it.

Saturday. Enſign *Maxwell* proceeded South, together with his Detachment of Soldiers. News came in the Evening of another ſad Accident, that happened to a poor Man, who was at Work (among others) for Mr. *Haberſham*, by his Appointment, on a Tract of upwards of five hundred Acres of Land, which was newly run out by the General's Order, next adjoining to mine near *Vernon* River; and in

the

the falling of a Tree, the Man was killed
by a small Branch of it. The Intent of
this Land being run out, was, that it might
be ready for Mr. *Whitfield*'s converting to
a proper Use whenever he came; and
whatever Use that shall be, this that Mr.
Haberſham purſues is preparatory to it.
Nothing more worth noting; but ſufficient
for this Day, may be ſaid, was the Evil
thereof.

Sunday. Mr. *Haberſham* continued, as
he had done, to read the Prayers of the
Church, and a Sermon.

Monday. Captain *Davis* having now
got his Snow ready for ſailing, after a pretty deal of Time ſpent in equipping her for
the Deſign of privateering; ſhe fell down
to *Tybee* in order for a Cruize; but not being yet ſufficiently manned, he would wait
there for more Hands, which he expected:
She was a neat-built Veſſel, ſailed well, and
of good Force, if well manned, carrying
about twenty Guns mounted on Carriages,
beſides Swivels; and required at leaſt a
hundred Men. A Jury of twelve Men
were impanelled, and ſent to ſit in Inqueſt
on the Body of the poor Man, who loſt
his Life on *Saturday*; who found it *Accidental Death*, and ſaw the Body buried: His
Name was *Gardener*, had ſome Land allotted him at *Skeedoway*, where he lived
a little while, and cleared a ſmall Piece

of

of two or three Acres; but grew weary and deferted it, more than two Years fince, as divers others have done; and lived of late by letting himfelf out to Hire.

11.
12.

Tuefday, } Nothing more than com-
Wednefday. } mon requiring my Atten-
tion in Town, my principal Care thefe two Days was, to promote and haften forward the Work I had begun at my new Planta-tion; which at firft fetting out was attend-ed with many new Expences; and I found it neceffary to begin *de novo* with thofe Hands which I was to employ there, by providing them with new Axes, Houghs, *&c.* and a new Set of Cloathing from Head to Foot, both Linen and Woollen, to be added to what they were now wear-ing out, of what was laft provided for them: And as they were henceforward to be employed at fuch a Diftance from hence, that they could not be fupplied fo frequent-ly as formerly with what they might want, it would be alfo neceffary to lay in fuch a Store of Provifions, as might be fufficient for their Wants a while to come, of all Kinds.

13.
Thurfday. A little Diforder, occafioned by a Cold coming upon me, made it ad-vifable to keep home; where I could al-ways employ myfelf ufefully, when well.

Friday.

Friday. The same: Nothing interrupting me from abroad, I made what Advances I could with my Pen and Ink; and found myself much better as the Day ended.

Saturday. Mr. *Jones* having a Desire to see *Abercorn* (which he never had) at his Request I went up the River with him; and the rather, because one *Bunyon*, a Builder of Boats and a Settler there, had newly, by the General's Order, built a large Ferry-Boat, fit to carry about nine or ten Horses at a Time, which was intended to be kept at *Palachocolas*, it being a proper and convenient Pass on this River from that Fort: Here we found the said Boat newly finished, and by her Appearance on the Water, we judged she would well answer the Purpose she was intended for. As there was no Place in the whole Province, of the like Allotment of fifty Acres each, which in my Eye seemed so desirable, being a most pleasant Situation on the Banks of such a River, with as good Land belonging to each Lot, as is readily to be found in most Parts of the Province; I never saw it but with Regret, that there never yet had been a Number of Settlers there deserving it; but generally they happened to be loose, idle People, who after some short Abode wandered elsewhere, and left it: It consists of twelve Lots, the two Trust-Lots bounding each Extream; and

P 4   there

1739. there are at prefent five Families only remaining there, nor has there often been
Decemb. more at one Time. As the Truft-Lands
feem to be now in fome better Way of
cultivating by their own Servants, than hitherto; I propofed it to Mr. *Jones* to fend
down a few *German* Families to work on
the Truft-Lots there; which by helping to
fill the Place, very probably might induce
others the fooner to occupy Lands there
alfo: He agreed with me in Opinion, and
faid he would write of it to the General.

16.   *Sunday.* We made what hafte we could
home; but the Tide not favouring us in
due Time, it was paft Noon ere we reached *Savannah*; and a wet Day.

17.   *Monday.* Moft Part of the Day employed with Mr. *Jones* in methodizing Accounts, which were preparing as faft as
we could to fend to the Truftees. In the
Evening I had once more an Inclination
to make a Vifit to our nightly Club;
where in this Time of Scarcity of News
from all Parts, I thought I fhould not fail
of fomething, either true or falfe; for rather than want, they could coin: I found
them now reduced to a very fmall Number, three or four only; who upon my
coming in (whatever Subject they had been
upon before) turned moft of their Difcourfe
into a doleful Story of the fad State they
faw poor *Georgia* fallen into, and how People

ple were deserting it Day by Day: Which not having Sagacity enough of myself to discover, I said I wished to know who they were: And after a pretty long Pause upon it, they named two or three, adding to them all the *Jews* in general; which I said little to then, intending to be better informed: And by Degrees passing from one Point to another, at length the Trustees Answer to their Representation was to be animadverted on; which with Patience I heard them a pretty while take in Pieces, and reason upon in their own Way as they liked, offering sometimes a Word or two myself in Vindication of what needed none: Till at last they came to that Length as to tell me, in plain Words, they thought it not a fair Answer, nor Way of proceeding in the Trust, to publish an Answer in Print, to what so very few in *England* had seen in Writing; and that in Justice they should have set one against the other, and printed them both together, whereby the World would then judge who was in the right: Which I thought such a Piece of Impudence, that I could no longer bear; and so I took my Leave, not likely to trouble them, or myself about them again in haste.

Tuesday. After dispatching some necessary Business at home, being pretty eagerly whetted at what passed last Night; I 18.

went

went out with a Resolution to discover, as far as I could, what Foundation appeared for such a Talk of Desertion, as I was then entertained with: And I was very well assured, that not one of the *Jews* who were People of Industry, or of any Value among us, had any such Thoughts or Design, being easy and contented in the present State they lived; some of them Planters, and others in a Way of Trade; only one, who was a Barber, and lived wholly by Shaving, but never improved his Lot; another who neglected his Land wholly, and followed no visible Business; and a third, who had not the least Property among us, but was a Wanderer; these three I understood had received lately some Advice from their Friends in *Jamaica*, inviting them to come thither; which they were pondering upon, and unresolved in: And among the common Freeholders, I could hear of none except *Robert Potter*, who was an elderly Man, lately made one of the Constables, by the General's Favour, to encourage him; from whence he seemed to expect a Maintenance, that he had no Title to otherwise; and therefore could not obtain it: He (it is confessed) had of late shewn some Tokens of Uneasiness, and given it out, that he would not stay here and starve, but rather try his Fortune with Captain *Davis* in his Privateer;

teer; who being now upon failing in few Days, we fhould foon fee how far he was in earneft.

Wednefday. My chief Employment great Part of the Day, was to haften on the Work I had taken in Hand, of a new Plantation; wherein I was not willing to admit of loitering. Towards Evening I received by a trading Boat juft arrived, Letters from Lieutenant *Kent* at Fort *Augufta,* informing me, among other Things, that it was currently reported in the Nations near us, the *French* were once more marching with a great Body of Men to attack the *Chicaffaw Indians,* whofe Fidelity to us, and whofe Bravery againft their Enemies, had been thoroughly experienced: Wherefore we could not but be in fome Pain for their Defence: Inclofed I found a Letter alfo for the General, which I made no Doubt imported the fame News, and I fhould forward with all the Difpatch I could.

Thurfday. Often in Conference with Mr. *Jones,* and bufy in Accounts; when between while we fell into Difcourfe about thofe who were faid to be leaving us; the Principal of whom being *Robert Potter,* and he having now declared openly his Refolution of feeking his Fortune in privateering, I afked Mr. *Jones* to tell me freely his Opinion of him, that (without telling him

him mine) I might know how well our
Sentiments agreed: And without Hefita-
tion, he anfwered plainly, that he knew
him to be a fly, old Knave, and that he
only wifhed he might hold his Refolution
of going; which rather than he fhould not,
he would give Money out of his own
Pocket, that the Colony might be rid of
him: Which Opinion of his, I entirely
concurred in; the fame Reafons inducing
us to think fo; among which fome we
fpecified.——As to his Religion, he put on
at Times a Shew of conftant Attendance
on the publick Worfhip of the Church,
perhaps for a Month; and then would
abfent himfelf from it more than twice as
long, profeffing himfelf a Diffenter; but it
is generally fufpected he had no Title to
the Word Proteftant, for it is certain he
was bred a *Roman Catholick* in *Ireland*, and
many People do not fcruple to fay, that
he is actually in Orders under that Church,
even now: He is univerfally looked on as a
great Hypocrite, affecting to go in a tat-
tered Habit, and complaining of Poverty;
whereas it is well known, he has good
Store of better Apparel in his Cheft; and
as to his Pretence of Want, fcarcely any
one gives Ear to it, believing rather that
he has a Mifer's Hoard, which he dares
not make proper Ufe of: Neverthelefs, utterly to deftroy all fuch Shams, it is well
known

known Mr. *Jones* employed him feveral
Months at the Rate of nine Shillings *per* Week, as a conftant Guard on the Office were the publick Accounts were examining, and where all the Books were fecured, to take effectual Care left any unfair Dealing fhould be ufed, or Embezzlement made to the Detriment of the Truft; and upon the late Promotion of Mr. *Fallowfield* to the Magiftracy, a Vacancy of one of the Conftables happening, the General made him a Conftable, to which was annexed a Payment of 10 *l. per Annum*, intended as a Mark of his Favour for not fubfcribing the late Reprefentation, his Excellence kindly overlooking all other Defects: But Mr. *Jones* had fome Time before difcharged him from his Employment at the Office, upon difcovering fome evident Tokens of his Infidelity: This 10 *l.* of itfelf, however, was fufficient for feeding him, and only one Daughter, which he had (a Girl of about ten Years of Age;) and if he would have added any Thing to it, by cultivating a little Land, as he had formerly done, and with Pleafure he now might, having a few Acres well cleared, he had a fair Profpect of living comfortably; but this laft Year he wholly neglected that, and now thought himfelf hardly ufed, for not being maintained as he expected. This being the true State of Mr. *Potter*'s Cafe, I cannot
apprehend

apprehend the Colony will suftain any Damage for the Want of him. Two others likewife, that a pretty while fince engaged in the Privateer Service, would as little be miffed: One of them, whofe Name is *Elifha Fofter*, and by Office a Tythingman, at whofe Houfe Capt. *Davis* lodged, was perfuaded to think he could not mifs making his Fortune in that Way, and entered as Quarter-Mafter, whofe Office was, upon taking a Prize, to ftand between the Captain and his Men, and fee that every one had his Dividend right: What Improvement he has made afhore on his Lot, is, a pretty good little Houfe to live in; but in five or fix Years that he has lived here, he never cultivated one Acre of Land, chufing to get Money any other Ways, if he could, by fome Traffick; which from the little vifible Appearance of, was generally thought to be unwarrantable, being ftrongly fufpected to be one of the Number of fuch as furnifh this Place with Spirits; and whereof he took fo plentiful a Share himfelf, that it was common with him to appear publickly drunk in the Streets in open Day. The next to be named is one *Garrett*, a Sort of Quack, who had little Skill and little Practice, fettling here about three Years fince, or more; had a Freehold Lot granted him in this Town, which he kept not long, and then threw
it

it up, refusing to do the Guard Duty, or discharge it by another: But both he and *Foster*, we now hear, are already wavering whether or not to pursue their intended Voyage. These were some of the good People, whom the Company I kept last *Monday*, were persuading to believe the Loss of, would be of sad Consequence: But we happened not to think alike; and I had good Reason to believe, that if they stopped short from proceeding to Sea, it was not for Want of Encouragement from *them*, who delighted in nothing more than to seduce all they could from continuing among us.

Friday. Early this Morning arrived a small Boat from the South *(John Rea* Patroon) with several Passengers, mostly belonging to this Place and Neighbourhood: We all sought eagerly for News, having not had any fresh Intelligence of late; but they could tell us little more than that the General was just returned safe, from the Expedition he had been upon near St. *Juan's*, where the *Spanish* Guard Sloop lately lay that was stationed there; but now was gone, and no Enemy appeared: The General, we were told, advanced with his little Body of about two hundred Men, partly Mariners, and some Landmen, with a few *Indians*; but scarce any of the regular Troops, except some Gentlemen Cadets,

21.

dets,

dets, and three or four Commiffion Officers, who obtained the Favour to attend
him; and with thefe he advanced within a
little Way of *Auguftin:* In marching, our
Indians fet up the War Whoop; which
thofe of the Enemy's Side underftood fo
well, that they who were near took to their
Heels, and ran into the Town for Safety;
only one of our *Indians* overtook one of
their Negroes with a Ball, which ftopt his
Flight and killed him. After reconnoitring
thus far, and finding none to oppofe, his
Excellence probably did not think it pru-
dential to wait, and fee whether or not
they would take Courage and intercept
them with a ftrong Body: Wherefore he
retreated homewards, but not in fuch hafte
as to neglect taking in Fort St. *George* by
the Way; which was the utmoft of our
Limits for a while, and given up again
upon fome Terms of Accommodation as
were then agreed to: Here the General re-
placed now a few Men, as a Look-out, to
keep Garifon, and obferve what the *Spaniards* are about.—This was what we could
pick out from thefe Paffengers, who faid
they came off in half an Hour's Time after the General's Arrival, who was much
fatigued, and went to take his Reft:
Wherefore we next hoped for fome more
authentick Advices thence by the next Opportunity. This being his Excellency's
Birth-

Birth-Day, was obferved by firing fome
Guns, and his Health was drank under the
Flag, without any Profufenefs of Powder
or Wine; which he forbid upon any publick Solemnity.

Saturday. Upon Advice received, that
a fmall Skooner had been obferved lurking for feveral Days paft within *Uffybaw
Sound*, and fome that belonged to her had
been afhore at one of our Plantations in
that Neighbourhood, where by making
Shew of their being in want of many
Things, they gave good Caufe of Sufpicion
that they had no good Defign; Captain
Davis was applied to, to fend out his
Sloop, now at *Tybee*, to prevent her getting
away by Sea: At the fame Time a Boat
well armed went within Land, to lay hold
of her; and Meffieurs *Parker* and *Jones*
(two Magiftrates) required the Mafter, as
well as the Men belonging to her, to be
brought afhore at the neareft and moft
commodious Place of landing, where they
might be examined; for which Purpofe
the faid Magiftrates rode thither; and finding their Orders punctually executed, by
Noble Jones, who had a Plantation near
the Place, they there examined them, and
found her navigated by four or five Hands
only, without any Appearance of Arms:
Neverthelefs, as fhe came from *Hifpaniola*,
laden with *Spanifh* contraband Goods, con-

signed to Meffieurs *Woodward* and *Flower*
at *Port-Royal*, fhe was feizable; and moreover her lying there fo many Days, gave
Grounds of Sufpicion, that they were found-
ing the Depths of that Inlet, or fomething
elfe was in their View, which they would
not own, but pretended that they miftook
their Port : She was ordered round to *Ty-*
bee, and to be fecured, till we had the General's Orders concerning her. This Afternoon Mr. *Chriftie* came to my Houfe, and
brought with him Meffieurs *Fallowfield*,
Theo. Hetherington, and *Andrew Grant*, as
Witneffes to his peremptory Demand of the
Conftitution appointing him firft Bailiff;
having, as he faid, fulfilled the Conditions
required of him, in making out a Copy
of the Proceedings of the Court to this
Time; and putting into my Hands a Packet with feveral Sheets of Paper written,
the Contents to me unknown, which he
put into a Cover of brown Paper immediately; and being then fealed with divers
Seals, he delivered it to me, directed to the
honourable Truftees, and told me he expected I would fend it : To which Mr.
Fallowfield, in a moft infolent Manner (as
it is his ufual Way) added many rude Ex-
preffions in a Sort of menacing, which I
little regarded; but directing my Anfwer
to Mr. *Chriftie*, I told him, that it was my
Duty to tranfmit faithfully to the Truft
what-

whatever was put into my Hands for that 1739.
Intent, and accordingly would take Care of
this; but what Name to give it I could not Decemb.
tell, unlefs I was better informed; for it
did not appear to me, that it was a full
Copy of the Court Proceedings; to which
he replied, that Mr. *Hetherington* then prefent could teftify that it was examined by
his Book; but I alledged, that Mr. *Hetherington* could be no Judge whether or not
that Book was duly kept, or contained
what ought to be recorded; for it was
known, that the Book itfelf, as well as
this now called a Copy, were all made out
fince the late Stop put to delivering him
the Conftitution of firft Bailiff; and it was
out of fuch Fragments, as it was to be
feared were never to be reduced into perfect Order; moreover, that it was well
known alfo there were feveral Fines due to
the Truftees, and other Sums paid into
Court, which he never yet accounted for,
or charged himfelf with; which none
could fo well difcover how well they were
taken Notice of, as the Magiftrates themfelves, who I apprehended had a Right at
all Times to call for that Book, and have
Recourfe to it: To which he replied pofi-
tively, that neither the Magiftrates, nor
any one living, fhould look into his Book:
And to conclude, I told him my laft Orders from the General were, that all thefe

Matters

1739. Matters fhould remain as they now ftood, till the Truftees Pleafure was farther known; that neverthelefs I would write to the General who was near, for his Advice as foon as he pleafed; and that I would not fail to lay before the Truftees what now paffed, by the next firft Packet that I fent for *England*: And fo they left me.

23. *Sunday*. Mr. *Haberſham* continued to read the publick Prayers, &c. during the Abfence of a Minifter. Some Perfons came up to Town from *Tybee*, belonging to a Sloop Privateer which came from *Providence Iſland*, that anchored at *Cockſpur* laft Night : Their Bufinefs was with the General, to get their Commiffion improved and ftrengthned by him; but miffing him here, they would lofe no Time in going to find him at St. *Simon's*: They had taken fome fmall Prizes from the *Spaniards* (as they faid) which they fent home; but they told us a Privateer belonging unto *Rhode-Iſland* had the good Fortune lately, though but a fmall Sloop with forty Hands, to take a rich *Spaniard* lately on the *Spaniards* own Coaft, with fuch a Quantity of Silver aboard, that they fhared four hundred Dollars apiece, befides folid Plate for the Ufe of a Church, and many rich Brocades, &c.

24. *Monday*. The moft remarkable Occurrence of this Day was the Arrival of a
Sloop

Sloop from *Philadelphia*, belonging to Mr. 1739.
Whitfield, which he had bought, and sent
hither, filled with great Variety of Necef- Decemb.
faries for fuch as were to fettle here: She
brought feven or eight fuch (Men, Women,
and Children) befides two that had been here,
and now returned from *England*, namely, a young Son of Mr. *Bradley's*, and one
Robert How, who it might be hoped from
Mr. *Whitfield's* Inftruction was become a
new Man; for he carried but a bad Character with him from hence. They made
Report, that Mr. *Whitfield* was coming, in
Company with two or three to attend him,
by Land, thro' *Maryland*, *Virginia*, *North*
and *South-Carolina*, hither; which is computed at leaft fix hundred Miles; and that
we might expect him here in about a
Week more.

Tuefday, Chriftmas-Day. Publick Divine 25.
Service was obferved, as at other Times.

Wednefday. The Skooner that was ta- 26.
ken on Sufpicion of unwarrantable Practices laft *Saturday*, and apparently loaden
with *Spanifh* Goods, being ordered round
hither, arrived; and Col. *Flower*, of *Port-
Royal*, who was the Owner, having Intelligence what a Situation fhe was in, thought
it Time to beftir himfelf, and came hither
alfo; who alledged many Things in his
own Favour, plaufible and fit to be confidered; but as the General was now in the

Pro-

Province, no Judicature here would venture to decide so nice an Affair, without first taking his Opinion and Advice: Wherefore Colonel *Flower* determined to wait on his Excellence at *Frederica* with all convenient Speed; when at the same Time the Magistrates, who had acted in it so far, would inform the General of all Proceedings. By Colonel *Flower* I received the Packets sent from the Trust by Captains *Ayres* and *Gregory*, with Letters of *September* 14, and *October* 6; together with a Letter from Mr. *Hopton* (as he never failed) now informing me, that Captain *Ayres* made eleven Weeks Passage of it, by whom he had the large Packet, and also a Box for the General: And Captain *Gregory*, who arrived in eight Weeks, and was within very few Days of the other, brought him the small Packet: All which he forwarded to me by Mr. *Jonathan Bryan*, who was to deliver it to Mr. *Wyre*, his Correspondent at *Port-Royal*; and who accordingly took this first Opportunity of sending it to me by the Colonel: But Mr. *Bryan* being on Horseback, could not take the Box with him; wherefore Mr. *Hopton* waited the first Convenience of sending it.

27.   *Thursday.* The whole Day taken up in writing Letters, and preparing many Things which required being sent to the South, wherewith a Pettyagua was now loading, and

and a small Boat was ordered also at the
Colonel's Request and Expence; by which
he purposed to make quick Expedition to-
morrow Morning; and I designed, by the
same Conveyance, to transmit to the General what I had received for him Yesterday.

Friday. Colonel *Flower*'s Design of setting out for *Frederica*, being baulked by a
very wet Day, which prevented his going
on Horseback as far as *Noble Jones*'s Plantation, who was to accompany him in his
Passage thence, for which Purpose the Boat
was sent round thither Yesterday; I delivered the General's Packet, and other Letters for him, to Mr. *Parker*, who had engaged to shew the Colonel the Way to *Noble Jones*'s, his own Plantation also lying
in that Neighbourhood; and he promised
to put what I gave him the Charge of, into *Noble Jones*'s Hands, to deliver it all
safe to the General. Bad Weather and
Christmas Holidays meeting, occasioned a
Conjunction also of Friends at one another's Houses, and scarcely any one to be
seen abroad, nor any Thing passed worth
Note.

Saturday. Took Horse, and rode to
my Plantation (intended) at the Mouth of
Vernon River, being the first Visit I made
my People since I sent them to begin there,
after they had first fenced in the full Quantity of Land allotted; which was the sooner

done,

done, by Means of an Ifthmus of near a Mile extent, that we fet our Fence on, and fo parted it from the Wildernefs. I found them well covered from the bad Weather, by a ftrong Palmeta Hut, which they had made as foon as they arrived; to which in the next Place they would add a convenient Enlargement with Clapboards in few Days more, and then to work in falling Trees, clearing Ground, &c. I had five Hands there, befides one that I had hired for an Overfeer, on fuch Terms as would make it his Intereft to take Care they all did their Duty; and that he alfo put a helping Hand to it himfelf. As this was the very utmoft Settlement in the Northern Divifion of this Province, towards the Sea-Coaft, and required their keeping a good Look-out that Way againft the *Spaniards*; as well as backwards againft any ftraggling *Spanifh Indians* that fhould attempt to come upon them unprovided; I furnifhed them with two Fufees and Bayonets of my own, and a Couple of Mufkets I got from the Stores for them, with Powder and Ball fufficient; telling them, that in Cafe of any Danger, I hoped they would behave like Men; which they promifed me very chearfully; and I affured them they fhould want for no Encouragement from me, that they deferved. Returned home in the Evening; and being

informed

informed by the Tything-man upon Duty, that there was like to be a weak Guard
to-night, through feveral Peoples Neglect,
&c. I gave him Charge to make a particular Return to me, of all that was fit to
be taken Notice of, when he went off his
Guard; refolving to fee the late Orders left
us by the General, relating to thofe Affairs,
ftrictly obferved.

Sunday. Mr. *Norris* not yet returning,
the publick Service, and a Sermon upon
Juftification, was read by Mr. *Haberfham.*

Monday. The Year ended without any
Thing remarkable, after too many that I
would gladly have taken no Notice of, had
it been confiftent with the Duty required
of me: But while fome among us were
too bufy in promoting Difcord, and tempt-
ing divers to think they might live happier
elfewhere (which few here of real Value would give Ear to; but on the contrary faw fome returning; heard of others
who were become very miferable, not
knowing how to get their Bread, and had
no Reafon to expect much Countenance
here, from their former ill Courfe of Life;
befides what Accounts we frequently had
of feveral of them that were taken away
by Death, in the late common Calamity of
Sicknefs, which fell upon the People of
Carolina, and *Charles-Town* efpecially) kind
Providence beftowed the Blefling of Health
in

in fo large a Share upon this Province, that fo few were not known to have died in one Year, fince the planting of the Colony. The Camp neverthelefs at St. *Simon*'s grew fickly, about the Fall of the Leaf, and the Soldiers were addicted to Agues, which rendered many of them weak; but very rarely proved mortal, they that had tafted of the current Diftemper recovering apace.

Tuefday. Great Part of this Day fpent with Mr. *Jones* in adjufting divers Accounts which had been examined fome Time paft, in order now to haften them away with what Speed we could to the Truftees; who by their laft Letters required us fo to do; wherein we had found great Intricacy: And it is a Piece of Juftice due to Mr. *Jones*, to acknowledge, that without his Application to that Bufinefs, I fee little could be done in it by either of thofe Colleagues joined in Commiffion with him: For as to myfelf, who have no Pretence to the Rank of an Accomptant, I only tread in the Path that he firft traces out, very often through many Turnings and Windings; and when the Light opens, fo that Truth may be more eafily difcovered from Error, whether by Accident or Defign, I then make ufe of what little Capacity I have, to inform my Judgment, in fuch Manner that I may not fet my Hand

Hand blindfold to I know not what; in 1739.
which Purſuit I never fail to join him,
whenever he calls upon me ſo to do, and January
tells me he has Leiſure.

Wedneſday. In Conference with Mr. *Jones* 2.
on ſundry Affairs, he acquainted me in what
Manner he was accoſted by Mr. *Chriſtie*;
who bringing two Witneſſes with him,
namely, *Andrew Grant* and *Theoph. Hetherington*, in the ſame Manner as he did to
me on the 22d *ult.* he produced an Account
which he ſhewed; wherein he made the
Truſtees Debtors to him in a large Sum
upwards of 100 *l.* Sterling; and he (Mr.
Jones) looking on it as what there was no
juſt Foundation for, told him in a ſatirical
Way, that they would have done well, if
they had brought their ſeveral Concubines
with them, as a farther Evidence of what
paſſed; wherein *Grant* and *Chriſtie* were
moſt barefaced and ſcandalouſly culpable;
the firſt of them having two Baſtards by
one Woman, who all cohabit with him;
and the other with as little Shame had taken to his Bed another Man's Wife (who
was run away ſome Time) with whom
he lived in open Adultery *(vide* 10, 11, 12,
13 of *Oct.)* *Chriſtie* then aſked him how
he dared iſſue any Money without his Pri-
vity; to which the other replied, that he
was not looked on as a Man fit to be truſt-
ed in thoſe Affairs, who was known to

have

have made feveral Concealments of Money belonging to the Truftees, which had come to his Hands; and withal he let him know in plain Words, that his Character was grown fo bad, the General declared he would never fuffer his Name to ftand on the fame Paper with his. The Time drawing near of our Court fitting again next Week; from thefe feveral Attacks lately made, it was imagined fomething was intended by them when that Day came, thefe Proceedings being well known to be the Refult of our Committee of Safety; which though reduced now to a fmall Number, yet like Vipers near expiring, continue to fhew a Difpofition to Mifchief as long as they can: Of which Number Mr. *Chriftie* (as before obferved) has for a confiderable Time paft made himfelf one; and I wifh I could wholly clear one of our new Magiftrates (Mr. *Fallowfield)* from any the like Imputation, who has been obferved to be a pretty frequent Attender on that Club; but how far a Partaker of their Counfels, Time will beft fhew; Facts, and not Suppofitions only, being the Guide I muft follow.

3.   *Thurfday.* The Day at length came, that had been long expected, when Captain *Davis* and his People took Leave of this Place for a while, *Potter* and *Fofter,* two of our Officers (before mentioned) making

Part

Part of their Crew; and both the Snow and Sloop lay at *Tybee* ready for failing, fitted out by *Davis*, who took the Command of one of them himself, and *James Williams* had that of the other: It was expected they would find good Hands, and enough, at *Providence*, where they were bound first; but they were yet poorly manned, neither could it be expected they were to be found here. A *New-York* Sloop that had been at *Frederica*, and difposed of moft of her Cargo of Provifions there, —— *Tinley* Mafter, ftopt at Anchor in our River; and the Mafter brought no Letters, but reported, that the General was preparing, when he came thence on *Tuefday* laft, to fet out on another Expedition againft the Enemy, much ftronger than before, refolving (as it was believed) at any Rate to drive the *Spaniards* out of two Forts they had on St. *John*'s River: Wherein it feems fome Attempt had been made a little while fince, by a fmall Party, under the Command of a Subaltern or two, who found the Forts fo fortify'd and garifon'd, that it was impracticable to attack them with Succefs, by naked Men, under no Defence or Cover; for which Reafon they then returned *re infectâ* after one (a Serjeant) being mortally wounded, who is fince dead: What this Mafter farther reported was, that a Duel was fought lately between Meffieurs

Leman

Leman and *Sutherland* (two Enfigns) and that Mr. *Leman* lay dangerouſly ill of his Wounds.

4.

Friday. *Samuel Lacy* coming in his Pettyagua from *Charles-Town*, brought Letters with him thence for the General, to be forwarded for his Majeſty's Service; ſome Letters alſo for me, but of no great Import; and ſeveral for other People; but no Ship arrived from *England* ſince Captain *Gregory*, nor any farther News than what *he* brought with him.

5.

Saturday. Moſt of my Time this Day, as well as for ſeveral preceding, was taken up with Mr. *Jones*, in getting forward ſuch Accounts as we poſſibly could, of thoſe which had been examined ſome Time paſt, but had not been yet put into due Order: And what yet remained to be examined, ſuppoſing them to be alike perplexed (at leaſt ſeveral of them) it was not in our Power to foreſee with any Certainty, what Time it would take to finiſh them: In the mean while I was unwilling my next Letters ſhould go without ſome Specimen of what we had been doing; which on the other Hand muſt occaſion a Delay more than uſual in ſending away my Packet.

6.

Sunday. No News yet of Mr. *Norris's* Return from the South, or of Mr. *Whitfield* from the North: Wherefore Mr. *Haberſham*

berſham continued, as he had done, to read the Service of the Church, and a Sermon after it.

Monday. This being the ordinary Day of the Court's ſitting, the Magiſtrates met, and opened it in due Form; but upon calling over the Names of the Perſons ſummoned, both on the Grand and Petty Jury, ſo many failed to appear, that they could not make out a Number ſufficient for either; and obſerving that the Perſons on thoſe Liſts, were many of them ſuch as were well known to be at preſent far out of Town, they conceived that the Recorder (who had always taken that Part upon him of giving out thoſe Liſts to be ſummoned) had now picked out enough Abſentees to prevent the Court's proceeding any farther: Wherefore being now aſſembled together, they took Care that other Liſts ſhould immediately be made, of the Freeholders, ſufficient to prevent any ſuch Defect when they met again; which by Adjournment they appointed this Day Fortnight. Mr. *Jones* returned, and I with him, to haſten on, as faſt as might be, ſome of thoſe Accounts the Truſtees expected.

Tueſday. The ſame: And I learnt nothing material from without. A *New-York* Sloop with Proviſions, *&c.* came up the River, —— *Ware* Maſter; who after privately higgling about among our Keepers

of

of Stores, and furnishing them with what they best liked, offered the Remainder to us; which we rejected with Scorn.

9.   *Wednesday.* Colonel *Flower* returned from the South, where he had been to wait on the General, about his Affair before-mentioned *(Dec. 26 & seq.)* and brought Letters from the General: In one of which to Mr. *Jones*, he gave some Directions relating to that Skooner, which he communicated to Mr. *Parker* and me; Copies whereof he promised to send to the Trustees: And this Evening, at Colonel *Flower*'s Request, the three Bailiffs and I met him, in order to consider what to be done therein; when it was proposed by Messieurs *Jones*, *Parker*, and self (in order to make the Colonel as easy as could be, in so difficult an Affair, which we were not fond of deciding) that the Case should be stated, and sent to Mr. *Rutledge*, a Lawyer in *Charles-Town*, whom the General has employed on several Occasions; desiring him to advise with the Officers of the Customs thereon, and to let us know how far we might proceed without Blame: But the Colonel thereupon said, that if that was the Resolution to be taken, he would save us that Trouble; for he well knew, that as he could not deny but there were some contraband Goods aboard, *viz.* a small Parcel of Coffee and Soap, that alone would,

in

in the Opinion of the Lawyers and Custom-House Officers, condemn the Vessel; but he hoped we should not carry Things on with that Rigour; since (as he said) those Things were taken in by the Master, without Direction from him; and the Bulk of the Cargo was Molasses and Sugar, which if suffered to be entered, would be of Service to the Colony. Hereupon Mr. *Fallow-field* declaring, with his usual Warmth, that the Affair was properly cognizable by him as Naval Officer, and none else; that he would enter the Molasses and Sugar; and as for those Goods that were contraband, he would take them into his Custody till farther Order; and the Blame (if any) he would take upon himself; that he knew what he did, being a better Judge of those Matters than any one here, &c. and appearing so very positive in it, Messieurs *Jones* and *Parker* were of Opinion not to enter into any Controversy with him, but to let him take his own Course; and if any new Difficulty should arise, they would meet upon it again to-morrow Morning: In the mean Time Messieurs *Jones* and *Parker* desired I would note what passed, that they might be justified.

Thursday. The same Persons meeting again this Morning, continued in the same Opinion as Yesterday; and Mr. *Fallowfield* undertook the Whole of what was to be done:

10.

done: But upon its being urged by us, that those contraband Goods could no where be so safely and properly lodged, as in the Truftees own Cuftody; Mr. *Fallowfield* thought fit to yield that Point, and promifed they fhould be brought to the Truft's Stores; and as for the reft, he undertook the Colonel fhould give his Bond to the Truftees, for paying the Duty on thofe Goods, which Bond he would deliver to me. —— *Ware*, Mafter of the *New-York* Sloop, going to the South, to fee if he could difpofe of the Refidue of his Cargo there, I took the Opportunity of fending by him a Packet to the General, wherein were enclofed fundry Letters that came to my Hands from different Parts of the two Provinces for him, fince the laft I fent on the 28th *ult.* In the Afternoon arrived Mr. *Norris* (long wifhed for) from the South, and with him Mr. *Eyre* the Cadet, in his Way again to the *Cherokee* Nation, by Order from the General: By whom I found the Story confirmed in all its Parts, as related to me, and noted the 3d Inftant; Mr. *Eyre* having been one at the Attack of thofe Forts: He told us, that Mr. *Leman*, who had been ill in a Fever, occafioned by the Wound he received in that Duel, was upon Recovery; and confirmed likewife the other Enterprize the General was intending, and which he actually was fet out

on,

on, upon *Tuesday* the 1st Instant, with a-
bout two hundred good Men, Soldiers and
Volunteers, for the Purpose before related.

Friday. Towards Noon arrived Mr.
Whitfield, accompanied by three or four in
his Travels; and it luckily happening, that
Mr. *Norris* arrived Yesterday from the
South, it was quickly seen with what Temper they met: When, to the Disappointment of some People, who are pleased best
with Contention, upon Mr. *Whitfield*'s shewing the Authority he brought with him,
Mr. *Norris,* without the least Emotion,
told him, that he should by no Means enter into any Disputes to disturb the Peace
of the Church; nor had he ever wrote
once to the Trustees concerning it, from
the first Notice he had of what was in
Agitation; wherefore it was far from his
Intention to enter into any Controversy with
him; but on the contrary declared, that
his Ministry at *Savannah* ceased from that
Instant, declining to officiate at Evening
Prayer this Night, but left it to Mr. *Whitfield* to take Possession of the Church immediately; who accordingly did so, when
a greater Congregation than usual most
Days were met, many (I fear) more out of
Curiosity than Devotion. He delivered to
me in the Afternoon a Letter from Mr.
Martyn, Secretary to the Trust, dated
June 1, relating to the Land appointed for

R 2   his

his Ufe, and whereon to fet the Orphan-Houfe, &c. which after I had read, he alfo did; and I told him I would not be wanting in any Thing on my Part to promote what the Truft appointed, and to give him what Affiftance I could; but as to the five hundred Acres, Mr. *Haberfham*, without conferring with me upon it, when the General was here, applied himfelf to him, who approved of the Place he had made Choice of, ordered it to be run out, and then figned a Warrant, which he directed me to give the Conftable, empowering him to give Poffeffion of it to Mr. *Haberfham*; which was done accordingly in fome fhort Time after: And that Mr. *Haberfham* had already began fencing and clearing upon it. After his reading the Letter from Mr. *Martyn*, he defired me to let him take a Copy of it; which I would not refufe him.

12. *Saturday.* Mr. *Whitfield* loft no Time in fetting forward the Work which he profeffed to have much at Heart, about an Orphan-Houfe; and rode out to view the Land which Mr. *Haberfham* had taken Care to provide againft his coming, confifting of five hundred Acres, that he had taken Poffeffion of in his own Name; where Mr. *Whitfield* gave fuch Orders and Directions as he thought proper. I met with very little Interruption from abroad in what I
had

had to do at home; so that I stuck to it 1739. pretty closely: Only Mr. *Fallowfield* called on me, to shew the rough Draught of a Bond which he was preparing for Colonel *Flower* to execute, pursuant to what was agreed on last *Thursday*: But I soon found it differed pretty much from what I expected; for it was not made to the Trustees, but to the King; which he said, upon considering of, he thought most proper: I then asked him, whether or not he knew that all Recognizances, either for the Peace or otherwise, which in *England* were made to the King, were here always taken in the Name of the Trustees; and that he had little to say to, but he thought it not a parallel Case: Then I asked if he did not intend to deliver the Bond, when signed, into my Custody; which he plainly told me he saw no Occasion for: But as I had the Honour to serve the Trust in the Station appointed me, I apprehended all Things of that Kind, which so immediately concerned the honourable Trustees, and their Interest, would be properly lodged in my Hands: Then I asked him whose Servant he thought himself to be? from whom he received the Powers by which he acted? and to whom he believed he was accountable? To all which he seemed to turn a deaf Ear, and only wished I would inform him, whether the Form of the

R 3 Bond

Bond was right or not: But as he had not fulfilled the Promise and Engagement he was under, I thought it my wisest Way not to meddle, or offer to mend what he had so warmly taken on himself, exclusive of all others.

13.   *Sunday.* Mr. *Whitfield*'s Name, which of late had made so much Noise in *England*, could not fail drawing all Sorts of People to Church, who professed Christianity, to hear what Doctrine it was that he preached: When both in the Morning and Afternoon, he made our Justification by Faith only, the Subject of his Discourse; taking those Words in St. *Matthew* for his Text, "What think you of Christ?" Which he pressed home with great Energy, denouncing Anathema's on all such as taught otherwise. In the Evening, at his Request, I drank Tea with him; where Mr. *Norris* also came; and delivering back to me Mr. *Martyn*'s Letter from the Trust, which he had taken Copy of, he told me he was so well satisfied with the Situation of the five hundred Acres, which he found provided for him by Mr. *Habersham* against his coming, that he would lay aside all farther Thought where to build his Orphan-House, being determined to fix it on that Land, and not meddle with what *Robert Hows* had resigned up to the Trust (which Lot therefore now became void.) As this five

hundred

hundred Acres was about ten Miles from
the Town, after some Pause, he reflected
a little upon some Inconvenience which he
should thereby bring upon himself, forasmuch as he purposed, where the Orphan-
House was, to have a Chapel (or Oratory)
and also an Apartment for himself, intending to make it pretty much the Place
of his Residence, when in these Parts;
Wherefore he seemed to wish for some
Help in discharging the Office of his Ministry at *Savannah*, whilst he carried on
the good Work he was upon; and for the
better effecting whereof, it would be expedient for him, after some Months Abode
here, to take another Travel, in order to
get the Fund augmented for that End:
And addressing himself to Mr. *Norris*, he
made him an Offer of exercising his Function here with us, at all Times when he
pleased, and did not see (he said) but it
might be done very well, by his being
sometimes here, and sometimes at *Frederica*, as formerly it had been done by Mr.
Wesley, &c. But Mr. *Norris* replied, that
since the Trust had been pleased to appoint
him specially at *Frederica*, he thought himself bound not to neglect his Charge, which
next under God he was accountable for to
the Bishop, who for his future Encouragement, had obtained a Stipend of 50*l. per
Annum*, to be paid him by the Society for

propa-

propagating the Gospel in Foreign Parts, additional to what the Trust allowed.

Monday. An exceeding heavy Rain kept every body within Doors all the Day; which Mr. *Jones* and I spent good Part of nevertheless together; and upon my asking (now Colonel *Flower*'s Skooner was unladen) whether or not Mr. *Fallowfield* had put those contraband Goods into the Trust's Stores, as he engaged; Mr. *Jones* told me, that there was no such Thing done; to which I replied, that then he had not kept his Word with me in any one Thing insisted on, which he had promised.

15

Tuesday. What I thought most worth present Observation, arose from the extraordinary Preparations making to build the Orphan-House, &c. wherein Mr. *Whitfield* indeed shewed himself much in earnest; and it may be presumed, he expected it would be finished in few Months; in order to which, there was hardly one Sawyer of any Value in Town, but all hired, and engaged by him to go over and work, where he meant to erect that Building: Most of our Carpenters, Bricklayers, &c. were likewise engaged by him, and a great Quantity of Scantling Timber, ready sawn, was coming (as I heard) for the more Expedition, from *North-Carolina.* The House that Mr. *Bradley* had lived in, being empty, Mr. *Jones* complimented the first Comers

ers with the Use of, for the present; and Mr. *Whitfield* chose, upon his Arrival, to carry those Friends that came with him thither also, as well as to be with them himself, leaving Mr. *Norris* in Possession of the Parsonage-House (which could not hold more than two or three) till he could conveniently move what he had there, and carry it with him to *Frederica*: But the great House not being finished within, and incommodious on many Accounts, especially by letting the Rain come through the Roof, which was flat; Mr. *Whitfield* agreed with *David Douglass* for the Use of his House (much the largest of any private Lot in Town) at the Rent of 20*l.* Sterling for half a Year only.; when I heard he might have rented it for a whole Year under 30*l.* which plainly shews (in my Opinion) that he depended on the new Building to be ready for him within that Time; and *Douglass* took the Advantage of exacting so unreasonable a Rent on that Occasion.

Wednesday. This Day was mostly taken up in rectifying many Things relating to our Militia, and the Guard Duty; which, without good Looking into, too many were apt to be negligent in: Wherefore I thought it my Duty to examine particularly into all such Neglects, as I apprehended were growing among us; ordering a Return to be made

16.

con-

conſtantly to the Conſtable every Morning, by the Tything-man going off Duty, giving an exact and true Account how many, and who were upon Guard of his Tything, and who were abſent; as alſo to certify what Occurrences he met with in the Night; what Boats came, or went (by Permit) and who were in them: And foraſmuch as in theſe dangerous Times, it was not improbable but ſome Incendiaries might be employed by the Enemy, ſecretly to make what Deſtruction they could; I gave Orders, that there muſt be a punctual Obſervance of the Patrol walking the Rounds on the Skirts of the Town, once in two Hours at leaſt: And as I found by an Inſpection, which I had before ordered to be made, that ſeveral Arms were wanting, eſpecially among ſome who had Freehold Lots lately granted them by the General; I took Care this Inſtant they ſhould be furniſhed out of the Stores, where they muſt be accountable, and produce them again when required: Then I recommended it to the Conſtable *Samuel Mercer* (who ſince *Potter*'s going off to Sea, was the only one, till the General ſhould appoint another) that he would be frequent in viſiting the Guard at uncertain Hours in the Night, that they might not know when to expect him, and to ſee if they were alert, or not; which I told him I ſhould think it

my

my Duty alſo to do ſometimes: He promiſed me to obſerve it; and I did not
doubt it, for a more diligent Officer in that
Poſt I never knew in *Savannah*.

Thurſday. Mr. *Whitfield* going again to 17.
his new Plantation, took Mr. *Mercer* the
Conſtable with him, to ſhew him the
Way; but when he came there, what he
aſked of him, was to give him Poſſeſſion
of that five hundred Acres, as he had before done to Mr. *Haberſham*, who was now
ready to ſurrender it to him, for the Uſe
of the Orphan-Houſe: But *Mercer* deſired
to be excuſed, giving his Reaſons for it:
Whereat Mr. *Whitfield* was much diſpleaſ-
ed; and as ſoon as he came home in the
Afternoon, he ſent, deſiring me to come
to him; and when I came, he complained
much of his being ſo dealt with; but I
explained the Cauſe of it to him as well as
I could, which in Subſtance was thus. ——
Mr. *Haberſham* (his Agent here) from the
Time of Mr. *Norris*'s firſt Arrival by Appointment from the Truſt, had ſhewn many evident Tokens of Diſreſpect to him,
and was (not without good Reaſon) ſuſ-
pected of ſtirring up, and abetting, a little
Party of angry Zealots; from whence idle
Stories were frequently ſpread abroad, tending to leſſen Mr. *Norris*'s Character, which
they put in Contraſt with Mr. *Whitfield*'s,
to make *his* appear with the greater Advantage,

vantage, whom they expected to return a-
gain, with more Power than ever. Be
that as it would, I had the Truftees Orders
to countenance Mr. *Norris*, and to join
with the Magiftrates in giving him all the
Affiftance we could, for the Support of his
Miniftry, &c. I did fo; and in fome of
my Letters to the Truft, vindicated him
for his unblameable Conduct: Whereupon
Mr. *Haberfham*, finding me an Advocate
for Mr. *Norris* (I perceived very plainly)
appeared fhy in Converfation with me, and
never uttered fo much as one Word to me
about his Intention of running out any
Land for Mr. *Whitfield*'s Purpofe, till the
Work was began; tho' I then had by me
the Commands of the Truft of the 14th
of *July*, fignifying, that Mr. *Whitfield* was
to confult me in that Affair: But the General being here a while after, Mr. *Haberfham* rather chofe to go to the Fountain's
Head (wherein no one can blame him;)
and the firft Notice I had of what was
doing, was from the General himfelf, who
ordered me to make out a Warrant for
giving Mr. *Haberfham* five hundred Acres
of Land, in fuch a certain Place, under
the ufual Reftrictions, as I had done to
others; which I did; and when the General had figned it, I delivered it to Mr.
Haberfham, who by Virtue of it, in a
fhort Time after, got *Mercer* the Conftable,

ftable, whom it was directed to, to go and give him Poffeffion of it; after which, Mr. *Mercer* re-delivered the Warrant endorfed, as duly executed, for me to keep among many others. This being really the Cafe, I told Mr. *Whitfield*, that I could not think but *Mercer* had acted very cautioufly, and with Prudence, in ftopping where he did: For how could he juftify it to the General, to give Poffeffion of the fame Land to another Perfon, without the fame, or equal Authority? Mr. *Whitfield* faid little more to it, but I faw he was pretty uneafy; and thereupon I told him, that nothing fhould be wanting in me to clear the Way with what Expedition I could, and give him what little Affiftance I was able.

Friday. This whole Day produced nothing obfervable, but that the late heavy Rains which had fallen this Winter, as well as the Summer foregoing, rendered our Ways to the feveral Lots almoft unpaffable. We began now to look with fome Impatience for fome News from the South, and to hear what Succefs the General met with, in the late Expedition he went upon the 1ft Inftant. 　18.

Saturday. Little to obferve, more than Yefterday; only hard Rains continuing, occafioned feveral People travelling on Horfeback, to be in great Danger of drowning, their Horfes fwimming in fome Places, which 　19.

which had scarce ever before been known under Water; and all the low Lands were so flooded, that it was feared we should hear of great Losses of Cattle; the like having not been known (as it was said) since the first planting of the Colony. I attended Mr. *Jones* again about the publick Accounts, being urgent (as often) to send away such as were gone through, and wishing that I might not be obliged to send away my Packet at last without any.

20. *Sunday.* Mr. *Whitfield* did the Duties of the Day, with more than ordinary Diligence, by reading Prayers at Seven in the Morning; at Ten again, with a Sermon after it; at Three again, the same as at Ten; and a Lecture at Seven in the Evening; besides the Sacrament, which he administred to betwixt thirty and forty People after the second Morning Service: His Sermons both before Noon and after, in the same Manner as on *Sunday* last, were wholly on the Doctrine of Justification and Regeneration; which we hoped would ere long be followed by an Exhortation to the Practice of all Christian Duties, that so our Faith might be shewn by our Works; otherwise a dry and inactive Faith, it is to be feared, might prove a dangerous State. This Evening Mr. *Bradley* returned from *Carolina.* I

Monday.

Monday. The Court now sat again, when upon calling over the Names of those that had been summoned to serve upon the Grand Jury, seventeen appeared : And whereas it had been frequently complained of, as well by Mr. *Norris* in his Time of Ministry, as now of late by Mr. *Whitfield*, that several Persons in this Town lived most scandalous Lives with their Whores, and went on *impunè* in open Defiance of all Laws both divine and human, to the great Reproach of the Place in which they lived; and therefore hoping that the Magistracy would take Notice of it, since there could be no Process against such notorious Offences, by any ecclesiastical Law, where those Offences were committed : The Court now sitting thought it high Time to take some Cognizance of it; and Mr. *Parker* (who since the Time of the Trustees Appointment of a new Set of Magistrates, declined as much as possible taking upon him to act, but in such Cases only where it was unavoidably necessary) desiring to be excused from giving the Charge as usual to the Grand Jury, looking on himself in no other Light, than as one substituted by the General to fill that Place on the Bench, till the Trustees Pleasure was farther known (as noted on the 15th of *October* last) and Mr. *Fallowfield* declining to take that upon him, which he

knew

knew himſelf not well qualified for: Mr.
Jones undertook that Part; and among o-
ther Things proper to be recommended to
their Conſideration, inſiſted ſtrongly upon
it as their Duty, to make a Preſentment to
the Court, of all ſuch Offences as came to
their Knowledge, either through common
Fame, or ſuch Evidence as might be produced, which were committed againſt the
known Laws of God and Man, or were
contra bonos mores; particularly ſpecifying
Adultery, and Incontinency: After which,
Mr. *Whitfield*, ſitting near the Bench, roſe,
and made an Oration, ſetting forth the
Heinouſneſs of ſuch Crimes, in very pa-
thetick Terms; ſhewing that we muſt never expect a Bleſſing on this Colony, unleſs
the civil Power would give all poſſible Aſſiſtance, in rooting out this accurſed Thing;
concluding, that it was his firm Perſuaſion,
the ſlow Progreſs that was made in the
Advancement of the Colony, was owing
to God's not permitting it to proſper whilſt
ſuch barefaced Wickedneſs was, through
Neglect, ſuffered to remain among us;
which every good Man was ready to allow:
But I found a pretty many who thought ſo,
ſeemed not well pleaſed at his taking upon
him to harangue the Grand Jury with what
would more properly have come from the
Pulpit; and I myſelf then feared, it would
have

have a different Effect upon the Grand
Jury from what was hoped and expected.

Tuefday. What I feared came to pafs;
for upon the Court's adjourning Yefterday
to give Room for the Deliberations of the
Jury, they fell immediately into warm Debates on what had happened; which held
all that Day, and came to nothing; and
it was late in the Afternoon this Day, ere
they agreed upon any Thing; when they
came into Court, and delivered in a few
Prefentments of ordinary Matters; but not
a Word concerning what was of much
greater Confequence: Whereat the Majority of the Court appeared difpleafed, and
adjourned to a long Day, namely, the 4th
of *February,* to take Time and confider
what Expedient could be attained, how to
bring their good Defigns to pafs. In the
Evening the Magiftrates all affembled at
my Houfe; and in Obedience to the Commands of the Truftees, knowing Mr. *Bradley* to be returned to Town, they fent for
him; who readily came; and was given
to underftand what the Truft expected
from him, *viz.* that he muft find Security for his not leaving the Colony till his
Accounts were made up: Which he feemed fomewhat fhocked at, and plainly told
them, he muft then conclude himfelf utterly loft; for that he knew not one in
the whole Town who would be his Bail;

1739.
January

which indeed we all thought alike in: But that occasioned a sorrowful Reflexion, what Sort of Behaviour then he must have shewn among them, not to find one Friend in this Time of Need, who would appear to give him kind Assistance: The Magistrates were all unwilling to push Matters against him with the utmost Severity, and immediately commit him; wherefore in great Tenderness, they allowed him till to-morrow to get what Security he could.

23

Wednesday. In Conference with Mr. *Jones* this Day, about the Affair of sending off to the Trust so many of the Accompts as had passed Examination; I found him, I thought, a little doubtful in himself concerning it, whether or not we ought to send them in such a Manner by piece-meal, or defer it a little longer, till the whole List of Debts sent us by the Trustees, to be examined and looked carefully into, could be perfected; which it was to be hoped in Time we might see an End of: But as to Messieurs *Causton* and *Bradley*'s Accounts, he plainly told me, he almost despaired of getting to the Bottom of either. And if he had such Thoughts of his own Inability in such Work, much more Reason was there for me to think so of mine, who never pretended to judge of Accompts, which were so intricate especially: But my Opinion was,

was, that it was incumbent on us to send what was ready, that thereby the Truſtees might ſee, and make ſome Judgment of what we had done; and to haſten forward the Remainder as faſt as we were capable: Moreover I told him, that I had deferred writing a pretty while longer than uſual, which I could offer no Excuſe for, excepting my great Deſire, that another Letter might not go from me unaccompanied with ſome of thoſe Accounts, which had been fully looked into: And he promiſed me it ſhould be ready ſome Time next Week, to take out of the Clerk's Hands. Mr. *Bradley* failed in getting Security this Day, as was ordered; and it was to be feared, another Day's Indulgence on that Occaſion, would produce nothing better; which I was ſorry to ſee.

Thurſday. Since it ſo happened, that Mr. *Whitfield* was miſtaken in his Expectation on laſt *Thurſday*, in the Manner I then noted; at his Requeſt I went with him and Mr. *Haberſham*, attended by two or three more of thoſe who followed him hither, to ſee what he had begun to do on the five hundred Acres, and to know whether any Means could immediately be uſed for giving him Poſſeſſion; which he appeared very uneaſy at, to find any Delay; telling me, that as the Truſt had recommended him to me to ſee it done, he

would

would apply no where elfe: In Anfwer to
which, I told him I was ready to attend
him this Day, and any other that he fhould
afk, and would readily do the Thing required; but his own Agent Mr. *Haber-*
fham, by the precipitate Meafures he had
taken, had put it out of my Power to do
it inftantly: For as Mr. *Haberfham* had
obtained a Grant of that particular'd Land
from the General, which I knew nothing
of, till the General himfelf ordered a Warrant to be made out, for giving Poffeffion
of that Tract to Mr. *Haberfham*; which
Warrant the General figned; who fhall
dare take upon them, of thofe that ferve
the Truft, to make void that Act of his,
but he himfelf? who undoubtedly would fet
all right, as the Truft intended it, as foon
as he is informed truly of the Cafe. This
Argument (however) did not fo fatisfy,
but that Mr. *Whitfield* fhewed plainly he
was uneafy: Wherefore, to give him all
the Satisfaction I could, I propofed it to
him, that his Friend *Haberfham* might
make a Surrender to him of all that Tract
of Land for the Ufes intended, refigning
thereby all the Right, Title, and Property, which he has, or ever had in the
fame; which I would be prefent at, and
ready to teftify: Accordingly when we
came there, Mr. *Haberfham* did fo in
Form, delivering to Mr. *Whitfield* a fmall
Shrub,

Shrub, which he plucked up, and therewith declaring, that he furrendered all his
Right, &c. in thofe Lands, to him, for
the Purpofe intended: Which though I
knew could not be deemed taking a legal
Poffeffion, forafmuch as no Surrender of
any Lands (as I apprehend) can be made to
another Perfon, without being authorized
by the Truft, or fome Perfon to whom
fuch Power is delegated; yet they appeared
content with it for the prefent; and I had
only farther to obferve, that I found the
new-intended Work already carrying on
with a good Number of Hands, Artificers
and Labourers; which Mr. *Whitfield* not
thinking yet fufficient, he was fending for
Men out of other Provinces, to haften it
as faft as poffible. In our Way home,
falling into fome Talk of the ill Succefs
our Attempts met with on *Monday* laft, in
getting Prefentments from the Grand Jury,
againft fuch Men as were become fcanda-
lous for their Debauchery; I underftood
Mr. *Chriftie* had been with him, and promifed him to put away his Houfe-keeper
(as he called her) that there might be no
farther Occafion of Scandal; infinuating,
that thofe Reports which were fpread of
him, were very injurious, and without any
real Foundation: But I fear rather, his
Guilt gave him Apprehenfions, that Truth
could not be withftood, when Proof could

be

1739.

January

be produced, from more than one pofitive Evidence, of his Houfe-keeper and himfelf having only one Bed between them, which they made ufe of together for a long while, and were feen fo to do by a Man and Boy Servants, who then lived with him.

25.

Friday. Mr. *Whitfield*, having at his firft Coming, given Notice in Church, that he would adminifter the Sacrament there conftantly on all *Sundays* and Holidays; there was a Communion early at Morning Prayer, being the Feftival of St. *Paul*. The Occurrences of the Day were no more than common, and therefore not worth obferving.

26.

Saturday. The great Rains ceafing for fome Days paft, a fmart Froft fucceeded, with a clear Sky, and pleafant Weather; but being attended with a frefh North-Weft Wind, it was piercing cold, and the Ice, which generally goes off in the Day, returned at Nights with more than ordinary Rigour. Thefe fudden Extreams of Weather, neverthelefs, had no ill Effect on the Inhabitants of this Place, which was never known more healthy, having fcarcely one fick Perfon in it; nor did any Thing happen this Day deferving more Notice than the preceding. Capt. *Thompfon* now was expected daily with his Ship from St. *Simon's*.

Sunday.

JOURNAL.

Sunday. Mr. *Whitfield* called a Congre- 1739.
gation again, four Times, at the same
Hours as on *Sunday* laſt; and in his Ser- January
mons before Noon and after, purſued the 27.
Doctrine of Juſtification and a New Birth.
Capt. *Thompſon* arrived at *Tybee* in the Evening, and came up in his Boat, late at Night,
together with Lieutenant *Horton*, from *Frederica*; Mr. *Horton* having the General's
Leave to go with *Thompſon* for *England*;
and to return again, after he has diſpatched
what Buſineſs calls him hence.

Monday. A Boat was ſent down to 28.
Cockſpur, to bring up Capt. *Heron*, and Mr.
Carteret, with their Ladies, who all came
with Capt. *Thompſon* from *Frederica*; and
the Ladies were bound for *England* with
him; and I allowed myſelf the Liberty of
being pretty much with them this Day,
where I had the Pleaſure of hearing the
whole Relation of the Manner wherein the
General proceeded, in his late Expedition
againſt the *Spaniſh* Forts, on the River St.
Juan's: One of which (it ſeems) was deſerted by the Enemy, ſince the late Attempt againſt them; who judged it not
tenable, in Caſe we returned with another
Viſit: But the other they defended with
good Reſolution, till our Forces played
three or four ſmall Pieces of Cannon upon them; which going thro' and thro',
they then ſent out a Flag of Truce, in or-

der to treat of furrendring; but the General would allow of no other Terms, than at Difcretion; which they were obliged to fubmit to: It was held only by twelve Men, but fo fortified with Logs of Timber, as to be Proof againft Mufket-Shot; and he who commanded, told the General, that had he not brought Ordnance with him, he would have withftood any Attack that could be made, if there had been double the Number againft him there was. The General caufed fome new Works of Fortification to be made, and left a Garifon of thirty good Men, under a proper Officer, to defend it. This Fort is efteemed of great Confequence, as being a Pafs where all muft come, who would go to *Auguftin* by Land, whether they are difaffected *Indians* out of the Nations, or runaway Negroes from *Carolina*; which is fuch a Benefit to that Province, that it is hoped they will contribute handfomely to ftrengthen the General's Hands, fo as to enable him to put thefe Provinces out of all Danger from *Auguftin* in Time coming; for nothing now ftands in our Way thither, and it is currently talked, *delenda eft Carthago*. Began my Letters to the Truft, but had not Time to finifh them.

29. 　　*Tuefday.* Capt. *Heron* proceeded early to *Charles-Town*, on the Affairs which he was charged with from the General; and

in

in the Afternoon Mr. *Eyre* took his Way 1739.
up the River in Pursuance of the General's
Orders, making what Speed he could to January
the *Cherokee* Nation of *Indians*; which the
great Floods we had lately, forbad him to
attempt, since his Arrival here the 10th Instant, till now. Messieurs *Horton* and *Carteret* continued here with the Ladies, and
probably might for a while, waiting the
Time when *Thompson* would be ready to
sail. A Boat being upon going to the
South, it took me up Part of this Day in
writing Letters to the General and others,
and preparing several Papers to be sent.

Wednesday. From Mr. *Whitfield*'s giving 30.
Notice in Church last *Sunday*, that this
Day was to be publickly observed; it was
expected he would have officiated himself; but he chose rather to visit his People at the new Settlement, leaving Mr.
Norris to perform the Duty at Church,
who read the appointed Service, and a
Church Homily after it, against Rebellion:
In the Evening Mr. *Whitfield* read the
usual Prayers, and expounded on the second Lesson, as constantly at other Times;
but took no Notice of any Part of the
Service appointed for the Day; from
whence every body concluded he had no
Regard to it.

Thursday. I delivered my Letters, &c. 31.
this Morning, which I had prepared on
Tuesday,

Tuesday, to the Care of Mr. *Upton*, who was going South in a Pettyagua of his own, which he had bought lately, and was now loaden mostly with Corn, for the Use of the Camp and Garisons, under the Conduct of a proper Patroon; he himself going as Supercargo, and carrying on a Traffick in various Commodities, betwixt *Charles-Town*, this Town, *Frederica*, &c. which has often been a Matter past my Comprehension to dive into, knowing him to have very little or no Fund of his own; and it must be not a trifling Sum, that can enable him to do what he does: The General (it is well known) has shewn him Favours, since his quitting what he had in the Neighbourhood of *Frederica*; and given him the Grant of an Island called *All-Honey*, Midway betwixt this and that, where he purposes to keep a large Stock of Cattle, Hogs, &c. which must require also a Purse, at first setting out; but whence that comes, may possibly be better known hereafter, than at present: In the mean while that Mr. *Upton* has the good Fortune to find such Aid, he is certainly not to be blamed for making as good Use of it as he can: People very often advance their Fortunes by joining with an able Partner. The Day produced nothing material relating to the Publick.

Friday.

Friday. This being the Anniversary Day
of the Colony's first Landing here, under
the Conduct of *James Oglethorpe*, Esq; the
Gunner asked me whether or not he should
fire any Guns, as had been formerly accustomed; to which Mr. *Jones* (then with
me) answered, no; but I was of a different
Opinion, and thought the Answer would
more properly have come from me, as the
General had left the Command of all the
Militia with me, in his Absence: Who
when here last, told us, that now in Time
of War, Powder ought not to be wasted
in needless Salutes, &c. Upon which Mr.
Jones made that the Foundation of his
Opinion, calling it a Saving; which I had
before shewn a particular Regard to, by
divers Restrictions made, where I thought
it proper; which would be found Savings
indeed, worth Notice; but to shew a Contempt of this Day, by such a poor Pretence, which in Effect was a bad Compliment to the General himself too, I thought
a mean Act, and might carry such a Reflexion, as could not easily be justified:
Therefore the least I could do, was to order five Guns to be fired; which I did, as
a Memorial; hoping that Ages to come
will celebrate this Day annually here, in a
better Manner. In the Evening a select
Company of such as had Confidence in one
another's sincere Disposition towards promoting

moting the Colony's Welfare, met, and took a chearful Glafs to its Founders, Protectors, and Benefactors Healths, Meffieurs *Carteret* and *Horton* (now in Town) joining us; and nothing appeared among us but Love and Good-humour.

2.   *Saturday.* After the Fore-part of the Day fpent with my Pen and Ink at home, the Remainder of it . I dedicated to Improvement of Land; and having now moft of my Strength employed upon my five hundred Acres, unwilling neverthelefs to throw up what I had been doing for two Years paft nearer home, I refolved to try what I could do with one Hand, upon the five-Acre Lot, which was perfectly cleared, but had made a very poor Return hitherto, for the Labour and Coft beftowed upon it: My Defign now being to drefs and cultivate fuch Parts of it, as I hoped for any Benefit from, and by Degrees to make an Orchard of it all, confifting chiefly of Mulberries; whereof I had already planted a pretty many the laft two Years, and now was preparing a good Number more for the prefent Seafon. In this Amufement I paffed away a few Hours, and returned home as Night came on.

3.   *Sunday.* Mr. *Whitfield* performed the divine Offices as before; but being taken with a fudden Diforder upon me, during the Service at Eleven, I was obliged to go

out

out of Church home; where, after a few Hours, with a little Help of warm Things inwardly applied, I quickly found Relief; and at the Seven a Clock Evening Lecture, I went again, having never yet been there; when the Work he took in Hand, was expounding on a Chapter in St. *John*'s Gospel; and, indeed, he did it, I thought, with great Perspicuity; but when he came towards a Conclusion, he could not shut up without a Touch on his darling Topick of Regeneration, which must spring from a vital Principle in the Heart, infused by the Holy Spirit; till which is made sure to us, we are all in a State of Damnation: And the Way to attain this, is by a strong Faith, without Regard to good Works; which will occasion great Pangs in the New Birth; and when by struggling with God in Prayer, we have obtained his Grace, we shall find the Holy Spirit sensibly moving upon our Hearts, as it did upon the Face of the Waters: Which if any one denies, in plain he told us he lied; for that the Warmth of the Spirit was as sensibly felt, as the Beams of the Sun upon our Bodies: But this, he said, was a Doctrine which very few of our modern Clergy approved of; whom he inveighed against terribly, as slothful Shepherds, dumb Dogs, &c. who led their People dreaming on in a carnal Security to Destruction; and that

that he was firmly perfuaded in himfelf, very few great and rich Men, and as few of our learned Doctors, for an Age and more paft, could ever fee Heaven; among whom, the Author of the *Whole Duty of Man*, he verily believed, had fent Thoufands to Hell: Then he exhorted fuch of his Hearers as were true Converts, to be on their Guard againft all Temptations, which they muft furely expect, to try them, whether or not they were ftedfaft; telling them they muft meet with Contempt and Derifion, on their thus fetting out in their Way to Glory; and by and by Perfecution would follow: For Men in high Places would be offended at all Oppofition made to their Delufions; and then we might expect undoubtedly it was at hand. Thefe Things were very fhocking to many People, who were otherwife well difpofed.

4.

Monday. The Court fat again, as *per* Adjournment; difpatched fome little Affairs, and farther adjourned to the 22d Inftant, not finding any Means to revive what they were difappointed in at their laft Meeting: Some little Good, however, came to pafs, if true what was faid, that Mr. *Chriftie* in the Fright, put off his Houfekeeper. In the Afternoon the Magiftrates and Mr. *Whitfield* (by their own Appointment) met at my Houfe, to confider of the Orphans Affair; when Mr. *Jenkins,*

the

the only furviving Truftee, fhewed a great
Defire he had to be quit of that Bufinefs,
as he had indeed defired many Times before; and now upon Mr. *Whitfield*'s telling
him, that he was ready to take all that
Trouble off his Hands; he promifed to
bring, and deliver into his Care, all that he
had been accountable for, to-morrow; from
which Time Mr. *Whitfield* engaged to free
him from accounting any farther, and his
Accounts hitherto were to be looked into
as the Court fhould direct. During this
Convention, in difcourfing on the Subject-
Matter of their Meeting, a little Difputa-
tion arofe betwixt Mr. *Whitfield*, and Mr.
Parker, who had two Orphan-Boys with
him (their Name was *Tondee*) the eldeft of
which being a well-grown Lad of fifteen
or fixteen Years of Age, Mr. *Parker* faid,
he thought it would be a great Hardfhip to
have that Boy taken from him, now he is
grown capable of doing him fome Service,
after living fo long with him when he
could do him none: To which Mr. *Whitfield* faid, that the Boy would be fo much
the better for him and his Purpofe, as he
could be employed for the Benefit of the
other Orphans: But *Parker* took that to
be no Anfwer, to what he thought himfelf aggrieved in, and fhewed a little more
Warmth than I thought feafonable at that
Time; which I blamed him for: His Argument

gument was, that where the Child was taken Care of as he ought, by a good Master (which the Magiſtrates might judge of) and without any Charge to the Truſt; he did ſuppoſe ſuch a Boy not to be reckoned an Orphan that Mr. *Whitfield* was entitled to by the Truſt: Mr. *Whitfield* then produced the Deed he had from the Truſt; which was the firſt Time I had ſeen it, though I obſerved my own Name to be mentioned in it for divers Purpoſes.——But enough of that.

5.   *Tueſday.* Nothing of any Conſequence occurred this Day. Wrote to the General by *George Cuthbert.*

6.   *Wedneſday.* Capt. *Thompſon*'s Ship having been detained at *Cockſpur* ever ſince the 27th paſt by contrary Winds, came up this Day, in order to deliver what remained in her, of ſuch Things as, *per* Advices I received, were deſigned for this Place; which I had heard nothing more of ſince my being on board at *Tybee* the Beginning of *October* laſt: And we would make no Delay now in clearing the Ship, that ſhe might return home again, which was intended directly from this Place, where ſhe would find a Loading of Rice from the neighbouring Plantations in *Carolina*, without going to *Charles-Town.* Having ſome Notice, that there was like to be a thin Guard this Evening, I went about Bed-
Time

Time to look into it, and found it fo indeed, fcarce half the Number upon Duty that ought to be: Which was fuch a Neglect, as gave me much Difturbance in my Mind, and I chiefly imputed it to the Advantage they took, of our having but one Conftable at prefent to act, fince *Potter*'s going off *(viz. Mercer)* who was vigilant, whenever he could be fo; but by reafon of his new Plantation at a Diftance, muft neceffarily be out of Town fometimes, or it would come to nothing: So that I was every Day in hopes of receiving from the General, a Conftitution of another Conftable, which by taking their Turn, would make it eafy to them both. I could at prefent only give it in ftrict Charge to the Tything-man, to fee and keep a good Look-out, with thofe Men he had; and to make a particular Report to me to-morrow Morning of all that happened: And it was incumbent on me to ufe all Means, pleafing, or difpleafing, that might oblige all Perfons to perform that fundamental Duty required upon Guard, which was fo effential to the common Safety of all. While I was at the Guard, a Scout-Boat from *Frederica*, as the Officer told me, arrived, whom I fent to enquire; and he farther acquainted me, that the Patroon was gone with Letters to Mr. *Jones*; but if he had any for me, I believed he would think to morrow Morning Time enough to deliver them : Such was the Cuftom, and fuch the Difference.

7.

Thurfday. As I imagined, fo it was : About Eight this Morning, the Mafter of the Scout-Boat gave me a Letter from the General; wherein, among other Things, he was pleafed to give a particular, and very pleafing Detail, of his late Proceedings againft the Enemy, defcribing the Situation of all thofe Parts near *Auguftin*, with the feveral Forts, moft of which had been abandoned ; but one which he had attacked and taken, was of very great Importance, to fecure a Pafs there, which would prevent any Annoyance from the *Spaniards* upon the Back of this Colony : He moreover ordered a Defcription to be fent me, of the Fortification of the Town and Caftle of *Auguftin*, and the Strength of the Garifon, how many and what Troops they confifted of : All which I could communicate with Delight to fuch as wifhed to hear it. Spent the Day in frequent Conference with Mr. *Jones*, tending to haften on the Accompts.

8.

Friday. Met the Magiftrates at Breakfaft with Mr. *Whitfield*, by his Defire ; where the Affair of the Orphans was again refumed ; and two or three of fuch as had any in their Keeping, having fhewn an Unwillingnefs to deliver up thofe who were now grown

up

up pretty well in Years, and therefore capable of doing them good Service, especially as the planting Season was coming
on; it was the Opinion of all present, upon having Recourse again to the Truſt's
Deed to Mr. *Whitfield*, that there was not
any Exception made; but all Orphans
were included, who either were, or had
been, chargeable to the Truſt: One Exception only was allowed, *nem. con.* nevertheleſs, to be juſt; and that was in the
Caſe of one *Little*, an Orphan, under the
Care of *Samuel Mercer* (Conſtable) who
having a particular Friendſhip for the Father, and ſeeing the Child in bad Hands,
by Leave of the Magiſtrates at that Time,
took him into his Keeping; and though
he was very young, promiſed he ſhould be
a Charge to nobody; wherein he has not
only kept his Word, but having no other
Children, beſides what came with his Wife,
who was a Widow; he has taken the
ſame Care of him as of a Son; and from
a Cow and Calf, which the Child had at
his Parents Death, he has ſeen them ſo
well looked after, that from the Increaſe
which he has in few Years paſt, probably
before he comes to Man's Eſtate (and he
is yet not more than eight or nine Years
old) he may be looked on as a Man of
good Subſtance to begin the World, and
make no contemptible Freeholder: This,

therefore, all agreed to be a fingular Cafe, and fit to remain as it was. In the Afternoon arrived *Peter Emery*, in a trading Boat, bound for *Augufta* from *Charles-Town*, whereof he was Patroon, and brought with him a Letter from Mr. *Hopton*, dated the 1ft Inftant, and enclofing feveral Letters thence to the General; among which one from himfelf: With this he alfo fent a Box for the General, which I took Notice of in my Notes of the 26th of *December*, and which he had attempted to fend to St. *Simon*'s by the *Tartar*; but that Ship being driven back to *Charles-Town* by foul Weather, he now took this Opportunity of fending it to me thus, to be forwarded from hence.

9. *Saturday*. *Samuel Lacy* being ready to fail for *Charles-Town*, with his Pettyagua, I was glad to fend my Packet and Letters by him, dated fo long fince as the 28th of *January*; and to accompany it, I fent one other Packet alfo from Mr. *Chriftie*, which he had left to my Care; writing at the fame Time to Mr. *Hopton*, to forward them *per* firft Opportunity for *London*. Wrote Letters to the South, and enclofed feveral to the General, which had come to my Hands fince the 5th, when I wrote by *George Cuthbert*, intending to fend thefe off by the Scout-Boat that came hither from thence on laft *Thurfday*, and was to return

turn on *Monday*. Mr. *Parker*, I underftood, had delivered up *Tondee* the Orphan
to Mr. *Whitfield*'s Care; which he did,
he faid, left the Truftees fhould be offended at him more and more; but complained, that it was a great Lofs and Difappointment to him; as indeed it muft be
in his planting, to be deprived of the Benefit of fuch an Youth's Labour, now
grown to a good Stature, fo as to do conftant Guard-Duty for his own Lot. *(Vid.
Feb.* 4.)

Sunday. Mr. *Whitfield* took Care that   10.
the Day fhould be duly obferved, by performing Divine Service four Times, as before; and with great Vehemence, which
fome call Power, inforced his Doctrine of
Juftification by Faith, which good Works
would follow of courfe; feeming determined to lay down this, as a Foundation for
Chriftians to reft on; and therefore allowed himfelf little Variation in handling
his Subject, which he moft folemnly pro-
nounced to be fo effentially neceffary to
Salvation, that without a firm Belief of its
Truth, no Perfon ought to make ufe of
the Lord's Prayer, and call God his Father, when he was undoubtedly a Child of
the Devil. From henceforth I refolved
not to turn Obfervator, or be at any Pains
in endeavouring to collect, what poffibly
in his Warmth might fometimes drop from

him:

him: Nevertheless I should still think it my Duty to attend the publick Worship, whatever my Sentiments were of the Preacher: But I feared every body would not be of the like Mind.

11.   *Monday.* *Samuel Lacy* went not for *Charles-Town* till this Morning early, to whose Care I had delivered my Packets for *England*: And this Afternoon I delivered my Letters for the General, to *John Latter*, Master of the Scout-Boat, together with the Box that I received on *Friday* by *Peter Emery*; the Boat being to set off this Evening: Which Mr. *Whitfield* made a seasonable Use of, having it lately in his Thoughts, to go and pay his Respects to the General at *Frederica*: Wherefore he rode to his new Plantation, where the Orphan-House was building, intending to stay and rest this Night among his Workmen, there, or thereabout, in that Neighbourhood, probably at Mr. *Burnside*'s; where the Scout-Boat, that was to go round, might take him in to-morrow Morning. This being the right Season for planting Mulberries, wherein the General had given me Direction to deliver out of the publick Garden, what Seedlings or Suckers could be had thence this Year, to all such as I judged would make a good Use of them; I made that my Employment good Part of this Day.

Tuesday.

Tuesday. After little more than a Month past, since Capt. *Davis* went out a privateering with two Vessels *(vide Jan.* 3.) they were now both returned to *Cockspur*, and the two Commanders come to Town again; in order to get their Ships refitted, having been terribly buffeted in a long Continuance of bad Weather, which drove them quite off the Coast, more than one hundred and fifty Leagues; so that their Sails and Rigging were utterly ruined; and for want of able Sailors, they were almost out of all Hopes of getting into Harbour again, having not found Men to add to their Strength, since they went so weakly out; and it may be supposed our two brave Officers, *Potter* and *Foster* (who not content with the Station they were in, imagined they should soon become great Men) have taken a Surfeit of going to seek their Fortunes at Sea, which we may soon expect they will confess: At the same Time it is to be feared, that unless some Means can soon be found of getting able Men, to carry on such an Enterprize, it cannot be to good Effect.

Wednesday. Scarce any Thing to observe. Capt. *McIntosh* from *Palachocolas* arrived, on his Way to the General in the South, in order to clear his Accompts; and take his Leave of these Parts, after several Years Continuance, purposing to take the

T 4　　　　first

firſt Opportunity of going for his native Country in *North Britain*, upon Advice he had received, that his Brother the Chieftain of that Clan was dead, or near dying; and whom, as next Heir, he was to ſucceed in Title and Eſtate. Wrote Letters to the South, to the General, Mr. *Hawkins*, &c. and incloſed ſeveral which I had lately received for the General. In the Night arrived *Jacob Matthews* from the *Alatamaha*, where he and his Wife were ſettled far up in that Country, by the General's Approbation, to keep a Store; and he was now come to ſpend a few Days at their former Habitation on this River, and then to return again.

14.
Thurſday. Capt. *McIntoſh* going off this Morning for *Frederica*, I ſent my Letters by him, which I had prepared Yeſterday; and attended Mr. *Jones* good Part of the Day in getting forward the Accounts; as indeed moſt other Days, what ſpare Time I had from other indiſpenſable Buſineſs, was that Way employed; that we might be ready againſt Capt. *Thompſon* ſailed, to ſend what was poſſible for us to do, wherein he could not always be alike intent. In the Afternoon he came to me under a great Diſorder of Mind, complaining of a moſt outrageous Inſult made upon him at the Stores by *Jacob Matthews*: Who having been among our incendiary Gentlemen at
Jenkins's

Jenkins's (which is the Company that he always kept, when in Town formerly, and *Robert Williams*, and he, and *Tailfer*, were never long afunder) he got very drunk, and it is too probable was fpurred on now, by thofe continual Mifchief-makers, to do fome Exploit, that might fhew what he dared; and (as Mr. *Jones* told me) it was in this Manner.—At firft he picked a Quarrel with one of the Truft's Servants, who was attending a Waggon drawn by Oxen, for the publick Work; afking him how he dared to drive his Oxen? and, without farther Words, knocked him down with his Fift; when Mr. *Jones*, being near, interpofed, and afked him what he meant, by thus abufing a Servant of the Truft, whom he was bound to protect? telling him, he muft expect to anfwer it in another Place: Whereat *Matthews*, curfing and fwearing, told him he would beat him too; and immediately coming at him, in Spite of two or three with-holding him, gave him a Blow in the Face, and a Kick in the Belly: After which he was huddled away by fome of his Friends, put into his Boat, and fo fent off to his Dwelling up the River. Enquiring of Mr. *Jones* what Pretence *Matthews* had to call the Oxen his; he informed me, that thofe Oxen were affigned by the General for common Draught, to the Care of *John Mellidge*, a young Fellow,

low, Son to one of them that came firſt over; who being a diligent Youth, the General had, among other Marks of his Favour, given him this farther Encouragement; and the better to be aſſured of the Uſe of thoſe Oxen, *Mellidge* had branded them with the two firſt Letters of his Name, *J. M.* which *Matthews* now ſaid was *Jacob Matthews*; though he knew moſt undoubtedly they were not of his branding. It is moſt likely the Venom lay next his Heart, ever ſince the former Diſpute about Cattle; when he thought a ſcandalous Aſperſion was caſt at him, and his Friend *Williams*, by Mr. *Jones*, which he kept in Memory *(vid. April* 23.) but whoever was in the Right then, it is certain that *Matthews* was much in the Wrong now. In the Afternoon arrived Mr. *Cadogan* (Enſign) from *Charles-Town*, where he had been ſent ſome Time ſince, with divers Diſpatches to the Governor, Council, &c. demanding ſome Aid from them againſt the *Spaniards*; on which Occaſion Capt. *Heron* alſo followed him (as noted *Jan.* 29.) and Mr. *Cadogan* was now on his Way South, Expreſs to the General, with Letters from the Government at *Charles-Town*, ſignifying, that the Council and Aſſembly had agreed to raiſe 120,000 *l.* Currency (15,000 *l.* Sterling) for his uſe in carrying on the War: Which was within

a

a Trifle, I hear, of what the General aſk- 1739.
ed: And they have agreed alſo to aſſiſt
him with a conſiderable Number of white
Men (ſome ſay five hundred) well appointed for Action, together with ſome Hundreds of Negroes for Pioneers. So far is
well; but with it (if it is true what we
hear) there comes a Stain which takes away
the Luſtre of a good Act being done with
an hearty Unanimity; for it is ſaid, the
Affair was carried on by the Majority of
only one Vote: So cloſe does their Ill-will
to this Province ſtick to many of them.
After a few Hours ſtopping here, Mr. *Cadogan* made what Expedition he could to
the General at *Frederica*.

Friday. Nothing came to my Know- 15.
ledge worth obſerving: My own Time was
ſufficiently taken up in purſuing the Work
I was daily upon, to get forward ſuch Mat-
ters as it was intended to ſend by Capt.
Thompſon. Mr. *Whitfield*'s Sloop, Capt.
Gladman, arrived with more Stores from
Carolina.

Saturday. Gave myſelf a little Vacancy 16.
from other Buſineſs, to attend what was
doing abroad, and ſpent good Part of the
Day at the five-Acre Lot, in planting Vines,
Mulberries, &c. reſolving (as before noted)
to try if I could not make that little Spot
turn to ſome good Account, which hitherto
had

1739. had difappointed me in what I might rea-
February fonably have expected from it. *(Vid. Feb. 2.)*
17.   *Sunday.* Upon Mr. *Whitfield*'s going
South the Beginning of the Week paft,
Mr. *Norris* took Care of the Church here
in his Abfence, and read the Morning and
Evening Service; as he alfo preached this
Day twice: But he told me, he had not
fo much as any Knowledge given him of
Mr. *Whitfield*'s Intention to be abfent: So
ftrangely were they difpofed towards each
other. Another unhappy Accident fell out
to-day to be added to divers of the like
Sort formerly: A Boy that belonged to
Capt. *Thompfon*, and attended in the Cab-
bin, was drowned: The Ship lying at the
new Wharf, in order to take in her Loading, People went in and out, on a Couple
of Planks laid for that Purpofe; and this
poor Boy misftepping, fell in, and was loft.
Mr. *Upton*, with his Pettyagua, arrived, in
order to carry more Provifions to the South;
as Mr. *Perkins*, who arrived Yefterday with
his Pettyagua, came on the fame Errand,
both from *Frederica*; where (it is to be
prefumed) a large Magazine is neceffary,
for the Maintenance of fuch a Number of
Men, as the General fhall think proper for
any Enterprize.

18.   *Monday.* Nothing particular to obferve;
but it was too evident in general not to
obferve that there was yet but a poor Appearance

pearance of planting likely to be this Spring,
from the Inhabitants of *Savannah:* I mean
from such, as have no other Dependence
but their own Labour; whereof I purpose
to make some necessary Remarks occasionally, as the Year advances; that so the
full Truth and Causes being laid open, the
Consequences will naturally follow, which
either promote or retard the Progress of
this Colony in Agriculture: Such as are
going on with it, have divers of them applied to me for Mulberries; which by the
General's Order I got what Quantity of
we possibly could; and I take Care to deliver out such a Number of Plants, whether
twenty, thirty, forty, fifty, or to an hundred, for their Use, in such Proportion as
I know they have laboured in clearing their
Land. One Thing here I cannot but
take Notice of with some Pleasure, which
is, that I find an uncommon Tendency
lately sprung up among our People of all
Ranks, towards planting Vines; wherein
they shew an Emulation, if they get but a
few, of out-doing one another; and I
would be glad to encourage them in that,
or any Thing commendable; more especially where cultivating Land has its Share,
whatever be the Product: And I tell them,
that against another Season, I make no
Doubt but Provision will be made, in such
a Manner, to get the choicest of Vine-

Cuttings

Cuttings for their Encouragement; that
with their own Diligence added to it, they
may reaſonably hope in a ſhort Time to be
each of them Maſter of a Vineyard: To
promote this, nothing ſeems to be wanting but Store of Cuttings, from Vines beſt
eſteemed; which may be procured, I hope,
againſt another Seaſon: In the mean while,
I expect this Year to ſee a very conſiderable Increaſe of this Plant, and the Fruit of
it ſhewing ſome Tokens of a large Recompence to the Planter in due Time.

19.
Shrove-Tueſday. After diſpatching what
I thought needful at home the firſt Part of
the Day; in the Afternoon I applied myſelf
to the Magiſtrates, for their Aſſiſtance in
promoting the Guard Duty, wherein great
Neglect had been from ſundry Perſons, as
appeared by ſeveral Reports made to me,
from divers of the Tything-men, on coming off their Guard; which Reports I
ſtrictly required always: And upon our
preſent Enquiry, finding there was juſt
Cauſe of Complaint, we fixed upon a few
of the moſt culpable, to make Examples
of, by the Magiſtrates iſſuing their Warrant, to levy by Diſtreſs two Shillings for
every ſuch Neglect committed by each of
them; hoping it would be a Means of Reformation, when they found that paying
the Penalty of two Shillings, was double
to what it would coſt any of them, who
choſe

chose rather to hire a Man in their Stead, than personally to perform it themselves, that Duty coming about once in eighteen Nights: And the Magistrates, at my Request, issued such Warrant accordingly.

Wednesday. Mr. *Patrick Houston* coming to Town from his Plantation near *Vernon* River, whom I looked on as a good Neighbour there, and who had made good Improvements, by cultivating a considerable Tract of Land, *&c.* called on me this Morning; and knowing he had been lately at *Frederica,* we naturally fell into some Talk about what was doing there, and how great Things the General had in view: Among other Matters, telling him, that I had heard from several, there was a Box directed to me from the honourable Trustees, wherein were said to be many Papers, which I had no Advice of by any Letter; that the Box came by the Ship St. *George,* which arrived at St. *Simon*'s ever since the Beginning of *January,* and was now gone again; but that I had never heard what came of that Box (if any such was come) nor any Letter relating to it: He readily told me, that there was such a Box directed to me, which he saw lying in the Stores at *Frederica;* that what was in it he knew not; but it was generally said to be full of Papers, and it was believed, of some Value; for that the

Master

Master of the Ship said he had given his Receipt for it in *London*, and therefore he must have a Receipt for it again, upon his delivering it; which Receipt he understood Mr. *Hawkins* had given him, and taken the Box out of the Ship. Upon hearing this so particularly, it was indeed a Matter of Admiration to me, what could be the Meaning of such dark Work; and I began to think what a notable Correspondent I was likely to find in him whom the Trust had appointed: Many Things occurred to my Thoughts on this Occasion.——But no more of that now.

21.   *Thursday*. A Letter came to the Magistrates from Mr. *Christie*, now at *Thunderbolt*, acquainting them, that he was not well, and therefore could not attend the Court that was adjourned to to-morrow. It was generally talked of, and believed, that he and Mr. *Hetherington* were preparing both to go for *England*; and as his Housekeeper and he yet stuck close together, it was imagined, that he purposed to take her also with him, notwithstanding what was given out of his Intention to part with her; that Fright being pretty well over. Spent as much of the Day as I could with Mr. *Jones*, in getting forward what we could, to go by Capt. *Thompson*.

Friday.

Friday. The Court was opened, and adjourned farther to the 10th of *March.* This Evening the Company returning home, that had been on their Pleafure up the River, this very cold Weather, at Mr. *Matthews*'s for two or three Days and Nights paft; I cannot well let it pafs unobferved, having the Appearance in it to many People, of fomething pretty particular. The Invitation was from *Matthews,* not many Days after the Infult he had made on Mr. *Jones*; and the Company was of a very odd Mixture: Firft, Dr. *Tailfer* and his Lady; next, Mr. *Carteret* and his, together with Capt. *Heron*'s Lady and her Daughter (the Captain not being yet returned from *Charles-Town)* then Mr. *Upton* and his; Capt. *Thompfon,* and Mr. *Norris,* making alfo Part of the Company fome of the Time. I could not learn from any of them, that they dealt much in Politicks; the very oppofite Way of thinking (fo well known among divers of them) forbidding it; but what People thought remarkable was, that it looked like a Piece of Daring in *Matthews,* to fhow the World he had no Concern upon him, for that violent Outrage he had been fo lately guilty of; for which Mr. *Jones* (if he had thought fit) might have fent an Officer, and fpoiled their Entertainment, by taking mine Hoft into Cuftody, *&c.* but he rather

chofe to fend a Narrative of it to the General, and leave it to him in what Manner
to refent it. The Truth is, *Matthews*'s
Wife has always been in great Efteem
with the General, and not without good
Reafon; for being half *Indian* by Extract,
fhe has a very great Influence upon many
of them, particularly the *Creek* Nation,
our next Neighbours; fo that there always has been a frequent Refort of thofe
People to her Houfe; and the General
would advife with her in many Things,
for his better dealing with the *Indians*; taking her generally for his Interpreter, and
ufing her very kindly on all Occafions. A
few Years fince, after her late Hufband
Mufgrave's Death, fhe thought fit to marry
this Man, a hail, lufty, young Fellow, an
Englifhman, and her Servant: Such a Promotion from Obeying to Commanding,
had the ufual Effect, which feldom fails;
and he foon grew vain, dreffing gaily
(which ill became him) and began to behave infolently among all he kept Company with, looking on himfelf at leaft equal
to the beft Man in the Colony, from the
Subftance he was poffeffed of with his
Wife: And Mr. *Williams*'s Plantation lying
contiguous to his on this River, by Degrees there grew an Intimacy betwixt them,
as Neighbours; and in Procefs of Time,
when Mr. *Williams*, unhappily with others
in

in Conjunction, began to fow Difcord, and
draw as many as they could, of the People in Town, into a Diflike of their Tenure, with many other fuppofed Grievances which they wanted the Power to rectify to their Humour; *Matthews* made one
among them: And at that Time our Malecontents fo blowed up their new Favourite
among them, that he was taught to believe he ought to be diftinguifhed, and gra-
tified in whatever he afked; and that he
fhould look upon himfelf, as a Man capable of doing great Service to the Colony,
or refenting it feverely, in Cafe he found
himfelf flighted, having fuch a powerful
Body of Men to ftand by him: But whatever Credit he gave to that, he has feveral
Times experienced that he was fadly mif-
taken; for when in his drunken Frolicks,
he has fometimes attempted any Sort of
Authority or Command, over fuch as came
occafionally that Way from the Nation,
he feldom has failed of a good Thrafhing
from them, to convince him of his Error:
For though they fhew fome Regard to
Mary (as they call his Wife) they fhew
none to him: And yet it is fuppofed, the
good Company he came from drunk the
other Day, when he did that Exploit, had
filled his Head again with fome of their
former Doctrine, that he was not to be in
Awe of any Man he had to do with.

1739.

February
22.

U 2 From

1739.
February

From hence some Estimate may be made of what may be at any Time necessary to observe, of the future Behaviour of Mr. *Matthews*.

23.

Saturday. Being somewhat cloyed with the close Application, I tied myself down to, of Business with my Pen and Ink, the Week past; I gave a Loose to my Inclination this Day, and passed away good Part of it very agreeably, at my little five-Acre Lot, in planting more Vines, Mulberries, &c. and walking among some of the adjacent Lots, to see what Preparation was made by any towards planting Corn, or the like: A few such I found, but wished it had been many more; it· being high Time now to get ready for that Work; and it would be soon seen who intended it, and who not.

24.

Sunday. Mr. *Whitfield* not being yet returned from the South, Mr. *Norris* continued to do the Office of the Day; and preached such orthodox Divinity to his Hearers, as they might well understand, and ought to put in Practice.

25.

Monday. Followed what I had to do, and lost no Time at home, where I spent most of the Day, and found nothing so remarkable in it, as the exceeding sudden Change of Seasons; the Weather for a pretty while past, being mostly frosty, since those heavy Rains, and extream cold, thro'

a

a ſtrong North-Weſt Wind, which continued preciſely till this Morning, the very
laſt Night being as ſevere as any paſt :
And after the Sun aroſe, the Wind getting
round to the Southward, the Weather became immediately as warm as we ordinarily find it in *England* at *Midſummer :* From
whence I reckon Winter is now quite over;
and it is to be wiſhed, that the Summer Heats
may not come on ſo faſt upon us, as to
cut our Spring ſhort.

Tueſday. Capt. *Æneas Mᶜ Intoſh*, who   26.
went hence the 14th to wait on the General, returned this Day, and brought Letters from his Excellence at *Frederica*, importing various Directions to Mr. *Jones* and
me, ſo ſuited to each as he ſaw proper. I
was very ſorry to hear what the Captain,
and the Maſter of the Boat which brought
him, reported had lately happened in the
South, *viz.* that Lieutenant *Dunbar*, being ſent out with a Party of Men, in a
well-armed Pettyagua, and a Scout-Boat to
attend him, in order to reconnoitre the
Coaſt, and ſeveral Creeks which fall into
the *Alatamaha*; they came to Anchor,
where the commanding Officer ſaw good;
and the Scout-Boat, with ſome Soldiers in
her, was ſent off, to make what Diſcove-
ries they could, of the Banks of the River,
and to know how far it was to any convenient Place of Landing : But at the ſame

Time

Time strict Orders were given, that at their Peril they should not offer to go ashore, or come any where within Musket-Shot of it: Nevertheless these poor infatuated People seeing great Plenty of Oranges in the Woods, growing naturally, and full of Fruit; they went ashore to gather some, but very soon found the Consequence: For espying some *Spaniards* and *Indians* coming towards them, they retreated to their Boat, and were put off; when the Enemy fired upon them, and killed two Men; one of whom was a Soldier shot in the Breast, and the other was the Master of the Boat (appointed by the General) who was shot into the Hind-part of his Head: Which shews the Situation they were in, the first at the Oar, the other at the Helm; whose Loss is particularly lamented by his poor Wife, and two small Children that live here; where the Man was a Freeholder, and his Name *Francis Brooks*, formerly a menial Servant of the General's. It was farther reported by the said Persons, that they met with a *Spanish* Launch, that had nobody in her; which they took, and might have been sufficient to shew them, there were some that belonged to her not far off. The General was not pleased to mention it in his Letter to me; but told me, he should write me farther by Mr. *Whitfield*, who was upon his Return hither; and who I found,

found, by what he wrote me, he thought had gone beyond what the Truſt intended, in taking ſome Orphans into his Keeping, who were well grown, and might have been of good Service this planting Time, to the Maſters they lived with. I cannot paſs over this Circumſtance of the Oranges, without a little Obſervation, having frequently heard the ſame related, of their growing common in the Woods: It is agreed by all, that no Beaſt will feed on them, or crop them; neither will the Dropping of any Trees annoy them, except the Pine, which will ſuffer no Tree to grow by him: Wherefore I purpoſe to make an Experiment this Seaſon of putting ſome Hundreds of good Orange-Seeds into the Ground, two or three in a Hole, in ſuch Places as I judge proper, in my new Plantation by *Vernon* River; which differs not a great deal in Latitude from the *Alatamaha:* And whereas the ill Succeſs we have hitherto had with Oranges in this Part, is ſaid to proceed from being too remote from the Salt; as well for the Influence of that Air, as that the Froſt is never ſo ſevere, as here farther up on the Freſhes; the Situation of my Land is open to the Sea: And from all this put together, I am not without Hopes that Oranges, by ſome lucky Incident or other, may in Time be the Product of *Georgia*; though this ſevere

U 4 Winter

1739. Winter has left very few young ones alive,
either in the publick Garden, or in any
February private about us, in Spite of all our Care.

27. *Wednesday,* Capt. *Mc Intosh* made the
best of his Way this Morning for *Palachocolas,* in order to surrender the Command
of that Fort to his Brother, whom the
General had given a Commission to suc-
ceed him: Before his going hence, we
learnt another Piece of News, that he
brought with him from the South, far
more agreeable than the other Account
which he gave, of that unhappy Disaster,
viz. that a Party of the Enemy lately,
having a Packet of Letters in their Charge,
from St. *Mark*'s, and not knowing that
the Fort of St. *Francis de Pupa* was taken
by us, went directly thither; where they
found themselves Prisoners: And it is said,
the Letters they had with them, were of
the greatest Consequence; discovering a
Design of a great Body of *French,* and
Spaniards, to join somewhere near that
Place, and march about the Middle of
April towards the *Savannah*; which they
were to cross, either at *Augusta,* or *Palachocolas,* and so come upon the Back of
both these Provinces. We could learn no
farther Particulars, nor make any certain
Judgment what Credit was to be given to
this Report: But it certainly behoved us to
be on our Guard; and we did not doubt,
if

if the General got fuch Intelligence, we fhould be advifed of it from him, and receive his Orders thereon. A fudden Report went about Town this Evening (whence it arofe I know not) that he would be here in two or three Days.

Thurfday. My prefent Thoughts being pretty full of Contrivances, how to improve that little domeftick five-Acre Lot, which lay fo near under my Eye (while that of much more Importance was far remote, where my chief Strength was employed) I went thither early in the Morning, and after entertaining myfelf there fome Hours, when the Heat of the Day came on, I returned home to my ordinary Employment, where I had little to obferve at prefent. ·Mr. *Whitfield*, with his Friend *Seward*, came to Town in the Afternoon, not having it in their Power to accomplifh their Intention fooner, fince they went South on *Monday* the 11th Inftant: By them I received a Letter from the General of the 18th Inftant, fignifying, that he had given 150 *l.* by his Bill on Mr. *Verelft*, as Money advanced towards building the Church; and recommending it to me to affift in forwarding that Work; having at the fame Time Regard to the Seafon of the Year, in not difcouraging planting, by hiring labouring Hands, *&c.* and in his Letter to me *per* Capt. *Mc Intofh*, which I

received

1739.
February

received on *Tuesday* last, he was pleased to tell me his Opinion freely in relation to the Orphans, by sending me a Paper inclosed, which was a Duplicate of what he had sent Mr. *Jones*; at the same Time advising me to acquaint the Trustees with what is done relating to the Orphans, the Orphan-House, and the Church: Which I have noted most commonly in the foregoing Pages, particularly on the 4th and 8th of this Month; and sundry other Places, since the Time of Mr. *Whitfield*'s Arrival on the 11th of *January*; and shall for the future be observant not to fail therein.

29.

Friday. A Negro Slave that belonged to the late Mr. *Dyson*, whom he kept in a clandestine Manner to and fro betwixt the two Provinces, being laid hold on by the Magistrates, after his Master's Decease here, and kept in Custody; the General sent Orders to Mr. *Jones* to sell him; wherein consulting me, I was of Opinion it should be at a publick Sale by Auction: In Pursuance of which, publick Advertisements being fixed up Yesterday, that the Sale would be this Morning; it was so; and among several Bidders, Captain *Thompson* advancing highest, he bought him for 23 *l.* 5 *s.* Sterling. The rest of the Day produced nothing extraordinary.

Saturday.

Saturday. I could not learn any Thing this Day fit to take Notice of here. Capt. *Thompson* began to think of falling down the River, Part of the Way to *Tybee*, for more Depth of Water, doubting, as he was far advanced now in his Loading, left he might be taken up by fome Shoal; and being paft fuch, he would take in the reft of his Loading there. Wherefore I was now, together with Mr. *Jones*, to get ready with all Diligence, what Papers we meant to fend by him.

Sunday. Mr. *Whitfield* went on without flackening his Rate of four Times a Day, weekly, in praying, preaching, expounding, and adminiftring the Sacrament: Wherein he took great Pains, exhorting his Hearers to a ftedfaft, faving Faith; the fame as when he preached here laft, on the 10th of *February*, and before: Wherein I wifhed he had fpared his Invectives againft the Clergy.

Monday. Divers of our Pieces of Artillery lying ufelefs, either without Carriages, or fuch as were unfit for Service; I had for fome Time paft given Directions, to remount as many as needed it on Ship-Carriages (or Trucks) which would be far lefs expenfive than Field-Carriages, and as proper for the Ufe intended them here, as the other: Which being now prepared, I ranged them in decent Order under a Shed,

from

from whence on any Occafion they might with Eafe be immediately run out, and in the mean while the Carriages be preferved from the Weather. One of the fmarteft Pieces on a Truck-Carriage, I chofe out to place commodioufly on the new Wharf under the Bluff; where it might be brought fo to bear, as to command the River upwards and downwards, whenever there was prefent Caufe for it; and all the reft were under the conftant Care of the Guard, at their ufual Place of Duty; which indeed was now fo open and expofed, that I hoped the General would grant Leave, when I faw him again, to let it be inclofed with a flight Palifade at leaft, at very little Coft; which would keep idle People among ourfelves from committing any Annoyance, and playing Tricks, as fometimes they were too apt to practife: And all Strangers coming and going would fee that we were difpofed to be in earneft.

4.   *Tuefday.* Mr. *Minis* going South this Morning, in order to difpofe of the Provifions which arrived lately in a Sloop there, Capt. *Tingly* from *New-York*; which Goods were configned to *Minis*; I wrote Letters by him to the General, in Anfwer to thofe I received by Capt. *McIntofh* and Mr. *Whitfield.* A Boat arrived from *Frederica,* wherein were two Cadets (Meffieurs *Wemys* and *Goldfmith)* fent by the General

for

for *Charles-Town*, whither they were hastening without Delay; by whom we learnt,
that the General was coming quickly after,
and bound to the same Place; which we
judged was in order to confer with the Government of that Province, concerning the
future Attempts intended against the Enemy, how the Council and Assembly had vo-
ted such an Aid. Another Boat came in
from the South this Morning, which was
also bound for *Charles-Town*, on Traffick;
in which was one Mr. *Ramsay*, who brought
me a small Packet from Mr. *Hawkins*, in
Return to what I wrote him of the 13th
ult. and inclosing several Lists, which by
the Trustees Order I had called on him
for: But as to the Box sent me from the
Trustees by the Ship St. *George*, which arrived the Beginning of *January* at St. *Simon*'s, and which Box I had so particular
an Account of very lately by Mr. *Patrick
Houston (vide Feb.* 20.) and I had wrote to
Mr. *Hawkins*, to be careful in sending it to
me *per* first Opportunity: The Answer I
now received from him was this, in a Post-
script. " I have inclosed one of the Pa-
" pers from the Trustees, not being cer-
" tain whether the Box is come to your
" Hands: About forwarding the same I
" have spared no Pains." This carries with
it such a Show of ———, that I know
not what to make of it, or what to call
it:

it: By his saying that he had sent me one of the Papers, I suppose I am to understand, that the Box contained them and nothing else: If so, why are they not sent me? or how can I believe him at such an Uncertainty, whether the Box is come to my Hands or not, after what I have heard from Mr. *Houston?* These are Mysteries too deep for me to fathom.

5. *Wednesday.* Capt. *Thompson* loosed his Ship from the Wharf, got up her Anchor, and attempted to fall down the River, in order to take in the rest of his Loading below: But through the Negligence of the Pilot (as it is said) the Ship ran aground on the Edge of a Marsh near the Town, tho' there was Water more than sufficient in the right Course, and the Wind very fair, an easy Breeze at West: What makes it the worse is, that it happened to be just at high Water, and the Top of the Spring Tide; so that when the Water ebbed, the Ship laid fast on the Mud, and there remained but little Expectation of her floating again till next Spring Tide. It must not, however, be inferred from hence, that the Navigation of this River is attended with uncommon Difficulties, Ships that draw as much or more Water than this, having frequently passed up and down, without any Obstruction, as I well know; and the Entrance in at *Tybee* over the Bar is allowed

to

to exceed all on this Coaſt, many Leagues Northward and Southward; beſides the great Advantage of ſo fine a Land-Mark there, which it is to be hoped will ſhortly be well repaired and ſtrengthned, before it is too late to mend it. Mr. *Patrick Graham*, Surgeon, who has made very conſiderable Improvements in building on his Lot in this Town, as well as been a conſtant Planter for two or three Years paſt, having Mrs. *Cuthbert* (Siſter to the late Capt. *Cuthbert*, deceaſed) for his Patient, dangerouſly ill in a Fever, at that Time a Lodger in his Houſe; the Doctor took the Opportunity of preſcribing Matrimony to her, as a Specifick which he was ſure would compleat her Cure; and on conſenting to take his Advice in it, they were married at her late Brother's Plantation: Mr. *Jones* and I (only) were preſſingly invited to the Wedding; which we complied with; though we could hardly perſuade ourſelves to be ſo long idling; and we rowed up to *Joſeph-Town* this Forenoon, timely enough to take Part of a good Dinner with them; but the Ceremony of the Wedding was over, the Marriage performed Yeſterday by Mr. *Norris*, and conſummated the ſame Evening: So after two or three Hours ſpent, we returned to the Place whence we came.

Thurſday. Meeting Mr. *Fallowfield* this Forenoon, he ſhewed me a Letter he had received

6.

received from Mr. *Williamson* at *Charles-Town*, and pointed out a Paragraph for me to read (by Direction I suppose from the Writer) full of Scurrility and Abuse; asking how I dared with-hold Mr. *Christie's* and his Constitutions, which were sent them by the Trustees? That I ought to know my Duty to my Masters better, and should be taught to know the Superiority of the Magistrates, under whom I was to act only as Secretary and Letter-Carrier to the Trust; with Abundance more such polite Strokes of his Wit: Which I only smiled at, and told his Crony who imparted it to me, that I hoped I needed not him for an Instructor in my Duty; that the State of that Affair was, by Order from the General, laid before those whom I thought it an Honour to serve as my Masters, which I should endeavour to do with Fidelity; nor would I be terrified from so doing: And that as soon as I knew their Pleasure, I should most undoubtedly obey it; which Mr. *Fallowfield* made no Reply to; and so we parted, at the Stores; where, with Mr. *Jones*, I spent great Part of the Day, in perfecting those Accompts which were intended to be sent by Capt. *Thompson*.

Friday. The common Talk of the Town Yesterday, being of what passed between our two Ministers on *Wednesday*, whilst Mr. *Jones* and I were at the

Wedding-

Wedding-Houſe abroad; Mr. *Norris* thought proper to give me a verbal Relation this Day of the principal Parts of their Conference; which being *ex parte* only, I muſt not take upon me to judge betwixt them: But as he deſired me to take in Writing what he related, and his Credit ſhould ſtand at Stake for the Veracity and Impartiality of what he deſired might be noted; I would not refuſe him, nor would I to do the ſame on the other Side, in Caſe it ſhould be aſked of me at any Time; which I had the leſs Reaſon to expect, becauſe Care was taken when they met, that two Witneſſes, namely, Mr. *Haberſham* and Mr. *Brownfield*, were to be preſent, that they might teſtify what they heard; whilſt Mr. *Norris* was not ſo guarded, who told me as follows.—" That on *Wedneſday* laſt, under-
" ſtanding Mr. *Whitfield* had a Deſire to
" ſee him, he went to wait on him; when
" he was received with common Civility,
" and a Cup of Tea, &c. That he had
" been there but a very little while, ere
" the two Perſons above-named came in
" as Witneſſes of what was ſaid; when
" (all farther Ceremony laid aſide) he was
" flatly charged with having preached falſe
" Doctrine here, during the Time of Mr.
" *Whitfield*'s being abſent in the South:
" Wherein Mr. *Norris* finding himſelf ſo
" ſtruck at, confeſſed he was pretty much

" startled, and asked what Testimony
" there was of it? To which he was an-
" swered, the two Persons before-men-
" tioned were Witnesses of it, as also the
" following named, *viz. Gladman* (Master
" of Mr. *Whitfield*'s Sloop) *Hunter* (an A-
" pothecary that came with Mr. *Whitfield)*
" the Widow *Vanderplank*, and lastly Mr.
" *Jones*, who lodges at her House. Mr.
" *Norris* then required, that they should
" give him some Particulars in Writing, of
" what they alledged; but they said they
" should not do that; nevertheless they in-
" sisted upon it, that his Foundations in
" general were false: Then Mr. *Whitfield*
" pressed him to produce his Notes; but
" he said he did not think it proper to do
" that, which might give them an Advan-
" tage over him, as they were maliciously
" disposed to wrest every Thing he had
" spoken, to a wrong Meaning; but upon
" their pointing out what they had ta-
" ken such Offence at, he would stand or
" fall by what appeared in the Sermons he
" had preached: Then he told them, that
" he had preached here eighteen Months
" among them, and never was suspected of
" false Doctrine till now; that he would
" appeal to the most competent Judges in
" this Town, or Neighbourhood, touching
" the Orthodoxy of his Sermons; but ex-
" cepted particularly against Mr. *Jones*,
" who

" who was bred a Diſſenter, and had ever
" ſince his being here, ſhewn an utter An-
" tipathy to him; and more particularly
" when he preached that Sermon on *Matt.*
" vi. 23. (which is what he ſuppoſes they
" are ſo angry at) as ſoon as he had named
" his Text; Mr. *Whitfield* ſaid, Mr. *Jones*
" had told him himſelf, that he took a
" Book, and read, during the whole Ser-
" mon; which muſt incapacitate him to
" obſerve the Connexion of his Diſcourſe,
" and render him an incompetent Judge:
" And from that Time Mr. *Jones* never
" came near the Church whilſt he ſupplied
" it. Mr. *Norris* farther alledged, that
" he had received double Orders from the
" Biſhop of *London*; and upon a ſtrict
" Examination before his Lordſhip and his
" Arch-Deacon, had given a full and ſa-
" tisfactory Account of his Faith: To
" which Mr. *Whitfield* replied, that he be-
" lieved ſo; but that he took the Biſhop
" of *London* to be no better a Judge, or
" knew more of Chriſtianity, than *Maho-*
" *met*, or an Infidel; and that he was
" now proving him to be ſuch, having
" wrote two Letters, which he had ſent to
" *Charles-Town* to be printed: Then Mr.
" *Norris* aſked him, whether or not he
" had read that Biſhop's Œconomy of our
" Redemption? Which he ſaid he had;
" but that he was quite wrong, and that

X 2   " that

" that Book was sufficient to send Thou-
" sands to Hell; as also Archbishop *Til-*
" *lotson*, and the Author of the *Whole Du-*
" *ty of Man:* Mr. *Whitfield* also told him,
" that he was at Work for the Devil, and
" capable of doing abundantly more Hurt
" than *Dyson*, or any such immoral
" Livers: Which Saying of Mr. *Whit-*
" *field*'s, proceeded from Mr. *Norris*'s ask-
" ing him, what he had to alledge against
" him, as to his Way of Life and Con-
" versation? When all he had to object,
" was that he played on the Fiddle, and
" at Cards with the Ladies, and kept po-
" lite Company; adding this for a Con-
" clusion, that he (Mr. *Norris*) had assisted
" him twice in administring the Sacra-
" ment, but that he never should again,
" or receive it at his Hands." I found
nothing fit to make any Remark on, of
the ordinary Occurrences of the Day; nor
shall I offer any on this that I have wrote:
But I wish it may stop here, without any
farther Distraction among us.

8.   *Saturday.* Good Luck, and a strong
easterly Wind, having beyond Expectation
lifted up Capt. *Thompson*'s Ship from where
she lay, by the Help of a high Tide, he
was now got down lower in the River; so
that what Mr. *Jones* and I could get ready
to send by him, would admit of little Delay. It was currently reported about Town,
that

1739.
March

that Mr. *Chriſtie*, together with Mr. *He-therington*, were gone off privately for *Ca-rolina*, in their Way to *England*; but I was not readily inclined to believe it, for he had more than a Year paſt frequently given out ſuch Speeches himſelf, of his Intention ſo to do; all which coming to nothing, few People now gave Credit to any ſuch Talk: And a particular Eſteem which he had for *Hetherington*, with whom he ſpent a Day or two ſometimes at *Thunderbolt*, occaſioned his going thither lately, to give no Umbrage: But about Evening we had certain Advice of it, that they were both gone, and had taken their Bedfellows with them (one his Wife, formerly *Roger Lacey*'s; and the other his famous Houſe-keeper, whom he had for a good while ſtuck cloſe to.) By this Flight I fear *Thunderbolt* is now almoſt deſerted.

Sunday. In my Way to Church this Forenoon, Mr. *Andrew Grant* met me, and ſhewed me a Letter he had juſt received from Mr. *Chriſtie*, of Yeſterday's Date, from a Plantation on this Side *Port-Royal*; where he and his Companions ſtopped a little, as they were going for *Charles-Town:* Incloſed he had one from him to deliver to me, wherein were ſome Keys; wherefore I forbore opening it immediately, but deferred it till we came from Church, reſolving with myſelf to have ſome-

9.

somebody with me, as a Witness of what the Contents of it were; more especially as this Mr. *Grant* was employed by Mr. *Chriſtie*, to be a Witness (among others) of what paſſed, when *Chriſtie* made his late Demand on me, to deliver him that Conſtitution, which appointed him firſt Bailiff, &c. *(vide Dec.* 22.) and I well knew, that all Steps taken in ſuch Affairs, were the Reſult of that wiſe Council at *Jenkins's,* whereof this *Grant* was a ſtedfaſt Member. After Church, I took with me Mr. *Jones,* together with Mr. *Grant,* to my Houſe; and opening the Letter (which was very ſhort) I found three Keys, which he wrote me were the Keys of the Office, Records, and the Orphan-Box: I ſaid little about it to Mr. *Grant,* but locked up the Keys, intending to give them to-morrow to the Magiſtrates; when (as it happened) they were to aſſemble, *per* Adjournment of the Court. Capt. *Norbury,* and Lieutenant *Horton,* came to Town both this Morning; the latter from *Charles-Town,* in order to proceed for *England* with *Thompſon;* and the other from his Command at *Port-Royal,* with ſome of his Family, whom he purpoſed to ſend by the ſame Ship. Mr. *Whitfield* preached, and prayed, as hitherto, ſticking fervently to the Doctrine of a New Birth, and Juſtification by Faith, provided it be ſuch, as to

2   produce

produce an Evidence within ourselves, that the Spirit of God is working in our Hearts; which he insists on, we may feel with a real Sensation; and till that is wrought within us, we are in a State of Damnation.

Monday. The Magistrates met at the Court-House, *pro formâ*, according to their last Adjournment; but not finding any Matters designed to come before the Court, to be such, as by being deferred would bring, or occasion, any Loss or Damage to any Complainant, they adjourned farther to the next Day, which must have been otherwise their ordinary Time of sitting in *April:* But before they did so, they looked (at my Request) into the many Defaults that were made by several, in not observing their Guard Duty; divers of whom were fined, to pay double the Money which they might hire a Man for, to have done Duty in their Stead; and it is hoped they will take more Care hereafter. The Wind changing suddenly from East to North-West, with much Lightning, betokened Storms.

10.

Tuesday. We found ourselves not mistaken in Yesterday's Prognosticks of the Weather; for a furious Wind from the North-West blowed all this Day, and so piercing cold, that no Day in the past Winter exceeded it, which it was apprehended would

11.

produce

produce a fevere Froft. An old Woman of Mr. *Whitfield*'s Houfhold, who came hither, among others, when he did, dying laft Night, was buried this Evening, with a folemn Funeral; thirty or forty little Boys and Girls walking in Pairs, partly Orphans, and others, whom with their Parents Requeft or Confent, he had taken under his Care, fung Pfalms as they went on to the Church; then followed Mr. *Whitfield*, and after him the Corpfe, half a Dozen diftinguifhed, chofen Men holding up the Pall; and a Number of mixed People, to clofe the Proceffion, joined them as they came by: Many People were gathered together at the Church, waiting; where after the ufual Prayers, Mr. *Whitfield* gave them a Sermon, *à propos*, on the Words *Watch and pray*: After which, the Corpfe was carried to the common Place of Burial, and there interred in the ordinary Manner. This was all that came to my Knowledge of this Day's Production, which I thought worth Notice, if it can deferve any.

12. *Wednefday.* Mr. *Whitfield* intending for fome Days paft, to take a Paffage for *Charles-Town* in his own Sloop, bound that Way, but with-held by contrary Winds, went off in her this Morning very early, the Wind at Weft, and a cruel Froft; which it is to be feared may prove pernicious again to the Vines, and all Kinds of tender

tender Plants. *Robert Potter*, late Constable, who so lightly esteemed the Promotion
the General had given him to that Office,
as to go a privateering, and came lately
sick ashore, died at the Widow *Montaigut*'s
Plantation, where he was designed by her
for an Overseer of her Negroes; and his
Corpse was brought down from thence,
and buried here this Evening.

Thursday. The Rigour of the Weather   13.
abated, but continued frosty still. Allowed
myself little Intermission this whole Day,
from attending with Mr. *Jones*, to examine
carefully those Accompts which had passed
our Enquiry, that no Errors might escape
uncorrected.

Friday. Kept close at home, copying   14.
my Journal, *&c.* (heavy Work! but such
as I dared not commit to another.) Mr.
Minis returned home about Noon from
Frederica; by whom I wrote to the General when he went thither (as noted the
4th Instant) but he brought me no Letter,
except one from Mr. *Houston*; who remembring what Conversation we had together
when he was here (as noted the 20th *ult.*)
was so kind to enquire of Mr. *Hawkins* at
Frederica, why that Box was not sent me?
To which Mr. *Hawkins* replied, it was
consigned to the General, and was in his
Custody: So Mr. *Houston* now wrote me:
And the same Answer, I apprehend, would
have

have been more ingenuous from Mr. *Hawkins* before, than such Trifling as he then used *(vide March* 4.) I then should have ceased from asking any farther after it; which possibly I may have given Offence in, to his Excellence, by such repeated Enquiry: But I would not incur his Displeasure knowingly; and conceiving it to be my Duty to ask after any Thing that I hear is directed to me by the honourable Trustees, and meets with Accidents or Delays by the Way; I ought to hope it will not be imputed to me as a Crime. Wrote my Letter to the Trust, expecting Capt. *Thompson* would sail in a Day or two.

15.   *Saturday.* It was Work enough for this Day, to finish what we had been preparing to go by Capt. *Thompson*, who intended to take his Leave to-morrow.

16.   *Sunday.* Mr. *Whitfield* not returning yet from *Charles-Town*, Mr. *Habersham* read the Prayers at Church, and a Sermon after it: Mr. *Norris* determining with himself not to meddle any farther here, since the Treatment he had lately received; some Particulars whereof he had related to me on *Friday* the 7th Instant.—Capt. *Thompson* not yet come.

17.   *Monday.* This Morning Mr. *Norris* took his Departure hence; and bringing me the Keys of the House he had lived in, desired I would not deliver them to any of
Mr.

Mr. *Whitfield*'s Followers, but to Mr. *Whitfield* himfelf, when he came home; for that he did not know how far the Malice which they bore towards him, might prompt them to farther Injuries. I took all poffible Care to avoid interfering with any of their Difputes on either Side; but kept my own Thoughts to myfelf, not ill pleafed that he was going; for it was evident, fo long as he fhould continue in this Place, there was like to be no Peace among us.—Delivered my Packet now to Capt. *Thompfon*.

Tuefday. Having now feen every Thing to the beft of my Power difpatched, that was to be fent by this Ship for *England*; I was very glad of a little Refpite from that Employment, and went in the Morning early, to fee how Things ftood at the five-Acre Lot, which I cultivated, at a little Diftance from the Town: There I fpent the greateft Part of the Day moft agreeably, in feeing my planting go forward, and putting various Seeds, with my own Hands, into the Earth, partly experimental, and partly with Expectation of the Ufe of them hereafter in my own Kitchen. At my Return I was informed, that Capt. *Thompfon* went off in the Forenoon; and taking with him fome of his principal Paffengers that yet remained here, namely Mr. *Horton*, and fome Ladies, who

had

18.

1739. had lived at *Frederica*; he purposed to sail
March as soon as he got aboard his Ship at *Cock-spur*. In the Evening Mr. *Norris* came back to Town again, disappointed in his Passage South, by reason of the Pettyagua wherein he was going being laden; and meeting with cross Winds, they were obliged to lie at Anchor, uncertain when to proceed farther.

19.   *Wednesday*. By a Boat which came up the River this Morning, we were informed, that Capt. *Thompson* was not sailed, the fair westerly Wind that we had Yesterday, shifting to the North-East, so he could not get out at *Tybee*, till veered again to some more favourable Point: In the Afternoon the Captain came again up to Town, to look after a runaway Sailor, that had left him very injuriously, at this Time especially: But little Hopes appearing of his being retaken, he returned to *Tybee* in the Night Tide, very intent upon sailing the first Offer of a Wind.

20.   *Thursday*. Early this Morning, by an Express Messenger we were informed, that the General was on his Passage from *Frederica* to *Charles-Town*, and would stop an Hour or two at *Thunderbolt*, where he would be glad to see Mr. *Jones* and me: Accordingly we set out immediately on foot, not waiting till Horses could be got; and found him where he had appointed:
From

From whence, after an Hour or two's Conference, and receiving his Commands in divers Matters, he proceeded; and we returned home about Noon. Capt. *Thompson*, I underftood, lay yet windbound at *Tybee*.

Friday. Not having had it in my Power for a good while paft, to fee how my Affairs went on at my new Plantation by *Vernon* River; I took this Day to myfelf for that Purpofe, and rode thither: The extream Point of which, Southward from *Savannah*, is near about twelve Miles; where I defigned the Place of Habitation to be. Here indeed I was much pleafed, to fee what Progrefs they had made, fince I faw them laft; having now built feveral good Huts, fufficient to withftand any Weather, and for various Ufes; the principal one being made with whole Logs, very ftrong, and capable of fome Defence, in Cafe of any fudden Attack made by vagrant Enemies, whether *Indian* or *Spaniards*; with feveral Loop-holes for the Difcharge of fmall Arms; and my Servants there, every one provided by me with fuch; which I found clean, and in good Order; and the Appearance of a ready Difpofition in them all to make a good Ufe of thofe Arms, if Occafion required: Another Hut made of Clapboards for the Servants to reft in: Another to keep Stores of all Kinds needful: Befides proper Receptacles, for

for my Poultry, Swine, &c. which I saw
an Increaſe of in each Kind happily begun;
and a very reaſonable Cauſe of hoping,
that Multiplication may take Place next
after Increaſe: Near adjoining they had
ſunk a Well, the Sides of which they had
ſupported with a ſtrong Timber Frame;
and at about ſeventeen or eighteen Foot
Depth, they came at excellent Water, not
in the leaſt brackiſh, though within the
Space of a hundred and fifty Yards of the
Salt: There was an Opening made of a-
bout ſeven Acres, wherein Abundance of
large Trees were fallen, and the Ground in a
good Forwardneſs of being cleared; which,
together with ſome more that we hoped to
add to it, was intended to be planted with
Corn, and Potatoes: So that it appeared
from the Whole, they had not been idle
ſince their being there; for it was after
Chriſtmas they began Plantation-Work at
that Place, where it was intended to ſettle: And herein appeared the Uſe of a
good Overſeer, who will both direct, and
alſo employ his own Hands in carrying on
the Work. I was now called upon, to
give the Place a Name; and thereupon naturally revolving in my Thoughts, divers
Places in my native Country, to try if I
could find any that had a Reſemblance to
this; I fancied that *Bewlie*, a Manor of his
Grace the Duke of *Montague* in the *New
Foreſt*,

Foreſt, was not unlike it much, as to its
Situation; and being on the Skirts of that
Foreſt, had Plenty of large Timber growing every where near; moreover a fine
Arm of the Sea running cloſe by, which
parts the *Iſle of Wight* from the main Land,
and makes a beautiful Proſpect; from all
which, Tradition tells us it took its Name,
and was antiently called *Beaulieu*, though
now vulgarly *Bewlie*; only by leaving out
the *a* in the firſt Syllable, and the *u* in
the End of the laſt. After a few Hours ſpent
at *Bewlie*, my direct Way home (which I
took) was through the five hundred Acre
Tract of Land, taken up by Mr. *Whitfield*
for the Uſe of the Orphan-Houſe; which
Land adjoins to mine, as we return northerly: And here I found the Building of
that Houſe carrying on with great Application, and Abundance of Hands; which
it is expected will in few Months effect the
Deſign: But I conceive it would have
turned to as good an Account for the Publick, if a little leſs Haſte had been made
in that Work, which takes up ſo many
People at this Seaſon, when one would
wiſh to have ſeen them as intent upon
planting: Some among them probably
might have taken a little to it; but I could
not promiſe for many, ſuch a Backward-
neſs ſtill appears among the ordinary, labouring People, who are apt to let themſelves

felves out to Hire, preferring that at all Times when they can, to Cultivation of Land; telling us plainly, that they are fure of Pay for their Pains, when they work that Way; but if they truft to planting, their Families may ftarve. The Day fo fpent, I returned home in the Evening.

22. *Saturday.* Mr. *Whitfield*, and his Companions, returned from *Charles-Town* in his own Sloop; by whom I learnt, that during the few Days he ftaid there, he had preached nine Times in various non-conforming Meeting - Houfes, and collected good Sums of Money towards the charitable Work of an Orphan-Houfe being promoted; at one Sermon particularly, upwards of 70*l.* Sterling: The *Carolina* printed News-Papers coming with them, I could not but obferve an Advertifement in one of them, fignifying, that Mr. *Whitfield* had publifhed two Letters there; one of them fhewing that Archbifhop *Tillotfon* knew no more of Chriftianity than *Mahomet*; and the other fhewing the fundamental Errors of a Book, entitled, *The Whole Duty of Man*; which confirmed my Belief of what I before doubted the Truth of, when it was told me, that he made one of his Boys throw that Book into the Fire, with great Deteftation. Mr. *Hopton* fent me by this Opportunity, a few private Letters from my Friends, which came by a Ship lately
arrived

arrived from *Cowes*, to his Hands; but
none from *London*; whence several Ships
were daily expected. What I found wrote
me (as reported) relating to the honourable Trust, was so exceeding shocking, that
I dare not commit it to Paper, hoping it
will prove to have no Foundation, and deserve not the least Credit : Neverthelesss,
the hearty Zeal which must always attend
my Actions, in the Station wherein I have
the Honour to serve them, leaves me under great Impatience till I receive their farther Commands; when I will not doubt
but such an Ecclaircisment will appear, that
no Room will be left for Jealousies and
Fears. Capt. *Thompson* sailed out at *Tybee*
this Day for *England*.

Sunday. The Church Service was per- 23.
formed by Mr. *Whitfield*, without any Variation from his usual Method of enforcing
the Necessity of a New Birth.

Monday. A frightful Story was pub- 24.
lished this Morning, of the *French*, and *Indians* in their Alliance, having fallen upon
the *Chicasaws*, cut off divers of our *Eng-
lish* Traders among the Nations, particularly *Thomas Andrews*, one of the most noted of them; and were going on with a
View of farther Mischief, &c. But I had
now so long experienced the Use which I
found was made of these bugbear Tales,
that I was resolved to trace it as far as I

could, to its firſt Source; which at length I diſcovered to be from that Mint of Scandal and Lies, which has for ſo long Time paſt created that Uneaſineſs in many People of this Colony; and who made it their Buſineſs ſtill to terrify weak Minds, infuſing ſad Apprehenſions of the Dangers that ſurrounded us, and ſticking at nothing they thought would make the Place odious to the Inhabitants: Inſomuch that it appeared evidently, it was a peculiar Pleaſure to them, whenever they knew any Deſertion of a Family likely to happen; which very probably alſo was by their Advice and Perſuaſion. As for the preſent Story, I could not find any Foundation for it.

25.

Tueſday. It may be proper here to inſert a Copy of what the General wrote to Mr. *Jones,* as his Sentiments, relating to Mr. *Whitfield*'s Proceedings concerning the Orphan-Houſe: Extract whereof, the General was pleaſed to order, ſhould be given me, that I might make it known to whom it might concern, *viz.*

S I R (Mr. *Jones)*

" As for *Mellidge*'s Brothers, I think
" your Repreſentation is very juſt; that
" taking them away to the Orphan-Houſe
" will break up a Family, which is in a
" likely Way of living comfortably: Mr.
" *Whitfield*'s Deſign is for the Good of the
" People, and the Glory of God; and I
　　　　　　　　　　　　　　　" dare

" dare say, when he considers this, he will
" be very well satisfied with the Boy and
" Girl's Return to their Brother *John Mel-*
" *lidge*, since they can assist him: Upon
" this Head I am to acquaint you, that
" I have inspected the Grant relating to the
" Orphan-House; Mr. *Seward* said, that
" the Trustees had granted the Orphans to
" Mr. *Whitfield*; but I shewed him, that it
" could not be in the Sense he at first
" seemed to understand it: It is most cer-
" tain, that the Orphans are human Crea-
" tures, and neither Cattle, nor any other
" Kind of Chattels; therefore cannot be
" granted: But the Trust have granted the
" Care of the helpless Orphans to Mr.
" *Whitfield*, and have given him five hun-
" dred Acres of Land, and a Power of col-
" lecting Charities, as a Consideration for
" maintaining all the Orphans, who are in
" Necessity in this Province; and thereby
" the Trustees think themselves discharged
" from maintaining of any: But at the
" same Time the Trustees have not given,
" as I see, any Power to Mr. *Whitfield* to
" receive the Effects of the Orphans, much
" less to take by Force any Orphans who
" can maintain themselves, or whom any
" other substantial Person will maintain:
" The Trustees in this, act according to
" the Law of *England*; in Case Orphans
" are left destitute, they become the Charge

Y 2   " of

"of the Parish, and the Parish may put
"them out to be taken Care of; but if
"any Person will maintain them, so that
"they are not chargeable to the Parish,
"then the Parish doth not meddle with
"them: And since taking away the Court
"of Wards and Liveries, the Guardian-
"ship of Orphans is in their next Rela-
"tions; or themselves, at certain Age, can
"chuse their Guardians; and the Chan-
"cellor, Judges, Magistrates, &c. have the
"same Inspection over the Effects and
"Persons of the Orphans, as they have
"over those of his Majesty's other Sub-
"jects: And the Effects and Persons of
"Orphans are as much under the Protec-
"tion of the Laws, as those of any other
"of his Majesty's Subjects."

In Pursuance of his Excellency's Opinion thus signified, *John Mellidge* was advised to wait on Mr. *Whitfield*, and desire
that he would permit his younger Brother
and Sister to go home to him, that they
might be helpful to one another: But upon his so doing this Day, he told me, that
Mr. *Whitfield* gave him for Answer, his
Brother and Sister were at their proper
Home already, and he knew no other
Home they had to go to; desiring him
to give his Service to the General, and
tell him so.

Wednesday.

Wednesday. I betook myself again to
Agriculture, and passed away a few Hours
at the five-Acre Lot very agreeably, in improving it to various Purposes, as my Inclination or Fancy led me to conceive, hoping to come at an experimental Knowledge of what would turn to most Advantage, and be therefore worth my chiefest
Care hereafter. Beside the usual Sorts of
Bread-Kind planted, I thought Cotton deserved a Place not too scanty; at leastwise
I would try, whether it would turn to any
Account or not; for the *West-India* Cotton,
which is perennial there, dies here every
Winter (as I have found) and the annual
Plant which will grow in this Country,
produces Plenty enough; and the Cotton is
at least equal to the other, if not better;
but so full of Seeds, that it cannot be cleansed by the ordinary Way of a Gin, nor by
any other Means than picking out with
Fingers; which is Work only for decrepid,
old People, and little Children; for which
Purpose Mr. *Whitfield* intends (he says) to
provide a good Stock of it, for Employment of the least of his Flock. Some Hundreds of Mulberries and Vines I had before
planted, for two Years past, besides of this
Season; to which I added now, upwards
of fourscore of Vine-Cuttings more, which
I received the latter End of the last Week
by a Ship arrived lately at *Charles-Town*

1740.
March
26.

from

from *Cowes*, all fresh, and ready to put out; so promising, that I hope few or none of them will fail; and if they are taken from those Vines of my own former planting (as I expect) I have almost Vanity enough to promise myself they will hardly be exceeded by any that are brought into this Colony from foreign Countries: Sir *William Bowyer* of *Bucks*, who was curious in Gardening, especially in Vines, brought some choice Cuttings himself out of *Italy*, which he was pleased to make me a Present of a few of; and they proved excellent in two or three Kinds: Wherefore I hope the nearer Approach of the Sun will not make them degenerate here, after more than forty Years flourishing in a more Northern Climate.

27.   *Thursday*. The Town was now grown so thin of People, that few were to be met with in the Streets, except some small Remains of the political Club, who commonly assembled in the Evening in the most publick Parts, making a tinsel Appearance; which drew more Ridicule than Respect from all Men of Sense; and after a little Heat, they seldom failed in adjourning to *Jenkins*'s, there to pursue their usual Debates, how to improve whatever Mischief they took in hand. —— Most of our labouring Men, and Artificers, were in full Employ at the Orphan-House, ten Miles off;

off; fo that Planting went on heavily, with a fmall Number of fuch as were left at home: And from what I yet faw, it did not appear to me, that we were to expect more than a Dozen, or thereabout, of the five-Acre Lots in the Neighbourhood of this Town, planted with Care (for fuch as are planted with more Hafte than good Speed, and not well cultivated at firft, as well as attended clofely afterwards, I look upon to be of but very little Value.) Nevertheless, I had yet pretty good Hopes, that we fhould find a while hence fomething done, among fome of the larger Tracts of Land, that would be worth obferving; divers who occupied fuch (fome by Virtue of a Grant, and fome in Expectation of a Leafe, being permitted to go on) having fet themfelves to Work in earneft, with fuch Help as they can get; which it were to be wifhed they could find more of.

Friday. Little Likelihood appeared of any Alteration in Favour of planting yet a-while (which Yefterday I took Notice of) the firft News I heard this Morning, being of an able Man voluntarily loft; which looking fomewhat like a Paradox, may need a little Explanation. The Man's Name is *John Sellier*, who holds a Free-hold Lot here, by Virtue of his Marriage fome Years fince with the Widow *Tibeau*, who has a Son grown a good hard Youth,

1740.
March

28.

and trained up to Labour by his Father-in-Law *Sellier*. This Lad feeing many other Boys, befides Orphans, accepted into Mr. *Whitfield*'s Houfe, there to be inftructed and maintained, in Confideration of their Labour (which feveral of them were capable of undertaking a good Share of) whether through his Parents Leave, or any other Perfuafion, does not appear; entered into that Houfe; where, after about a Month's Continuance, finding there was no Intermiffion, but every Hour of his Life was fully taken up, betwixt Things temporal and divine; grew weary, and returned home to his Parents, liking it better to work for them, or any other Mafter where he got a Penny: But his Father-in-Law *Sellier* has fhewn a different Way of thinking, and is grown lately fo fignal a Convert, through the Power of the Word as delivered by Mr. *Whitfield*, that he has bid adieu to all worldly Care; and refolving from henceforth to be content with Food and Raiment for his Labour, has given himfelf up to Mr. *Whitfield*'s entire Difpofal for his Service, on the faid Condition of being fed and cloathed for Life. This Man has been as regular and orderly in his Behaviour, and Pains-taking in planting conftantly, as moft of the Inhabitants, according to his Ability; and what he did plant, was done carefully and well; wherein

to

to encourage him, the General was pleased to make him one of our Tything-men: He is a ſtrong, healthy Man, betwixt forty and fifty Years of Age; has left his Wife, &c. regardleſs of this Colony, to make one in building up the *New Jeruſalem*: Young *Tibeau*, who left that Station which his Father-in-Law has now taken, continues with his Mother; and it is to be hoped they will be able to plant their five-Acre Lot without him. Methinks, it is great Pity this Place ſhould be bereft of the Labour of ſuch Youth, who are of Age and Strength ſufficient to maintain themſelves.——But I muſt not run beyond the Length of my Tedder.

Saturday. Mr. *Norris* who returned, baulked in his intended Paſſage (as noted on the 18th Inſtant) and waited ever ſince for the Opportunity of another Boat going, went off this Morning for *Frederica*. The ſame Day (after he was gone) it was commonly talked, that Mr. *Whitfield* would be going in few Days on another Progreſs among the Northern Plantations, in *Penſylvania*, *New-York*, &c. Capt. *Davis*, after ſo long labouring in vain, to fit out his Privateers, for want of Men and other Requiſites on that Occaſion, now began to turn his Thoughts other ways; and it was given out, that with the few Hands he had, he would go a trading Voyage to St.

29.

1740. St. *Kitt*'s, or some of the *West-Indian* Islands.

March 30.

Sunday. Mr. *Whitfield,* this Day, declared his Intention of leaving us for a while, preaching a farewel Sermon, in the same Manner as St. *Paul* exhorted the Elders of the Church in *Acts* xx. taking for his Text the 26th and 27th Verses of that Chapter, and carrying the Parallel betwixt the Apostle and himself as far as it would go; signified, that he expected Persecution wheresoever he went; therefore knew not, whether ever those among whom he had preached the Gospel here, should see his Face any more, or not: However, as the Work was great which he had in hand, it must take up some Months, at least, before he could return.

31.

Monday. Received a Letter this Morning from Lieutenant *Kent* at *Augusta,* brought by two or three Men newly come thence, who had left *Carolina* lately, complaining how hard a Matter it was for a labouring Man to live there, the Negroes doing all the Work: And Mr. *Kent* recommended them to me, to obtain some Land for them at *Augusta,* from the General, where they had a great Desire to settle (as indeed it was become very desirable by many others, from the Goodness of the Soil.) I told them they came hither in a good Time, for that the General being gone to

Charles-

Charles-Town, we now expected him back every Day. The reft of Mr. *Kent's* Letter was more difpleafing, informing me of an unhappy Accident that befel one of their Men lately at the Fort; who upon firing one of their little Pieces of Cannon, and the Gun burfting, had his Head ftruck clean off. The remaining Part of what he wrote was, that from what he heard, he was doubtful left the *Cherokee* Nation fhould fall off, and not perform what the General expected from them, in fending him an Aid of feveral hundred Men, to march with him againft the *Spaniards*.

1740.

March 31.

Tuefday. Mr. *McLeod*, Minifter at *Darien*, coming lately to Town in a Vifit to Mr. *Whitfield*, and to fee this Part of the Country, which he was a Stranger to; there was a notable Ride out this Day, to the Orphan-Houfe, by a pretty many, who were defirous to attend on that Occafion, and fhew their particular Regard to their Teachers. After fuch Orders given there by Mr. *Whitfield*, as he thought proper, for carrying on the Work (which was in great Forwardnefs by fuch a Number of Artificers and Labourers conftantly employed) they returned to Town again in the Afternoon; where nothing was to be heard of worth Notice till Evening; when Mr. *Whitfield* (after expounding on the Leffon for the Day out of the *New Teftament,*

April 1.

ment, as his ufual Manner was) took Occafion to reproach his Audience with their Hardnefs of Heart, and little Marks which they fhewed in Improvement of Grace; infomuch that they came behind all, to whom he had preached the Word elfewhere; for he feldom failed of Numbers in thofe Places, who followed him with Weeping, defirous to know how they muft be faved; but he found very few fuch here; Thofe few that had found themfelves prickt to the Heart, and began to be enlightened by the Holy Spirit, he charged to take Care of Backfliding; telling them they muft expect many Trials and Temptations; to be fcoffed at and derided, and probably perfecuted too; wherefore they muft not forget to affemble and meet together, ftrengthning and comforting one another: And for the reft, he told us, he had often thought this Colony would never be fuffered by Providence to profper, till God had planted it with Seed of his own.——The Conftruction of which I muft humbly fubmit to my Betters.

Wednefday. About Eight this Morning Mr. *Whitfield* went on board his Sloop, accompanied with Mr. *Seward*, and taking with them Mr. *Haberfham*, formerly SchoolMafter here, hitherto deputed by Mr. *Whitfield* to officiate in his Abfence; but now feemed chofen out for other Purpofes elfewhere:

where: The Wind being fair, they sailed immediately; and the Place they were said to be bound to, was some Part of *Pensylvania*, but far short of *Philadelphia*, to which Town they meant to travel by Land, gathering the Brethren together, and preaching the Gospel in their Way: From *Pensylvania* they were to proceed to *New-York*, and so on to *New-England*; if my Information is right: By the same Information I learnt, that Mr. *Whitfield* had farther Views in taking up a Tract of Land in some one of the Provinces, and erecting a School or Nursery for the Instruction of young Negro Children, in the Christian Religion; which Works of so extensive Piety, are most undoubtedly to be highly esteemed: At the same Time it is to be wished, that whilst he is gone far off to make Proselytes, he may retain a few charitable Thoughts at least towards this poor Place, and not look upon all the Inhabitants, as Castaways not worth regarding; except the little Children which he has taken to himself, and about half a Score full-grown Persons, Men and Women (some of which came with him, and a few others became early Adepts) who are distinguished by the Name of True Believers; and separating themselves from among their Neighbours, they appear with a different Aspect, and converse as little as

may

may be with any but one another.——But it would make a Volume to purfue this Theme, which I meddle with unwillingly in thefe fhort Notes; having no Prejudice, or the leaft Ill-will to Mr. *Whitfield*; but on the contrary, a Defire to join with him in all Chriftian Fellowfhip and Communion; as I have evidently fhewn, though (I am forry to fay) I have thought myfelf, on divers Occafions, to be coldly received: Whatever Remarks, therefore, I may have made on this Affair, or may hereafter, it has been, and fhall be, only the Refult of what I think a confcientious Difcharge of my Duty, without any finifter Views, or particular Refpect of Perfons. Notice being brought me in the Afternoon, that fome Perfon (unknown yet) had fet Fire to a large Tract of old Canes, growing in the Swamp at the Weft Side of the Town; which was become fuch a terrible Conflagration, by reafon of a ftrong Wind driving it on, that nobody dared to go near it; I fent immediately, and got what little Strength together I could, to do our Endeavours about it; when indeed we gave over all Pretence to extinguifh it; but as there was a new Bridge that lay in its Way very much in Danger, which was built about a Year or more fince, at an exorbitant Expence of the Truftees; we applied ourfelves, if poffible,

fible, to fave that from perifhing; and by taking timely Care, we fo managed Matters, as to conduct the Flames clear on each Side, at fome little Diftance from it: After which, we had nothing to fear from its raging in thofe Swamps; neither, if it threatned the upper Lands, was there a fufficient Pabulum to maintain it. Thefe Fires are a common Practice in all thefe Countries, as well for deftroying Vermin, as to allow young tender Grafs to grow for the Cattle: But I conceive it would need fome Regulation.

Thurfday. Moft of my Time taken up 3. this Day, in getting together Provifions of all Kinds, to be fent to my People at *Bewlie* by Water; being far round: Wherefore I thought beft to fend fuch a Store as might hold out a few Months, and prevent my being too frequently called upon to fupply their Wants, and interrupted at fuch Seafons when I could ill attend them.

Friday. This being a Day much re- 4. garded by the Church of *England*, it was expected that it would have had fome Notice taken of it, by fuch as Mr. *Whitfield* had conftituted to take Care of all divine Affairs here in his Abfence; but I was forry to find not the leaft Regard fhewn to it at Church, nor any Part of the particular Service appointed by the Rubrick, read; either Pfalms, Leffons, or Collects. Though it is a sad Truth that this Place has little Piety, to deserve being looked on as a People zealous in good Works; yet it is to be hoped there may be some well-meaning Persons in it, who find a Comfort in frequenting the Church, and joining in the publick Service, when duly performed; that are equally grieved when they see the Liturgy mangled, and giving Way to ———. We know not what next.

5. *Saturday.* Finding little abroad that required my Attention, I made the best Use of my Time at home; where my Pen and Ink seldom stood still. In the Evening pretty late, the General arrived from *Charles-Town,* on his Way back to the South; whither he was hasting, and designed to make but a short Stay here: There was little Room to have much Talk with him this Night; but we found him well satisfied with his Reception in *Carolina,* and the Aid he was assured of from thence: So that the Siege of *Augustin* was now again talked of, as a Thing certainly designed.

6. *Easter-Sunday.* Prayers appointed by the Church of *England* were read, Morning and Afternoon, by Mr. *Simms,* deputed by Mr. *Whitfield* to perform that Office in his Absence, and who likewise was charged by him with the principal Care of the Orphans: Mr. *McLeod,* Minister at *Darien;*
having

having not yet left the Town, was pleaſed
to give us two Sermons after Morning and
Evening Prayer. *Simms* was one who
came from *England* lately in Company with
Mr. *Whitfield*; had the Appearance of a
modeſt young Man, and one of very few
Words, eſpecially with any but of the Brotherhood; but whether he was a Butcher
living in *Clare-Market*, or not (as it is currently ſaid here) who left all, by the Im-
pulſe of the Spirit, to follow whereſoever
he thought it called him, I can ſay nothing of; but the Truth or Falſity of it,
may upon Enquiry be made eaſily appear;
as alſo it may, whether one *Peryam*, another Inſtructor of the Orphans, was bred
a Lawyer, and found out at a Mad-Houſe,
from whence his Liberty was procured,
that he might, with the greater Fervency
of Devotion, unite among thoſe who are
become approved Converts.

Monday. The General was ſo thronged 7.
with Affairs of various Kinds, which he
would allow himſelf but a ſhort Time to
diſpatch whilſt here, that it was difficult
to have Acceſs to him for Advice, in many needful Caſes, how to conduct myſelf
hereafter. He was pleaſed now to deliver
me a ſmall Packet, ſent from the Truſt,
and dated the 28th of *September* laſt, which
came by Capt. *Wright*, who brought with
him the Box of Papers at the ſame Time,

1740.
April

the Beginning of *January* laſt; which Box I have not yet: In this Packet was a Letter from Mr. *Verelſt*, by Order of the Truſt; Invoice of Goods on board that Ship; Notice for Perſons to claim, to be fixed in the Town-Court of *Savannah*, and Copy of the ſame to be publiſhed in the *South-Carolina* Gazettes, &c. And the Contents of the Box, not yet received, *viz.* a Deed-Poll relating to forfeited Lots: And alſo two hundred of the printed Reſolutions for the Inhabitants, relating to the Grants and Tenure of Lands, &c. Theſe Things could not be otherwiſe than a little ſurprizing at firſt; till I became aſſured in myſelf, that the General would certify it ſo to the Truſt, as to take off all Blame from me.

8.
9.

Tueſday, } Both theſe Days were en-
Wedneſday. } tirely taken up in attending the General, and receiving his Inſtructions, how to behave when he left us; which he intended the next Morning early; but a Boat arriving late in the Evening on *Wedneſday*, from *Auguſta*, which brought Letters importing, that Mr. *Eyre* was on his Way from the *Cherokees*, with a hundred choſen Men of that Nation, who were the Forerunners of ſeveral hundred more to follow; that he had moreover about ſeventy of the *Chicaſſaws* with him, and twenty white Men, Volunteers: And alſo being adviſed, that ſeveral Hundred

I

of

of the *Upper* and *Lower Creek* Nations
were preparing to join him: Withal, that
the Report of the *Chicaſſaw* Nation being
deſtroyed by the *French*, and one of our
principal Traders *(Thomas Andrews)* cut off
among them, was a malicious, falſe, and
groundleſs Report, ſpread to intimidate and
diſcourage the People of this Colony: Such
good and ſeaſonable News coming, occaſioned his Excellence to conſider farther,
and incline to pauſe a little upon it, before
he would ſet out.

Thurſday. The Advices of Yeſterday
had now ſo far wrought on the General,
that he reſolved perſonally to go up the
Country, in order to meet thoſe that were
on their Way hither, and prevent their
coming to this Town; which would create an unneceſſary Expence, and alſo retard
them from making ſuch Expedition as he
wiſhed: Wherefore he deſigned to alter
their Rout, and point out the March they
muſt make croſs the Country, over the River *Ogeechy*, to *Darien*, &c. which when
he had ordered as he ſaw good, he purpoſed to take this Town in his Way South
himſelf; by which Time he expected the
Reinforcement from *Carolina* would begin
to be on their Way to the Place of general
Rendezvous, appointed by him at St. *John's*
River. After having diſpatched many Orders and counter Orders, which ſo ſudden

of

of his Purpose, therefore muſt unavoidably produce; he ſet out in the Evening by Water up the River, having before ſent Orders for Horſes to be ready for him to mount, where he thought fit.

11.   *Friday.* The General, upon delivering the Packet, as mentioned on *Monday* laſt, underſtanding from me what Orders the Truſt had been pleaſed to ſend, relating to my publiſhing the Notice to be given, that all Grantees of Lands were required to enter their Claims in one of the Town-Courts of *Georgia*, &c. for the more effectual Performance of which Publication, they had alſo directed me to get it printed in the *South-Carolina* Gazette: His Excellence was pleaſed now to tell me, that if the Truſtees had known the Circumſtance of Affairs at preſent here, he was ſure they would have thought farther of it: And directing his Diſcourſe in a particular Sort to me, aſked me if I did not know, that Dr. *Dale* was the Writer of that Gazette? Which I anſwered I did: Then he aſked me, what my Opinion of him was, with Regard to this Colony? To which I made no Scruple in ſaying, that I looked on him as one of the moſt inveterate Oppoſers of any good that might befal it; and that he was generally ſo eſteemed: Then his Excellence replied, how eaſy a Matter would it be for a Man of ſuch a Diſpoſition, that delights

delights in Scribbling and Scandal, to give
such a Turn to the true Intent of it, either
by Addition or Omiffion of two or three
Words, as to render it ridiculous? And
then he would be the firft Perfon to print
such Remarks on it as he thought good.
For thefe Reafons he was pleafed to fay,
that he thought it advifable not to print it
at *Charles-Town*, but to poft up divers
written Copies of it in the ufual Places
of publifhing any other Affairs in this
Town that required it: Upon which, I
did fo this Day; and at the fame Time
(which was his exprefs Command) wherefoever I fixed one of thofe Notices fo
written, clofe by the Side of it I placed
one of thofe printed Anfwers, which the
honourable Truftees had long fince given,
to that notable Reprefentation, fent by this
Town and Neighbourhood, of Grievances
which they thought they lay under. This
was all I remembered fit to take Notice of:
The Box, with thofe other Papers often
mentioned, remaining ftill at *Frederica*,
nothing yet can be faid farther of that.

Saturday. Some Inhabitants of *Frede-*
rica, who had been two or three Days
here, on Bufinefs of their own, returned
this Morning in the fame Boat they came;
and Mr. *McLeod*, who had fpent fome
Time among us, took the Opportunity,
by the fame Boat, of returning to his Care

1740.

April

12.

at

at *Darien.* In the Evening Mr. *Thomas Holmes,* one of our *Indian* Traders among the *Cherokees,* together with —— *Craig,* a *Carolina* Trader inhabiting at *New-Windsor,* arrived with Letters to the General from Mr. *Eyre,* and also to me (doubting where the General was to be found) whereby we were informed, that he was coming down with a certain Number of *Indians,* and twenty white Men (as before noted on the 9th Inftant) to go on immediate Service under the General; and that they are to be followed by a good Body more: By the fame Hand I had also Letters from Mr. *Wigan,* fignifying the prefent State and Difpofition of the *Creeks,* among whom he had lived many Years a principal Trader; and also a Letter from Lieutenant *Willy* to the fame Purpofe: By all which it appeared, that fome ill-meaning People had been tampering with the *Indians* of thofe feveral Nations, and endeavouring to excite them to a Rupture; but (it was hoped) in vain.

13.   *Sunday.* The Office of the Day was performed by Mr. *Simms,* appointed thereto by Mr. *Whitfield;* who read fuch Parts of it as he faw good; but mangled, omitting the Pfalms, and fuch other Parts as it may be fuppofed he thought unneceffary. Towards Evening a Meffenger arrived, with a Letter to Mr. *Jones* from the General, then

at

at the *Uchee* Town, belonging to a Tribe
of *Indians* so called; where he met the Body of *Indians, Cherokees,* &c. mentioned on
Wednesday last; and acquainting us, that
they would pursue their intended March as
far by Land as *Musgrave's* (i.e. *Matthews's*)
where he would have some Pettyaguas sent
to meet them on *Monday* Evening, and
bring them thence on *Tuesday* to *Savannah.*

Monday. The General arrived in his
Cutter, about Three a Clock this Morning,
at *Savannah*: About Eight, after taking a
little Rest, he conversed with such as had
received his Commands, and had any Matters of Consequence to lay before him: In
the Afternoon, the Pettyaguas which he
had before ordered, were dispatched up
the River to *Matthews's*; and nothing more
happened memorable.

Tuesday. I had the General's Orders
to receive the *Indians* under Arms, with as
many Freeholders as could readily be got
together, other spare Men and Inmates being not allowed on this Occasion: And
upon Beat of Drum, we got soon together
about forty; which indeed was more than
expected, considering how many were a-
broad at work, some one Way, and some
another, especially at the Orphan-House;
and Minors also, who were not of sufficient Stature, though judged capable of
doing Guard Duty in their own Right,

were

were excluded here. At Eleven a Clock they landed, under the Conduct of Mr. *Eyre*, and Mr. *Samuel Brown* an *Indian* Trader of Diſtinction; when I received them; and the greateſt Part of the Town were gathered together, out of Curioſity, to ſee them: They were a Body of luſty, lively Fellows, with all their Faces moſt diſmally painted with Vermillion and Blue, variouſly, as each fancied, to make himſelf appear terrible (as is their uſual Cuſtom) and well armed with Firelocks and Hatchets: The Freeholders marched firſt, four in a Rank; then the *Indians* in the ſame Manner, with each Party a Drum in the Centre, which alternately beat the *Engliſh* March, till we came to the Court-Houſe, where the General ſat to receive them; and the Freeholders then forming two ſtrait Lines, the *Indians* paſſed betwixt them into the Houſe, and the Drums ceaſed: During the March up the Town, fifteen Pieces of Cannon were diſcharged: When they were all ſeated, the General talked kindly to them a while by an Interpreter, and they had Pipes and Tobacco given them, which they all took readily: After that was over, I had Orders to conduct them to the Place prepared for them to reſt in; which I did, in the ſame Manner as before; and there they found what neceſſary Refreſhment was provided, &c. After which, I
diſcharged

discharged our People, to follow their own
Business, and took my Leave.

Wednesday. What I thought most worth
regarding, was some private Intelligence I
got, that there was a Combination carrying
on, among our incessant Workers of Mischief, to form another Representation of
Grievances, in a different Strain from their
former, and of more dangerous Consequence; forasmuch as that was speculative
only, and imported divers Propositions, so
far culpable, as they were the Production
of a rash Presumption: But this (I understood) was intended to strike at the Foundation of the executive Power in this Place,
by heaping up Abundance of illegal and
arbitrary Proceedings, deserving immediately to be remedied; and laying them to
the Charge of all those in any Authority,
who hitherto boldly withstood their mis-
chievous Purposes; wherein even the General himself (if my Information proves true)
will hardly escape their vile Calumny: It is
said moreover, that the People at *Darien*
act secretly in Concert with them; and that
an Agent from thence, whose Name I yet
forbear mentioning (though I observed for
several Weeks past his frequent coming and
going to and fro) has been very busy here,
on this good Work. Among other Pieces
of curious Politicks, I am told farther, they
want an Officer to be created, under the
Title

Title of Sheriff; but how far his Power is to extend, or be limited, I cannot yet learn; nor whether, in these Times of War, he is to be elective, Dictator-like, or not, is not yet revealed: But in case it comes out such a finished Piece as we may expect, it will then be seen what the Authors dare to drive at; which a little Time will shew. Late at Night arrived some Expresses; by one of which the General was advised, a large Body of the *Creeks* were preparing to march, and join his Excellence in the South: And by another he was informed, that several half Gallies, and Sloops, well armed and manned, came out of the Harbour at St. *Augustin*, and in a Calm attacked one of our Frigates of twenty Guns, commanded by Capt. *Warren*, who was upon a Cruise off that Place: That they fired several Shot at him, and with a nine Pound Ball went through and through his Ship betwixt Decks, killing one Man only: But the Captain so behaved, that they found a warm Reception; and after about twenty of their Men slain, they were glad to sheer off; and not able to get in by the Way they came out, they took Shelter in a small Cove near by, where they were pent up. About Two in the Morning the General dispatched an Express to *Charles-Town*, to hasten the Force he expected, and to acquaint the Commanders of those Frigates

that

that were ſtationed there, how needful it was for them to turn out, and give what Aſſiſtance they could in preventing any Succours getting in, or any uſeleſs Hands out of *Auguſtin*, where he began to grow impatient till he could make them a Viſit.

Thurſday. Much Hurry, and crowding of Buſineſs, took up the whole Day : The General determining with himſelf not to loſe an Hour that could be ſaved, in ſetting forward the Operations of War, and putting himſelf at the Head of what Forces he had, with all poſſible Expedition : Wherein nothing happened particularly fit to be taken Notice of here. Capt. *Davis*, with his Snow and Sloop, were now all put to Sea from *Tybee*; but whither bound, very few knew.

Friday. Orders being given for the *Indians* to embark on board the Pettyaguas which brought them, and ſufficient Proviſions for them on their Paſſage, *&c.* that was the Work of the Forenoon ; and about Two a Clock they all ſailed, under the Diſcharge of eleven Pieces of Cannon : In little more than an Hour after, the General took his Cutter, and followed, expecting to overtake them at Anchor, as ſoon as the Tide they had with them was ſpent ; for the Wind being ſoutherly, and againſt them, till they were paſt *Skeedoway Narrows*, they muſt depend on the Tide alone, unleſs

unleſs it veered to a more favourable Point.
Out of the eight Companies of fifty-two
private Men in each, which were to be
paid by the Government of *Carolina*, the
General had engaged to raiſe two of them
on this River, under the Command of Meſ-
fieurs *Richards* and *La Feit*, appointed Captains: Which ſucceeded ſo well, that *Richards*, who lives at *Puryſburgh*, had that
whole Town to follow him, leaving only
Women and Children, with a few old Men,
to keep Poſſeſſion at home; ſo that he had
a Surplus to ſpare, towards forming the o-
ther Company; to which three or four
were added from *Ebenezer*; and the
Remainder, even this Town, in the low
Eſtate it is, without all Doubt will make
up; for we ſeldom fail of rambling Fellows
among us, ſufficient for ſuch an Enterprize,
and ready to ſhew their Bravery againſt
the *Spaniards*: All ſuch, together with
ſome of our young Men inhabiting here,
readily and voluntarily ſhew their good
Diſpoſition, by enliſting themſelves for four
Months (which is the Time limited for
this Expedition, and) within the Compaſs
of which, the Succeſs againſt *Auguſtin* is
expected to be known. In ſuch a Juncture,
when we daily hear of divers Gentlemen,
Volunteers, taking to Arms at their own
Expence, from *Carolina* and elſewhere, in
order to ſignalize themſelves againſt the
Enemies

Enemies of their Country; it might have been hoped, that some of our reforming Gentry, in their Gold and Silver buttoned Coats, and gay Waistcoats, would have made some little Advance, beyond the Parade, which they daily tread here, and displayed their Abilities, *tam Marte quam Mercurio:* But herein only they are modest.

Saturday. Being under a little Disorder, by reason of an accidental Bruise in one of my Legs, I sat all Day at home, where I never was at a Loss to find Employment; and did not hear of any Thing abroad more than common.

Sunday. Mr. *Simms* read the common Prayers of the Church regularly this Day, and a Sermon both in the Forenoon and after, still setting forth the Necessity of a strong Faith, &c.

Monday. A Report had flown about for a Week past, that *Donald Stewart* (Master of a small Sloop, often made use of as a Pilot, and a Freeholder) was cast away with his Sloop, and drowned; but being contradicted by several, little Credit was given to it; till now it was unhappily confirmed. He was hired by some Persons in this Town, who were on their Way thus far to settle at *Augusta*, to go and fetch their Families and Effects from the Place where they had left them in *Carolina (vide March*

1740. *March* 31.) On which Occasion, this poor
April Man sailing, within *Port-Royal Island*, in
crossing a Sound, under a hard Gale of
Wind, ran upon some Shoals, and staved
his Vessel, his Son and another escaping
with their Lives; but himself and one Man
more drowned.

22. *Tuesday.* One of the two Companies,
appointed to be raised on the Banks of this
River, being not yet compleat, which was
to be commanded by Capt. *La Feit*; the
enlisting Officer applied to me for the
Guard-Drum to beat up for Volunteers;
which I very gladly made him a Compliment of; hitherto no such Means of Invitation having been used, but all that enlisted, came without a Call; but now the
Town was grown so exceeding thin, the
Orphan-House taking off hence such a
Number one Way, and so many more
going into the War chearfully and commendably another, that we were almost
become uncapable of finding Hands sufficient to carry on the ordinary Guard-
Duty; and Planting was regarded by very
few.

23. *Wednesday.* A Boat was sent off early
this Morning to the General at *Frederica*,
with an Express from *Charles-Town*, by
whom Mr. *Jones* and I wrote Letters needful. The ordinary Club, which meet at
Jenkins's, rode out, with Landlord at the
Head

Head of them this Day, by Invitation, to
an Entertainment provided for them at
Mr. *Fallowfield*'s Plantation, about eight
Miles off; where it may be presumed, it
was taken into Consideration, what Steps
farther to make in these dubious Times towards settling this Colony upon such a
Foundation as would best please them: It
having been observed, that at these select
Meetings out of Town, usually something
extraordinary has been the Subject Matter
of their Deliberations; and it is not ques-
tioned, but their aspiring Temper is somewhat offended, at a Rebuke one of their
Fellow Workers lately met with from the
General; who overtaking the Pettyaguas
with the *Indians*, on *Friday* Night last,
and espying on board one of them, a
Man whom his Excellency thought not
proper to mix with that Company, knowing him to be a close Attender of the Club,
and a busy Person, often passing to and fro
betwixt this and the South, which rendered
him suspicious of being employed to no
good Purposes; he ordered the Master of
the Pettyagua to set him ashore that Instant, at the first Place of Landing; which
happened to be on the Island called the *Isle
of Hope*, whereon Mr. *Fallowfield* is one of
the three that are settled there, and where
now this Company met: But whether or
not it was only to celebrate the Festival
of

1740.
April

24.

of St. *George*, they beſt knew: Hoiſting up the *Britiſh* Flag, was all I thought needful in the Town of *Savannah*.

Thurſday. Enliſting of Men was now the principal Affair in hand; which had ſo drained the Town, that it was hard to find a Man more to enter: Wherefore it was reſolved by the Officer, to make a Viſit to the People at work about Mr. *Whitfield*'s Plantation at the Orphan-Houſe; which I would have nothing to ſay to, but left them to do as they pleaſed, being unwilling to ſhew the leaſt Diſcouragement in ſo important a Service; and not over-fond of meddling, where my appearing in it (I had Reaſon to apprehend) would be ill conſtrued as a Sort of Sacrilege, in breaking in upon ſuch a Work, carrying on for ſo pious an Uſe: Moreover, I knew it was a Matter much in queſtion among the Directors of that Work, whether or not it was lawful in the Sight of God, to take up Arms with an offenſive Intent, or on any Occaſion, but purely in Defence of our own Lives. In the Afternoon an Officer in the new-raiſed Troops of *Carolina*, arrived from *Charles-Town*, by the Way of *Puryſburgh*, with Letters expreſs from thence for the General, which was incumbent upon us to forward, with what Expedition we could: But indeed, the daily Demand upon us for Boats, and Men

to

to go in them, was so disproportioned to
our Abilities (being now so far bereft of
People for ordinary Uses) that we were
hard put to it to do, what we wished, more
readily for the publick Service. One or
two of the Letters now brought us for the
General, I observed by the Superscription,
came from *England* by the *Charming Phil-
ly*, Capt. *Colebatch*; which gave me Hopes,
that I might also have some thence for me
fall into Mr. *Hopton*'s Hands at *Charles-
Town*, who would not slip the first Opportunity he could meet with, of forwarding
whatever he received.

Friday. The Letters we received Yesterday *per* Express from *Charles-Town*, we
sent over Land by the Way of *Darien*;
and other Letters for the General, which
came by the South, expecting he was here,
we sent back also by the same Hand, together with more Letters now wrote from
hence. The enlisting Officer stuck to his
Purpose of Yesterday, and marched with a
few Volunteers, and a Drum attending
him, to beat up for more Soldiers at the
Orphan-House, where he would find a
Number of People; but what Disposition
any of them were in for War, or what
Success he met with, we yet had not learnt.
What occurred in Town was not worth
remembring.

Satur-

Saturday. Capt. *La Feit*, and his Sub-altern Recruiting Officer, taking Breakfaſt with me, I was informed by them what Succeſs they had attending Yeſterday's Ex-pedition to *Betheſda* (which is the Name given to that Place by Mr. *Whitfield)* and it proved almoſt fruitleſs, one or two Fel-lows only taking on: They took Notice to me of the People in general there, being provided with one and the ſame Anſwer; which it was ſuppoſed was taught them to give, by their Employers, ·when invited to take Arms; which was, that they had good Proviſions, and a Place to ſleep in, with ready Money Pay for their Work, where they were, which they were not deſirous to change for the Hazard of being knocked on the Head, and the Certainty of being continually expoſed to bad Wea-ther, either Heats, or heavy Rains. By reaſon of ſeveral Tythings now rendered incapable of doing effectual Duty on our Guard, for want of Hands ſufficient, it behoved me to make ſome new Regulation, for carrying on ſo neceſſary a Service: For when the utmoſt was done in our Power to raiſe Recruits, which might contribute to Action againſt our Enemies in the South; it was Time to conſider a little our own Safety, in being watchful with thoſe Free-holders which remained, that we might not be ſurprized by any Party of *Florida*
Indians

Indians ſtraggling, to come on our Backs, nor by any armed Boat coming up the River, ſculking to do Miſchief; who coming upon us unaware, and unprovided, might carry all before them; whereas on Diſcovery of approaching, imminent Danger, we yet hoped, by putting Arms into our ſpare Mens Hands, and calling in all others employed within little Diſtance, we might make a Stand with at leaſt one hundred and fifty Men, ſufficient to repel any ſuch Attempt: Upon looking carefully, therefore, over the Liſt of Freeholders, with the Conſtables; it was thought adviſable, that three or four of thoſe Tythings, with the feweſt Hands left in them, not compe- tent to make a reaſonable Guard, ſhould be totally reduced for this preſent Occaſion, and the few Freeholders left in them, ſhould be divided among other Tythings, ſo as to make them ſufficient, and called upon to do Duty with them: This we ap- prehended could produce no Inconvenience, but muſt bring their mounting on Guard a little quicker about; but that could not be holpen, and was therefore ordered: As alſo the Orders before given, I now renewed in the ſtrongeſt Terms, requiring a frequent Patrole from the Guard every Night, and that the Conſtables would be careful in vi- ſiting the Guard often, and making con-

ſtant

ftant Report to me in Writing of what paffed.

Sunday. Mr. *Simms* obferved the Directions given him by Mr. *Whitfield,* in reading the Prayers of the Church, and a Sermon (out of what Author I know not) in the Forenoon, and after, maintaining the Doctrine of Juftification by Faith alone, in ftronger Terms than had been delivered yet; excluding from Heaven all who came not fully up to that Pitch of Faith, and fuch might reft affured of Sanctification next following, and of their being numbered among the Elect. In the Afternoon a Skooner from *Charles-Town,* laden with fundry Stores for the Ufe of the Army, and bound for the South; having been out a full Week with contrary Winds; fearing they fhould want Water, came up the River for a Supply of that, with Intent to go down again to-morrow, and wait for the firft Wind at *Tybee.*

28.   *Monday.* Volunteers no longer now offering themfelves to enlift, and a few more yet being wanted to compleat the Company; what few Servants remained among us, who were the Property of private Perfons, had Temptations offered them, to exchange their prefent Service for one more valuable; which, without fome Stop put to it, muft have been of mifchievous Confequence: And the General well knowing
ing

ing that, had forbidden it: Moreover, instead of twenty-five Men, which his Excellency said he thought would be an handsome Quota for this Town, if so many
could readily be spared, they had already
enlisted upwards of thirty: Wherefore some
of the Magistrates thought proper to repre-
sent to the Officers, that there was a Necessity of their interposing, to prevent great
Injury accruing to Masters; for if indented
Servants had the Liberty of going off on
this Occasion, possibly there would hardly
be one left in Town: Out of seven that
remained with me, after the Loss of three
by Death and Desertion, I made the Captain a Present of one for this Expedition,
who was a lively Fellow at any Thing but
what I most wanted him for, *viz.* Work;
and all would have gone the same Way
readily. Late in the Evening came Letters
from the General, by the Return of a Boat
lately sent to *Frederica*; wherein were some
short Orders for Mr. *Jones* to observe, *&c.*
but what was most acceptable to us, was
telling us in few Words, " All goes well,
" and the *Spaniards* desert daily."

Tuesday. Most Part of this Day was 29.
taken up by me in going over a List of all
the Inhabitants, and taking personally,
from Tything to Tything, as true an Account of the State of each, as possibly I
could, for the Satisfaction of the honoura-

ble

1740.

April

ble Truftees: Which Work I had of late attempted feveral Times in vain, by reafon of fuch frequent Changes and Alterations happening, during fome Months paft, in this Town and Neighbourhood; infomuch that it baffled my utmoft Endeavours, to make out a Lift perfectly correct; and even now, I cannot warrant but this may need fome Emendation, before it is many Days out of my Hand.

30.

Wednefday. More Letters and Expreffes from divers Parts arrived, for the General; among which one for me from Lieutenant *Willy* in the *Creek* Nation; fetting forth feveral Attempts made by the *French*, to draw thofe People, as alfo the *Chicaffaws*, off from any Alliance with us, and what large Prefents they had made them, of Stores of all Sorts, for Food and Cloathing; and great Plenty of Guns, Ammunition, &c. endeavouring, at any Rate, to make Peace with the *Chicaffaws*, who were ftrongly attached to us, and whofe Bravery in the Field they had experienced many Times to their own Coft; and from what Affurances the General had received from them, they ftill appeared firm in their Friendfhip with us, feveral of their People being gone to ferve in the Wars under him, and more were expected to follow: Moreover, at this very Time, another fmall Party of the *Chicaffaws*, joined by as many *Eu-chies*,

chies, were on their Way down to the
South, under the Conduct of one *Hewet*,
an *Indian* Trader, who came to Town in
the Night paſt, whilſt they followed after.
So many Men as were liſted for Soldiers,
living idle about Town, and frequent Diſ-
orders happening from thence, by their
getting drunk; it was much to be wiſhed
that their Officers would ſend them away
to their Duties; more eſpecially ſince it
was found that the Authors of all Licenti-
ouſneſs, and Contempt of the Civil Power,
at our noted Club, were never wanting to
encourage, and make Sport of, any Diſtur-
bance given to our Peace and Quiet; ſo
that every Thing tending to a Riot, appeared to be what they aimed at.

Thurſday. Having found no convenient
Leiſure for about ſix Weeks paſt, to ſee
what my People at *Bewlie* were doing; I
choſe this Day to make them a Viſit;
where I had the Satisfaction to ſee they had
not been idle, but had planted as much
Land, as could well be expected, in the
Time they were there, conſidering what
Work they had to do, at firſt ſitting down
on a Plantation, in building convenient
Huts, and other neceſſary Conveniences of
Life; falling Abundance of large Timber,
diſbranching that, whereof they had burned
and deſtroyed great Part, and clearing the
Whole from all Shrub-Wood, and other

Impe-

Impediments of Planting; besides their farther going on, and adding to it daily: So that I had good Reason to hope, before the Season of Planting was quite over, I should be yet better pleased with my new Plantation. In my Return home, I stopped at the Orphan-House, which I found carrying on with a great Number of Hands for various Uses, at an unknown Expence; but undoubtedly it must be proportionable to the grand Appearance it already makes, by the two Wings that are now carried up and covered, intended for several Offices: The Body of the Dwelling-House, which is hitherto carried up with substantial Brick-Work for Cellars, &c. to a certain Height, a little above the Surface of the Land, will be very large, and disposed into such Apartments as are, or shall be judged proper, each fronting Angle whereof is to have a Communication with the Offices in the before-mentioned Wings, whether by a Colonade, after the Manner of *Buckingham-House*, or not, I have not learnt. Rain had been much wanted a long while, none falling since the Beginning of *March*; which dry Spring occasioned such as regarded Planting, to fear their Labour would prove fruitless; but we now happily found what we wished for, great Plenty of it overtaking me in my Travel, and I was well
pleased

pleafed to get home in the Evening, thoroughly wafhed to my Skin.

Friday. A bleffed Rain continued moft
Part of the Day, which confined every body at home : Towards Night Letters were
brought me out of the *Creek* Nation from
Lieutenant *Willy*, Mr. *Wiggan*, and others,
by one *Finlay* ; the Contents whereof were
fetting forth many Particulars, relating to
the prefent dubious State and Difpofition of
thofe *Indians*, which it behoved me to lay
before the General by the Opportunity that
firft offered. It feems old *Chigellie*, their
chief *Mico* at prefent, had of late fhewn
an unufual Coldnefs towards meddling in
the Wars that we were engaged in againft
Spain ; telling fome of his People, that
they had no Bufinefs to interpofe among
the white Mens Quarrels : Which Behaviour of his, it is fufpected arofe from fome
French and *Spanifh* Emiffaries among them ;
but the main Body of his People were eagerly bent upon joining the General ; and his
Nephew *Malatchie*, who was the Son of
old *Bream*, the former *Mico*, ftuck clofe
to them, and put himfelf at their Head,
refolving in the firft Place to go himfelf,
and have a perfonal Talk (which is a Term
they ufe) with the General at *Frederica* ;
and whither he was accordingly gone : After which, if he liked the General's Talk,

he

he would return and try who had the best Interest in his Country, he or *Chigellie*.

Saturday. Capt. *Heron* (now said to be Major in the General's Regiment) arrived from *Frederick* Fort at *Port-Royal* in a ten-oar'd Boat, filled with Soldiers, having been sent by the General to fetch a certain Number of the Company commanded by Capt. *Norbury*, to join the other Forces in the South; and he had brought away thence forty-two, what he had not with him, being in a Pettyagua that was coming after. Mrs. *Matthews* arrived in the Afternoon from the South, by whom came several Letters and Orders from the General, and withal, *Malatchie*, accompanied by three or four head Men, and noted Warriors of their Nation, who had been to get a Talk with the General, agreeable to what I noted Yesterday; in which he had made such quick Dispatch, and was so well pleased, that he was now making the like Speed home, resolved to put his Purpose in Execution; and if *Chigellie* opposed him, to cut off his Head: For the farther Explanation whereof, it should be observed, that when old *Bream*, the Father of *Malatchie*, died, his Son was then a Youth; and thereupon *Chigellie* had the Power put in his Hands by the old Men, till *Malatchie* came to the Age of Maturity: During which Time, the young Man has signalized himself himfelf to be a great Warrior, and behaved fo well, that he is now looked on as the greateſt Man of that, or moſt other Nations; which makes him highly eſteemed among them: Nevertheleſs (he ſays) he never intended to take the Government out of old *Chigellie's* Hands, but let him die poſſeſſed of it, had he ruled for the Good of his Country; but now, if he ſhews no longer Regard to the pleaſing his People, it is Time to put an End to his Power; and he thinks himſelf of Age ſufficient to take his own Right, being near Thirty: And as his Ability, as well as his Good-will to the *Engliſh*, is not to be queſtioned; ſo his Perſon is very engaging: His Stature but a little ſhort of ſix Foot, his Make clean, and perfeċtly well ſhaped from Head to Foot, as he appears when naked to his Skin; and when he puts on a Coat and Hat, his Behaviour is ſuch, that one would rather imagine from his Complaiſance, he had been bred in ſome *European* Court, than among *Barbarians*: At the ſame Time, though the Features of his Face were inviting, and ſhew Tokens of Good-Nature; yet there is ſomething in his Aſpeċt which demands Awe. By Mrs. *Matthews* we were moreover informed, that two Men of War were newly arrived at St. *Simon's*; and that the General was preparing to ſet out in few Days for the appointed Place of Rendez-vous:

vous: To whom I wrote by Capt. *Heron*, inclosing thofe Letters I received for him on *Friday* laft.

4.

Sunday. About Two this Morning Capt. *Heron* went down the River, proceeding with his Men for the Camp: And about Eight *Malatchie* went up the River, with his Attendants, intending to ftay a Day or two with Mrs. *Matthews*, whilft a Scarlet Coat, *&c.* with other Prefents for him by the General's Order, were making ready. Mr. *Simms* read the Prayers of the Church, and Sermons on the fame conftant Topick of Faith and Free Grace.

5.

Monday. Nothing of any Kind happened within my Obfervation worth remembring; fo that I had full Leifure at home, to take fuch Matters in hand, as required Difpatch, to be fent for *England*.

6.

Tuefday. Some of our few Freeholders left, beginning again to grow flack in their Duty of keeping a good Guard; upon looking over the Defaulters returned to me by the feveral Tything-men, I had them fummoned before the Magiftrates; when we made the Pockets of thofe that were moft culpable, pay for their Negleft; for it was Time now to be ftrict: And whereas divers of our Tythings were grown much thinner than others, and too weak to make a competent Guard; it was thought beft, in this Cafe of Neceffity, to vary a little

little from the ordinary Cuſtom, and by
reducing two or three of thoſe Tythings,
who had perhaps not more than two or
three Freeholders occupying them, in the
Out-parts of the Town, and joining ſuch
with another Tything, which was a little
ſtronger; by ſo doing, I found, upon a careful Calculation, that we could make out
eighteen Tythings capable of doing conſtant Duty round, with an Officer and
eight Men; which I would be content
with, inſtead of ten that was the original Eſtabliſhment; but a leſs Number
would not be ſufficient, ſome of the Guard
having my Orders to keep the Patrole conſtantly going round the Town in the Night:
This being reſolved, I took Care to ſee Liſts
made out, and given to the ſeveral Tything-
men, of the Names of thoſe eight Men appointed to do Duty under each of them;
which would make a Round of eighteen
Days before they mounted again, and could
not be thought hard: But it is not to be
underſtood from hence, that every Night
produced freſh Men, many of our People
doing frequent Duty upon Hire, or otherwiſe, for others, who perhaps lived remote, or had Avocation on ſuch Buſineſs,
as induced them rather to pay a Man for
ſtanding in their Stead, than ſhewing any
eager Diſpoſition to perſonal Service, unleſs

an

an Alarm were to call them out in good Earneſt.

Wedneſday. Two or three *Indian* Traders arrived from the *Creek* Nation, in order to renew their Licences; by whom I had another Letter from Mr. *Wigan*, relating to ſome farther Apprehenſions they were under of Diſturbances ariſing among them: But as *Malatchie* was now preparing to be with them ſoon, whoſe Fidelity we could rely on, we promiſed ourſelves, and were very confident, that all Doubts of that Sort would ſoon vaniſh. One of Mr. *Fallowfield*'s Boys, from his Plantation in the *Iſle of Hope*, came and brought me a Letter, which he ſaid was left the Day before, by Mr. *Hird* of *Frederica*, who was paſſing by in a Boat for *Carolina*: Upon opening it, I found it was a Letter from Mr. *Verelſt*, dated the 22d of *October* laſt; which (he ſaid) he took the Opportunity of writing by a Ship with Stores of War for the General; and I knew that muſt be Capt. *Wright* in the St. *George*, whoſe Name has been ſeveral Times mentioned before on ſome ſuch like Occaſion: It happened, indeed, to be only a private Letter, acquainting me, that he had ſeen my Son then newly arrived in *England*, who he thought knew of no immediate Opportunity of writing to me; wherefore he very kindly ſent me himſelf what he thought
would

would be the firſt Advice I ſhould have of
his being well; but therein he happened to
be miſtaken ſeveral Months, which is of
leſs Significance, ſince it proved of no Detriment to the Publick; but inevitably it
muſt recur to my Thoughts, what I formerly noted, concerning what I was to
expect by that Ship, &c. whereto I ſhall
add no more now. — About Noon arrived
a trading Boat from *Charles-Town*, bound
up the River (——— *Johnſon* Patroon) by
whom I had Letters from Mr. *Hopton* of
the 29th and 30th *ult.* acquainting me,
that he had ſent by that Boat three Boxes,
one of which directed to me, came out of
England in the *Colcheſter* Man of War,
Capt. *Symonds* Commander; who meeting
with bad Weather, and receiving great Damage in his Rigging, was forced to put
in at *Virginia*; but had ſent that Box by
Sir *Yelverton Peyton*, Commander of the
Hector, bound for *Charles-Town*, from
whom Mr. *Hopton* had received it, and
now ſent it by this firſt Conveyance to
me: In which Box I found a good and
welcome Parcel of Stationary Ware, a large
Packet for the General, and ſeveral other
Letters; among which one from the Secretary, Mr. *Martyn*, to me, and one from
Mr. *Verelſt*; both dated the 5th of *December* laſt; together with ſundry Papers, relating to Mr. *Robert Williams*'s Accounts,
which

which were to be examined, &c. Mr.
Hopton farther wrote me, that the other
two Boxes now fent, came a few Days
before by Capt. *Somerfet*, a trading Ship;
one of which was for *Peter Joubert*, a
Freeholder here; and the other was directed for *Ebenezer*: I was moreover informed by Mr. *Hopton*, that there were yet
in his Cuftody two more Boxes, or Cafes,
which alfo were brought by Capt. *Somerfet*,
but one of them more efpecially, being
of great Weight, and the Patroon of this
Boat therefore not caring to take it in, being already deep laden; I might expect
them both by *Peter Emery*, who was coming this Way very foon. Befides this, Mr.
Hopton referred me to feveral Particulars,
which he had wrote me of the 21ft paft;
when at the fame Time he fent me (as he
now wrote) fome Letters from Mr. *Verelft*,
by Enfign *Tolfon* to *Port-Royal*, and engaged him to forward them from thence:
But as yet I had no farther Tidings of
any fuch Letters.

Thurfday. Capt. *La Feit* intending to
carry off what Men he had raifed, for the
South, this Evening; the Fore-part of the
Day was wholly taken up by me, in
writing divers Letters that Way; which,
together with the Packet I received Yefterday, for the General, I committed to the
Care of *James Carwils*, one of our Freeholders,

holders, who had been an old Soldier, and
formerly a Serjeant in the Army, and was
now going, not a lifted Soldier, but a Volunteer, to be difposed of as his Excellence
faw good; and as there was Room enough
to employ experienced Men, among thefe
yet undifciplined, there was little Reafon
to doubt of his being kindly accepted. It
was no fmall Trouble to the Captain and
his Officers, to get his Men together, out
of the feveral little Holes in Town, where
many of them had been too long debauch-
ing themfelves; fo that the Tide being far
fpent, they were obliged to wait, after their
being on board, till the next Tide ferved;
when they went off before Morning.

Friday. A Skooner in the Service of
the Province of *Carolina*, arrived here from
Port-Royal by Order, to take in Major *Ri-*
chards's Company, who were expected down
from *Puryfburgh*, and fo to the general
Rendezvous in the South, where the Forces
intended for this Expedition were now
drawing together apace. By this Skooner
I had the Packet fent by the Hands of
Enfign *Tolfon*, to be left at *Port-Royal*, and
forwarded from thence; as Mr. *Hopton* had
wrote me in his Letter of the 21ft of *April*,
which accompanied this Packet, as noted
by me on *Wednefday* laft: Under which
Cover I found a Letter to the General, one
to Colonel *Cook*, and one to another Perfon

in the Regiment; besides two for myself from Mr. *Verelst*, one of the 10th, and one of the 12th of *December*; all which came by Capt. *Somerset*, who had been four Months from *England*, in the *Carolina* Packet, on his Passage, last from *Madera*.

10.   *Saturday.* Capt. *La Feit* and his Men now gone, and all spare Hands, for the Camp; the Orphan-House also drawing off a considerable Number, very few remained in Town, to be seen in our Streets; from whence little could be observed.

11.   *Sunday.* Mr. *Simms* went on in executing the Office appointed him by Mr. *Whitfield*, reading the Prayers and Sermons before Noon and after; wherein we found always hitherto the Substance the same, with very little Diversity of Phrase from such former Discourses; which many People seemed to grow weary of hearing.

12.   *Monday.* Mr. *Upton* came to Town from the South, and brought us the News of the General's being gone, with what Forces he had ready, to Fort *Francisco del Pupa* (taken a while since from the Enemy) upon the River St. *Juan's*, being the Rendezvous appointed, where others from divers Parts were daily joining him. In the Evening Major *Richards* arrived at *Savannah* from *Purysburgh*, with Part of his new-raised Company, the other Part being sent off some Time before; and with these he was

I   to

to proceed to-morrow in the Skooner appointed, as noted on *Friday* laſt. All well-meaning Peoples Hearts were now full of good Wiſhes for Succeſs in this Enterprize, of ſo great Importance for the Security of his Majeſty's Dominions in theſe Parts, and the Enlargement of his Power, to bridle the Pride of the haughty *Spaniard*.

Tueſday. His Majeſty's Declaration of War againſt *Spain*, which had lately been publiſhed in moſt of the neighbouring Parts, but never yet here, was by the General's Order read this Day, with due Solemnity at our Guard-Houſe, in Preſence of the Magiſtrates, all the Town-Officers, and moſt of the Inhabitants, under a Diſcharge of all our Cannon, with chearful Acclamations of the People; wherein the new-raiſed Men, under Command of Major *Richards*, joined us; and in the Evening they proceeded Southward, in the Skooner before provided: But before their going off, a little Ruffle happened between our Magiſtrates and the Major, on the following Occaſion. Mr. *Groneau*, one of the Miniſters of *Ebenezer*, coming to Town a Day or two ſince, on ſome Buſineſs, with a Boat rowed down by ſome of their own People, as uſual, came to me complaining, that Major *Richards* had impreſſed one of his Men into the Service, and took him by Force aboard the Skooner,

B b 2   intend-

intending to carry him off; whereupon I recommended him to the Magiftrates, who I told him I was fure would not fuffer a Freeholder of this Colony to be carried away againft his Will: Accordingly upon hearing the Complaint, and finding it to be juft, (for the Man was aboard on the Deck, with two Men as a Guard over him) they fent two Tything-men to demand the Fellow's Appearance before them afhore, where they themfelves then ftood, that they might enquire into the Truth, the Veffel lying faft at the new Wharf: But feveral of the lifted Men obftructed them in their Way, and fet up a great Shout, crying out to their Comrades, *Couragio:* Whereat the Magiftrates feeing themfelves fo comtemned, called particularly to one of the Tything-men (known remarkably for a robuft, daring Man) and bad him lay hold on one of the moft infolent among them, and to bring him before them; whereupon *John Lyndal* the Tything-man inftantly collar'd him, and betwixt him and his Partner, they brought him up the Hill, when the Magiftrates directly committed him into Cuftody: Upon which the Major then appeared, and offered fome Words in Juftification; which made it rather worfe: Wherefore feeing it in vain to contend, he gave up the Man again to Mr. *Groneau*; and upon afking it as a Favour,

vour, the Magiſtrates gave him his Soldier out of Cuſtody. So Peace was concluded, and the Service went forward.

Wedneſday. After ſeveral Days waiting for an Opportunity to ſend the General that Packet which I received on *Friday* laſt, with ſeveral other Letters encloſed, for Colonel *Cook*, &c. I took Occaſion by Mr. *John Pye*, one of our Clerks, now going by the General's Order from hence, to tranſmit it all to his Excellency. Several Matters of Controverſy and Litigation being at this Time brought before the Magiſtrates, aſſembled on that Occaſion at the Stores, I thought it proper to attend them there, at their Deſire, more eſpecially having ſomewhat to offer to their Conſideration, which I conceived would require it: Among the reſt, one *Marmaduke Canon*, an Orphan, and Freeholder here, happening to be ſeen now in Town, I had him brought before them, that due Enquiry might be made concerning him, and the Way of Life he was in, many Stories, and uncertain Reports, often paſſing, which we wanted to get to the Bottom of; and it may not be improper to make a ſhort Minute here, how it appeared to us upon Examination. The Boy was taken by Mr. *Cauſton* (with the Allowance and Approbation, it may be ſuppoſed, of his Brother Magiſtrates at that Time) into his Houſe,

with

with Intent to maintain him; for which undoubtedly his Master had Reason to expect some Service from him: This commenced several Years since, long before I saw *Georgia* in the Year 1736; at which Time I observed him there a lively Youth; from which Period, Mr. *Caustion* then beginning his Improvements at *Ockstead*, the Boy was sent thither, and there employed in hard Labour, as others were; where he has continued ever since, excepting when sent to Town on an Errand. Upon Mr. *Whitfield*'s coming with those Powers lately from the honourable Trustees, to take all the Orphans under his Care, Mr. *Caustion* was the only Person who refused to comply, and persisted in not surrendring him; though some others, who had equal Pretence, gave up theirs, howsoever against their Inclination. The Boy now appeared much dejected, looked poorly, and in miserable Rags, weeping: Upon asking him whether or not he was misused, he seemed under a Terror, not daring to complain; but it was alledged by some of the Bystanders, that his Mistress tyrannized over him with great Cruelty, whilst his Master gave little Heed to Things of that Kind. He was grown a tall Lad, at least five Foot high, and could hardly read his Primer: I asked him whether or not he had received a Gun, which I ordered to be be delivered to him, by the General's Direction; who told me I should give a light *Indian* Gun out of the Stores, to each Orphan Boy that was capable of handling it, who was a Freeholder, that they might be trained, in their younger Years, to do Guard-Duty; which would become habitual, and teach them to be ready in Defence of their own Property: This I had observed, and such of them as I allowed of, were delighted at it: And upon my telling this Boy, that I must not lose a Soldier, but that he must appear this very Evening with his Gun, upon Guard, it being his Turn to come on; and that he must go home, and fetch it from his Master, acquainting him that he came by my Order; he promised to do so, and went his Way; returning in the Evening with his Gun, and did his Night's Duty with the rest very orderly.

Thursday. Young *Canon*, on his Appearance this Morning, and declaring his Desire of leaving Mr. *Causton*, and putting himself under Mr. *Whitfield*; one of the Persons who were left in Charge of the Boys by Mr. *Whitfield*, was sent for by Mr. *Jones*, to whom the Lad was delivered, and he took him with him. All was husht and quiet now in Town, and every body following their own Business, without any Thing happening extraordinary.

Friday.

1740.
May
16.
17.

Friday, } The only Occurrence I
Saturday. } found to obferve thefe
two Days was, that fome Boats from *Carolina* ftopped at *Thunderbolt*, waiting an
Hour or two for the Tide in their Way
South; wherein was Colonel *Barnwell*,
with near thirty other Gentlemen; who
acquainted us, that near thirty more were
gone at the fame Time in the *Tartar* Pink,
all Gentlemen Volunteers, to ferve under
the General in this Expedition.

18.

Sunday. Mr. *Simms* continued to read
the Prayers of the Church, and Sermons,
as before.

19.

Monday. *John Rea*, who went lately
Patroon of a Boat to *Charles-Town*, returned from thence, and brought with
him what Mr. *Hopton* had committed to
his Care, that he had lately received by the
Ship *Ann and Marianna*, Capt. *Campbel*,
newly arrived, *viz.* feveral Packets of Letters, and a Box containing Blank Sola Bills
to the Value of 1000 *l.* Sterling, with many Letters enclofed therein, and Packets
to me for the General, and divers other
Perfons near him: All which it was incumbent on me to haften forward as foon
as might be; as I would alfo take Care to
fee what came for others in this Neighbourhood duly delivered to them: Among
the reft, there was a Packet for Meffieurs
Bolzius and *Groneau*, at *Ebenezer*; and
Mr.

Mr. *Hopton* took this Opportunity of sending another of thofe three Cafes which
came for them in Capt. *Somerfet*'s Ship, as
noted on *Wednefday* the 7th Inftant; but
the largeft was yet in Mr. *Hopton*'s Cuftody, till he could find a fuitable Conveyance. What Letters came for me were
two from Mr. *Verelft*, one of the 28th of
December, and the other of the 25th of
February laft: In the former of which
was enclofed Copy of Mr. *Robert Ellis*'s
Account, &c. and the latter contained Matters of the utmoft Importance, relating to
the Truft; which, to be fure, my Duty and
Fidelity required me to pay the ftricteft
Regard to, and to purfue the Inftructions
fent me, with all Diligence. By this I
now partly underftood what was meant in
that Letter, and Paffage therein, then hint-
ed to me (as noted on the 22d of *March*
laft) wherein the Writer acquainted me,
that it was currently reported the Parliament would make an Enquiry into the
State of this Colony; which many People
feemed to fpeak lightly of, as if it was
likely never to come to any Good.———
Thefe are fome of the Fruits of our de-
teftable Club, who have fo long been labouring to get the Direction of all into their
own Hands; reftlefs under any but their
own headftrong Will, which produced that
memorable Reprefentation, calculated (I am
fully

fully convinced) purely to set *Williams* and *Tailfer* at the Head of the Negro Trade, which they meant to be the sole Importers of; and finding themselves therein mistaken, Malice and Revenge succeeds to such a Degree, that their whole Study appears to be making Mischief at any Rate, and even the utter Destruction of the Whole, were it in their Power, would give them Pleasure: But let them take Care, lest they trip in their Career, and fall headlong at once.

20. *Tuesday.* Mr. *Brownfield* called on me, and shewed me a Letter he had received from my Son, which came not in any Packet directed to me, but (as I observed) was directed to the Care of one *Mackenzie*, Merchant in *Charles-Town*; from whom Mr. *Brownfield* had it, and it was dated the 28th of *December*. The Substance of it was to inform him, of a Design carrying on, to obtain a parliamentary Enquiry into the bad State of this Colony, &c. which he made no Scruple to inform him, he was, among others, a Promoter of, and professed, that what he did therein, he did not desire should be concealed, for that he meant it openly and publick. This, without any Thing else to employ my Thoughts, was more than sufficient for one Day's Disquiet; whereof none can judge, but such only as have the Misfortune to deal with

an

an unruly Son of his own. At our laſt 1740.
parting, and frequently before, too well
knowing the Impetuoſity of his Temper,
I begged and conjured him to promiſe
me not to meddle in any Affairs relating
to the Colony, or to keep Company with
any, whom he knew to have Pique or Ill-
will againſt it: For I knew *Robert Williams*'s Intention was, to be in *London* in
the Winter; and as I alſo knew, that there
was a Familiarity betwixt them here, my
Heart foreboded that no Good would come
of their meeting in *London*, being not unlike in Warmth, but very unequal in Craft.
He knew my Opinion of all that Set of
People very well, and how narrowly I obſerved all their Proceedings here; which he
often, when with me, would blame them
for (in good Earneſt I verily believe at that
Time) and engaged to me in the moſt
ſolemn Manner to keep at a Diſtance from
all ſuch Company, mind his own private
Affairs only, and return to me in the
Winter. What a Shock, therefore, muſt
an old Man feel from ſuch a Blow given
by his own Son? No Letter from him to
frame any Excuſe to me for what he has
done, or to offer at any Vindication of himſelf (and ſo far, perhaps, he judges right,
that it is inexcuſable) but the World, nevertheleſs, will not fail to cenſure the Father
as an Adviſer in this, however contrary to

his

May
20.

his conftant Profeffion, his open Zeal, and even to his Oath; which muft render me infamous, unlefs the honourable Truftees pleafe to entertain more kind and charitable Thoughts of my Simplicity; which from the many Inftances of their paft Benevolence towards me, it would be a Crime in me not to hope for their Continuance of.

21.　　*Wednefday.* Yefterday's Affair fat fo heavy upon my Spirits, that it rendered me incapable of Action; nor could I fhake off that Pain of Mind which I laboured under, all this Day; wherein it fo happened, that no Tranfaction in this Place, was of fuch Confequence, as to need any Remark of mine.

22.　　*Thurfday.* Our Court met, as *per* Adjournment; fat an Hour or two; little to be done; and adjourned farther to the 7th Day of *July* next. This being the Seafon of the Year, when the *Indian* Traders ufually came to renew their Licences; two of them, newly arrived, were this Day with me; one of whom, that had laft Year taken Licence from *Carolina*, doubting he was not well warranted from thence to trade in thofe Towns therein named; now threw it up, and defired a Licence might be granted him from *Georgia*.

23.　　*Friday.* Another Party of Gentlemen Volunteers paffed this Day by *Thunderbolt*, on their Way to the General, which renewed

newed my Sorrow, in thinking how much more commendably my Son might have been fo employed, than in what he has been bufied about at *London*, or elfewhere in *England*. Conferring with fome *Indian* Traders, and adjufting Matters with them, in order to obtain new Licences, or Permits, to continue their former for a Year longer; took up much of my Time this Day. Mr. *Jones* acquainted me, that he had taken a Refolution (after confidering well what I had fhewn him, of Mr. *Verelft*'s writing to me from the Truft, in his Letter of the 25th of *February)* to go South, and wait on the General, and take his Advice, as well on that, as divers other Matters now depending: To which I had no Objection at prefent, but defired him to be as expeditious in his Return as poffible; for that he knew how daring and infolent our good People at *Jenkins*'s were lately grown, even to the Cafting out Threats againft all who oppofed them.

Saturday. Being difappointed in my Expectation of fending off a fmall Packet for *England*, which I had got ready in a Hurry, dated the 14th Inftant, and been forced to keep by me ever fince I prepared it, directed to the Truft's Secretary, Mr. *Martyn*; I now fent it away by the *Carolina* Scout-Boat, *Thomas Bifwick* Patroon, who was bound to *Port-Royal*, where he
engaged

engaged to deliver it fafely to Mr. *Wire*, whom I knew to be a conftant Correfpondent there, with Mr. *Hopton* of *Charles-Town*, and would be careful in fending it to him, together with a Letter accompanying it, that I wrote to Mr. *Hopton:* So very difficult was it now become, for me to carry on a regular Correfpondence any where; all Boats here, and hereabout, being impreffed for the publick Service in the South. This Afternoon I had a full Inftance given me, what the prefent Difpofition was of our mifchief-making Cabal: Mr. *Tailfer*, attended by *William Sterling*, and Landlord *Jenkins* himfelf, thought fit to call on me; the firft as the principal Catechift to examine me; and the other two as able fefquipedarian Evidence, qualified in a tumultuous Manner to promote an Uproar; if they were of Opinion that I acted clandeftinely, and kept back any Thing from them, that the Truftees required me to communicate. Being therefore interrogated, what Letters and Orders I received from the Truft in their laft Packet; and whether, among other Things, I was not enjoined by them to lay divers Affairs relating to the prefent State of the Colony, in open Court before them, for their being enabled to give fuch Anfwers to them as they thought proper? Without difputing by what Authority they took

upon

upon them to take such Examination of
me; I told them plainly, that whilst I
continued to serve the Trust in my present
Station, I should never think myself subject
to give any Answer at all, to what they
demanded in the first Place, of knowing
what Orders or Letters I received at any
Time, but such only as immediately required it: And as to what they more particularly insisted on, *viz.* my exposing to publick View those Affairs before-mentioned,
I said flatly, that I had received no such
Orders; wherein I conceived I departed not
from strict Truth: For upon reading over
again and again those Orders to myself, I
cannot any Way put such a Construction
upon them, as would oblige me to it; neither can it (I think) be justly supposed that
the Trustees meant to have it so; which
would be an effectual Means of defeating
the Purpose they intended by it, and would
put it out of the Power of well-meaning
Men to disintangle Truth from Error, were
these good People to have the Preference of
all in scanning over those Particulars, which
more especially the Trustees expect shall be
set in a true Light; towards which we are
not to look for any Help from them.
They had little more to say to me at present, visibly much out of Humour; and
so they left me, with this farther Admoni-
tion, that if I had no such Orders from
the

1740. the Truſtees yet, moſt undoubtedly I ſhould
May very ſoon: By which I might underſtand,
that their Intelligence came from good
Hands, near the Fountain-Head.

25. *Whit-Sunday.* Mr. *Simms* went on in
reading the Church Service, and two Sermons, Morning and Afternoon, upon the
Reſurrection. Mr. *Jones* determining to
ſet out to-morrow on his Expedition Southward; this Evening I committed thoſe Packets to his Care, which I received lately by
John Rea from Mr. *Hopton*, who had them
out of the *Ann and Marianne,* Capt. *Campbel,* from *England*; with which I wrote
alſo to the General himſelf, encloſing divers
Papers needful.

26. *Monday.* This Holiday-Time (a Word
made uſe of by ſeveral of my Acquaintance)
I was inclinable to comply with the Mode,
and take a Day or two to myſelf: Wherefore I took a Ride to *Bewlie,* to ſee how
they went on at that Plantation, where I
had not been ſince the 1ſt of this Month:
And upon my telling Mr. *Jones* that it
was twelve Miles by Land, and at leaſt
thirty by Water, and that the Boat in its
Way to *Frederica* muſt paſs very near by us
there, he was perſuaded to ſend the Boat
round, and take Horſe with me to *Bewlie,*
where he might refreſh himſelf: He did
ſo, and the Boat came thither four or five
Hours after us; from whence he proceeded
in

in her as foon as the Tide would admit,
which was not till near Night; and then,
not willing to ride through the Woods fo
far alone home, I chofe to ftay all Night
where I was, having a very good Roof
over my Head; and making a good Neft
of Palmeta Leaves, whereon was laid a
Blanket, I laid myfelf upon that, and flept
very heartily.

Tuefday. No Want of Diverfion to employ my Time and Thoughts: It was a
Pleafure to fee my Corn coming on, and
other Things that were planted, very promifing, the live Stock increafing, and all
hitherto in a hopeful Way: Befides the A-
mufement it gave me, in forming Schemes
for many future Improvements in Gardening, and more curious Cultivation of Land,
for the Production of Vines, Mulberries,
Cotton, &c. of all which, I had provided
a fmall Nurfery, in the little five-Acre Lot
near home. Mr. *Mercer*, and another
Neighbour or two, who had Improvements
in thofe Parts, calling on me in the Afternoon, we travelled home together, and
got to Town in very good Time in the
Evening.

Wednefday. No Appearance of any
Thing at prefent to difturb our Quiet;
every body followed his own Bufinefs; and
all I had to obferve was, that Mr. *Bradley*'s
Door being locked up, it was not doubted

but he was gone off to *Carolina*, where he had been for a good while past providing for a Retreat; even before those Orders came from the Truft, requiring him to give good Security, for his not going out of the Province, till his Accompts were made up: Which the Magistrates demanding of him, and often putting him in Mind of, being unwilling (if possibly it could be avoided) to commit him to Prison; and plainly seeing, that he could find not one Man to appear for him (such was the Opinion that every body had of him) they indulged him, upon making large Promises, and giving his Parole of Honour, to appear when required, so far as to enjoy his Liberty of walking the Streets, and employing himself about his Accompts, &c. but upon his asking several Times for a Permit to take a Boat (which is strictly expected from every body) and that being not granted him, he now took Leave without asking, and went off clandestinely by some back Way. It has been sufficiently proved, that had he staid here ever so long, he would have done nothing towards clearing up any Doubts, or Objections, that might be made, but make new Obstacles continually: Wherefore there remained no other Method of going on, in Behalf of the Truft, but to state it as well as it could be done, from his own Accompt delivered in,

com-

comparing it with the Store Books, and leaving proper Room for him (if he thought fit) to make any Remarks of his own, upon any Part where he thought himfelf aggrieved. This being fo done, and ready to receive any fuch Remarks of his, I am apt to think he found it pinch too clofe for him to evade coming to an Iffue; wherefore he left it upon our Hands, as not worth his farther Care, or Notice.— A Man of fuch a finifhed Character, that he moft eminently merits a due Appellation!

Thurfday. Nothing ftirring that was new, and no Intelligence from the Camp for a little while paft; it was Time to expect fome framed at home would be fent out, and pafs currently; which had often fucceeded to the Wifh of the Publifhers, whofe principal Bufinefs it was, to fpread Terrors, that might difcourage weak People, and keep them under continual Alarm: No lefs now than four or five of our People who were gone to War, were faid to be killed by the Enemy, who lay in Ambufh for them; but where or when, none could tell: Neverthelefs the Report went about fo ftrongly, that fome good Wives bewailed the Lofs of their Hufbands with Tears; and I found it no eafy Matter to undeceive them prefently, till the firft Flafh of the Report was pretty well paft,

and

and I found convincing Arguments to fhew them there was no Truth in all they heard, but it was contrived with only a wicked Defign, &c. which at length pacifying *them*, I was not well contented myfelf, to fee three or four audacious Perfons daily going on *impunè*, to difturb the Minds of the People, which they made their Paftime and Delight: But if I can luckily fix upon one of them, with good Proof, to be the Author of fpreading fuch falfe News, I fhall not doubt but the Magiftrates will find Law fufficient to reftrain them for the future, as well as give them their Demerits for what is paft.

30. *Friday.* Nothing occurred of any Moment, but every body wifhed for fome Intelligence what was doing in the South, to clear up thofe Doubts which had for fome Days paft arifen among us, by the Means before-mentioned, which I could find no Grounds for.

31. *Saturday.* The Time was now come, when Truth muft appear, by the Arrival of a Perfon who came immediately from the Camp *(William Ewen)* who had formerly been a Servant in the Stores, and now came away in hafte from Mr. *Houfton*, whofe Employment was to deliver out Provifions to the General's Regiment; fo that he brought no Letters from the General, but made Report, on his own Knowledge,

in

in Subſtance as follows, *viz.* That the General was broke up from the late Camp
on the Main, oppoſite to the Iſland St.
George, and advanced nearer the Enemy:
That upon receiving Intelligence there was
a large Cow-Pen not far off, which had
more than a thouſand Cattle belonging to
it, ſuppoſed to be the King of *Spain*'s own,
for the Uſe of the Gariſon of *Auguſtin*,
and defended by a Fort called St. *Diego*;
his Excellence reſolved to take that in, and
accordingly marched to attack it, making
uſe of a little Stratagem, as well as Force:
Which was, by appointing three or four
Drums together beating here and there in
divers Places in the Woods, and now and
then a few Men appearing ſuddenly, and
then withdrawing out of Sight again;
which the Enemy in the Fort were ſo con-
founded at, not doubting but they were in-
veſted by a greater Number of Troops than
we really had, they made but a feint Op-
poſition, by firing a few Guns over our
Mens Heads (which whether ſo intended
or not, is uncertain) and upon being ſummoned to ſurrender, they did not long he-
ſitate ere they did ſo, on Condition of being treated as Priſoners of War, and (what
they principally inſiſted on) not to be delivered into the Hands of the *Indians* with
us; which was granted; and they were in
Number forty-ſix *Spaniards*, and four Ne-

groes,

groes, moſt of whom were ſent on board our Men of War, only the Commander had his Liberty to walk to and fro in the Camp, on his Parole given to the General; and one other, ſaid to be a Gunner, and upon good Examination found to be an expert one, upon his Requeſt to take on in our Service, the General readily accepted of him; and from what private Intelligence he got of him, ſhews him great Countenance; a very agreeable Inſtrument at this Seaſon. The Camp is now ſaid to be within thirteen Miles of *Auguſtin*, and the General has been ſeveral Times to view it, at a very little Diſtance: Great Numbers of Boats of all Kinds and Sizes lie ready for any Service, within the Mouth of the River St. *Juan*, and two Men of War (the *Phœnix* and *Flamborough*) without all, to protect them; ſome being employed in fetching Mortars, Bombs, and other Stores of Ammunition to the Camp, from *Frederica*, and where elſe they had been landed: Several other Men of War are conſtantly cruiſing, to prevent any one getting into, or coming out of *Auguſtin*; wherefore it is preſumed we ſhall now ſoon hear of the Town's being actually beſieged, which all our Troops are briſk and intent upon: In the mean Time, after ſuch a prodigious Seizure of Cattle, our People eat roaſt Beef in Plenty, and are likely to do

ſo

fo a while to come, as well as mount *Spanish* Horfes, which they alfo took great Numbers of.

Sunday. All Fears being now blown once more over, fuch as were fo difpofed, went quietly to Church, to hear the Prayers read by Mr. *Simms*, and two Sermons, as ufual.

Monday. Advice being brought me by *Jacob Morris*, an *Indian* Trader among the *Cherokees*, who arrived late laft Night, that he had brought down with him out of that Nation twelve Men, whom he had left at Mr. *Matthews*'s, and defired I would fend a Conveyance for them hither; I affured him no Delay in the Service fhould be imputed to me, which was in my Power to prevent: But the great Difficulties we lay under for want of Boats here, which were moftly employed already in the South, muft unavoidably check fuch Expedition in many Cafes, as otherwife we fhould readily make: Soon after, we made Shift to get a Boat however, to go up thither, large enough to bring them all down with the next Tide. In the Afternoon I received Letters from Lieutenant *Willy*, in the *Upper Creeks*, and Mr. *Wigan*, a Trader in the *Lower Creeks*, both fetting forth divers Artifices ufed by the *French* Emiffaries to create a cold Indifference in that Nation towards us: Whereof Notice has before been taken *(vide May* 2, 3 and 7.) but as *Malatchie*

latchie was not arrived, who was every Day expected, when these Letters were wrote that I now received; we expect his Presence among them, on his Return, will alter the Face of Affairs there very soon. In the Evening the Boat came down with those *Indians* from *Matthews*'s, whom I received in the accustomed Manner of greeting, went with them to the House provided for them, and took Care that they had Provisions of Meat, Drink, Pipes and Tobacco, to their Content, after the Rate which had always been allowed.

3. *Tuesday.* A Riot happening lately in the *Lower Creek* Nation, by several unlicensed Traders insulting some of those legally appointed, wounding, assaulting, and binding two or three, and threatning immediate Death to them: For which Violence, Endeavours have been used to seize the Offenders, but hitherto only two of them have been laid hold on; one of whom was catcht at *Frederica*, or near it, whose Deserts the General will best judge of: Another, since taken up in the Nations, was now brought down a Prisoner here, whom the Magistrates have taken in hand; and finding that he was not a Fomenter of the Mischief, but came at the latter End of the Fray, they thought fit to accept of Bail for his Appearance at our next Court, he offering such as was unexceptionable.

tionable. Two or three others, the moſt 1740.
culpable, are yet ſought after, and it is hoped, through Mr. *Kent*'s Diligence at Fort
Auguſta, they will be apprehended in a little Time. My immediate Care at preſent,
was to haſten away thoſe few *Indians* that
came laſt Night; wherein I would not loſe
an Hour willingly: But we were now left
in ſuch a low State, without almoſt any
Boats or Hands to row them, all our
Strength· on the Water being employed in
the South, that it was not inſtantly in my
Power to ſend away this Handful of People after them; but I would leave no Stone
unturned, till ſome Expedient or other
might be found, to accompliſh my Purpoſe. Mr. *Williamſon*, newly arrived from
Charles-Town, called on me in the Form
of a Viſit; and falling of courſe into ſome
Talk of what paſſed ſeveral Months ſince,
relating to the Recorderſhip, &c. I aſked
him, whether or no at that Time he did
not tell me, in caſe he had been in my
Place, he muſt have acted as I did? which
he now confeſſed; but told me the Caſe
was ſince altered, by Mr. *Chriſtie*'s going
off: To which I replied, that the whole
Affair having at that Time been laid before the honourable Truſtees, I could not
perſuade myſelf to think, it would become
me, to take the leaſt Step farther in it, till
I received their Orders fully thereon: And
it

it was well known, that the utmost Extent of my Office, was to be a Vehicle of their Commands, which some People fancied the Title of, the Trusts Letter-Carrier, was a synonymous Term for *(vide May* 6.) We parted in good Humour; and in the next Place I was to expect what an extraordinary Council held at *Jenkins's* would produce.

4.   *Wednesday.* Having Intelligence, that Capt. *Davis* was come into the River at *Tybee*, after much Time lost at *Charles-Town*, his Men being impressed into the Men of War, and himself engaged in much Controversy at Law, which put a full End now to any farther Thoughts about Privateering: He therefore purposed to make the best of his Way to the General in the South, hoping, that as he had shewn him many Favours, he would receive him kindly, and admit the Sloop he had with him into the publick Service, among so many others employed. This I thought a providential Piece of good News for us, whereby it was hoped we might get these *Indians* off our Hands, which we were at so much Loss about before; and therefore I wrote a Letter immediately to the Captain, and sent it by the same Person who came up, and brought us this News, (which was *Elisha Foster*, one of our Freeholders, that sailed with him in some Office) desiring that we might have the Benefit

Benefit of such a Conveyance, which would be shewing a ready Disposition to promote the Service, and making a Compliment to the General, which without Doubt he would take kindly; and that they should be no Expence to him, for they should be fully victualled from hence. This I conceived was so reasonable a Request, that I assured myself it could not be refused; but must wait for his Answer. In the mean while, the Devil had been hard at Work in finding out fresh Means to disturb Peoples Minds, with Rumours of strange Things we were to see very soon, namely, that his Majesty being made sensible of the Hardships which his Subjects of this Colony labour'd under, he was determined to put an End to the Trust, and would establish such Rules, and Forms, as he saw proper to be observed, under a new Governor, whom he would appoint. Howsoever ridiculous this must appear to Men of good Understanding, yet there were not wanting some honest Men of the common Rank, who in a Sort of Consternation came to be informed of the Truth of what they had heard, expecting I would tell them *all the Truth*; but when they found I had nothing to say to it, but laughed at them, for suffering themselves to be so easily imposed on, when they so well knew from whence these vile Stories so frequently

frequently fprang; they went away with equal Shame in themfelves, as Indignation at the Authors, whom they beftowed their Curfes upon bitterly. This is looked upon by many People as the utmoft Stretch of Politicks our Wifeacres of the Club have attempted, vain as it is, but defigned to try how well it would relifh among us. Whether or not Mr. *Williamfon*'s Prefence added any Weight to their Deliberations, does not appear to us without; but undoubtedly they are all big with the Expectation of fomething that is to come to pafs (very foon, as they give out.)

5. *Thurfday.* The Relict of *John Weft*, a while fince deceafed, died this Morning, after a fhort Illnefs; but whether fhe was a Widow or Wife, many People doubted; though fhe cohabited with Mr. *William Kellaway*, a Trader and Freeholder in this Town; and it was faid they were privately married by the *French* Minifter at *Puryf-burgh*, which fome queftioned the Truth of. Mr. *Whitfield*, to the Surprize of moft People, came to Town in a Boat from *Ty-bee*, where he left his Sloop that he failed in from *Penfilvania*, and was a Month or two fooner than expected. Upon my making him a Vifit in the Afternoon, to bid him welcome; he told me, that he had collected upwards of 500 *l.* Sterling for the Ufe of the Orphan-Houfe, on his preaching

ing feveral Sermons, notwithftanding the Oppofition he met with: Whereat obferving it was what I feemed to take particular Notice of; he farther added, that he fhould not think himfelf a Preacher of the Gofpel, unlefs he met with Oppofers: I underftood he had travelled by Land to *New-York* from *Philadelphia*, and back again; after difpatching his Friend, Mr. *Seward*, firft to *Old-England*, before he himfelf vifited the *New*; which he told me was in his Intention the latter End of this Summer, after he had tarried a while here. His Sloop, that he came in, was fully loaden with Provifions of all Sorts, for Food and Cloathing, and ten Paffengers (Men and Women) of divers Trades, ufeful to his Purpofe, *viz.* Taylor, Shoemaker, Glazier, &c. In the Evening (after paufing and hefitating a while) he buried the Corpfe that died this Morning; but after it was in the Ground, and the Service over, he made a Sort of Declamation againft a loofe and debauched Life and Converfation; not fparing the Deceafed, as one who had given publick Scandal to good People, by her Deportment for fome Time paft: Mr. *Kellaway*, her fuppofed Hufband, being at prefent attending the General, as an Interpreter of the *Spanifh* Language, which he is a good

Mafter

1740.
June
6.

Master of, having lived among them several Years in Time past.

Friday. This Morning early *Peter Emery*, with his Boat, arrived from *Charles-Town*, to whom Mr. *Hopton* had committed the Care of the following Particulars, which he wrote me came by the *Charles*, Capt. *Haramond*, on *Sunday* the 1st Instant, and were now delivered to me, *viz.* a large Box directed to the General, and a Letter with it for him; a Box of a less Size directed to me, wherein were Blank Sola Bills to the Value of 1060*l.* Sterling; and with it divers Letters for Messieurs *Jones*, *Parker*, *Fallowfield*, *Christie*, *Bolzius*, &c. and among others, one for me from Mr. *Verelst*, importing the Orders and Directions of the Trust to be observed by me: Withal a new Constitution, appointing Mr. *Parker* first Bailiff, and revoking that which was formerly sent Mr. *Christie*: Also a Constitution appointing *John Pye* to officiate as Recorder, during the Suspension of *Thomas Christie*; and Revocation of Mr. *Williamson* from that Office: Moreover, a Grant of three hundred Acres of Land to the Rev. Mr. *McLeod*, Minister of *Darien*, for the Benefit of him and his Successors, dated *October* 10, 1739, together with a Counterpart for him to execute, &c. I lost no Time in delivering out the Letters, whereat I observed some People appeared as if thunder-

thunder-ftruck, finding themfelves fo defeated in their Defigns: For it was evident
beyond Contradiction, that had the Scheme
fucceeded, which fome few had formed
in their Imaginations, the whole Determination of all Matters would have refted in
the Will of our political Club, who knew
how to lead two of thofe as they pleafed,
who they expected would fit on the
Bench of Juftice; Mr. *Fallowfield* by too
often frequenting that Company, imbibing
many Notions tending to create much Difturbance in this Place, and had of late
fhewn himfelf a Creature of theirs, whom
he advifed with on all Occafions: But I
am unwilling to fay more of that now, hoping he will fee his Error, when he finds
it in vain to fet himfelf in Oppofition to
two of his Brethren; either of whom he
is in no Degree comparable with, in Underftanding or Judgment: And if Mr. *Williamfon*'s being among us for fo many Days
paft, was owing to an Opinion that about
this Time the Truftees Orders would come
for eftablifhing fuch a Court of Juftice, as
he and a few others looked for; I faw no
Obftacle now to his returning when he
pleafed to *Carolina*, till he faw Matters go
more to his Liking. As to myfelf, nothing could be of equal Comfort to me,
under my prefent Anxiety of Mind, with
the kind and tender Regard which Mr. *Verelft*

1740.
June
7.

relſt wrote me the honourable Truſtees expreſſed on that Occaſion.

   Saturday.   Having received a Letter
from Capt. *Davis*, readily conſenting to
what I aſked of him a Day or two ſince,
relating to his Conveyance of thoſe *Indians*
to the South, that were lately come hither,
I ſent them off this Day in a ſmall Sloop,
to be put by her on board the Captain at
Tybee, namely, eleven *Cherokee Indians*, and
nine *Chicaſſaws*, together with their Con-
ductors, and a few other white Men that
accompanied them out of their Nations,
making in all about thirty Men : And with
them I ſent the Box that I had newly received for the General; as alſo the Letter
that came with it; together with Letters,
and various Diſpatches to his Excellency,
from myſelf, and others in theſe Parts; all
which I charged Mr. *George Currie* with
the Care of, whom I always had looked
upon as a ſedate, ſober Perſon, to be confi-
ded in : Which is more than I can ſay of
many of our *Indian* Traders, that are too
much addicted to a looſe Way of Living.
This Afternoon I entertained myſelf by
looking into my little Plantation and Nurſery near the Town, where I ſpent a few
Hours; which, though ſo nigh, was more
than I could find Leiſure to do for a Fortnight paſt.

                                Sunday.

Sunday. Mr. *Whitfield* appeared to be returned to his Miniſtry here, with double Vigour; and after reading the Common Prayer, what he delivered *extempore*, as well in Prayer as Sermon, ſeemed to be with uncommon Vociferation and Waſte of Spirits; enforcing the Doctrine of original Sin, and the Neceſſity of a Regeneration, Converſion, and Juſtification by Faith in Chriſt, &c. otherwiſe Hell was ready to receive us. It matters little how far I thought all he ſaid was ſound Divinity; but unleſs he abates ſome of his Threats to keep Heaven Gates ſhut, againſt all whom he ſhall think unworthy to enter in, I fear the Conſequence will be bad.

Monday, } The violent Heat of Wea-
Tueſday. } ther more than ordinary, which People felt for a few Days paſt, made the moſt Hardy ſubmit to it, and leſſen their Labour: And I found ſuch Influence from it on my own Spirits, that every Thing I attempted becoming irkſome, I acquieſced in an indolent State, as others did, waiting a little refreſhing Change of Air: My Thoughts, however, were not aſleep, but ſufficiently buſied about thoſe weighty Matters, which thoſe Letters contained, lately ſent me from the Truſt; and I began now with ſome Impatience, to look for Mr. *Jones*'s Return from the General, after more than a Fortnight's Ab-

1740.
June 8.

9.
10.

fence, that we might join in our Endeavours, to anfwer what was required. By a Boat arrived this Day *(Tuefday)* from *Port-Royal,* we learnt, that Capt. *Davis*'s Sloop at *Tybee,* with the *Indians* on board, was not yet failed thence; but the Captain told him he intended to put to Sea this fame Night; whereat I began to grow a little uneafy, wifhing him gone.

11. *Wednefday.* This Day we had Intelligence again of another Rifing of the Negroes in *Carolina,* which, unlefs foon fuppreffed, has the Appearance of greater Danger than any of the former; forafmuch as this broke out near *Charles-Town* itfelf, about *Afhley* River, *Dorchefter,* and the circumjacent Parts, where at leaft a hundred and fifty were got together in Defiance: But as they were yet unprovided with Arms, and there was no Corn on the Ground ripe, for their Subfiftance, it was hoped they would quickly be difperfed: And the Country being all alarmed and in Purfuit of them, they had already taken about fifty, whom they were daily hanging, ten in a Day. Such dreadful Work, it is to be feared, we may hear more of in Time, in cafe they come to breaking open Stores to find Arms, as they did the laft Year; and are able to keep the Field, with Plenty of Corn and Potatoes every where; and above all, if it is confidered,

I how

how vaftly difproportionate the Number of white Men is to theirs: So that at beft, the Inhabitants cannot live without perpetually guarding their own Safety, now become fo precarious. What Inference may be drawn from hence, with relation to this Colony, will be beft done by the honourable Perfons who make the Welfare of *Georgia* their Study. I had this Afternoon the Pleafure of feeing a Beginning made, of a Work long wifhed for, *viz.* building a Church at this Town, a few Load of Stones being brought, and laid down in the Place where it is intended to ftand.

Thurfday. This Day began with the melancholy News of more Duelling, at the Camp in the South, and the fatal Confequence of it. Enfign *Tolfon*, of Capt. *Norbury*'s Company, having a Quarrel with Mr. *Eyles*, a Surgeon in the Army, they fought; and the latter was killed on the Spot; a Man of very good Skill in his Profeffion, and well efteemed. Not many Days after, *Peter Grant*, lately of this Town, and a Freeholder, afterwards made Naval Officer at *Frederica* by the General, and fince changing, to be a Cadet in the Army; having a Quarrel with one Mr. *Shenton*, a Cadet likewife; which Mr. *Shenton* endeavoured (as far as he well could) to avoid deciding by the Sword; but the other admitting of no Terms of Reconciliation,

they

1740. they fought, and the Aggreſſor dropt dead.
June Theſe Tidings came by a ſmall Boat, on
its Way from the Camp to *Charles-Town*,
which ſtopt and left it at one of our Out-
Plantations; and is looked on with great
Pity: It is not very long ſince Enſign *Leman*, in a Rencounter, being wounded in
his Leg, and a Mortification enſuing, he
was forced to ſuffer an Amputation, and
ſupply its Place with a wooden one. Surely
our Enemies will hear this with Pleaſure.
After three or four Days Detention at *Tybee*, by contrary Winds, I was now adviſed, by a Boat from thence, that Capt.
Davis, with the *Indians* lately taken by
him on board his Sloop, ſailed Yeſterday to
the South; which I was very glad to hear.
In the Evening Mr. *Jones* arrived from
thence, having been about ſeventeen Days
on this Expedition.

13.   *Friday*.   In frequent Conference with
Mr. *Jones*, I learnt the General's Opinion
in divers of thoſe Matters which had been
laid before him, for our better Conduct;
and withal, his Excellency's near Approach
to the Fortreſs of *Auguſtin*; wherein various Conjectures were made, whether they
ſhould meet with an obſtinate Defence,
or the contrary; but a very little Time
now, would let us ſee the Event, which
every good Man had much at Heart. It
was obſervable, that ſince the Anſwers I
had

had given to thofe Queftions, demanded of 1740.
me on the 24th *ult.* thofe Examiners, or
fome of the fame Fraternity, were often
on Horfeback, taking a Progrefs through
moft of the Plantations, as well near, as
more remote, looking on themfelves as Sur-
veyors, and Infpectors, appointed fo to do;
and it was not improbable, that their Cor-
refpondents in *England* had fo advifed them,
in order to fee how well the different Reports would agree, which muft be expected
from hence hereafter; when without Doubt
no Pains would be wanting in them, to
accumulate Abundance of Grievances, to
obviate any Pofitions, or Sentiments offered,
by Perfons who retain a juft Opinion of
the impartial Proceedings of the honourable
Truftees.

Saturday. A Sloop from *New-York* 14.
(—— *Tingley* Mafter) arrived with fundry
Sorts of Provifions for Sale; but no Beef,
or Pork; which being greatly wanted, we
were much difappointed in our Expectations, not knowing which Way to come at
any this Summer Seafon: Wherefore, after
fome few Things of leaft Value were taken
off his Hands, he defigned to proceed with
the Bulk of his Loading to the Army in
the South, confifting of Flour, Rice, Bif-
cuit, ftrong Beer, Wine, &c. which would
be welcome there, to make ufe of with
their choice Food, that they were lately

fo

fo happily fupplied with at St. *Diego* from the *Spaniards* (much Good may it do them.) As for us here, though it is too early yet to meet with Beef that is thorough fat; we are obliged for Subfiftance to kill now and then a Steer, perhaps once in ten Days, which we debet ourfelves with as Cafh, and fell out, to the People who are able to pay for it, in fmall Pieces, for immediate Ufe; otherwife it will corrupt, Salt not availing to cure during thefe Heats. I cannot pafs over this, without offering my poor Opinion humbly thereon to the honourable Truftees (as I think I have done fome Time formerly) that if they would pleafe at a proper Seafon in the Winter, or early in the Spring, to fend us a Veffel of pretty good Burden, laden in *Ireland* with good Beef, fome Tallow, a little Butter, and nothing elfe; it would be gladly received, and accounted for as Cafh, and put us out of all Anxiety about Meat, which we always fuffer at this Time of Year, for about four or five Months, when it is not to be had for Money by the moft induftrious among us, otherwife than as I have faid.

15. *Sunday.* Mr. *Whitfield* performed the Divine Service, with fuch a devout Emotion of Spirit, as nobody could juftly blame him for: After which he dwelt a while on *extempore* Prayer (as ufual;) and in his Preach-

Preaching, I was very glad to obferve him more temperate in his Utterance, than fometimes he appears: Nor did I think his Reafoning a Jot the lefs enforcing, without Ranting.

Monday. Another Set-out this Morning, with two or three of our new-appointed Infpectors from *Jenkins*'s, to make what Obfervations they thought proper, and report to their Principals, how they found Matters at their Return : Which without Doubt they meant to apply to a right Ufe, for perfecting the Work of Reformation, which they had fo long been labouring in, for the Good of the Colony. Late in the Evening Mr. *Whitfield* took Boat up the River, to make a Vifit at *Ebenezer*, accompanied by Mr. *Groneau*, one of the Minifters there, who was come hither to wait on him. I could not find any Thing elfe all this Day to make Remark of.

Tuefday. The Weather happening to be rainy, was a little Baulk to our Infpectors, who thought it beft to repofe themfelves at Mr. *Fallowfield*'s Plantation thefe two Days; where it may be prefumed they found Matter in Difcourfe, to make farther Improvement on in due Seafon : All we could know of their Proceedings was, that they returned home again this Afternoon, as wife as they went. Spending an Hour or two with Mr. *Jones* at the Store (as I frequently

16.

17.

ufe

ufe to do) he told me Mr. *Whitfield* had made him a Vifit there the Day before, complaining to him, that he thought himfelf hardly ufed by him (Mr. *Jones)* during the Time of his Abfence in the Northern Provinces; by taking away one of the Orphans out of his Houfe, in an authoritative Manner, whereas he could have no fuch Authority; which might in Effect deftroy the Deed of the Truft to him. Mr. *Jones* alledged the General's pofitive Orders to him, to do what he did: But that availed little with Mr. *Whitfield,* who faid he was refolved to write thereupon to the Truft. Wherefore, being no Party myfelf in this Affair, it may not be amifs to recollect what I remember about it.———— *Mellidge,* a Freeholder here, and one of the firft forty, at his Death left feveral Orphans, whom the General (then only Mr. *Oglethorpe)* fhewed particular Marks of his Favour to, for their Father's Sake, whom he looked on as a valuable Man; and in the Procefs of a few Years, the eldeft Boy proving to be an active, diligent, and well-grown Youth, he was become ferviceable, in many Cafes, to his good Patron, and employed by him varioufly, as Occafion required: The eldeft Sifter began now likewife to be capable of managing the Houfe at home, and guiding the young Family: Whereupon the General

neral laft Spring encouraged them to begin, and try what they could do about Planting, intending feemingly thereby to fhew, what might be expected from Boys, if encouraged, and well looked after. About that Time it happened, that Mr. *Whitfield* came, with the Power which the Truft had granted him, for taking the Orphans under his Care; among whom the Younger of thefe two Brothers *(Mellidge)* was taken by him for one, leaving the Elder at home; who complained, that his Brother being taken from them at this Time, when he could be of fo much Ufe; it would be a Means of breaking up a Family that were now come to the Point of fhifting for themfelves: Which agreeing exactly with the General's Thoughts (then at *Frederica)* he fent Orders to Mr. *Jones*, to take the young Lad home to the Family, which now would be no Charge to the Publick: And on that Occafion was pleafed to write his Sentiments relating to the Orphans; which (as I remember) I enclofed Copy of to Mr. *Verelft*, for the Perufal of the Truft; whofe Opinion we fhall now hope for, upon Mr. *Whitfield's* laying this Cafe before them.

Wednefday. A profound Quiet; and nothing ftirring all Day worth taking Notice of.

Thurfday.

1740.

June 19.

Thurſday. After having at ſundry Times conferred with ſome Perſons, whom I thought I could repoſe the greateſt Confidence in, relating to what the Truſt had been pleaſed to impart to me, of the Parliament being appealed to, by ſome of our Malecontents, who ſought all Ways to give them Trouble: And by Degrees informing ſuch as I knew to be open-hearted, well-meaning People, what Means the honourable Truſtees propoſed, to defeat their malicious and baſe Deſigns, namely, by our atteſting the Truth, of what we knew to be ſuch, in ſeveral Articles they had ordered to be laid before us: (In the doing whereof it behoved me to act with the utmoſt Caution, leſt a *Judas* ſhould be found among us) I thought as little Time as poſſible ſhould be loſt in reducing ſome of our Thoughts into Writing: For which Purpoſe I conceived, that three or four at a Time meeting, would be ſufficient; who were ſtedfaſt to the Truth, and utterly averſe to all ſuch Clamour as they ſaw made of late; which they rightly apprehended muſt produce great Miſchief, if ſuffered to go on: Thus in ſome Meaſure prepared, I reſolved, in a Day or two more, to make a Beginning, and try whether or not we could produce ſomewhat towards the Support of Truth, at leaſt as valid as what our woful Patriots brought forth at *Jenkins's*,

to

to difguife it. Mr. *Williamfon*'s Stay fo long among us here, gave Occafion for various Reports (now in other Folks Turn) to fly about, and affign fome Caufe for it, right or wrong : Some faid he was fending for his Wife to come to him ; from whence others concluded, that *Charles-Town* was too hot for him —— at this Seafon ; and fuch Stories ftill improving as they go, a great many Things were talked of to his Difcredit ; which, without fure Grounds, I would not, in common Charity, be the Reporter of ; Time will difcover greater Myfteries than this.

Friday. The *New-York* Sloop that arrived here laft *Saturday*, after difpofing of a few fmall Wares, which were of little Value ; and intending to fail for the South this Day, I wrote by her to the General, &c. giving my Letters in Charge to Mr. *Minis*, a *Jew* Freeholder of this Town, to whom the Loading was configned. Two or three *Indian* Traders, wanting to renew their Licences, and pretty much fluftered in Drink (which is pretty common among them) took up more of my Time this Day with their Impertinence, than I could well afford. 20.

Saturday. To purfue my Defign of *Thurfday* laft, with as little Delay as poffible ; I now called to my Affiftance three fuch as I had no Doubt of their Qualifications 21.

tions

tions or Good-will, to promote that neceſſary Piece of Service, namely, Meſſieurs
Parker and *Jones*, firſt and third Bailiffs,
and *Mercer*, firſt Conſtable: When we
ſpent a few Hours together, in an hearty
Concurrence of Opinion on what was under our Conſideration; which we hoped,
in due Time, to reduce into ſuch Form, as
we might be able to juſtify to every Perſon
unprejudiced, who had a real Diſpoſition
to maintain Truth: And at parting we reſolved to meet again, and communicate
our Thoughts to each other, as often as
conveniently might be. Mr. *Jones* afterwards, in Diſcourſe on various other
Matters betwixt ourſelves, ſhewed a great
Diſlike of ſeveral of Mr. *Whitfield*'s
late Proceedings; more eſpecially with Regard to calling his Authority in Queſtion,
concerning what he did lately about young
Mellidge (which I took Notice of on *Tueſday* laſt) and Mr. *Whitfield*'s having wrote
a Letter to the Truſt thereon, complaining
of Mr. *Jones*, without acquainting him
that he intended ſo to do, before their late
Conference on that Affair; which Mr.
Jones reſented very much; and I plainly
found, by his warm Expreſſions, it was
likely to come to an open Rupture between
them: One, on all Appearance, ſetting little Value on any Power, either eccleſiaſti-
cal or civil, which claimed a Superiority
over

over him; and the other, not much heed- 1740.
ing what Obedience was paid to Church
Government, refolved not to abate one Iota June
of what he thought due to the Civil Magiftrate.

Sunday. Mr. *Whitfield* ftuck clofely to   22.
his Vocation, in praying and preaching *extempore*, as was his Cuftom, after the appointed Service was firft read: But the Sur-
plice for fome Time paft feemed to be laid
afide as ufelefs. The Morning Service was
on one of the Beatitudes, concerning hungring and thirfting after Righteoufnefs;
which he treated of to very good Purpofe
a while; till at length he had wound himfelf up into one of his ordinary Rhapfodies,
touching a New Birth, Conviction, Con-
verfion, Free Grace, Juftification by Faith,
&c. which, be the Subject what it would,
all his Difcourfes terminated in: And now
he told us plainly, that unlefs we were fo
far advanced in the Knowledge of Chrift,
as to have a full Affurance that we felt the
Holy Spirit move within us, we were as
uncapable of hungring and thirfting after
Righteoufnefs, as the Stones in a Wall;
without which, neverthelefs, we were all
in a reprobate State, &c. &c. In the Afternoon he took St. *Paul*'s Words to *Timo-
thy*, in his 2d Epiftle, 3d Chapter, and
12th Verfe, for his Subject: Wherein addreffing himfelf to thofe few particularly,
                                        who

who were his ſtricteſt Diſciples, and ſcarce-ly allowed themſelves to converſe with any that had not found the Spirit yet upon them, he ſhewed what the Word Perſecu-tion imported in its full Latitude; and that from the Apoſtle's aſſerting, all who will live holy muſt ſuffer Perſecution, it was plainly begun already, in oppoſing the Doc-trine he taught, and ridiculing the conver-ted Saints, who endeavoured to live up to it: Bidding *them* be of good Cheer, to ſtand faſt together as Brethren: And as for himſelf, he was expecting all cruel Treat-ment from his Adverſaries, who were ſet on by the Devil; all which he was ready to undergo. This Point he had lightly touched on, twice or thrice before; but now he was grown more vehement; which occaſioned ſome Talk after Church was over, ſeveral Conſtructions being put upon it; and among others, Mr. *Jones* would needs have it, that *he* was one pointed at, next under the General himſelf.

23.   *Monday.* From the Time of my Arrival here in the Truſt's Service, on *November* 1, 1737, I had divers Times notified the Danger I apprehended from the Decay of the Sea-Mark at *Tybee*, leſt it ſhould come to Ruin for Want of timely Care to pre-vent it, which would bring a Reproach from all the trading People in theſe Parts, for ſo ſhameful a Neglect, and alſo might

prove

prove of very bad Confequence to many: But all I could fay upon it, proved of no Effect, fome publick Work or other ftill taking Place, as more immediately needful; infomuch that not any Survey had been taken of the Condition it was in; till now, upon the Truft's making particular Mention of it, in their late Letter; and thereupon my urging it again, it was agreed by Mr. *Jones* and me to go down this Day; as we did; and taking fufficient Workmen with us, who were competent Judges of the State it was in; it was very grievous to me to hear every one of them declare, that it was not in the Power of Man now to repair it, it was fo far gone to Ruin: And it would hardly have been thought credible by me, what I now faw myfelf, how greatly the Deftruction of it was increafed, fince the laft Time I faw it, which was in *October* laft, when I conceived it might have been fomewhat holpen; and fo I reported it at my Return, after going on board Capt. *Thompfon*, at that Time there: But every Part, both of the upper and lower Work, was now fo perifhed, and all the Joints become fo rotten, that it was rather to be admired it yet ftood as it did, many of the Braces frequently dropping; and it muft now be expected, as foon as the ftrong North-Weft Winds come, which we ufually look for

in

1740.

June 23.

in Autumn, it muſt tumble all together. Under theſe melancholy Apprehenſions we returned home.

Tueſday. The Heat of the Weather a-bàting, which had confined me at home all Day; towards Evening, in my Walk to catch a little Breeze of Air, I accidentally met Mr. *Williamſon,* who ſoon found ſomething to ſay to me; and ſo we fell into Diſcourſe from one Thing to another; wherein he took Pains (as I thought) to make me believe, how much better Opinion he had of *Georgia,* where he once lived, than *Carolina,* where the Buſineſs he was in obliged him at preſent to be reſident: Then he inveighed againſt the Vanity of the Inhabitants, and the inveterate Ill-will they almoſt in general bore to this Colony; which they would talk of with great Contempt, though at the ſame Time they were under ſtrong Apprehenſions, that in a few Years it would outdo them in Trade and Manufactures too, who in ſuch a Length of Time had attained to nothing but Rice. I told him, in my Turn, that we were under no Pain at ſeveral of our People deſerting this Place, laſt Year particularly; moſt Part of whom have experienced, to their Coſt (ſome with the Loſs of their Lives) what an unhappy Change they made: Some are eſcaped out of their Miſery there, and returned to poor *Georgia,*

glad

glad to be admitted again to work for their
Bread among us; and one Family or two
more, as I am advised from them, are purposing the like just now. I could not refrain from adding, that if we can be so
happy to get Possession of *Augustin*, I did
not doubt but we should quickly see some
of the fine Folks at *Charles-Town* looking
out for a Place to sit down in, more in the
Way of a *Spanish* and *West-India* Trade,
than where they are; and might be glad
to submit to the Constitution of *Georgia*,
which so much Pains had been taken to ex-
plode. He replied, that he was firmly of
that Opinion; and whatever some might
think of *him*, he would not quit what Interest he had in Land here, for 200 *l.* Sterling: Then he told me, that I guessed
right in what I said; for that to his Knowledge, several were hunting about for Titles
of Grants of Lands, run out here formerly; and among others, he said the Attorney-General had sent his Service to me by
him, and advised me, as a Friend, not to
be at any farther Expence in making Improvements, as I was going on at my Plantation; for that he had a good Title to a
large Tract of Land there (I think he
said a Barony) wherein mine, which I
held from the Trust, was included: I smiled, and desired him to return my Compliments to that Gentleman; and to assure

him, I fhould not ftop my Hands at *Bew-lie*, nor be in any Pain about the Title to it; and fo we parted. —— *Fas eft & ab Hofte doceri.*

25.   *Wednefday.* Very little worth taking Notice of; But I found, upon fome Talk I had with Mr. *Jones,* that no good Underftanding was yet to be looked for, betwixt him and Mr. *Whitfield*; for that he had fent this Morning to one of Mr. *Whitfield*'s principal Actors to come to him, whom he had difcourfed with very freely, and plainly told him divers Things, wherein he thought Mr. *Whitfield* to blame, as to his outward Conduct and Behaviour, efpecially with refpect to the General, whofe Name, at any Time when mentioned, he feemed to make light of; and if it was made ufe of in any Inftance, where his Approbation was judged needful, Mr. *Whitfield* commonly would exprefs his Diflike of it, by faying —— What have I to do with the General? or Words to that Effect: Seeming to infift on it, that in all Cafes he fhould have Regard only to the collective Body of the Truftees. Mr. *Jones* added farther (as he faid to me) that he could not but take Notice of Mr. *Whitfield*'s going on fo unadvifedly as he did, in paying fuch an *extravagant* Price for Stones, which were now bringing, in order to begin building a Church, without ever confulting,

fulting, or advising, with any one but himfelf; when he knew he was directed by the
Truftees, to confer with me thereon; and
the General moreover had directed both
him (Mr. *Jones)* and me, to be affifting to
him in promoting that Work; efpecially in
the Laying out and Difpofal of the 150 *l.*
lately advanced towards it from the Truft,
who, as Guardians of all the Benefactions
for that Purpofe, have moft undoubtedly
a Right to appoint Officers of their own,
to infpect and controll the Difburfement
thereof, *&c. &c.* All which, the Perfon
whom it was faid to, was charged to acquaint Mr. *Whitfield* with; and it is to be
prefumed he did fo. Here it may be proper to explain the Occafion of the Word
extravagant being made ufe of as above.
One *William Gough,* a Freeholder here,
who near two Years fince left this Place,
and went to *Carolina,* taking up his Abode
at *Port-Royal,* where he made a poor Shift
to live, by teaching little Children to read;
had it neverthelefs ftill at heart, to return
again fome Time or other to *Savannah,*
where he hoped to fee more Profperity; on
which Account, to preferve his Claim, he
took Care that his Guard-Duty fhould be
performed duly: For which End he left
the Care of his five-Acre Lot to *Duchee*
the Potter, who in Lieu of Rent would
provide for the faid Duty; and has conti-

E e 2   nued

nued fo to do : But *Duchee* having before made fome Trial what that Lot would produce, found in it a plentiful Quarry of Iron Stone; went to work upon it, and turned out a confiderable Quantity of fuch Stone; which was then looked upon as a Rarity; and he fold a great deal of it to divers People for various Ufes; fome for building Chimnies, and fome for other Purpofes; at the Rate of two Shillings *per* Load, and at one Shilling *per* Load for digging, befides Carriage; by which he got a pretty deal of Money : And that put fome others upon Experiments, whether or not the like could not be found in their Lots : Among whom, Mr. *Mercer* happened to find fome on his Lot, at leaft equally good with the other; which he offered to any one that would dig it, and fetch it away, at Sixpence a Load; and which we intended to make ufe of at that Rate, for fuch publick Work as we were directed to carry on, *viz.* about the Houfe lately Mr. *Bradley*'s, *&c.* and would exceedingly differ from the Rate which Mr. *Whitfield* was to get them at from Mr. *Duchee*.

26. *Thurfday.* An odd Humour being lately fprung up among fome of our People for Horfe-Racing, feveral Days fucceffively; it gave me a Jealoufy of fome farther latent Defign; when I obferved it was promoted by that defperate Crew, whofe whole
Study

Study and Employment was to difturb the
Quiet of the Place, and keep the Spirits of
the Well-meaning in a continual Flutter.
The Horfes were ordinarily mean and low-
prized, fuch as are moftly adapted to common Ufes, for Hire, &c. the Riders alfo
ready, for Payment in Drink, to contribute
to the Diverfion : The Race a little more
than a Quarter of a Mile, from the Gate
of the publick Garden, to the Midft of
Johnfon's-Square. This anfwered the Purpofe of the Bettors (Dr. *Tailfer* and his Affociates) very well, and occafioned a Gathering together of a Number of People,
idling ; among whom, a great Number of
Children, in the Way of Danger (as I
thought.) After the Race was over, it was
very remarkable, that inftead of going to
Jenkins's, *Tailfer* directed the Bets to be
fpent at another publick Houfe ; for this
Reafon only, as I could find ; becaufe he
could there find more People to talk to,
than at their Club ; feveral not fcrupling to
go here, who would have thought it a
Scandal on themfelves to be feen in their
Company at the ufual Place of their meeting. Seeing Matters thus carried on, I had
the Curiofity to try if we could not penetrate farther into what they were doing :
Wherefore Mr. *Jones* and I went in the
Evening to the fame Houfe (Mr. *Parker*
being out of Town at his Plantation ;) and

1740.
June
26.

E e 3   taking

taking a little Room adjoining to this Affembly, we called for a Glafs of Wine, fitting to obferve what paffed: Where we
foon difcovered what I gueffed to be their
Bufinefs; and could hear diftinctly their
Prolocutor, difplaying his Parts moft vehe-
mently to his Audience, in a long Harangue; to fhew how grievoufly ill-ufed
this poor Colony had been, for a great
while paft, through the arbitrary Proceedings of thofe who had the Government of
it: And now at laft, after all, they could
imagine, that People were to be fweetened
by fome trifling Amendments which they
thought fit to make, in relation to the In-
heritance of their Lands: But he would
make it appear it was the bafeft Tenure in
Chriftendom; and that it was not in the
Power of any Man living to be fafe in
what he held, it being liable to fuch a
Multitude of Forfeitures, which the Gran-
tors would, at their Pleafure, take Advantage of: But he hoped in few Months to
fee a new Leaf turned over, and that Juftice would be done by a fuperior Power:
And as for thofe Tools who worked under them here (meaning, without Doubt,
fuch as had the Execution of the Truft's
Commands) it was in vain for them to
conceal their Inftructions; for all muft now
very foon come to Light, &c. with Abundance more fuch like Ribaldry, too long

2   to

to dwell upon here; all tending to inflame his Hearers, and excite Disturbances. I could not find, however (with all this Contrivance) that any Person of good Character had joined their Company; only two or three loose, idle Fellows, were got among them, who had more Regard to their Share of Drink in the Wagers lost, than to the Doctor's Eloquence: But the stanch Members of the Club stuck together, as at other Times. After about an Hour's Stay, my Companion having no longer Patience to bear such Roasting among others; we walked off, and left them to make what they pleased of it.

Friday. The same Humour of Horse-Racing going forward, my Apprehensions increased, of the Consequence proving pernicious, from such mad, tumultuous Work; and I could not forbear imparting my Sentiments of it to Mr. *Jones*, as a Magistrate; recommending a Stop to be put to it, as a Breach of the Peace; by their publishing an Advertisement, forbidding such illegal Assemblies; which undoubtedly ought to be deemed so, in the Heart of the Town, how warrantable soever they might be at a Distance out of it: Wherein he seemed to be tacitly of my Opinion; but no other Magistrate being then to be found, it rested for the present; and the Sportsmen, as Yesterday, took a plentiful Cup in the Evening, imbibing (I fear) but little Good under fo fignal a Conductor.

Saturday. Capt. *Patrick Mackay,* going for *Charles-Town,* I wrote fome Letters by him to Mr. *Hopton,* and others. Meffieurs *Whitfield* and *Jones,* coming (in outward Appearance at leaft) to a better Underftanding, I was invited, with Mr. *Jones,* to Dinner at the Parfon's, where he acquainted us with his Intention of going the Beginning of the Week for *Charles-Town*: But whether he fhould go farther, or not, he was not fully determined, for that he purpofed to be back again here in about three Weeks. Private Information was brought me this Afternoon, that a Paper, ready drawn at *Charles-Town,* full of more fad Complaints againft our chief Rulers, and inferior Magiftrates alfo, was fecretly crept into this Place, with Intent to be handed about, and to get as many Names to it, as could be had among our Malecontents: But what Title it bore, whether it was by Way of Petition, or Remonftrance, my Informer could not yet learn; only he promifed to ufe his beft Endeavours to get farther Knowledge about it very foon, *viz.* whofe Framing it was, what the Subftance of it, and whom it was intended to be prefented to. One of this Kind of Productions, I before took Notice of, was beginning to appear about the Middle of *April* laft; but

by

by what Means it proved abortive, I could never learn.

Sunday. The publick Service was duly obſerved, as uſual; and Mr. *Whitfield* gave an inſtructive Diſcourſe on the barren Fig-Tree. After Church we had the ill News, by a trading Boat juſt arrived from *Charles-Town*, of a ſharp Action that happened lately near *Auguſtin*, wherein we loſt about ſeventy Men; and it was related thus, *viz.* That Colonel *Palmer*, a Gentleman of good Fortune in *Carolina*, and an old Officer there formerly, but now not commiſſioned in this new-raiſed Regiment, and ſerving as a Volunteer, was appointed by the General, with the Command of about a hundred Men, to take Poſt at a certain Diſtance from the Town, towards the Land: That in the Morning, about Day-break, or before, a Body of five or ſix hundred *Spaniards* out of the Town attacked them; when they defended themſelves bravely a while, and repelled them twice; but being over-powered with Numbers, a great Slaughter enſued, and two Thirds of our Men fell by the Sword; but not without making the Enemy pay dearly for their Lives: Among the Dead was Colonel *Palmer* himſelf, the Remainder making what Eſcape they could: And it is ſaid farther, that a great Number of the Enemy, at leaſt twice as many as on our Side, were ſlain.

flain. Thus we had it told us by the Patroon of this Boat: But as we feldom find
the Reports from that Neighbourhood verified in all Parts, and moreover having not
the leaft Intelligence of any Thing like it
fent us from the General's Camp (which
feems very ftrange) we are willing to hope
the next authentic Account we have from
thence, will make fome Abatement of this
difagreeable Story, and render it more favourable.

30.
Monday. Lieutenant *Kent* from Fort *Augufta*, arrived this Morning, by Permiffion,
for a few Days, to adjuft divers Matters,
relating to his own private Affairs, as well
as confult the Magiftrates in fome Affairs
concerning the Civil Power, wherein he
met with frequent Embarraffment how to
put it in Execution; there was fuch Jang-
ling among the Traders, and often Attempts of Violence with one another, to
decide Controverfies by Force, rather than
fubmit to any Judicature; having committed the Care of the Fort to a Serjeant under him, whom he could well confide in,
during his Abfence: He alfo had with him
three Men, that he brought Prifoners,
whom he had lately taken, after a diligent
Purfuit; and were Part of thofe who
committed that notorious Riot in the *Creek*
Nation fome Time ago *(vide June 3.)* but
one or two of the moft criminal were got
out

out of his Reach, and fled to *Charles-Town*; which they looked on as a fafe Afylum againſt all Profecutions from *Georgia*: Theſe who now appeared, found good Bail for their ſo doing again at our Court, near at hand now, and to abide the Judgment of the ſame. Mr. *Whitfield* went off for *Carolina* about Noon, taking one only Companion of his Houſhold with him (Mr. *Simms*) after having conſtituted Mr. *Haberſham*, to perform the Office of the Church in his Abſence, and Mr. *Brownfield* chief Steward of the Whole, who now gave himſelf up wholly to that Care, appointing *William Ewen* to manage his own private Affairs, about keeping Stores, who had formerly been Mr. *Cauſton*'s principal Agent in delivering out thoſe of the Publick: Since which, the ſaid *Ewen* went on very induſtriouſly with a fifty-Acre Lot at *Skeedoway*; but now all was given up to promote a Work thought to be of greater Importance; which was the Caſe with many others, not only of this Town, but of *Hampſtead, Highgate*, and divers Places beſides; ſo that the Work at the Orphan-Houſe ſeemed to be the great Gulph which ſwallowed up moſt of our common People, whether Artificers, Labourers, or Planters, that thought it more preferable to be ſo employed; which made the Town become thin indeed. The Humour of Horſe-Racing

1740.

Racing was yet kept up; but they thought fit to alter the Scene, and carry on the Show a little out of Town.

July 1.

Tuesday. Three or four more *Indian* Traders took up good Part of my Time this Day; which I could not well spare, from being employed about what I was directed to use my best Diligence in, to get ready such a State of the Colony, as the Trustees could abide by the Truth of, in any parliamentary Enquiry, &c. and therein my daily Employment should be doing something towards it. Mr. *Causton* having for some Months past forsaken the Town, and retired to *Ockstead*, it has often been reported among us, that he was in a decaying State of Health; which (it is to be feared) a great Anxiety of Mind has contributed to; and now we heard from thence, that he was so wasted away, and weak, it was believed his Life was near an End.

2.

Wednesday. Mr. *Mackenzie*, a Store-Keeper at *Augusta*, stopping here, in his Way home from *Charles-Town*, confirmed the bad News, as he had it there, which was reported to us by one of the trading Boats thence, on the 29th past, of the Loss of a great many Men; who (it was also said) sold their Lives at a dear Price, taking Payment of the Enemy by the Death of more than two hundred of them

them flain; which they could ill fpare:
The Lofs is faid unhappily to fall heavieft
(on our Side) upon the Men of this Colony; moft of thofe that were killed being
either of the *Darien* People, or of our
Troop of Rangers, or other fmall Parties;
none of the regular Forces, or of the *Ca-*
rolina Regiment, having any Share in the
Action. This rather quickens than abates
the Refolution of the Befiegers, who are
now animated with a Spirit of Revenge;
and we hear, that a large Battery of heavy Cannon had begun to play on the Town.
During thefe Tranfactions, we of this Place
can come at very little News that is certain, to be relied on, having not had any
Intelligence from the General fince Mr.
Jones's Return; and what we more admire
at is, that not any Letters come thence
from any of our People to their Friends.

Thurfday. After a pretty long Continuance of exceeding hot Weather, we were
bleffed this Day with a plentiful Rain, but
accompanied with terrible Thunder and
Lightning, which lafted a great Part of the
Night following; whereby the Earth, and
all thereon, was much refrefhed; and fuch
as had Employment for a Pen and Ink,
were fure to be undifturbed by any Avoca-
tions from home, or giving Attention to
what was doing abroad.

Friday,

Friday, } Being under some Indispos-
Saturday. } tion, I would not allow myself the Liberty of being abroad; but Messieurs *Parker*, *Jones*, &c. now and then
calling on me, we conferred betwixt while
on the principal Affair at present in hand, to
make what Progress in it we could: Wherein I wished for better Abilities, than I found
myself endued with, so to illustrate the
Truth, as to vindicate the Trustees Honour,
and expose the Malignity of those who attempted to impeach it. Thinking it of
little Significance now, to puzzle my
Thoughts farther, in putting together those
Fragments which I had been collecting, in
order to lay the State we were in before the
Trust, when the State of the Colony was
expected so fully to be explained and laid
open to them with our utmost Care and Diligence, at this Time to be used: I chose
rather to make up a Packet, with my Journal to this Time, and other Papers, &c.
together with a Letter to Mr. *Verelst*, which
might be ready at any Time to send off,
when Opportunity offered; and which indeed was all I attempted these two Days.

Sunday. Mr. *Habersham,* in Mr. *Whitfield's* Absence, read the Prayers of the
Church, and Sermons before Noon and after, out of some old Author; wherein, tho'
the Language was somewhat antiquated,
the

the Doctrine was good, tending to promote Piety and Virtue.

Monday. Our Court met this Day, as *per* Adjournment, and sat, to determine several Controversies among some of our Keepers of Stores at *Augusta*, and some *Indian* Traders who dealt with them; wherein I observed a Propensity pretty equal on both Sides, to over-reach one another, and scramble which of them should gain most. Attending the Court before Noon, and some of the Traders after, who came to renew their Licences, took up most of my Time all Day.

Tuesday. The Court went on with such Matters as they could not well avoid hearing; much of the same Significance as Yesterday, and worth little Notice from me: But what else occurred there, I thought required my particular Remark, being what possibly one Day or other I may be called to account for: When the Court was about rising, an Attempt was made, by two or three, to interrupt them in a clamorous Manner, and demand an Entry of their Claims to such Lands as they held: Which they received an Answer to in the softest Manner, to pacify them as far as might be, *viz.* that they would readily concur in so doing; but they apprehended, from what I had some Time since acquainted them with, that there was a Box directed to me, sent

sent from the Trustees, wherein were divers Papers, printed, intended to be dispersed by me for the Satisfaction of the People, relating to the future intended Tenure of Lands; and among other Things in the said Box, a Deed-Poll relating to forfeited Lots; which printed Papers concerning the Tenure of Lands, and Deed-Poll relating to forfeited Estates, they had never yet seen, and that they should have expected some plain Instructions thereon, when I published the Notice that I received from the Trust for the People to enter their Claims; but all appeared dark to them, as Matters now stood; and they were fearful lest they might commit some Error, &c. reserving them to me at last, to explain the whole Progress (or rather I should say Obstruction) of my putting in Execution the Orders sent me from the Trust, concerning this important Affair; wherein the one only Step I have been able to take about it, has been publishing the Notice in our Town which was written and enclosed from the Trust, about Claims, &c. and even that I never received till the 7th of *April* last, tho' the Letter it came in, was dated the 28th of *September* last; and no Box, or other Thing relating, has yet ever come to my Hand; of all which I took proper Notice on the said 7th of *April*, and 11th *Ditto*, in this Diary; as I had several Times before

fore in divers preceding Articles, and now
I related the Whole fully to them, for their
Satisfaction; being sorry to hear it even
whispered by some, that they found, if
any Benefit was intended them, it by some
Means or other was sure to prove abortive: And forasmuch as all Claims to be
made pursuant to this Notice must be before the 28th of *August* now drawing near,
I recommended it to the Magistrates to
make another short Adjournment of the
Court, that farther Consideration might
be timely had of it; for I greatly feared,
that this Check given to their Expectation
from the honourable Trust, might be a
Sowering to some, who had hitherto readily
acquiesced in all Determinations from them;
whereupon the Court adjourned to the 1st
of *August*.

1740.
July

Wednesday. About Two a Clock this
Morning, I was knocked up by a Party of
about eight or nine People, who fled from
Mr. *Whitfield*'s Works at the Orphan-House, terrified with the Apprehensions
they were under, of two Boats full of *Spanish Indians* coming upon them in the
Night; for that two of their young Men
who were fetching some Lime in a Boat
the Evening before, were pursued by those
Indians, and in their Fright fearing to be
taken by them, they got ashore, and run
to their Comrades at the said Works;

9.

whereupon thefe People now made what Hafte they could, to give us Information of it, bringing the two young Men with them: I went inftantly to fee what Pofture our Guard was in, fending, at the fame Time, our Magiftrates Notice, and to the Conftables to meet me: I was glad to find the Guard waking and alert, and immediately alarmed the Town, by Beat of Drum to Arms, which in lefs than a Quarter of an Hour brought betwixt thirty and forty together (and but few more could. be expected on the Spot, confidering where, and how many of our Freeholders were daily employed) I then fent out two Patroles, with an Officer and fix Men to each, to take a Round at a little Diftance from the Town, appointing them where to join, and return, &c. After the two Lads had been examined by the Magiftrates (who ftood to what they had before reported) upon a Confultation had, feven or eight of our moft expert Cattle-Hunters were fent out on Horfeback to fcout about thofe Parts, and fee if any farther Difcovery could be made, and in fuch Cafe to give us immediate Notice. In this Pofture we continued till about Ten a Clock, when on a fudden we were well informed, by two or three Perfons coming one after another from *Thunderbolt*, *Skeedoway*, and that Neighbourhood, that the *Indians*, whom the two

Lads

Lads took to be Enemies, were no other than some of those our Friends who live near us, and who at this Time were out a hunting on those Islands, and the adjacent Coast: We were also farther assured, that they had spoke with them, at the Place where their Camp was last Night, and where they made Fires to dress their Venison: Which Circumstance alone is sufficient to demand Belief of their not being Enemies; for it is a Rule among all of them, when they go to War, to make not the least Fire, which would discover them, and spoil their Designs, that are always projected to attack their Foes, when they do not look for them.——Thus all this imagined Storm blowed over, and every body went to their Homes in Peace.

Thursday, } Very little seemed worth
    Friday. } Regard now among us, in
Comparison of what great Things we were daily expecting some Intelligence of from the South; from whence (to our Admiration) no authentick Account had for a long Time past come to our Hands; but during these two Days, several private Letters were received by some of our People, from their Friends thereabout; which Letters came round about, having been as far as *Port-Royal,* and most of them agreeing, in the Main, on what Advices we got before, in the Manner I took Notice (the 29th of

10.

11,

1740.
July
10.
11.

June, and 2d of *July*;) but varioufly told now, as the Writers got Information, none of them having been perfonally in that Action. It was paft all Doubt, that it was a great Slaughter on both Sides; our People fought very bravely, and grown defperate, feeing themfelves fo over-powered, fold their Lives at a dear Rate, at leaft double the Number of the Enemy being flain, Sword in Hand, to what fell of our Men. It fell heavy upon our Party of Rangers, who were a Set of gallant, brave, young Men; and behaved fignally well: But the moft bloody Part of all fell to the unhappy Share of our good People at *Darien*, who almoft all to a Man engaged, under the Command of their Leader *John Mackintofh (More)* a worthy, careful Director among his People at home, and who now fhewed himfelf as valiant in the Field of Battle, where calling on his Countrymen and Followers to follow his Example, they made fuch Work with their broad Swords, as the *Spaniards* cannot eafily forget: This is certainly an unhappy Accident, not more however than the Chance of War often produces; and therefore it behoves us ftill to look forward, whence it is to be hoped, ere long, we fhall find a different Story to tell, all Accounts confirming, that the Siege of *Auguftin* goes on fuccefsfully by Sea and Land; that we are Mafters of the Harbour, where are feveral

veral warlike Gallies, &c. that muſt fall
into our Hands; that we are firing at the
Fort from a Battery of heavy Cannon;
that we had thrown a hundred and ſixty
Bombs, whereof not more than ſix or ſeven had miſſed falling into the Caſtle, &c.
and it is ſaid the General declared, that
he expected ſoon to be Maſter of the Place.
N. B. The above-mentioned Attack is ſaid
to have been on *Sunday* the 15th of *June*.

Saturday. We now at length attained
to ſome more ſatisfactory Account, than
any yet to be depended on, of the late Action with the Enemy, by Means of a Letter from Mr. *Patterſon* at *Frederica* to Mr.
Jones; which Letter had taken a Round
alſo to *Port-Royal*, as well as all others of
late, that were wrote from the South to
this Place; the Bearers being ſome of our
Carolina Gentry for the moſt Part, who
went as Volunteers, and made more Haſte
to return home, than was for their Credit,
carrying with them the News of this Miſ-
adventure, which they reported in ſuch
Colours, as their Fright ſuggeſted, few or
none of them having been Witneſſes of it;
which ſtruck a Damp upon ſome. weak
Minds that are apt to take the firſt Impreſſion too deep. What Mr. *Patterſon*
wrote Mr. *Jones* was authentick, being Copies of the General's own Letters to the
Magiſtrates of *Frederica*, and to Mr. *McLeod*,

Miniſter

Minister of *Darien:* Wherein, the Bravery of our People is set forth to their Honour, and the Loss of Men much lessened, from what was at first given out; which the General says he expected would be by a Parcel of runaway Cowards, many being since come in that at first were said to be slain. Colonel *Palmer*, a Gentleman in good Esteem, is among the Dead; but *John More Mackintosh*, the Leader of the *Darien* People, together with some of his Countrymen, and some also of the Rangers, are Prisoners in the Town; whence, his Excellence writes, he does not doubt but to release them soon: In the mean while he was pleased to write a Letter to the Governor, by a Flag of Truce, telling him, that he expected the Prisoners should not be ill treated; for that in case they were, he would hang up every Prisoner he had before the Gates of the Town; of which he had a great Number: Whereupon the Governor ordered our Men that were taken, to write to the General; who acquainted him, that they were kindly used. — And now we are imagining Things near a Crisis at *Augustin*; which raises our Expectations daily, of such Advices from thence, as will preponderate all past that was disagreeable. It was not an Observation of my own only, but the like made to me by some honest Men, that during the

the Obscurity which the Truth of these
Things lay under, our common Disturbers
took great Pains, with a Kind of Sneer,
to publish what they thought fit, in a
frightful Manner, as what their Friends
had (I know not from whence) wrote
them they might depend on, seemingly
full of deep Concern for poor *Georgia*:
All which, any Man of common Understanding could easily see thro': But the Light
now appearing through that Cloud, it was
yet more remarkable, that the counterfeit
Sorrow which they had then put on, now
visibly became real; and when other Folk
grew chearful, they so far forgot themselves, as to look sullen and out of Humour: What Inference may justly be drawn
from hence, I chuse to submit to those who
are the best Judges.

Sunday. Mr. *Habersham* performed the   13.
Divine Service, Morning and Afternoon;
reading after it two Sermons, one exhorting
to a due Obedience of God's Laws, and
the other setting forth his Omnipresence:
Both (I thought) better adapted to a Reformation of Life, than such nice Points concerning Justification, which were so often
taken in hand.

Monday. The last Week carried off most   14.
of our *Indian* Traders, and Store-Keepers
at *Augusta*, who had spent a little Time
with us: Lieutenant *Kent* also returning

Yester-

1740. Yesterday to his Command at the Fort there; and among others, Mr. *Williamson* likewise at length thought fit to go back to *Charles-Town*, after having employed himself here a long Time past, doing what Mischief he could in promoting false Rumours, and concerting Measures with our wicked Crew, how most effectually to alienate the Minds of well-disposed People, from shewing a due Regard to the good Intention of the honourable Trustees, whose Designs for the Welfare of the Colony they always talked of in an ironical Stile, or in such a Manner as to be on their Guard, left any Expressions should drop from them, which if animadverted on, they might have Cause to repent of; for they well know what they may expect, if they openly dare to revile those in the highest Authority over us. It now appeared, that the principal Cause of *Williamson*'s coming hither, was in Expectation that his Uncle *Causton* was dead, or dying; that so he might be ready to take Possession of what he could; but Mr. *Causton*, tho' grown very weak, yet leaving Room for his Friends to entertain some Hopes of his Recovery, gave him a cold Reception, and blamed his Conduct very much (as I am informed) for meddling so much as he did, with the Affairs of the Colony, and allowing himself the Liberty of censuring the Acts of the Trustees;

tees; much less would *Caufton* be persuaded by him, to be a Partaker in those wise Councils, which were carrying on among them at their Club; for (to give *Caufton* his Due) he had more Penetration than all of them put together, and could see afar off what their Politicks would end in: Whereat the other enraged, left him; and coming to Town, let loose all the Scandal he could think of against him at *Jenkins*'s, giving him the Title of both Fool and Knave, for not concurring with them, in appealing to the Parliament against the Truftees, who had dealt so hardly with *him*: Which *Caufton* was so provoked at, that when the other came a few Days after to see him, he forbad him his House, and ordered the Doors to be shut against him. Our Court sitting soon after, he then turned Sollicitor, in a Cause or two to be heard betwixt some of our *Indian* Traders, *&c.* But being timely admonished, thought it safest not to appear as a Pleader; tho' he confidently affirmed, that he had the Truft's Leave to practise as an Attorney. From thence-forward, as well as before, he busied himself as an Inspector among our selfelected ones, riding frequently to and fro, to note what he imagined would make for his Purpose; and at going off, left this Memento behind him; that he had made himself so far Master of all the Settlements,

Planta-

Plantations, and Families, in the Province;
how many, and whom they confisted of,
and what every one was employed about,
that he fhould get a faithful Account ready againft the next Enquiry into the State
of the Colony, to confront any fent by
other Hands, and prevent Gentlemen from
being mifled. What paffed betwixt him
and me, towards the latter End of his Mif-
fion here, I think not worth remembring;
but upon meeting him once or twice accidentally, and his attempting to obtrude a
Queftion or two upon me, which I took
to be enfnaring, I told him, that I thought
fuch Queftions would be beft anfwered before Witneffes, as (he knew) had been prac-
tifed by him and his Friends upon *me*; and
fo I turned my Back on him. Lieutenant
Kent, in his Way home, meeting with a
Letter fent to him out of the *Cherokee* Nation, thought it proper to be fent hither;
that if we faw it needful, we might tranfmit it to the General: It came to us this
Morning, and was from *Lodowick Grant*,
a Trader in that Nation; who wrote him,
that there were eighty of thofe People lately marched out in two Parties, on what
Defign, at firft not known; but it proved
to be againft the *French*, whom they attacked as they were coming up the River
to *Terriqua*, in three Perriaguas, two of
which they plundered and deftroyed:
What

What the Confequence may be we know
not, but think it forebodes no Ill to the
Englifh. In the Evening Mr. *Fallowfield*
came to Town from his Plantation on the
Ifle of Hope; which it may be proper to
take Notice here, is a Name given it
by the Settlers thereon, who are Meffieurs
Parker, *Fallowfield*, and *Noble Jones*: It is
a Peninfula, cut off from the Main with a
very little Ifthmus, which by a fhort Fence
makes the Ifland an entire Poffeffion to
them; and it is equally divided betwixt
them, which they hold by Leafe (or Expectation of fuch) from the Truft, having
occupied it two or three Years, and made
confiderable Improvements: The Ifle of
Skeedoway lies without it, and betwixt
them is the Way that all Boats pafs to and
fro, betwixt us and the South. —— What
News Mr. *Fallowfield* brought was very furprizing, *viz.* that about Noon there was a
Boat paffing from the Camp towards *Carolina*, wherein was young Mr. *Delagal*, a
Lieutenant in the General's own Regiment:
That upon hailing the Boat, and afking
what News? *Delagal* told him, the General was intending to draw off his Forces
from before *Auguftin*, and make them another Vifit in *October* next; which being
fomewhat ftartled at, he would have afked
him fome more Queftions, but that he
thought *Delagal* was fhy, and feemed unwilling

1740.
July

willing to talk any farther with him; but as the Men lay upon their Oars, he called on them haſtily to pull away, which they did. What he obſerved farther was, that he ſaw a Gentleman under the Awning, who lay ſtill, and did not ſhew himſelf. Upon this Report made to us, and ſo many odd Circumſtances attending it (among others I ſhould not forget that the Rowers appeared to Mr. *Fallowfield* not to be natural-born Subjects, being of a black and ſwarthy Complexion, ſomewhat of the Mulatto Kind) various were our Conjectures, too many to name: But moſt were of Opinion, that *Delagal* was not well warranted to give ſuch Intelligence. Neverthelefs it muſt needs leave us under much Perplexity of Thought, till we could come at the Truth.

15.

Tueſday. The dark Account we had laſt Night of Matters at *Auguſtin,* which came by that Boat Mr. *Fallowfield* had ſpoken with, ſeemed to vaniſh, with the Light of another Day: Two of the Men who rowed in her, who thro' much Sweat and Toil appeared with dirty Faces, and were taken to be Mulatto's, landing not many Miles off; this Morning we found one of them to be an *Engliſhman,* who had lived ſeveral Years up in the *Cherokee* Nation; and talking that Language perfectly, was made uſe of by the General as an Interpreter

terpreter with them at the Camp; where 1740.
thofe *Cherokees* having a peculiar Sicknefs a-
mong them, whereof feveral of them had
lately died, the reft, with the General's
Leave, were returning home, and were on
their Way hither; to which Place this Man
was fent as a Forerunner, to make Preparation againft their Arrival; the other, who
was his Companion, was an infignificant,
little, old Fellow, a Sort of Jack Pudding
at *Augufta*, whom the Inhabitants there
made ufe of on Occafion in a fervile Manner, and he was maintained out of their
Plenty; to which Place he was now returning, together with this People; but
what Motive carried *him* to War, I am not
able to guefs from thefe two; we made
fhift to underftand, that the General finding
Bombarding to have very little Effect on the
Works of the Fort, which were made
Bomb Proof, had put fome of his heavy
Artillery on board the Men of War, who
now (according to the Ufage of thofe Countries) were obliged to ftand farther off to
Sea, fearing left in cafe of a Hurricane
coming upon them at this Seafon (the ufual
Time of expecting fuch) they fhould be
catcht, and not able to get out from the
Bay; that the Enemy lately made an Attempt of fallying with a Party of Horfe,
but were foon glad to make hafte in again;
feveral of the Horfes carrying only their
Saddles,

July 15.

Saddles, without any Riders. That the coming away of these *Cherokees* would not be missed, for their Room would be more than supplied by three hundred from the *Creek* Nation, who were within few Days March of the Camp when these left it; and that the General seemed determined to carry on the Siege; which I must own I could hardly believe; unless he meant to turn it into a Blockade, and wait the coming of more Force from other Parts (as it was of late pretty much talked of) under the Lord *Cathcart*. The Person in the Boat who did not shew himself Yesterday, we now heard was Colonel *Barnwell* of *Carolina*, whom the General had been friendly with; and it was not doubted but both he and Lieutenant *Delagal* had with them some particular Orders and Instructions from his Excellency. Thus all was pretty well again, and most Folk must talk about what few of them understood.

16.   *Wednesday.* Peter *Emery* arriving last Night with his Boat from *Charles-Town*, brought me a Box sent me by my Son from *England*, with sundry Necessaries that I wanted, which came by a Ship newly come in, as Mr. *Hopton* wrote me; but no Letter, except one, advising me of the Contents. This Day produced nothing relating to the Publick worth regarding.

Thursday.

Thursday. The whole Attention of all People this Day, was to the various Reports that came by several Persons returning to *Carolina* from the Army; who in their Way home dropt such Accounts of Matters here and there among our Out-Settlements, as were very inconsistent, and much disagreeing; so that the Truth could not yet fully be come at, but gave Occasion of a great deal of Talk at random to no Purpose.

1740.
July
17.

Friday. Capt. *Tingley* arrived this Morning from the South, where he had been to dispose of his Cargo *(vide June 14.)* and with him came Mr. *Abraham Minis*, a *Jew* Freeholder here, whom the Cargo was consigned to, and who was looked on by all of us, as an honest Man: Wherefore we could make no Scruple of giving Credit to what was now told us, as real Fact. The Action which happened upon the Enemy's sallying out in the Night, and attacking our Party early in the Morning, so often canvassed amongst us here, differed very little in Circumstances from what we had heard; and it was very sharp; but the Number slain was too much magnified on our Side; for out of about one hundred and thirty, which the Party consisted of, it is now said that forty were killed, and ten taken Prisoners; among the first of whom, Colonel *Palmer* was one; and among

18.

mong the latter, Capt. *John Mᶜ Intoſh More*, the Principal of the *Darien* People; the reſt making their Eſcape. It is agreed by all, that the Enemy ſuffered twice as much; for our Men finding themſelves encloſed, fought deſperately, and made their Way thro' and thro' them, Sword in Hand: But the certain Loſs they ſuſtained, is not to be diſcovered; for remaining Maſters of the Field a-while, they buried their Dead, leaving us to do the ſame by ours; which we did ſoon after: But to countervail the Loſs of Colonel *Palmer*, the principal Commander of the *Spaniards* there was killed at the firſt Onſet, when our Men maintained a briſk Fire for ſome Time, before they engaged Hand to Hand; and it is ſtill ſaid the *Spaniards* were upwards of five hundred. They made a faint Attempt very lately of ſallying with a Party of Horſe, to perform ſome farther Exploit: But the General was ſo well provided for them, that they made more haſte back, than they had done ſo far, and a great many Horſes were ſeen to have left their Riders; as we were before told by thoſe two Men whom we talked with on laſt *Tueſday*; and what the ſame Men then told us of the General having ſhipped off his Artillery, and his Reaſons for ſo doing; as alſo of the Men of War ſtanding off farther to Sea, for Fear of a Hurricane, was now confirmed: Moreover,

over, the General feeing his Men beginning
to grow fickly, and finding little more could
be done, refolved to turn the Siege into a
Blockade (as I imagined would be the Cafe)
till they were recruited with good Health,
and fome additional Strength, intending after *Michaelmas* to have fomething more to
fay to them: In the mean Time, he was
marched, with his little Army, to his former Camp at St. *Juan's*.

Saturday. The only Thing that came
farther to my Knowledge worth obferving
from the South, was, that Capt. *Davis*,
whom on many Occafions, I have formerly at feveral Times, for a whole Year paft,
taken Notice of, as a Man, in my Opinion, carrying on dark Purpofes, which I
did what in me lay to obftruct, by the Affiftance of the Magiftrates; which produced a great Clamour from our Patrons of
Liberty at the Club, charging us with acting illegally, &c. (the Particulars whereof
were noted in my Journal of *Sept.* 10, 11,
12 and 13, 1739; and again on the 18th
Ditto:) But the General coming among us
again foon after, very much approved of
what we had done (as noted on the 24th
Ditto;) tho' afterward upon Affurances of
his Fidelity, he was pleafed to grant him
a Commiffion to act as a Privateer; which
he never did; his Character was fuch a-
mong the Sailors, that he could never get

1740.

July

19.

1740.
July

Hands fufficient for that Purpofe: This Man now lying with his Sloop near St. *Auguftin*, in Expectation of being employed, as many other were, by the General, we are now informed is taken into Cuftody by his Excellency's Order, for fending off two of the *Spanifh* Prifoners, in his own Boat, into the Town of *Auguftin*, by whom the Enemy would get the beft Intelligence they could wifh.——But I muft not anticipate what Evidence will appear, nor the Confequence.

20.

Sunday. Mr. *Haberfham* continued to perform the Office of Reader of the Divine Service, and a Sermon in the Forenoon and after, with good practical Doctrine; till in the Conclufion his Author left a Difrelifh to all he had faid, by denouncing Damnation to all who were not juftified by Faith.

21.

Monday. I had waited now ever fince the 28th of laft Month, to get a little farther Account, if I could, of the Paper, which I had private Intelligence of that Day, was fent among us from *Charles-Town*; but I could not find that its Poifon had operated upon any worth naming: It was fent to the Care of the Wife of *Edward Townfend*, whofe Hufband keeps a Perriague, and is at prefent employed among others by the General. *Probably* fhe may be better known by the Name of *Hodges*

Hodges (her former Husband) and it is very well known how exceeding kind Mr. *Ogle-thorpe* was to her, and her Family, for several Years; notwithstanding all which, she has, to an inconceivable Degree, most ungratefully upon all Occasions, reviled her kind Benefactor, and given herself most unwarrantable Liberties with her Tongue to defile his Character; which he used to hear of with Contempt, and beneath his Notice: But Mr. *Brownfield* marrying her Daughter, he foretold would be a Means of his becoming tainted with the Sourness of that Family; which I fear was too true a Prediction; for he is unhappily fallen into the same Way of thinking with Regard to this Colony, as other of our Malecontents are (or I should rather say was one of the earliest of them) but secretly, and avoiding all publick Clamour: But this good Mother-in-Law of his, exposes the Bitterness of her Heart continually, as far as she dares, and her House was a long while the Place of Resort for such as delighted in her Way of Railing, and would take a Part in it themselves; till at length a superior Genius prevailed at *Jenkins's*, which this was obscured by; but the Woman still retaining the same Faculty of scattering what Venom she can, the Author of this doughty Piece judged so far right, that she would be a Well-wisher to it at least: Wherefore

it

it was depofited with her, to fee what good Ufe fhe could make of it; and ftiled no lefs than An humble Petition to the King and Council, fetting forth what terrible Hardfhips the People of this Province laboured under, &c. as the Author's fertile Genius thought fit to difplay; who was faid to be Mr. *Bradley*, as my Informant told me, who averred that he knew it to be his Son's Hand Writing: But this Cockatrice Egg was crufhed, and not allowed to come to Maturity, by our fupream Divan; who would fuffer no Interfering in thofe weighty Matters, which they alone were fufficient for. Found an Opportunity of fpending a little Time at the five-Acre Lot near the Town, good Part of which I had converted to particular Ufes, as a Nurfery for greater Purpofes: The little Quantity of Corn growing there, I thought no farther worth my prefent regarding, than to obferve, that fince the Time I firft began planting, I had never known fo promifing an Increafe as now, of that Grain, and alfo Potatoes; fo that the like proving pretty general, I thought it great Pity that all thofe who were grown weary of perfevering in Cultivation, would now fee Caufe to wifh their Patience would hold out longer. After taking much Pleafure in feeing divers other Things come forward, fuch as Vines, Mulberries, Cotton, &c. I returned home,

not

not without wishing for such a Recess of- 1740.
tener; for it was more than a Month since
my last Visit there.

July 22.

Tuesday. What passed at the Time of
our Court's adjourning on the 8th Instant,
relating to the several Claims being received,
which divers were desirous to make, and
for which Purpose I obtained a farther
short Adjournment to the 1st of *August*,
gave me much Uneasiness, lest any Defect of Duty should in the End be imputed to me; wherefore I thought it proper
to fix up publick Advertisement, signed by
me, to give all People Notice, that Whereas
the Court now stood adjourned till the 1st
of *August*, it would then sit, and be ready
to receive Claims from all Persons who had
any to make for Lands, &c. held under
the Trust, provided they specified where
their Lots lay which they claimed, and
that the Persons so claiming signed the
same: This was all that I could think of
in my Power to do towards it at present.
Much Buzzing began again to appear in
our Town (among most People indeed
now) since the News came of the General's
having withdrawn a little from the For-
tress of *Augustin*; from whence it was not
unreasonable to infer, that whilst the General had a watchful Eye over the Enemy
by Land, they might possibly send out
Row-Gallies and Launches, &c. by Sea,

with

with which they might very much annoy
the Coaft, and make Depredations on our
Out-Settlements lying all along that Way,
of which mine ftood foremoft on a Point
facing *Uffibaw Sound:* Neverthelefs, I could
difcover no Terror among the Generality of
our People, who were moftly of Opinion,
that whatever Mifchief might fall on the
moft remote Parts, that lay expofed, they
would fcarcely venture fo far up as *Savannah,* and run the Rifk of being intercepted:
Wherein I concurred with them; and after
giving what Orders I found neceffary, for a
ftrict Infpection into every individual Man's
Arms, and for a Diftribution of what Powder and Ball was proper; as alfo fpecial
repeated Orders touching the Guard, *&c.*
all appeared in good Temper, whom it
might be expected from, but *fome* nothing
would fatisfy.

23.   *Wednesday.* Whilft my Thoughts were
employed as ufefully as I could for the Publick, in the Station appointed me, it was
not amifs to have fome Regard likewife
to my own little Affair: And having not
feen *Bewlie* fince *Whitfuntide,* which was
now eight Weeks ago, I rode out to make
them a Vifit there, and fee what Difpofition my little Family were in, under fuch
daily Rumours there. I found eight Acres
of Land as well filled with Corn, Peafe,
and Potatoes, as I could wifh, all thriving,
and

and likely to do well: More I could not
expect to see planted this Year, considering
what Time they began, and how many
Kinds of Works they had upon their Hands
at first setting down. The Men were easy,
and their present Work was to erect another
Edifice, partly for holding Corn, and partly for divers other Uses; after which, in
the next Place, I purposed to set up a
Dwelling-House, in such a Manner, that it
might be for a comfortable Reception of
myself and a Friend at any Time, as well
as whomsoever I thought fit to live in it.
Upon asking my People, whether or not
they would allow the *Spaniards* to come
ashore and eat the Fruits of their Labour;
they promised me very chearfully, to shew
them they would not part with all for
Nought; and having with them two Fu-
sees of my own, and two Muskets that I
sent them from the Stores, which I assured
them they should not want Ammunition
for, they engaged to behave manfully, if it
came to a Trial: And knowing him that
was appointed by me their Overseer, to be
a brisk Man, I was pretty confident in
them that they would not set an ill Example to my next Neighbours there, by running away sooner than they were forced.

Thursday. Hard Thunder-Showers falling 24.
in the Evening, stopped me at *Bewlie* till
this Morning, and then I set out homeward,

ward, in Company with my Neighbour
Mercer : We called in our Way at *Bethefda*
(the Name given to that Place by Mr.
Whitfield) next adjoining to *Bewlie,* where
I faw great Things done fince I viewed it
laft : The principal Houfe was a grand Edifice ; the Defign of the Apartments within
I am not Mafter of ; they were in fuch
Forwardnefs, as to be ready for raifing the
Roof this Week ; it is all well cellared underneath ; the Foundation Walls are of
Brick, which rife feveral Foot higher than
the Surface of the Land, and the Rooms
of both lower and upper Story are of good
Height : As we approach it, are fix good,
handfome Edifices, three of each Side, for
the following Purpofes, *viz.* a Work-houfe
for Women and Children, oppofite an In-
firmary of the like Dimenfions ; next a
Kitchen, oppofite to it another of the fame
Size, for Wafhing, Brewing, *&c.* the other
two I was not yet informed what Ufes they
were defigned for.   Thence travelling on,
we got home about Nine a Clock in the
Morning ; where I found about thirty of
the *Cherokee Indians,* arrived the Day before
from the Camp, being thofe whom we expected, from the Account we had of them,
as noted on the 15th Inftant.   They continued very fickly and weak, and one of
them died this Evening : They were conducted hither by Meffieurs *Samuel Brown,*
and

and *Jacob Morris*, two Traders in that Nation. The Heats were now grown so violent, that very few attempted to stir abroad; and I was contented to sit still, as others did, not hearing of any Thing that required Action without Doors.

Friday. Indolence prevailed with most People, which I took my Share of; and avoiding any Business abroad, I found sufficient always at home to employ my Time and Thought there, in getting forward what I had to do. Mr. *Whitfield* returned in the Afternoon from his Expedition to *Carolina*; but what Success he met with there, in preaching, to promote the great Designs he had in hand, I yet heard nothing of: Before his Coming, we had various Reports of the Opposition he met with from Mr. *Garden*, Minister at *Charles-Town*, who (it is said) by Virtue of a Power from the Bishop, cited him to appear, and answer for many Doctrines which he preached that were not orthodox, and also for his irregular Proceedings, which gave so great Disturbances to the publick Peace, as well as Divisions among Families: To all which Mr. *Whitfield* gave but little Heed; but offering to partake of the Sacrament, Mr. *Garden* refused him, &c. —— The certain Truth of these Things, we may probably soon be better informed in.

Saturday.

1740.

July

25.

Saturday. Our Declaimers of the Club, finding those Terrors, which they scattered among the People, did not operate so effectually as they expected, seemed resolved to try what Example would do; and it was publickly given out, that *Tailfer* and Landlord *Jenkins* were preparing to send their Wives and Families out of Harm's Way, into some other Province, I know not where, intending to follow, when they judged a proper Time. These cannot be numbered surely among our defensive Men, nor any who have the like Faculty of smelling Danger at a Distance; of such it is to be hoped there are but few, if such these are. I really think it would be for the Benefit of the Colony, that they all left it, notwithstanding the Decrease of People for some while past; for if they do not think their Property worth defending, I know not what Good can be expected from them; and most certainly a small Band, well united, is of more Force than a loose one more numerous, but easily dispersed.

Sunday. Mr. *Whitfield* attended on the Service of the Church, as usual; but being in a weak State of Health (supposed to be occasioned by the Fatigue he underwent in his late Progress) he was not able to preach in the Forenoon; and in the Evening Service he was obliged to break off, and return home.

Monday.

Monday. Every Day now brought forth some new Report or other, touching the prefent Situation of Affairs in this Colony, and how far any Danger from the Enemy might affect us in thefe Parts: But I found the Generality pretty equanimous, and in no wife fond of giving Credit to many Falfhoods that were frequently publifhed to affright Families (for Women will always have their Fears :) On the contrary, it was pretty evident with what Pleafure any News was received, which imported a Probability of acting in a little Time offenfively againft the *Spaniards :* Such was the Report of this Day, that came by a Boat from *Carolina :* Whereby we were informed, that a Ship arrived at *Charles-Town* from *Cowes,* brought Intelligence, that there was a very confiderable Body of Soldiers, that were draughted out of feveral ftanding Regiments lying in the Neighbourhood of *Portfmouth,* when he came away, defigned to embark foon, to enable General *Oglethorpe* to carry on his Enterprizes againft the Enemy. 'Whether there was any Foundation for this, or not, tho' much doubted, yet it is fcarce credible how much all were enlivened by it, whom any Regard was due to: And on this Occafion, looking over our Lift of Freeholders, I thought even in this our low Eftate I could mark out about feventy of them, who would be ready to defend their Country, and

ftand

1740. ſtand to their Arms in good Earneſt, if
July Occaſion called them out for that Purpoſe;
and it is of the Freeholders only, Inhabitants in *Savannah*, that I now ſpeak: For
upon reckoning all the ſpare Men, and Servants, *Dutch* and *Engliſh*, belonging to the
Town, there may be found more than e-
nough to double that Number, excluſive of
Highgate, *Hamptſtead*, &c. and the Town
of *Ebenezer* alone is able to furniſh betwixt
fifty and ſixty good Men.

29.   *Tueſday*. Capt. *Tingley*, who lately returned from the South, where he had diſpoſed of his Cargo, intending this Evening
to proceed homeward for *New-York*; it
would now be ſeen how many took this
Opportunity, by Flight, to leave us; as we
were told to expect Abundance would (by
thoſe who would be glad to ſee it.)   I took
Care, as I uſed to do, to be exactly informed who went; and as Permits were
refuſed to none who were weary of ſtaying
here, excepting ſuch only as had juſt Demands upon them, which were yet unſa-
tisfied, and no Perſuaſion, much leſs Com-
pulſion, had been uſed to ſtop any body
againſt their Inclination; there could be
no truer Teſt, whereby to judge of the
People's Diſpoſition than this.   And behold
it ended all in what follows: 1. *Joſeph
Stanley*, a Freeholder ſuperannuated, weak
and paſt any Labour; his Wife left him,
                                        and

and went to *England* three Years since, and
he now went to a Relation, who he expects
will keep him in his old Age: He never
did any Thing towards maintaining himself by Planting whilst here. 2. *Jacob
Bernal*, a *Jew*, of no visible Way of Live-
lihood. 3. *Hiam Bendannoon*, ditto, with
his Wife and two small Children. And
last of all (thank God) the eminent Mrs.
Townsend thought fit to leave us, whose
Tongue has been a Nusance to this Town
ever since I knew it; taking her young
Daughter with her now, and had not Patience to wait her Husband's Return home
from the South, where he with his Perriague had been employed; and what Loss
the Colony sustains by such a Desertion, of
whom no one has been a Grain of Corn
the better for, I leave to our wise Men
of the Club to discuss, being past my Dis-
covery. *N. B.* None of these now going
off, were reckoned in that Number of
seventy in Yesterday's Notes.

Wednesday. A Skooner passed by *Thunderbolt* from the South, wherein was said to
be about eighty of the *Carolina* Regiment,
on their Return home; which Regiment,
from all the Reports we had, proved of little or no Use to the General in carrying on
the Siege of *Augustin*, being always turbu-
lent and disobedient to Orders, many In-
stances whereof were notorious, but not
proper

1740.
July

30.

proper to be noted here, before due Enquiry made into all thofe Things, which it is expected will be in another Place, ere long; moſt of the gay Volunteers run away by ſmall Parties, baſely and cowardly, as they could get Boats to carry them off during the Time of greateſt Action; and Capt. *Bull* (a Son of the Lieutenant-Governor) who had the Command of a Company in that Regiment, moſt ſcandalouſly deſerted his Poſt when upon Duty, and not ſtaying to be relieved regularly, made his Flight privately, carrying off four Men of his Guard with him, and eſcaped to *Charles-Town*; for which he ought in Juſtice to have been tried as a Deſerter; but he was well received at home; and upon the Aſſembly's meeting, his Brother was choſen Speaker of that Houſe, in the Room of Mr. *Pinckny*, who was lately gone off (ſo the *Carolina* Gazette terms it) with two others of particular Note and Diſtinction in that Province, namely, Meſſieurs *Wragg* and *Whitaker*; the firſt one of the moſt conſiderable Merchants there, and the other a noted Lawyer, choſen by the Council to fill the Place of Chief Juſtice, till there ſhould be one duly appointed by his Majeſty: It is ſaid they are gone to *New-York*, to look for ſome Place to ſettle on, where they may be more eaſy, not liking (it ſeems) the Situation of Affairs at preſent, where they were.

were.——If Half that we hear of thefe
People proves true, it will afford Room for
many Inferences, which I would not be
too hafty in making till we know a little
farther.

Thurfday. Nothing to be heard of now
from all Quarters, but Abundance of flying Reports concerning the late Tranfactions
before *Auguftin*, which were fo different,
that in giving too eafy Credit to, a Man
would moft probably foon find himfelf
deceived: One only Report, every one who
wifhed well to the Place, was in Hopes
would prove true; which was, that we
might expect the General here in a Fortnight, and then we might affure ourfelves
many Truths would be laid open, which
yet lay concealed. Mr. *Whitfield*'s Sloop
came in from *Carolina*, by which feveral
of his Difciples in thofe Parts came; but
whether it was purely on a Vifit, or that
any of them had a Defign of continuing
among us, was not known; tho' the latter did not feem likely yet a-while, one
of them being an Anabaptift Teacher.

Friday. Purfuant to the Court's Adjournment on the 8th *ult.* to this Day, for the
Reafon then given, they now met; when
about feventy Freeholders delivered in their
feveral Claims to fuch Lots as they held,
&c. But forafmuch as many others did not
appear, either thro' Ignorance, or Miftake,

or

1740.
August

or other pardonable Occaſion, that none might think themſelves hardly dealt with, the Court adjourned farther for a Fortnight to the 15th Inſtant. Nothing elſe material to take Notice of.

2.   *Saturday.* Mr. *Whitfield* not coming to Church this Morning (occaſioned, as it is ſaid, by the late Indiſpoſition continuing upon him) Mr. *Haberſham* read the Confeſſion, Lord's Prayer, and a Chapter out of the Goſpel; after which the Preacher before taken Notice of, advanced to the Deſk (there being yet no Pulpit) and naming the five firſt Verſes of the ſecond Chapter of the firſt Epiſtle of St. *Peter,* for his Text, he proceeded to give us a Sermon, ſetting forth the ſame Doctrine we were taught for a long while paſt, concerning the Neceſſity of a New Birth, and being endued with that vital Principle in our Hearts here on Earth, without which no one could enter into Heaven, being altogether carnal and void of ſaving Grace : After Sermon ended *extempore,* he made uſe of a long Prayer in the ſame Way; wherein he gave Thanks to God for the great Progreſs, and wonderful Succeſs which the Publication of the Terms of Salvation had met with, from that Inſtrument whom he had made uſe of in theſe Parts, and who (he prayed) might be as a Poſt of Iron, or Wall of Braſs, in Defence of the Truth he contended for, *&c.*

3   *Sunday.*

Sunday. Divers of the *Carolina* Strangers, who came laſt Week, continuing with their Wives, *&c.* among whom Mr. *Jones*, Miniſter at *Port-Royal*, was one; Mr. *Whitfield* had two Divines with him on the Bench this Day, when Mr. *Jones* read the Prayers of the Church, who is a Man of a very good Character, and orthodox Principles : Mr. *Tilly*, the Anabaptiſt Teacher, ſat as an Auditor only, and Preaching was the Part which Mr. *Whitfield* took to himſelf, the like before Noon and after; when he ſeemed to exert himſelf in a particular Manner, labouring to make good the Doctrine, which more eſpecially he had taught hitherto.

Monday. Having in vain waited for a Month or more paſt, to find a ſafe Conveyance of a Packet to *Charles-Town*, deſigned for the Truſt, which I made up on the 5th of *July*; but hearing of no Boat going that I could confide in, till now, when I underſtood a fair Opportunity offered to-morrow, I reſolved to do what I could, in getting another Packet ready, to be ſent in Company with the former; and that was my chief Employment this Day.

Tueſday. What with one Hindrance or another, which unavoidably ſometimes called me aſide, I found this Day ſhort enough to finiſh what I took in hand Yeſterday; but at length putting an End to it, and Mr.

1740.

Auguſt 3.

4.

5.

1740.
August

Jones likewise having got ready what he had to send, I put it all up in a small Box, together with my former Packet of the 5th *ult.* and in the Evening delivered it to the Patroon of the Boat *(Peter Shepherd)* whom I had Confidence in, and who was to set off with the next Tide about Three in the Morning; by him I also sent another Box for Mr. *Eyre* (one of the honourable Trust) wherein were Sundries left in Charge with me by his Kinsman, a Cadet in the Army in the South; and with the Boxes I wrote to Mr. *Hopton,* as usual. Mr. *Whitfield,* with the Company about him, taking Horse early to go and view what was doing at *Bethesda* (where they spent the Day;) after the Morning Lesson was read at Church by Mr. *Habersham,* Mr. *Tilly,* the Anabaptist, supplied the Place of an Expositor on the second Chapter of the *Ephesians.*

6.

Wednesday. Returned now to my former Task, how to set the present State of the Colony in its due Light before the honourable the Trustees, as they required: Wherein I met with such Contrariety of Opinion, among divers whom I conversed with, touching some of those Questions that were to be resolved, that it was a great Difficulty how to reconcile them, so as to make one uniform Contexture of the Whole; which I had strong Inclination to do, that as little Dissension as possible might

appear

appear among those, whom I knew to be
Persons of a good Disposition towards the
Colony; and such as I knew too well to
expect they could be brought into any Measures but those they had been projecting I
know not how long past, I was determined
not to have any Thing to say to them. In
the Afternoon arrived Colonel *Vanderduffen*,
Commander of the *Carolina* Regiment,
which had been in the Service at *Auguftin*,
with whom he was now on his Return to
Charles-Town; and with him were several
of his Officers: They had been beating
the Sea several Days against a contrary
Wind, without getting forward; for which
Reason they came ashore here for some Refreshment. By Conversation with the Colonel, I was informed of several Things
which I was a Stranger to before, and found
him as ready as others, to condemn the
daftardly Behaviour of many of those runaway Volunteers, and to express a Resentment against the ill Conduct of some of his
own Officers; but from what he said, I
understood he was himself on very good
Terms with the General, whom he spoke of
with all due Honour and Deference; but it
raised a Concern in us to be told by him,
that the General was in so ill a State of
Health at *Frederica*, as he was at the Time
when he now left him, being (as he said)
reduced to an extraordinary Weakness, by

a continual Fever upon him, with fome Intermiffion, for two Months paft; during which Time his Spirits fupported him under all Fatigue; but the Difappointment of Succefs (it is believed) now galled him, and too great Anxiety of Mind preyed upon him.

7. *Thurfday.* Colonel *Vanderduffen*, and fome of his Officers, fhewing a Defire of viewing the Town, and Parts adjacent, which they were Strangers to, and admired the pleafant Situation of; I walked with them to fhew what I thought moft worth their Notice; and upon fome of them feeming to exprefs a great Pity, that fo fine a Place made no fafter Advances towards Perfection, I could not refrain from addreffing myfelf to fuch among them, as I knew to live in the Neighbourhood of *Port-Royal*; and faying (in Return) that I alfo thought it great Pity, fo commodious a Place as *Beaufort* was, fhould feem at a Stand; for that in fo many Years as I have known it, I did not difcover the leaft Increafe of Inhabitants; but the fame Show of a few ftraggling Houfes ftill appeared as when I firft faw it: And as for *Charles-Town*, it was well known by fome old People yet living, how many Years that Town lay in a languifhing State, with little Hopes of Recovery: The fame Obfervation was to be made on *Penfilvania*, now one of the moft flourifhing

rifhing Provinces in thefe Parts, from being
almoft in Defpair of ever rifing, &c. and
I made no Doubt, *Georgia* would alfo find
the Way to its true Intereft in a little more
Time; tho' I fhould never expect it would
confift in planting of Rice, which I apprehended they began to grow weary of now
in *Carolina*; when it was apparent that as
the Rate of Intereft of Money was at 10
per Cent. unlefs Rice would bring 40 *s. per*
Hundred, the Planters muft be ruined;
and the Increafe of that Product is grown
fo exorbitant, that for two Years paft it
will not exceed 30 *s*. From all which I
might naturally have inferred, that the Ze-
nith of that Province's moft flourifhing
State muft certainly be paft, unlefs they
turn their Strength, as *Georgia* muft, to
fome different Ufe from what is paft. After
fome little inoffenfive Raillery among us on
this Occafion, I dined with them, as did
alfo Mr. *Jones*; and towards Evening they
took themfelves Boats, and went down the
River to the Tender which they came in.

Friday. Little paffed worth Notice. Mr.   8.
Whitfield's Weaknefs continued upon him,
which he had brought on himfelf by fuch
an exceffive Vehemence in preaching and
expounding: He was fometimes obliged to
break off, unable to proceed; neverthelefs I
underftood he was preparing to fet out very
foon on another Progrefs Northward, in-

tending

tending now to visit *New-England* and those Parts. Mr. *Jones* (the Minister of *Port-Royal*) left us this Evening, with his Wife, and went home, to the Disappointment of many who wished to have heard some of his Doctrine; but why they did not, I could no ways learn: The other Strangers, who with their Wives came hither more than a Week since, to hear the Word from Mr. *Whitfield*, designed (as I heard) to attend him till he departed hence, ere they returned to their several Homes in *Carolina*. By a fresh Account this Day from *Ockstead*, we heard, that Mr. *Causton* was so far wasted as to leave his Friends little Hopes of surviving it much longer.

9. *Saturday*. Mr. *Tilly*, the Anabaptist Teacher, supplied Mr. *Whitfield*'s Place, in expounding a Part of the Scripture; for which he made Choice of the third Chapter to the *Philippians*, at usual Time of Morning Service: The ensuing Day produced nothing particularly remarkable.

10. *Sunday*. Mr. *Habersham* read the Prayers of the Church, and Mr. *Tilly* again preached. In the Afternoon the Congregation found some good Doctrine, from a regular Divine of the Church, Mr. *Jones* of *Port-Royal*, who went hence on *Friday* Evening, but meeting with a cross Passage, was forced to return hither about Noon, and now gave the People a good Sermon, exhorting them

to

to have a lively Faith in Chrift, to lead virtuous Lives, and to put their Truft in God's
good Providence for all Things needful.

Monday. Mr. *Whitfield* officiated at the
Morning Service in his ufual Manner, but
was yet very weak: About Noon Mr. *Noble*
Jones arrived here laft from *Frederica*, and
brought many Letters thence for divers of
our People; befides a Letter from the General to Mr. *Jones* and me each: Whereat
I conceived much Pleafure, having not had
the Honour of any from his Excellency
for feveral Months paft; neither could I
well expect it, as Affairs ftood: He was
pleafed to acquaint me, that he had ordered
the Bearer, *Noble Jones*, to raife ten Men
for a Guard and Scout-Boat; and that he
was to receive his Orders from me, where
principally to have a watchful Eye, that fo
we might have timely Notice, and not be
furprized; and the like Caution was taken
in divers other Parts, the General well knowing how very much the Safety of both thefe
Provinces is expofed to the Enemy's Half
Galleys, with a wide-extended Frontier towards the Sea; hardly to be defended by a
few Men; wherefore we muft wifh that
our Frigates, which are ftationed to cruize
on this Coaft, may be alert in their Duty
alfo, and not lie afleep in Harbour, which
I have known in former Times has been
laid to the Charge of fome Commanders;
but

but far be it from me to fufpect any of our
prefent Captains can be guilty of fo difho-
nourable an Indifference towards the Prefervation of thefe Countries. The Men
that came now with *Noble Jones* (in Number upwards of thirty) were all *Georgia*
Men, moftly of *Savannah Town,* and lifted
voluntarily here, towards compleating the
Carolina Regiment, which was one Caufe
of *Noble Jones's* having a Lieutenant's
Commiffion therein; and now their Time
is near expired, the Colonel *Vanderduffen*
required all of them to proceed with the
reft of the Regiment for *Charles-Town,* to
be paid off; but the General forefeeing, that
if they went thither, very few of them
probably would return hither again, except
fuch as were married, moft of the reft
being young Men, who were eafy to be
feduced; and moreover a pretty many Servants among them, both *Dutch* and *Englifh,* who had their Mafters Leave to go,
but not thereby to take the Remainder of
their indented Time to themfelves: For
thefe Reafons they were all of them put on
one Bottom, under this Officer's Care, who
was charged by the General to fee them
all fafe afhore on this Place; and if any
Doubt arofe at *Charles-Town* concerning
the Pay due, he would fee that looked
into; and *Noble Jones* was to go on himfelf

to

to *Charles-Town*, to fignify the General's
Sentiments to the Government there.

Tuefday. I found nothing ftirring all this
Day that deferved particular Notice; fome
of our *Carolina* Strangers, who found themfelves pretty well replenifhed with the Spirit, which they thought abounded from the
Doctrine they had learnt here, now left
us; and Mr. *Jones* the Minifter of *Port-
Royal* alfo, who was defeated in his Endeavour to return home laft Week, attempted
it again this Morning: But Mr. *Tilly* being found ufeful during Mr. *Whitfield's*
Weaknefs, continued yet as a Helper, and
Fellow Labourer.

Wednefday. The extream Heat of Weather more than common, for fome Days
paft, had fuch an Influence as to throw
me into a little Diforder, which would not
admit of my clofe Attention to any Bufinefs at prefent; neither did I hear of any
Thing material to obferve abroad.

Thurfday. This Morning began with a
very furprizing Piece of ill News; that the
Spanifh Prifoner, whom the Magiftrates
committed above a Year fince *(vide* 29th
and 30th of *July,* 1739.) upon ftrong
Prefumption of being a Spy, together with
an *Irifhman* his Companion, under the
Term of a Servant; and whom, under
Apprehenfions of a War likely to break
out foon, the General had given Orders

to

to be continued in safe Custody: They both broke out of Prison this last Night, and were fled: Some strong Grounds of Suspicion arising several Days before, of their having a Design to make some Attempt that Way; the Magistrates ordered them to have Irons put on, for their better Security; which upon View a few Days after, were found so near sawn off, that they might readily get quit of them; upon which fresh Irons were ordered, and withal an Iron Belly-band, with a Chain fixed in a Staple driven into the Floor: Notwithstanding all which Precaution, and they being also locked into a close Cell, they found Means to wrench the Staple of that Lock, and got into the outer Prison, where in a most incredible Manner they got free also from their Fetters and Chains, and before Morning found Means to get out at the Top of the Prison Room, by some of the Timber-Work being raised up, which could not be done but by some Help from without; nor could they have effected what they did within, had they not been supplied with proper Materials, by some Villains who assisted them; and out of Hatred to the Authority by which this Colony subsists, are wicked enough to turn Parricides, and wish to see Destruction brought upon the Whole: These are some of the Fruits of that seditious Club which
infested

infeſted this Place; and though I would
not, without plain Conviction, charge any
of that Aſſembly with being perſonally
aiding in ſo deteſtable an Act, I can very
readily believe the Perpetrators of it to be
well-inſtructed Diſciples of theirs, ready at
all Times to obſtruct (as far as in them lies)
every Thing done, however legally, which
does not ſuit their Humours; and now
more eſpecially upon miſſing a little while
that Succeſs, which was immediately expected at *Auguſtin*, I made no Doubt but
we ſhould ſee more and more daring Attempts made in various Shapes, to irritate
People (if poſſible) to commit ſome Outrage or other; and that very ſoon too. All
was done that could be thought of, in the
Power of thoſe in Authority, to endeavour
retaking theſe Fugitives, and Men ſent every Way on Horſeback, and Foot, and by
Water, to try if any Diſcovery could be
made; but as to my own Part, I own,
that my Hopes were very ſmall about it;
being poſſeſſed with an Opinion, that it
was an Affair concerted by ſuch as had
good Skill, as well as Will, to conduct it.
And the Conſideration of an enraged and
provoked Enemy being broke looſe, capable of giving the *Spaniards* ſuch Information at this Time, of all Circumſtances
here, muſt needs quicken the Apprehenſions of divers good People among us,
whom

1740.

August
14.

whom I look on as valuable Men, and dif-poſed truly to give Proof at any Time of their firm Attachment to the Colony.

15.   *Friday.* The Court ſat again, as *per* Adjournment, and received Claims from all who brought any ſuch, for what Lands they held under the Truſt, which were as many, or more, than at their laſt Sitting. Great was our Expectation of what would be the Succeſs of their Endeavours, who were gone in Purſuit of the Goal Breakers; but yet it proved vain.

16.   *Saturday.* What happened this Day among us, I thought a pretty plain Indication of my Imagination not being without ſome Foundation, from whence ſuch Thoughts aroſe on *Thurſday* laſt: For two or three of our *Indian* Traders, who took up their Lodging at *Jenkins*'s (who are generally, with a few Exceptions, a debauched, diſſolute People) having continued in Town ſomewhat longer than uſual, and got intimate with our Club Gentry there, who had taught them the Way of railing againſt all publick Tranſactions of this Place, and talking with Contempt in whatever Company they kept, of the Magiſtrates, and all in any Authority; it was no more than might be expected, if ſuch Inſolence ſhortly broke out into Action, and open Defiance of all Power whatever. Accordingly Meſſieurs *Parker* and *Jones*, having

ſum-

summoned one of these Traders to appear
before them, and answer the Complaint of
a certain Keeper of Stores at *Augusta*, who
was a well behaved Man, and ready to make
it appear how grievously he had injured
him, and fraudulently attempted to carry
off a great Quantity of his Goods: The
first Step taken by him was an absolute
Disobedience of their Warrant, which put
them under the Necessity of sending the
Constable to bring him by Force; which
was no sooner done, but two more of his
Comrades followed after him; and when
the Magistrates attempted to examine into
the Truth of Things, with all due Temper, they were interrupted in a scandalous
Manner, and set at nought by them all
three, swearing, cursing, and daring them
to do their worst, refusing to submit
to any Determination of theirs, and
even to lay aside their Hats in Token of
allowing them to be Magistrates, though
they well knew it. One of them was audacious enough to discover the Venom of
his Heart, by bitter Imprecations, and declaring, that he hoped to see this cursed
Town shortly in Flames, which nothing
should extinguish but the Blood of the Inhabitants; for which he was immediately,
and most deservedly, sent to Prison: Another of them, in the Time of his Ranting,
shaking his Fist at Bailiff *Parker*, and
threat-

threatning to call him to Account for theſe Things to-morrow, it was thought proper to ſend him to the Cuſtody of the Guard, for preventing of Miſchief: And in his Way thither he attacked the Conſtable, who being a Man of Spirit, and a good Officer *(viz. Samuel Mercer)* he ſoon ſhewed him he was miſtaken in his Man, and delivered him a Priſoner; which in a little Time brought ſome of his Club Acquaintance to pay him a Viſit there, being a Perſon in much Eſteem among them, and looked on by them as an able Railer, and Maker of Miſchief; wherefore they came not empty-handed, but brought both Wine and Landlord *Jenkins* himſelf with them, to keep up a good Heart in him. The third (who was the firſt Occaſion of this Uproar) refuſing to come to any Terms of Agreement whatever with his Adverſary, or to comply with any Thing propoſed by the Magiſtrates, wherein they ſought all Ways poſſible to give him Contentment, as far as Juſtice would permit; but he continued obſtinate and inflexible, bidding them do their worſt; though they would have been content with his giving his own Bond to come to a fair Account with the Complainant in any reaſonable Time; or would even have accepted of his entering into a ſingle Recognizance for his Appearance at any Seſſions three or four Months hence;
but

but refusing to accept of any such Indulgence, and persisting still in his contumelious Behaviour, there was no avoiding the Necessity they were under of committing him; which they did, to the same Place where they had sent his incendiary Companion. During these Transactions, another Fellow (a Stranger, who has some Concern among these Traders) came saucily up to the Centry upon Guard, who would not suffer him to go in without Orders; and in an impudent Manner, with Abundance of Oaths, telling the Guard to their Teeth they were a Pack of Scoundrels, and that he, and a few more such, as he knew where to find, would come and drive them all into the River: The Officer of the Guard laid hold of him, and bringing him to me, I sent him to the Magistrates to get his Demerits with the others; but it appearing he was pretty much gone in Drink, and an honest Man of the Town being near who knew him, upon Security given for his Appearance at a proper Time, he was dismissed; but after the Magistrates had done, I thought something farther necessary for me; for on one Occasion or another, observing a pretty many People gathered together, and it growing a little late in the Night, I was not without some Apprehensions of a yet greater Feud arising; wherefore I sent to the Tything-man next

upon

1740. upon Duty, ordering him immediately to
bring his People with him, which I waited
August till he did; and then doubling the Guard,
and leaving ftrict Orders to prevent any
Difturbance, a little after Midnight I went
home. No News yet of the Runaways.

17. *Sunday.* One of our Neighbour *Indians*
coming to Town this Morning, and hearing of what had happened of the late E-
fcape made by the two Prifoners, told us,
that he met two fuch Perfons as were de-
fcribed, about four Miles off, on the Path
leading to *Palachocolas*; by which we found
they had been lurking near, if not in Town,
till they thought the firft Heat of Purfuit
was a little over; and now upon the fame
Indian's telling us, he believed it was not
too late to overtake them, wherein he
would give what Affiftance he could, by
tracking, &c. we fent out immediately
frefh Parties, Horfe and Foot, in Queft of
them, under his Guidance, with frefh Hopes
of Succefs. Mr. *Whitfield* did his Office of
praying and preaching this Morning, but
was in a very weak State; and in the Afternoon was forced to go out of Church as
foon as he came in, leaving Mr. *Haberfham*
to read the Prayers, and Mr. *Tilly*, the A-
nabaptift, to perform the reft; who after
an *extempore* Prayer of more than an Hour,
and a Sermon of as great a Length, dif-
miffed his Audience; a great Part of which
(if

(if I miſtake not) would have choſen rather to have ſtaid at home. Whether he,
or who elſe, was appointed by Mr. *Whit-*
field to perform the Duty of a Miniſter
here, during his Abſence, I know not; but
notwithſtanding the low State he was in, I
found he was determined to leave us in a
few Days, and go to the Northern Provinces: For in a Kind of a farewel Sermon that he gave us in the Forenoon,
when he recommended us all to the Grace
of God, and in a particular Manner
charged thoſe of his own Houſe how to
behave as well towards each other, as the
Children he left under their Care; he ſig-
nified that he believed it would be a long
while ere he ſaw us again: And indeed unleſs he got a little Recovery of Strength
ſoon, which was ſo waſted by his inceſſant
Labour and Vehemence in preaching, I
much doubted whether or not he would
live to come back.

Monday. I could not learn any Thing, **18.**
during the Courſe of this whole Day, that
deſerved Notice from me here: The Pur-
ſuers of the Fugitives not yet returning,
we knew not what to expect. A fine
Shower of Rain falling, was exceeding delightful and refreſhing, the Heats for a
while paſt having been more than ordinary
violent; nevertheleſs the Town had the
great Bleſſing of Health to a Degree far

beyond its Neighbours croſs the River in *Carolina*, which it was to be wiſhed might not be impaired, as the Fall came on, through the immenſe Quantity of Peaches growing every where, which our People have long eaten with Greedineſs, alike with the Swine, that have in great Part been fed with them. All Peace and Quiet again, and *Saturday* Night's Ruffle forgot for the preſent.

19.　　　*Tueſday.* Mr. *Whitfield* went on board his Sloop very early, about Three in the Morning, falling down the River on his intended Voyage Northward, and taking with him Mr. *Simms* only of his own Houſhold, to attend him in his Travels; divers others, Men and Women, Strangers, went Paſſengers as far as *Charles-Town,* who had a good while been his Diſciples here, and now returned to their ſeveral Homes in *Carolina*; Mr. *Tilly* alſo took the ſame Opportunity, and left us; *Robert Gilbert* (one of our Freeholders, and Magiſtrate laſt Year) with his Wife, were the only Perſons who went with them, which they could give no good Reaſon for; not that their Loſs is of any great Significance, for he was originally a Seller of old Cloaths in *London,* here a botching Taylor, and no Planter, but a ſober, quiet Man, doing no Harm, nor much Good, more than doing his own perſonal Guard-Duty; and

if

If I am rightly informed, he hath formerly received many diftinguifhing Marks of Favour, very folid ones too, from Mr. *Oglethorpe*; for he came in a very poor State; but howfoever hard Thoughts fome Folks may have conceived of *Georgia*, it is plain he has found it a Place where he could live and make Money; whereof he is not wanting to carry with him to *Penfil-vania*, to which Place he thinks himfelf directed by the Spirit, which mixed with fome Ingratitude, I think to be his prefent Compofition. The next Movement of any of our fettled Inhabitants, it is expected will happen among our reftlefs Gentry of the Club, fome of whom, namely, Dr. *Tailfer* and *Jenkins*, I have before taken Notice were preparing to fend off their Wives and Families; but that not yet being done, it is now publickly given out, that they themfelves alfo are preparing to go with them, and were putting their Goods on board a fmall Sloop lying near, formerly built by Mr. *Robert Williams*, but never yet employed, whereof another of the Club was to go Mafter on this Occafion, whofe Skill in Navigation is fuppofed not to be great; and when I fee this come to pafs, I fhall think the Colony happily delivered from the moft mifchievous Set of People that ever fat down in it; for it muft inevitably caufe a Diffolution of that So-

ciety

1740. ciety when their great *Pan* is gone; nevertheless as they all stand Debtors in some
August Degree or other on the Trustees Books, it
is to be expected they must come to an
Account before they are suffered to depart;
though probably that may, among others,
be termed an arbitrary and tyrannical Act.

20. *Wednesday.* Some of our Pursuers being
returned *re infectâ*, who went out on
Sunday last, and others yet continuing a-
broad, after tracking them as far as the
River *Oguchee*, we did not despair utterly
of their coming up with them. One of
the Persons taken into Custody on *Saturday*
last, being discharged from the Guard on
Monday Morning, upon asking Pardon for
his Offence, and finding Sureties for the
Peace; another of them was this Day discharged out of Goal, upon his Submission
likewise, and complying with what was at
first required of him, confessing he found
himself mistaken in some whom he expected to take his Part, that in this Time
of Need would not so much as appear to
be his Bail; from whence it was pretty
evident who had been the Instigators of
that Disturbance, as we judged at that
Time; but the third superlative to the o-
thers, with his Menaces of Flame and
Blood, the Magistrates thought proper to
detain till he was made a little more sensible

ble of his Crime. What fell out more in
the Day, was of no Moment.

Thurſday. The reſt of the Horſemen
now returned from their Purſuit of the
Goal-Breakers, all agreeing in one Opinion, that they could not have paſſed the
Oguchee River, but they muſt have made
ſome Diſcovery of it; but the Swamps and
Thickets on this Side were ſo impenetrable,
that no Good could be done by attempting to look into them; and thereupon
ſome of our *Indians*, which they had with
them, undertaking to guard all thoſe Places
of difficult Acceſs, and to watch them
narrowly if they lay hid there (as was
ſuppoſed) what Hopes we now had remaining, were built upon the Diligence
of thoſe *Indians*. Mr. *Jones* calling on me
this Afternoon, and conferring a while (as
we frequently uſed to do with one another)
was gone not far from my Houſe, when
a Gun went off; and he returning immediately, aſked me if I knew whence that
Shot was, for that it was with a Ball,
which he heard whiz very near him: He
went away again but a little Way, when
another Shot was made from the ſame
Quarter, with a Ball alſo, and that I heard
clearly paſs over my Head as I ſtood at the
Gate of my Yard looking out; whereupon
I called on Mr. *Jones* (not yet out of Sight)
and when he came, upon laying theſe

Things

Things together, we thought the Circumſtances attending it were pretty remarkable; wherefore Mr. *Jones* taking the Tything-man with him, who is a Smith, and
whoſe Shop is over-againſt the Backſide of
my Houſe, in one of the Planks of which
Shop one of theſe Balls lodged that were
now fired, they went directly and ſeized
the Fellow, who was yet ſtanding on, or
near the ſame Spot from whence he had
fired, and had his Gun again ready loaden;
it was juſt without the Skirts of the Town;
the Houſe where I live at preſent is in
Huck's Tything, Nº 9. in *Percivall* Ward,
not far from the Court-Houſe: The Distance of Mr. *Jones* from me was as far as
Nº 6. in the ſame Tything, when the firſt
Shot paſſed by him, on his Way home:
Upon Examination, the Fellow owned that
he was not ſhooting at any Mark or o-
ther particular Thing whatever, but only
diverting himſelf with his Gun; when we
aſked him whether he thought it a reaſonable Diverſion or not, to ſtand without the
Town and fire Ball into it, levelling his
Piece directly: He had nothing to ſay more,
than that he did not mean any Harm:
But Mr. *Jones* not ſatisfied with that Anſwer, and which I neither could think a
very ſufficient one; he committed him for
the preſent, and took the Gun from him,
which I was told afterwards was found to

3   be

be loaden with Drop Shot (the fame as is
commonly ufed in killing of Deer) by
which it looked as if he refolved to make
fure of fome Mifchief the next Difcharge,
the two laft that he made paffing fo near
each of us, though at fo wide a Diftance
as we then were from one another. The
Fellow was a Servant to *Phelps* a *Scotchman*,
who for a Year or two paft had rented a
Houfe in Town, where he kept Store of
Cloth, and other like dry Goods, and was
one of the moft active and bufy Men of
our Club, being the fame whom the General fhewed fuch a particular Mark of his
Difpleafure to, as noted in my Journal of
the 23d of *April* laft; and of late finding
his Behaviour narrowly watched, he thought
it beft to withdraw to *Charles-Town*, quitting his Houfe, where he had little Store
left; and this Man was appointed to ftay
here, waiting his farther Orders. Divers
of our People, beft affected, are apt to draw
Inferences from this, which I cannot readily join in; for how malicious foever the
Mafter may be, I am unwilling to think he
had a particular and perfonal Antipathy towards me, or that his Servant would, at any
Inftigation, perpetrate fo bafe and wicked
an Act, as to deftroy a Man in cold
Blood, who had never injured him, and
hardly knew him.

I i 4 *Friday.*

1740.
August
22.

Friday. The Court sat again, to receive Claims from any who brought them, whereof divers yet came in. Mr. *Currie* (an *Indian* Trader) went privately out of Town, as the Magistrates were informed, to the Orphan-House, where some of Mr. *Whitfield*'s People had promised to assist him with a Boat, to carry him to the General at *Frederica,* with Intent to make Complaint to his Excellency of the hard Usage which some of his Fraternity had met with in those Proceedings against them, as noted on *Saturday* last & *seq.* but the Magistrates were under no Apprehension of his Displeasure, for having done no more than their Duty on such an Occasion, when the publick Peace was at Stake, and their lawful Authority set at nought.

23.

Saturday. This Day I devoted wholly to my little Ville at *Bewlie,* where I spent it with Pleasure, having not seen it since the 23d past : The principal Work now in hand was setting up a little Edifice of somewhat better Sort than any yet done, as Necessity required hitherto ; for I was also desirous to frame a small Habitation, commodious for myself and a Friend with me, when I saw it during my own Time, and useful to such afterward as were to take Possession. After a pretty hot Day, I chose to return pretty late in the Evening, having the Benefit of a bright Moon, and heard of nothing strange when I came home.

Sunday.

Sunday, St. *Bartholomew*. Mr. *Haber-ſham* now ſupplying Mr. *Whitfield*'s Place during his Abſence, he read the Prayers, and a Sermon before Noon and after; but out of what Author I knew not; it ſeemed to be entering upon a freſh Round of the Doctrine of Regeneration, Converſion and Juſtification, beginning again with our Saviour's Conference with *Nicodemus*. Having no freſh Intelligence ſince *Thurſday* of what Succeſs might be expected relating to the Recovery of thoſe Goal-Breakers, we began now to deſpair of any Good.

Monday. In the Afternoon arrived *Peter Emery* with his Boat from *Charles-Town*, and brought with him two Packets from the Truſt, which were committed to his Care by Mr. *Hopton*, who alſo wrote me a Letter, ſignifying his having received them about a Week before, and acquainting me, that a new Poſt-Maſter being lately appointed, he ſuffered no Letters to be brought aſhore, but what he fetch'd himſelf; wherefore all Letters and Packets, for the future, muſt be paid for; and that he was now obliged to pay 20 s. Currency *(i. e.* Half a Crown) for theſe two; he wrote me likewiſe, that the two Boxes I ſent him lately, one directed to Mr. *Verelſt*, the other to *Robert Eyre*, Eſq; as ſpecified in my Letter to him of the 5th Inſtant, he had delivered to the Care of Capt. *Samuel Ragly*

Ragly of the *Betty*, taking the Captain's Receipt for them, which he had inclofed to Mr. *Verelft* in a Letter; but was obliged to mention in the Receipt 10 s. Sterling to be paid for Freight of them, or he would not take them and fign it. In each of thefe Packets I found one for the General, with various other Letters to fundry People, one to Mr. *Jones*, and two fhort ones to myfelf of the 24th of *April* and the 5th of *May*, referring to divers Papers inclofed from Mr. *Verelft*, &c. I fent abroad all that came to hand for other People, and the Contents of what Mr. *Jones* and I receiv'd gave Occafion of our Conference good Part of the Evening; when we concluded upon it, that one of us would go and wait on the General ourfelves in a Day or two, with thofe Packets for him, having not feen or heard from him for a good while paft; and it was highly needful to inform him of divers Things paffed here of late, that we might be advifed the better *ore tenus*.

26.   *Tuefday.* Mr. *Caufton* being brought to Town a few Days fince in a very weak State, hoping that Change of Air, and the Converfation of his Friends might contribute towards his Recovery; I had the Opportunity of delivering him his Letter from the Truft, whereof I had received a Copy. He was reduced, indeed, to the Shadow of a Man, and there appeared little

Room

Room of his Amendment, otherwise than from him with whom all Things are possible. It was again given out, that Meſſ. *Stirling*, *Grant* and *Douglas*, had received in that Letter which I delivered them from the Truſt, a ſatisfactory Anſwer to what they had requeſted, touching their ſettling on *Wilmington Iſland*; which I knowing of could ſay nothing to: But as Dr. *Tailfer* was preparing now in Earneſt to leave us, and that Club muſt thereby come to an End, I apprehended no ill Conſequence, provided they were under a Covenant to cultivate Land, as well as raiſe a live Stock, which, perhaps, was their Aim only.

Wedneſday. Much Talk now of Dr. *Tailfer*'s Preparation to leave us ſoon, together with his cloſe Adherents; and more than ordinary Pains having been taken by them ſince the Siege of *Auguſtin* being raiſed, to ſet forth the deſtitute and indefenſable State this Colony was left in, and that we might ſurely expect the Enemy to come ſoon upon us; I made no Doubt but I ſhould find this doughty Club, at their Breaking entirely up, go off with ſome little Train of puſillanimous Attendants: My Wiſhes at the ſame Time were, that they might not leave one among us behind them ſo actuated by the like Spirit of Diſcord, as to be capable of propagating more Miſchief.

Thurſday.

Thurſday. *Noble Jones* being in Town,
whom the General had given the Command to of a Scout and Guard-Boat, with
ten Men, to watch the *Narrows* at *Skedoway*, and who was to take his Orders from
me as Occaſion might happen; I had many Things to ſay to him thereon, concerning a Boat which I had in my Eye at *Puryſburgh*, that was to be ſold, and I conceived would very fitly anſwer our Purpoſe,
wherein I gave him proper Directions, as I
alſo did about getting able and good Men
for the Uſe intended *(vide* 11th Inſtant;)
moreover acquainting him, that as it was
probable I might go South very ſoon, to
wait on the General, I ſhould in ſuch Caſe,
on my Return, expect to find his Boat and
Men at their proper Station; and therefore
recommended to him to uſe all poſſible Diligence in ſo neceſſary a Piece of Service;
which he promiſed.

29.

Friday. The Packets for the General
having lain in my Hands ſince *Monday*,
and ſeeing no Opportunity offer to ſend
them; upon conferring with Mr. *Jones* upon it, I obſerved he had it in his Intention,
to be the Bearer of them himſelf; but
having not waited on the General in the
South for more than a Year paſt (which
Mr. *Jones* had divers Times) and withal
having a more than ordinary Deſire at this
Time, to conſult his Excellency on thoſe
arduous

arduous Points, which the Truſtees in their Letters (of late received) had required me to be very explicit in, and for that Reaſon they had deſired me to crave his Help; I thought proper not to be too free with my Compliments at preſent, but ſaid plainly to him, that I thought it was my Turn; at which he acquieſced, and a Boat was ordered to be ready againſt the Morning Tide, very early. Dr. *Tailfer* now alſo began to ſend off his Goods and Luggage on board a ſmall Sloop lying at the Wharf, in order to proceed for *Charles-Town* in a Day or two, as it was ſaid.

Saturday. I took Boat at Three in the Morning, having with me Mr. *Clee*, who had ſome ſmall Affair of his own to tranſact at *Frederica*, &c. and knowing him to be well ſkilled as a Pilot to ſteer, and moreover an inoffenſive Companion, I was glad of him in both Capacities. *Noble Jones* was to go out of Town in the Morning on Horſeback, to meet me at his own Plantation, which is within a Mile or two Diſtance from the Guard-Houſe: We arrived at his Houſe about Nine, and he came ſoon after; when we went together to the Watch-Houſe; which I found in pretty good Order; but with little more Expence and Labour, it would be very uſeful, and capable of Annoyance and Defence; and after a little Time ſo ſpent, we

went

30.

went on with our Boat, and reached *Bear Ifland* that Evening, where we went afhore, refted during the Night; and,

31. *Sunday*, very early, we went forward, and refted that Night on *Sapiloe Ifland*, not venturing too far, by reafon the Wind arofe, and began to blow hard.

Septemb. *Monday*. Arrived at *Frederica* about Sun-
1. fetting; when underftanding the General was in but a weak State of Health, feldom converfing with any more than needful; and being myfelf alfo pretty much difcom-pofed and fatigued, I fent him his Packets by Mr. *Hawkins*, and afked his Leave to wait on him in the Morning; whereupon he was fo good to fend me a Bottle of Wine, and a Bottle of Cyder: And the beft Compli-ment I had to make him in Return, was to acquaint him I had a Bottle of *Savannah* Wine at his Service, made there, which I had brought with me, to prefent it with my own Hand from the Maker.

2. *Tuefday*. I did fo in the Morning; when I was readily admitted, and kindly received; but wifhed to have found his Excellency in better Health, for a lurking Fever that hanged on him for a long Time paft had worn away his Strength very much; fo that he indulged himfelf pretty much on his Bed, and feldom came down Stairs, but retained ftill the fame Vivacity of Spirit in Appearance to all whom he
talked

talked with, though he chose to converse with very few; wherefore I never was urgent to speak with him, when I called to ask his Servants how he did (which was pretty often) but only left my Name, &c. waiting for the Time when he found an Inclination to talk with me of the Business I came about, which he very well knew. From this Day, during my Abode there, it was in vain for me to attempt keeping a daily Journal, which must have been *pro formâ* only, and filled with incoherent Trifles, not worth remembring. One Day I took to go and make a Visit to the Camp at the South-East End of St. *Simon*'s, and paid my Respects to Colonel *Cook*, Major *Heron*, and some other Officers whom I knew, which is about eight Miles from *Frederica* by Land, but by Water (as I went) it is much farther round: Four Companies were here stationed, and the other two are at *Frederica* with the General, who are also encamped without the Lines of the Town, which the General is fortifying, by casting up a Trench, and making proper Works at due Distances. I was glad to see the Men so soon and well recovered from the Sickness which they brought with them from *Augustin*, very few of them being now unfit for Service, and the Companies much fuller than I expected, wanting little more than a fifth Part to recruit

the

1740.

Septemb.

the Whole; though the Company which marched at the Beginning of the Summer from *Port-Royal*, to join them, had loft fo many by Sicknefs, Accident of drowning, Defertion, &c. that it wanted near half its Complement at their firft taking the Field. From thefe two Camps, Detachments are made to fupply the Out Garifons near the Frontiers, *viz.* St. *Andrew*, *Fort William*, *Amelia*, St. *George*, &c. in Proportion to their Strength, and they are relieved as thought fit by the General. After nine or ten Days, his Excellency growing ftronger, began to talk more clofely of Bufinefs; and by Degrees taking the Affair into Confideration, which principally occafioned my waiting on him, I collected his Sentiments in many Things that I wanted to know, and withal informed him how far I could atteft and maintain the Truth of divers Things which would need it : Many Things were difcuffed during the laft few Days of my Stay, too long to enter into again here, but not fit to be forgotten by me; fo having gone through what was requifite, having the Pleafure of parting with his Excellency in a much better State of Health than I found him, I took my Leave; and,

17.

Wednefday, about One o'Clock, we put off again with our Boat for *Savannah*, and refted that Night at our former Camp on *Sapiloe*.

Thurfday.

Thurfday. We proceeded, and by the Help of a fair Wind we reached *Vernon* River; a little Way within the Mouth of which was *Bewlie*, where I took the Opportunity of looking into what was doing; but was forry to find fo much Sicknefs among them; one of my beft Servants ill; as was alfo my Overfeer's Wife, whilft he himfelf newly gone to Town for fome Help, was alfo taken ill there.

Friday. It was Noon this Day before the Tide would admit of our going on, with the Wind againft us; and then we proceeded, after leaving the beft Directions among them that I could, with Promifes of remembring them farther, of which they fhould have Tokens as foon as I got home. On our Way, we met with the Scout-Boat at her proper Station, which was appointed to guard that Pafs of *Skedoway Narrows*; and it was a Satisfaction to me to find the Orders I left with *Noble Jones (vide* the 28th of *Auguft)* fo well obferved: After rowing a few Miles farther, the Wind holding contrary, we were oblig'd to come to an Anchor, and wait another different Tide coming, to carry us on, fo we dozed in the Boat a-while; and putting forward again about Eleven at Night, we arrived at *Savannah* about Three or Four o'Clock in the Morning, being about the

1740. fame Hour we left it juſt three Weeks
Septemb. ſince.
20.

Saturday. The firſt News I met with
this Morning, as ſoon as abroad, was a full
Completion of what I foreſaw would come
to paſs, as I noted it on the 27th *ult.* For
ſoon after I went South, the Doctor and
his Crew made their Way North (it is ſaid)
to *Charles-Town*; his Attendants or Followers ſoon after, were *Grant, Douglas,
Sterling, Baylie,* and (to make the Set
compleat) Landlord *Jenkins,* with his Wife
alſo. It is needleſs to ſay what inſtigated
theſe People, who have ſufficiently ſhewn
their good Diſpoſition for ſome Years
paſt. Thus we at laſt ſee an End of that
curſed Club, which has ſo long been the
very Bane of this Place, and which might
have been happy ere now, had not the
poiſonous Influence of that Crew blinded
their Underſtandings. It is ſaid that the
Fear of the *Spaniards* was what drove
away theſe next following (all likewiſe
ſince my going from home) *viz.* Dr. *Nu-
nez* and his Son *Daniel, De Lion's* Wife,
Pye's Wife (Siſter to Mr. *Brownfield)* our
Conſtable *Duchee's* Wife; their Huſbands
yet ſtaying to wait a farther Event; and
Penroſe's Wife went off in Defiance of
hers; a notorious Termagant, whom I ſuppoſe he thinks himſelf well rid of: On the
contrary,

contrary, I this Day received the bad News of my own dear Wife's Death.

Sunday. Mr. *Haberſham* read the Prayers and Sermon in the ſame Way as before. Towards Evening *Laughlan Mᶜ Intoſh* alighted at my Door, and gave me a diſmal Relation of what had happened at Fort *Argyle*, upon the River *Oguchee:* Which in Subſtance was, That having been ſome Days abſent from the Fort on Buſineſs, partly at *Savannah* and elſewhere; on his Return thither laſt *Thurſday* Evening, he found the Doors all open, what Cheſts or Boxes were within rifled, much Blood ſpilt on the Bed, Floor, *&c.* and his Dog wrapt up in a Blanket with his Throat cut; from whence he concluded, that a Man and Woman Servant, whom he left there, were both murdered. How it happened that ſo few Hands were left there, or why he himſelf, who had the Charge of the Place, left them ſo defenceleſs, it was not a Time for me to enter into an Enquiry of; but I ſoon called the Magiſtrates together, that due Examination might be taken of all Circumſtances which could be come at: And then he depoſed, that they had found the Servant-Man's Body floating in the River a Mile or two lower, with no Head to it, which was ſuppoſed to have been cut off; but they could find no Token of what became of the Maid: He ſaid, that

when

when he went thither on *Thursday* last, he had in Company with him *William Francis* of this Town, who was appointed one to keep Garison there; and before he came thence now, two or three other Men arrived there, under the same Appointment: It was observed, that during his Examination, he appeared very much disordered, by an uncommon Flutter of Spirits, which raised a Jealousy there was something more than ordinary which he had not discovered; wherefore it was thought best to defer a farther Examination till to-morrow; and in the mean while a watchful Eye was appointed to be near him, as a Companion, that he might not slip out of Town, whilst at the same Time he knew not himself to be under Confinement. Various were Peoples Conjectures on this Occasion, and indeed the whole Town was alarmed, most Part of them concluding, that it must be some *Indians*, but what *Indians* they could not tell, unless our own Friends and Neighbours, which there were not the least Grounds to suspect. My own Thoughts (which divers concurred with me in) were, that the *Spanish* Doctor, and the *Irishman*, who broke Prison, and escaped hence (as noted the 14th of *August, &c. seq.*) finding themselves under great Difficulties how to subsist, and make a thorough Escape, had joined themselves to some Negroes lately
fled

fled from *Carolina*, who were wandring 1740.
Southward (as of late many of them had
deferted; infomuch that there was a Party Septemb.
of Horfe appointed always to fcout on the
Banks of the River, and guard the Paffes
out of that Province) and thefe fo joined
very probably might attempt fuch an Act,
efpecially when they would meet with no
Oppofition; and what induced me the rather to incline to this Opinion was, that
among the feveral Particulars of Plunder
carried off, which chiefly confifted of Eat-
ables, I took particular Notice they had
taken a Quire of Writing-Paper, which
could be of no Ufe to an *Indian*; and
moreover it is to be obferved, that when
an *Indian* kills, he always takes the Scalp
alone; but the Negro moft commonly takes
the whole Head. We were next to wait
for what farther Difcoveries we could come
at to-morrow.

Monday. The Magiftrates now met again, 22.
and took Depofitions in Form of what
Laughlan McIntofh had to fay; which he
made Affidavit of: And finding him very
abftrufe in many Things, and differing
from what he had reported Yefterday; they
became more fufpicious than before, that
fomething at Bottom was not right; wherefore Mr. *Parker* the Magiftrate, and Mr.
Mercer the Conftable, offering voluntarily
to go to the Fort themfelves, and endea-

vour to find out the Truth of the Whole, it was so agreed at my House; and as their readiest Way to come at it, was up the *Oguchee* from the Mouth of it, they purposed to go by Land to *Noble Jones*'s Plantation; to whom I wrote an Order to be assisting to them, with his Guard-Boat, and proper Hands; and accordingly they set out soon after. In the mean while proper Means were used to amuse *Laughlan*, and keep him in Town, till we should get some Report from *Parker* and *Mercer* how they found Matters at the Fort.

23.   *Tuesday.* I thought every Day now lost that was not chiefly employed in forwarding the great Work in hand, to set the present State of the Colony in a due Light before the Trustees, as they had required for some Time past; and therefore having got some of the principal Materials together, in the best Manner I could, it must next be my Care to get it perfected with all possible Expedition; and so I resolved.

24.   *Wednesday.* Nothing happened that required my taking Notice of in the Town, or abroad elsewhere, which I was not forry for, having enough to do at home every Day for some Time coming; and such Confinement happened now to be also requisite, on Account of a lame Leg that I brought home with me from my late Expedition, which was occasioned by a trifling
Acci-

Accident of a Bite from one of our flying 1740.
Infects (of which there is great Variety Septemb.
in this Part of the World) which occafioned a fmall Swelling, from whence en-
fued an extream Itching, and that was attended with Scratching, which added to
the Venom; and the Skin being thereby a
little broke, an Humour immediately followed it; fo that maugre what Mr. *Hawkins* applied to ftop it at *Frederica*, from the
Bignefs of a Pin's Head, it foon became a
Sore as broad as a Man's Hand, as it yet
continues; but by the Help of innocent
cooling Things made ufe of now, and proper Reft, I hope foon to fee it healed.

Thurfday. Meffieurs *Parker* and *Mer-*   25.
cer returned; and having examined, upon
Oath, the Perfons whom they found at the
Fort, and made the beft Enquiry they
could, upon comparing the feveral Affidavits together, it was found, that in
the main Points they agreed all. *Peter
Emery* at this fame Time having his Boat
freighted with fundry Goods bound for
Frederica, Mr. *Jones* and I both wrote
Letters to the General, advifing him of
what was needful in many other Cafes, as
well as in this, delivering all to *Emery's*
Care, and recommending it to *Laughlan
Mc Intofh* to go in the fame Boat, and re-
late all to the General himfelf; and fo he
refolved to do.

K k 4   *Friday,*

1740.
Septemb.
26.
27.

28.

29.

Friday, } Confinement at home be-
Saturday. } ing doubly neceſſary now,
as well on Account of my Lameneſs, as
to get forward what I had in hand; I
ſtuck to it, and heard of nothing abroad
that required my Attention theſe two Days.

Sunday. A Preſbyterian Divine, who
arrived from *Carolina* ſome Days ſince,
preached to the Congregation before Noon
and after; but my Infirmity would not admit of my going to hear him.

Monday. Freſh Intelligence being brought
us this Evening, that the *Spaniſh* Doctor,
who with his Companion broke Priſon, and
eſcaped hence ſome Time ago, had been
ſeen that Morning near the Cow-Pen at
Old Ebenezer; we began to conceive again
more Hopes of Succeſs in our Endeavours
to take them; wherefore upon Conſultation had, we made Choice of three of
the moſt active and expert Men in the
Woods that we had, to ride out well armed and provided with Food, to try what
they could do; and for their Encouragement, a Reward of 20 *l.* Sterling was promiſed upon catching them, or proportionable for either; being now pretty full in
Opinion, that the late Murder and Plunder
at Fort *Argyle* was perpetrated by that
Crew; one at leaſt, if not more, having
lately joined them; but who, we could
not tell.

Tueſday.

Tuefday. The Perfons appointed rode out this Morning in Purfuit of thofe Villains; and I refted in the fame Pofture at home as before, doing what I could in employing my Pen to a right Purpofe.

Wednefday. Still confined at home. Mr. *Caufton* having fpent a few Weeks in Town, for the Benefit of converfing with fome of his old Acquaintance, thereby hoping to get a little Strength; during his Continuance here had the Misfortune to lofe his Son (his only Child) who was taken in one of thofe intermitting Fevers, which are pretty frequent in this Part of the World, at this Time of the Year, whereof very few die; and being of a weak Conftitution, it carried him foon off, which fo affected his Father, that he returned mournfully to *Ockftead,* ill able to fuftain his Grief.

Thurfday. Nothing came to my Knowledge from abroad worth Notice, but every body following their own Bufinefs, as I did mine, and hoped foon to be on my Legs again.

Friday. At length the Time was come which brought the News we wanted, of thofe Villains being taken; two of thofe Men we fent out returning this Day, and acquainting us, that they came upon them about twenty-five Miles beyond the Cow-Pen at *Ebenezer,* at a Place called *Mount Pleafant,* or the *Uchee* Town (from fome of thofe

thofe *Indians* inhabiting thereabout) on the River *Savannah*, and is the ufual Place of croffing it to the *Palachocolas* : Here the Rain had driven them for Shelter into a Hut, and our Purfuers furprizing them, they were fecured without Refiftance ; tho' they had Arms with them, which they took at Fort *Argyle*, and where they readily confeffed they had murdered that Man and Woman, and made Plunder of what they liked. After binding them fafely, they left them under the Charge of one of their own Company, joined with feveral other well known trufty Perfons, whom they met on their Paffage by Water to *Savannah*, where they were bound ; and it was a convenient Opportunity of fending the Prifoners with them, whom we were to expect to-morrow ; but they utterly denied having any third Perfon in their Company, as it was reported.

Saturday. Great were all Peoples Expectations of feeing thofe Prifoners brought down, which were in Cuftody, as they that took them reported to us Yefterday ; but one of their Guard being a principal *Indian* Trader among the *Creeks* and *Uchees*, we judged he might be detained a little by his Bufinefs with them, before he fet out for *Savannah* ; and fo we would look for them to-morrow. A *New-York* Sloop, *Samuel Tingley* Mafter, arrived with Store

Store of Provifion for Sale, which effectually put a Stop to one current Lie, that
our late Deferters had fpread before their
Departure; that all Provinces looked on
us as a Place given up for loft, and none
of them would deal with us any farther
for any Support: At the fame Time the
faid Mafter told us, that he himfelf heard
fome of thofe that went thither from
hence, complaining already how much
dearer they found it living there than here,
and beginning to wifh they had not been
fo mifled. In the Evening Mr. *Cambel*
returned, who went hence for *London* with
Captain *Thompfon*, and arrived at *Charles-
Town* about a Fortnight fince; where he
fell ill, that Place of late being grown
very fickly again: And he told me, he
had brought feveral Packets for the General, which he had fent to *Frederica*, by a
Boat going that Way; and that he had
alfo one for me from Mr. *Verelft*, which
he had during his Illnefs delivered to another Boat, under the Care of *Young Ger-
main*, who was the Patroon bound hither; but that Boat being fomewhere detained (as he imagined) was not yet arrived
with the faid Packet, and he got hither
by another Conveyance, before her, which
gave me fome Uneafinefs: He farther told
us, that feeing fome of our late Club at
Charles-Town, they afked him if he was
not

1740.
October 4.

not mad to go again to *Savannah,* where all People that were left were ftarving, and the Place muft foon be depopulated? So inceffant were their vile Tongues employed in uttering their Venom againft this Colony.

A

S T A T E

OF THE

Province of *Georgia*,

Attefted upon Oath in the Court
of *Savannah, Nov.* 10, 1740.

T H E Province of *Georgia* lies
from the moft Northern
Stream of the River *Savannah* (the Mouth of which
is in the Latitude of 32
Deg.) along the Sea-Coaft, to the moft
Southern Stream of the *Alatamaha* (the
Mouth of which is 30 ½ Deg.) and Weftward from the Heads of the faid Rivers,
refpectively in direct Lines to the South
Seas.

THIS

THIS Province was Part of *South-Carolina*; but the Eastern and Southern Parts of it, inhabited by the *Creek Indians*; the Northern by the *Cherokees* and *Chickesaws*; the Western by the *Chactaws*; the *Blew-mouths*, and other *Indian* Nations, to the *South-Sea*. The *Creek Indians*, who always acknowledged the King of *England* for their Sovereign, yet made War with the People of *Carolina*, to obtain Satisfaction for Injuries done by their pedling Traders: The War was concluded by a Peace, which obliged the People of *Carolina* not to settle beyond the River *Savannah*; and no *Englishman* was settled within this District, that we know of, when the first Colony of *Georgia* arrived. The Country was then all covered with Woods. Mr. *Oglethorpe* agreed with the *Indians*, and purchased of them the Limits mentioned in the Treaty.

THE Town of *Savannah* was laid out, and began to be built, in which are now 142 Houses, and good habitable Huts. The Soil in general, when cleared, is productive of *Indian* Corn, Rice, Peas, Potatoes, Pumpions, Melons, and many other Kinds of Gourds, in great Quantities; Wheat, Oats, Barley, and other *European* Grains, 'tis found by divers Experiments, may be propagated in many Parts (more especially in the Uplands toward *Augusta*)

with

with Succefs. Mulberry-Trees and Vines
agree exceeding well with the Soil and Climate, and fo does the Annual Cotton,
whereof 'large Quantities have been raifed ;
and it is much planted : But the Cotton,
which in fome Parts is perennial, dies here
in the Winter; which neverthelefs the Annual is not inferior to in Goodnefs, but re-
quires more Trouble in cleanfing from the
Seed. Cattle, Hogs, Poultry, and Fruit-
Trees of moft Kinds, have increafed even
beyond Imagination.

SHIPS of about three hundred Tons can
come up to the Town, where the Worm
(which is the Plague of the *American* Seas)
does not eat; and the River is navigable for
large Boats, as far as the Town of *Augufta*,
which lies in the Latitude of 33 D. 5 M.
and is 250 Miles diftant from *Savannah* by
Water; fmall Boats can go 300 Miles further, to the *Cherokees*.

THERE is already a confiderable Trade
in the River; and there is in this Town a
Court-Houfe, a Goal, a Store-Houfe, a
large Houfe for receiving the *Indians*, a
Wharf or Bridge, a Guard-Houfe, and
fome other publick Buildings; a publick
Garden of ten Acres cleared, fenced, and
planted with Orange-Trees, Mulberry-
Trees, Vines, fome Olives which thrive
very well, Peaches, Apples, &c.

IT

It muſt be confeſſed, that Oranges have not ſo univerſally thriven with us, as was expected, by Reaſon of ſome ſevere Blaſts by Froſts in the Spring; yet divers with proper Care have preſerved them; and as we ſee them grow and thrive well, with many of our Neighbours of *Carolina* to the Northward, we are convinced that they will with us alſo, as ſoon as we are become more perfect in the Knowledge of propagating them in a right Manner; in order to which frequent Experiments are making; and we have already diſcovered not only what Kind of Soil agrees beſt with them, but alſo that they flouriſh moſt when they grow under Foreſt Trees, whereby we imagine they are protected from Blaſts; and 'tis obſerved, that they take no Harm from the Droppings of any, except the Pine; which ſuffers nothing to grow near it, unleſs of its own Kind.

Notwithstanding the Quantity of Silk, hitherto made, has not been great, yet it increaſes, and will more and more conſiderably, as the Mulberry-Trees grow, whereof there are great Numbers yearly planted.

Vines likewiſe of late are greatly increaſed, many People appearing to have an Emulation of outdoing their Neighbours; and this Year has produced a conſiderable Quantity of very fine Grapes, whereof one

Planter

Planter in particular made a Trial, to fee what Kind of Wine they would make, which he put into a large Stone-Bottle, and made a Prefent of it to the General; who upon tafting, faid he found it to be fome-thing of the Nature of a fmall *French* White Wine, with an agreeable Flavour; and feveral Perfons here, who have lived for-merly in Countries where there are a Plenty of Vineyards, do affirm, that all young Vines produce fmall Wines at firft, and the Strength and Goodnefs of it increafes as the Vines grow older.

THREE Miles up the River there is an *Indian* Town, and at fix Miles Diftance are feveral confiderable Plantations: At ten Miles Diftance are fome more, and at fif-teen Miles Diftance is a little Village, called *Abercorn*.

ABOVE that, on the *Carolina* Side, is the Town of *Puryfburgh*, twenty-two Miles from *Savannah*; and on the *Georgia* Side, twelve Miles from *Puryfburgh*, is the Town of *Ebenezer*, which thrives very much; there are very good Houfes built for each of the Minifters, and an Orphan-Houfe; and they have partly framed Houfes, and partly Huts, neatly built, and formed into regular Streets; they have a great deal of Cattle and Corn-Ground, fo that they fell Provifions at *Savannah*; for they raife much more than they can confume.

THIRTY Miles above *Ebenezer*, on the *Carolina* Side, lies the *Palachocolas* Fort: Five Miles above the *Palachocolas*, on *Georgia* Side, lies the *Euchee* Town (or *Mount Pleasant*) to which about a hundred *Indians* belong; but few of them stay now in the Town, they chusing rather to live dispersed. All the Land from *Ebenezer* to the River *Briers* belongs to those *Indians*, who will not part with the same, therefore it cannot be planted.

ONE hundred and forty-four Miles above *Mount Pleasant*, on the *Carolina* Side, is *Silver Bluff*, where there is another Settlement of *Euchee Indians:* On both Sides of the River are Fields of Corn planted by them.

THIRTY Miles above *Silver Bluff* is *New Windsor*, formerly known by the Name of *Savannah* Town, or *Moore's* Fort, where there are but two or three Families on the *Carolina* Side, and a small Fort.

SEVEN Miles above *New Windsor*, on the *Georgia* Side, lies the Town of *Augusta*, just below the Falls; this was laid out by the Trustees Orders in the Year 1735, which has thriven prodigiously; there are several Warehouses thoroughly well furnished with Goods for the *Indian* Trade, and five large Boats belonging to the different Inhabitants of the Town, which can carry about nine or ten thousand Weight

of

of Deer-Skins each, making four or five Voyages at leaft in a Year to *Charles-Town*, for exporting to *England*; and the Value of each Cargo is computed to be from 12 to 1500*l*. Sterling. Hither all the *Englifh* Traders, with their Servants, refort in the Spring; and 'tis computed above two thoufand Horfes come thither at that Seafon; and the Traders, Packhorfe-men, Servants, Townfmen, and others, depending upon that Bufinefs, are moderately computed to be fix hundred white Men, who live by their Trade, carrying upon Packhorfes all Kinds of proper *Englifh* Goods; for which the *Indians* pay in Deer-Skins, Bever, and other Furs; each *Indian* Hunter is reckoned to get three hundred Weight of Deer-Skins in a Year. This is a very advantageous Trade to *England*, fince it is moftly paid for in Woollen and Iron.

ABOVE this Town to the North-Weft, and on the *Georgia* Side of the River, the *Cherokees* live, in the Valley of the *Appelachin* Mountains; they were about five thoufand Warriors; but laft Year it is computed they loft a thoufand, partly by the Small-Pox, and partly (as they themfelves fay) by too much Rum brought from *Carolina*. The *French* are ftriving to get this Nation from us, which if they do, *Carolina* muft be fupported by a vaft Number of Troops, or loft: But as long as we

keep

keep the Town of *Augufta*, our Party in the *Cherokees* can be fo eafily furnifhed with Arms, Ammunition and Neceffaries, that the *French* will not be able to gain any Ground there.

THE *Creek Indians* live to the Weftward of this Town. Their chief Town is the *Cowetas*, two hundred Miles from *Augufta*, and one hundred and twenty Miles from the neareft *French* Fort. The *Lower Creeks* confift of about a thoufand, and the *Upper Creeks* of about feven hundred Warriors, upon the Edge of whofe Country, the *French* Fort of *Albamahs* lies : They are efteemed to be fincerely attached to his Majefty's Intereft.

BEYOND the *Creeks* lie the brave *Chicke-faws*, who inhabit near the *Miffifipi* River, and poffefs the Banks of it; thefe have re-fifted both the Bribes and Arms of the *French*, and Traders fent by us live amongft them.

AT *Augufta* there is a handfome Fort, where there is a fmall Garrifon of about twelve or fifteen Men, befides Officers; and one Reafon that drew the Traders to fettle the Town of *Augufta*, was the Safety they received from this Fort, which ftands upon high Ground on the Side of the River *Savannah*, which is there one hundred and forty Yards wide, and very deep; another Reafon was the Richnefs

and

and Fertility of the Land. The great Value of this Town of *Augusta* occasioned the General to have a Path marked out, through the Woods, from thence to *Old Ebenezer*; and the *Cherokee Indians* have marked out one from thence to their Nation, so that Horsemen now can ride from the Town of *Savannah* to the Nation of *Cherokees*, and any other of the *Indian* Nations, all on the *Georgia* Side of the River; but there are some bad Places which ought to be causewayed and made good, and which the General says he has not yet Capacity to do. This Road begins to be frequented, and will every Day be more and more so, and by it the *Cherokee Indians* can at any Time come down to our Assistance.

At *Old Ebenezer* there is a Cow-Pen, where the Trustees have a great Number of Cattle, and 'tis hoped with Care they will amount to six or seven hundred Head in another Year: But they were much neglected, there not being Horses or Men sufficient to drive up the young and outlying Cattle.

This is the Situation of the Settlements upon the River, at the Mouth of which lies the Island of *Tybee*, with the Light-House, which has been of the greatest Use to all Ships falling in with this Part of *America*. But from *Savannah* Southward,

there

there are several Plantations (besides the Villages of *Hampstead* and *Highgate)* several of which are settled by such of the Inhabitants of the Town, as being able to purchase Cattle, have petitioned for Leases of Lands, and are settled upon those Lands by the General's Permission, until the Trustees Pleasure be known concerning the Leases: The Terms they propose, is the Lease to be for twenty-one Years, renewable every seven Years, upon paying one Year's Purchase of the improved Value; the first seven Years to be free, and no Fine paid for the first Renewal. Besides these Settlements, there are some others of five hundred Acres *per* Grant from the Trust, which extend as far as the *Ogeechy* River; upon which River lies *Fort Argyll*, in such a Situation, as is intended thereby to command all the Passes in that Part of the Province.

THE next is *Darien*, where the *Scots* Highlanders are settled; the Buildings are mostly Huts, but tight and warm; and they have a little Fort: They have been industrious in Planting, and have got into driving of Cattle, for the Supply of the Regiment, *&c.* but this last Year most of them going voluntarily into the War, little was done at home, where their Families remained.

BELOW

BELOW the Town of *Darien*, is the Town of *Frederica*, where there is a ſtrong Fort, and Store-Houſes, many good Buildings in the Town, ſome of which are Brick; there is a Meadow near adjoining that is ditch'd in, of about three hundred and twenty Acres, of which there is good Hay made. The People have not planted much there this Year, occaſioned by the War ſo near their Doors, and being chiefly Tradeſmen, who make more by working, or ſelling to the Camp, than they can by Planting. There are ſome little Villages upon the Iſland of St. *Simon*'s, and ſome very handſome Houſes built by the Officers of the Regiment; and there has been Pot-Herbs, Pulſe, and Fruit, produced upon the Iſland, of great Uſe towards ſupplying the Town and Garriſon: But Corn, Beer, and Meat, they have from elſewhere.

BETWEEN this Iſland and *Jekyll Iſland*, is an Inlet of the Sea, called *Jekyll Sound*, which is a very fine Harbour, and is one of the beſt Entries the *Engliſh* have to the Southward of *Virginia*. This is an excellent Station for Ships to cruize on the *Spaniards*, it commanding the homeward-bound Trade, which muſt come through the Gulph of *Florida*, and near St. *Simon*'s; the Entry lies in 31 D. 10 M. The Place is barred, but upon the Bar there is Water ſufficient every Tide to carry in Twenty-

Gun

Gun Ships; and taking the beſt Opportunity, Forty-Gun Ships may be carried in to refit; — a great Conveniency to a Squadron in this Place. Upon *Jekyll Iſland* there is but very little good Land, not above three or four hundred Acres, the reſt being ſandy Sea-Beach. Mr. *Horton* has his Lot upon this Iſland, and has made great Improvements there. To the Southward of *Jekyll* lies the Iſland of *Cumberland,* and the Fort of St. *Andrew's,* ſituated upon a fine commanding Ground; and on the S. E. of the ſame Iſland, is another ſtrong Fort called *Fort William,* which commands *Amelia Sound,* and the inland Paſſage from *Auguſtine.* The next Iſland is *Amelia*; beyond that is St. *John's,* one of the *Spaniſh* Outguards; and between forty and fifty Miles from that is *Auguſtine.*

WE are now fully acquainted with the Colony, and what it will produce; the inland Part is hilly, till it riſes into Mountains, where all Kinds of Timber grow. Near the Sea the Ground is more level and flat, where Laurels, Cedars, Cyprus, Bays, and Live Oak, are of the Size of Timber-Trees: Among the Shrubs, ſome of the principal are Pomegranates, which will grow well in Hedges, Myrtle, prickly Pears, Shumach, Saſſafraſs, China Root, ſeveral Sorts of Snake Root, *&c.* There is commonly black Mould in the low Lands;

Lands; the rifing Ground is frequently
Clay, where Oak and Hickery moftly
grow; as it alfo does in a great Part of the
flat Land that is dry, where Walnut, Afh,
Gum-Tree, Oak of feveral Kinds, Hickery, Beech, wild Cherries, &c. are in great
Plenty to be found. The higher Lands are
of a fandy Surface, where Pines ufually
grow, all Parts producing Trees of fome
Kind or other, except the Savannahs, and
Marfhes, which bear Grafs; and many of
the low Land Swamps covered with Canes,
which are excellent Feed for Cattle in the
Winter. Where the Oak and Hickery
grow, the Soil is in general of a ftrong
Nature, and very well efteemed for Planting, being found by Experience to produce
the beft Crops of *Indian* Corn, and moft
Sorts of Grain, except Rice, which thrives
beft in fwampy Ground : This is only fpo-
ken of the lower Parts of *Georgia*, which
reaches from the Sea-Shore to the Foot of
the Hills, being a flat Country of fixty or
feventy Miles, or more, in Breadth. The
Hill Country is very different, there being
Marble, Chalk, Gravel, Rocks, and all
the fame Variety of Soil that is in *Europe*;
with refpect to the Proportion of the different Kinds of Soil, it cannot be given,
unlefs the Whole were furveyed; but the
American Dialect diftinguifhes Land into
Pine, Oak and Hickery, Swamp, Savannah,

nah, and Marſh. Near the Town of *Savannah* we have found Stone, which is
dug for Building; as there is alſo good
Clay, whereof Bricks are made; and a
Pottery Work is carried on with Succeſs,
where common Ware for moſt Uſes is
made in good Plenty, and exported to the
neighbouring Provinces; and the Maſter,
who is of an enterprizing Genius, has un-
dertaken, as ſoon as he has made proper
Furnaces, to make a ſuperfine Sort, of
ſuch as ſhall not be inferior to *Porcelian* it-
ſelf; but a little Time will diſcover his
further Performances.

THE Coaſt is low, with a hard, ſandy
Beach: When we approach it at twenty-
five Leagues Diſtance, we find Ground in
twenty-five Fathom Water, and it ſhoals
gradually to the Shore; the Sounding being
ſo regular, makes it a ſafe Coaſt to fall in
with, having good Anchoring all along,
and no Rocks. The Mouths of the Rivers *Savannah* and *Alatamaha* make a great
Number of Iſlands, and the Entries between them form good Harbours. To the
Southward of *Tybee* are the following Entries, *viz. Waſſaw, Oſſebah,* St. *Catharine's,
Sapello, Doboy,* St. *Simon's,* which is the
North-Entry to *Frederica; Jekyll Sound,*
which is the South-Entry to *Frederica,* to
which Place the Channel is navigable,
from the ordinary Place of Anchoring in
the

the Sound, for Ships of a good Burden up
to the Town.

THE Staple of the Country of *Georgia*
being prefumed, and intended to be, principally Silk and Wine, every Year confirms
more our Hopes of fucceeding in thofe
two, from the great Increafe (as has
been before obferved) of the Vines and
Mulberry-Trees, wherein Perfeverance only
can bring it to Perfection. Several other
Things might be produced, and perhaps
more immediately profitable to the Planters; but it is apprehended, that it is not
any Bufinefs of this Colony, nor any Benefit to the Trade of *England*, to interfere
with what other *Englifh* Plantations have
produced, fuch as Rice, &c.

As the Boundaries of the Colony are
now known, together with the Climate,
and Manner of Agriculture, more might
be done henceforward in one Year, than
could in feveral Years before we attained
to that Knowledge; but our People are
weak, being decreafed, by great Numbers
having been decoyed away to other Colonies: Many having taken to Idlenefs, upon
fhutting up the Store went away; but
thofe who ftayed, and now remain, are
ftill a Body of the moft valuable People,
that find Means to live comfortably, fome
by their Trades, fome by Planting, and
raifing live Stock, and fome by their Labour,

bour, either by Land or Water; and one of thofe remaining, are worth three that left us, for fuch Work: And if an Embarkation was to come in with the next Year, it would be of great Service to the Colony, the *Saltzburghers* wifhing for more of their Countrymen, and having been very induftrious.

THE Perfons fent from *England* on the Charity were of the Unfortunate, many of whom have by their Induftry proved that they deferved better, and have thriven; many alfo fhewed they were brought into thofe Misfortunes by their own Faults; and when thofe who quitted their own Country to avoid Labour, faw Labour ftand before their Eyes in *Georgia*, they were eafily perfuaded to live in *Carolina* by Cunning, rather than work: This has been a great Misfortune alfo upon many Perfons, who brought over Servants indented to ferve them, for a certain Number of Years, who being picked up in the Streets of *London*, or fome fuch Manner, their Mafters found them unfit for Labour, and many of them took fuch Opportunities as they could get, to defert and fly into *Carolina*, where they could be protected. Indeed, good and bad which came from *England*, were moftly Inhabitants of Towns there; but fuch feldom turn out good Hufbandmen with their own Hands; yet fome of them proved very ufe-

ufeful in a new Colony, fince they moft
readily compofe Towns, which is the firft
Thing neceffary to be a Receptacle for new
Comers: And from thence, when all Demands of Labour, for Building and Trade
are fupplied, the laborious People may en-
large into the Country, and raife Provifions for the Ufe of the Towns: Whereas,
if the firft were all labouring Countrymen,
they would naturally difperfe to the moft
fertile Land, and perhaps fucceed for a
While; but for Want of Neighbourhood
and Markets, would force moft of them to
remove, and the Country remain little or
nothing the better improved, as it happened in *Virginia*, till the Government,
with great Difficulty at laft, raifed Towns
in that Province.

It ought not here to be paffed over,
how ready the Country is to receive a
Number of *German* Families, accuftomed
to Hufbandry, fuch as ufually come once
a Year down the *Rhine* to *Holland*, and
embark thence for *America*, or the *Eaft-
Indies*; fome of thefe we have already had
Experience of, infomuch that the People
here would take off a good Number of
them: And it would be of great Service (as
we apprehend) to this Colony, at prefent,
to fend a Ship over, loaden with *Germans*,
on the fame Terms Mr. *Hope* does to *Philadelphia*, only taking Care that Provifions
for

for them on their Paſſage be more plentiful, and that they are leſs crowded than
on board his Ships: The Terms are, they
pay Half their Paſſage themſelves on em-
barking, and ſix Weeks after their Arrival,
to pay the other Half, which they generally do, with private Contracts to People;
but in caſe they do not, then they may be
bound by the Ship's Maſter for four or five
Years, if they are above twenty-one Years
of Age; but if under, they may be bound
until the Age of twenty-one if Men, and
eighteen if Girls. It muſt be at the ſame
Time confeſs'd, that divers of theſe Fo-
reigners have, during the Time of their
Servitude, ſhewn themſelves of a dogged
Diſpoſition, ſurly and obſtinate, diſcover-
ing an Averſeneſs to their Maſters Orders,
which proceeds (as we imagine) from a
Diſlike of their being ſubject to Strangers;
whilſt others again have behaved well; but
it may be alledged with Truth, that when,
or whereſoever among us, any of them
have worked for their own Benefit, they
are indefatigable, and out-done by none,
which joined with great Parſimony, fits
them for excellent Settlers when free.

To enable the induſtrious *Engliſh* Settlers
to go on with Planting, who are truly deſirous of cultivating Land; we humbly
conceive nothing could be a greater Inducement to it, than that the honourable
Truſtees

Truſtees would pleaſe to import yearly, ſo
long as they ſee good, a Number of *Engliſh* or *Welch* Servants, ſuch as are uſed to
hard Labour in the Country, and Strangers
to *London*, to be contracted with in *England*, to ſerve the Truſtees for five Years,
from two to four Pounds yearly Wages,
according to their Ability, for finding
themſelves in Apparel. Thoſe Servants, on
their Arrival, to be hired by the Inhabitants for one Year, the Perſon hiring to
pay over and above the contracted Wages,
one Pound yearly to the Truſtees, ſo that
in five Years the Paſſage-Money will be
paid. And to enable the Planters to pay
the ſaid Wages, it is humbly propoſed,
that a Bounty be ſettled on every Product
of the Land, *viz.* Corn, Peaſe, Potatoes,
Wine, Silk, Cotton, Flax, *&c.* to what
Value the honourable Truſt ſhall judge
meet to be limited in the following, or any
other Manner, *viz.* For the firſt
Years the ſaid Bounty to be payable for
Corn, Peaſe, Potatoes, *&c.* only; and
thenceforward to ceaſe wholly, and the
Reſidue of Years wherein any Bounty
ſhould be allowed, to be payable only for
Silk, Wine, Oil, *&c.* by which Means the
Planter ſo aſſiſted might be able to live,
whilſt at the ſame Time he propagates
Vines, Mulberry-Trees, *&c.* from which
he can expect no immediate Benefit before
they

they come to fome Maturity. A Rule to be made, that they who hire the faid Servants fhall employ them only in Plantation-Work of their own, and not let them out at Hire to work at handicraft Trades, or any other Bufinefs, &c. That each Servant fhall ferve one whole Year; and if they part at the Year's End, he fhall find himfelf another Mafter within   Days to ferve for one Year alfo, and fo on to the End of their refpective Times to ferve; by which Means good Mafters will not want good Servants, and 'twill be a great Means to make other Mafters become good, in order to get good Servants, or elfe be content with the bad, or none. If any Difputes arife between Mafters and Servants, fuch to be determined by the Magiftrates, according to the Laws of *England*, wherein the Magiftrate concerned as a Party fhall not appear as a Judge, or offer to interfere with the Opinion of the others, but acquiefce in their Determination, if it happens to be in Favour of the Servant, whom they ought to defend from cruel Ufage, and where they find fuch evil Treatment either thro' too fevere Correction, or want of fufficient wholfome Food, according to the Cuftom of the Colony, the Magiftrates to have Power of vacating fuch Services, and obliging the Servants to find another Mafter.

THE

THE kind Intention of the honourable Truftees to extend the Tenure of Lands in the Manner propofed (as fignify'd to their Secretary here) gave great Satisfaction to all reafonable Perfons who feem'd to defire no more, and only wifh to find that ratify'd, which they apprehend to be not yet done, and that occafions fome Anxiety about it.

WHETHER thefe Helps, or whatever other, the honourable Truftees fhall be pleas'd to afford us, the Ability of the Inhabitants to fupport themfelves muft ftill in a great Meafure depend on the Induftry and Frugality of each. Divers in the Province who underftand Planting, and are already fettled, provided they can attain to fome live Stock, can and do fupport themfelves. Men working for Hire, Boat-men, Pack-horfe-men, &c. fupport themfelves very well, if they will work; and more fuch would, were they to be found. Shopkeepers, Tradef-men, and Artificers, fuch as Tallow-Chand-lers, Soap-Boilers, Brafiers, Sadlers, Shoe-makers, Tanners, &c. live very well on their Bufinefs here, and many more might, were there more Merchants to import Goods for fupplying the *Indian* Traders, which would increafe the Refort to *Savannah*; whereas thofe Traders are now obliged to get the greateft Part of what they want from *Charles-Town* in *Carolina*. New Planters, and fuch as go on upon particular

Improvements, fuch as Wine, Silk, &c. will need fome Affiftance. Magiftrates, Conftables, and Tything-men, and others whofe Time is taken up in the publick Service, require fome Allowance for the fame. It is alfo needful for the Well-being of the Colony, that Roads fhould be maintain'd: Pofts for communicating of Letters, and Forts upon the Frontiers, as well towards the *Indians* as *Spaniards*, be fupported: As likewife other publick Works, which the People here are in no Degree able to bear.

WHEN the Eaft Part of the Province of *Georgia* was taken Poffeffion of under the Truftees Charter by Mr. *Oglethorpe*, according to the Limits of the *Britifh* Dominions in *America*, Forts were erected upon the Extremities to keep up Marks of Poffeffion: The Strength and Materials were of fuch a Nature, as the Men he had with him could make, and fufficient for Defence againft any Strength that could be brought againft them by the neighbouring *Indians*, or *Spaniards* in *Florida*.

THE firft Foundation of the Colony was upon Tenures, by which each Lot was to be occupied by a Freeholder, obliged to take Arms for the Defence of the Colony; and this Militia, with the Affiftance of our friendly *Indians*, held the Colony againft all Attempts of the *Spaniards* from

Auguf-

Auguſtine, who alarmed them almoſt every Spring, pretending a Claim, and therefore a Right to invade, without being ſaid to infringe the Peace; but did not take one Foot of Ground from us.

In the Beginning of the Year 1738, great Preparations were made at the *Havannah*, and Troops were ſent from thence and *Old Spain* to *Auguſtine*, for the taking Poſſeſſion (as they call'd it) of that Part of *Carolina* in which *Georgia* was comprehended, and which they gave out belong'd to them. Upon the Truſtees having early Notice of theſe great Preparations, they applied to his Majeſty to take upon him the Protection of the Colony, which in its Infancy was unable to repel ſo great a Force. His Majeſty thereupon ordered a Regiment to be raiſed, and poſted on the *Spaniſh* Frontiers, ſince which the War is broke out, and that Regiment, with the Aſſiſtance of Troops and *Indians* raiſed in *Georgia* and *Carolina*, in Conjunction with a Squadron of Men of War, attack'd *Auguſtine*, and after raiſing the Siege of that Place, remain'd in the Poſſeſſion of the Frontiers, as before the War; but for the Defence of the Colony now, it is neceſſary to have Veſſels that can act in ſhoal Water, on ſo large and extended a Frontier towards the Sea, and Rangers who can ride the Woods; as alſo Artillery, and all other

Things

Things neceſſarily appertaining thereto, and Means for augmenting our Fortifications equal to the increas'd Strength of the *Spaniards*.

Savannah, Nov. 10, 1740.

WE whoſe Names are hereunto ſub-ſcribed, being duly ſworn in open Court, do declare, that the above State of the Province of *Georgia* is true, according to the beſt of our own Knowledge, and from the moſt certain Informations we could obtain from others; and do deſire, that the Seal of this Court may be affixed thereto.

* Pat. Graham	George Johnſon
* Joſ. Fitzwalter	Samuel Parker
* James Carwells	Thomas Palmer
* Thomas Upton	William Stephens
* Giles Becu	Henry Parker
* Thomas Egerton	Thomas Jones
* Thomas Cundell	Samuel Mercer
Anthony Camuſe	James Campbell
John Burton	John Rae
Joſ. Pavey	Noble Jones
Robert Hainks	Thomas Young
John Mellidge	Thomas Ellis.
Tho. Bayley (Smith)	

N. B. Thoſe ſeven mark'd with *, at their own voluntary Deſire, were admitted to ſign it, and were ſworn before the Magiſtrates out of Court.

The

The Depofition of Lieutenant George Dunbar, *taken upon the Holy Evangelifts, be-*
fore the Recorder of the Town of Frederica, Jan. 20, 1738-9.

THIS Deponent fays, That he arri-
rived in *Georgia* the Beginning of
June laft, with the firft Detachment of
General *Oglethorpe's* Regiment ; and from
that Time, to the Beginning of *Auguft;*
all the Carpenters of the faid three Companies, and a certain Number of other Soldiers, were employ'd in building Clap-board
Huts for the faid Companies, and the other
Soldiers were employ'd in unloading Veffels
and Boats loaded with Clap-boards, and
other Neceffaries for Building, and Provifions of different Kinds, often up to their
Necks in Water : They were alfo employ'd
in carrying Clap-boards, *&c.* upon their
Backs to the Camp, in clearing Ground
from Roots of Trees, *&c.* for a Parade,
burning the Wood and Rubbifh upon it,
carrying of Bricks, and burning Lime :
And the Artifts who were excufed from
thefe Works, wrought at their own Trades,
without ftanding ftill, by Reafon of Heat.
The Hours of Labour were from Day-
Light, till between Eleven and Twelve ;
and from between One and Two, and
fometimes between Two and Three, till
Dark.

Dark, All that Time the Men kept fo healthy, that often no Man in the Camp ailed in the leaft, and none died except one Man, who came fick on board, and never worked at all; nor did I hear, that any of the Men ever made the Heat a Pretence for not Working.

AND this Deponent further fays, That he has been often in *America*, and frequently heard, that in the Negro Colonies, the Hire of White Men is more than that of Negroes. And this Deponent knows, that in *South-Carolina* White Ship-Carpenters and Caulkers have about one Third more Wages than a Negro of the fame Trade or Profeffion, this Deponent having often paid Wages to both; and alfo knows there is the aforefaid Difference in many Handicrafts, and verily believes it is fo in all; and affirms, that the fame is owing to the White Men exceeding the Negroes in the fame Profeffions, both in Quantity and Quality of their Work.

GEORGE DUNBAR.

Sworn before me the
Day and Year above
written,
    FRANCIS MOORE.

Extract

Extract of a Letter from Mr. Thomas Jones *at* Savannah *in* Georgia, *to the Truftees Accomptant, dated* July 1, 1741.

THE Truftees *German* Servants in general behave well, and are induftrious: Of thefe, eight or ten Families are more remarkably fo, and have this laft Year purchas'd a good Stock of Cattle, fome having fix Cows, the leaft two; and each having a Garden, where they raife fome Corn, Peafe, Pompions, Potatoes, &c. which with the Milk of their Cows is the chief Part of their Food: They are at little Expence in Cloathing; but this expofes them to the Envy and Hatred of our Negro-Mongers, and fuch who feek the Extirpation of the Colony, as well as of the drunken, idle Sort amongft us.

I AM informed by *Francis Harris* and *William Ruffell* (who are very converfant with them, and can talk the *German* Tongue) That they have lately joined, in a Letter writ and fent to their Friends and Acquaintance in *Germany*, perfuading them to come to *Georgia*, where they may, by their Induftry, live in greater Plenty, and more comfortably than they can elfewhere.

THESE Servants are very defirous, That (when the Time of their Service is expired) they

M m 4

they may have Lands allotted them within twelve or fifteen Miles of *Savannah*; where they may bring Things by Land-Carriage in a Vicinage, and that they may make one common Fence (as the People of *Ebenezer* have done) and be affifting to one another.

The Copy of a Letter from the Reverend Mr. Frederick Michael Ziegenhagen, German *Chaplain to his Majefty, dated at* Kenfington, January 11, 1741-2, *and fent to the Truftees for Eftablifhing the Colony of* Georgia *in* America.

GENTLEMEN,

HAVING feen Paragraphs in Print reprefenting the *Saltzburghers* as being uneafy with their Settlement at *Ebenezer* in *Georgia*, and defirous to remove therefrom; and fearing fuch Reports (if credited) might give juft Offence to your Honours their Guardians, as well as to their Benefactors in *Germany*, and thereby deprive them from having yours, and their Favours continued.

I THOUGHT it my indifpenfible Duty to acquaint your Honours, That by all the Letters and Journals I have received fince their Settlement at *New Ebenezer*, they have exprefs'd quite different Sentiments;

3   and

and not to trouble you with many Particulars, I beg Leave herewith to inclose you two Extracts of the latest Accounts I received from them in *November* last.

Extract of a Letter from the Reverend Mr.
Boltzius *at* Ebenezer, *dated the* 23d *of*
July, 1741, *to the Reverend Dr.* Francke,
Professor of Divinity at Hall.

" TOGETHER with these spiritual
" Blessings, and the salutary Ef-
" fect of the Word of God to the Con-
" version of many Souls, we enjoy also
" this Year, by the Mercy of God, many
" temporal good Things.

" The present War, and the Burden of
" it, hath not affected us yet, and we
" don't feel the least of it; and in the
" great Dearness the Colony suffered last
" Year, we have not been in Want of
" necessary Provisions. As to the present
" Year, we have a very hopeful Prospect
" of a good Harvest, every Thing in the
" Fields and Gardens growing so delight-
" ful, as our Eyes hardly have seen in this
" Country before. * If *Isaac*, by the Bless-
" ing of the Lord, received from what he
" had sowed, an hundred Fold, I believe, I
" dare say, to the Praise of the great Mercy
" of God over us, our *Saltzburghers* will
" get

* Gen. xxvi. 12.

" get thousand Fold, notwithstanding that
" the Corn, when it came out of the
" Ground, was eaten quite up two or three
" Times by the Worms, of which nobody
" can hardly form a right Idea, except he
" sees it with his own Eyes. Wheat, Rice,
" and other Grain, must be sowed very
" thin, because each Grain brings forth
" fifty, an hundred, or more Stalks and
" Ears. The Land is really very fruitful,
" if the Sins of the Inhabitants, and the
" Curse of God for such Sins, doth not
" eat it up, which was formerly the
" unhappy Case of the blessed Land of
" *Canaan.*

" AND I am heartily sorry to acquaint
" you, that I don't find in some of the
" Inhabitants of the Colony, a due Thank-
" fulness for, and Contentment with the
" many Benefits bestowed on them for se-
" veral Years together; although those who
" are industrious, and will labour for their
" Maintenance, may, as we do, live con-
" tentedly, and subsist under the Blessing
" of God, promised by St. *Paul, Heb.* xiii.
" 5. *I will never leave thee, nor forsake*
" *thee.* Which Blessing the Idle and Un-
" thankful are not intitled to."

Extract

Extract out of the Journal of Mr. Boltzius, *Minister of the Gospel at* Ebenezer
in Georgia.

"THE 10th of *August*, 1741. We
" have this Year Plenty of Peach-
" es, and as this Fruit doth not keep,
" some of our People try to make a cer-
" tain Sort of Brandy of them, others
" give them to the Swine : This is more
" than any body could have promised to
" himself, or others, some Years ago. Even
" at this Time, when I am writing this, a
" Man brings a large Dish of blue Grapes
" to me, grown wild in the Woods ; they
" are of a sweet Taste, and pretty like
" our *European* Grapes ; that I am very
" apt to believe, the wild Vine-Trees, if
" properly managed, would give good
" Wine. Thanks be to our gracious God,
" who gives us here every good Thing for
" our Support.
" The 9th of *September*, 1741. Some
" Time ago I wrote to an honoured Friend
" in *Europe*, That the Land in this Coun-
" try, if well managed and laboured, brings
" forth, by the Blessings of God, not only
" hundred Fold, but thousand Fold ; and
" I this Day was confirmed therein. A
" Woman having two Years ago picked
" out of *Indian* Corn, bought at *Purys-*
" *burgh*,

" *burgh*, no more than three Grains of
" Rye (called here *German* Corn) and
" planting them here at *Ebenezer*, one of
" thefe Grains produced an hundred and
" feventy Stalks and Ears, and the three
" Grains yielded to her a Bag of Corn as
" large as a Coat-Pocket, the Grains where-
" of were good and full grown; and fhe
" defired me to fend Part of them to a
" kind Benefactor in *Europe*. One of our
" *Saltzburghers* brought to me alfo a like
" Bag of Beans, all grown out of one
" Bean.

" TRUE it is, notwithftanding the Fer-
" tility of the Land, the firft Tillagers of
" it muft undergo and ftruggle with great
" Difficulties; but them that come after
" them will reap the Benefit thereof, if
" they go on to do their Labour in the
" Fear of God.

" THE Land is able to provide every
" good Thing, and more particularly is
" Pafturage very plenteous."

INDEX

INDEX

TO THE

SECOND VOLUME.

A,

B.

INDEX

INDEX.

Court

INDEX.

INDEX.

E.

EVANS, a young Man, kill'd by an Accident 53

Ewen, *William,* leaves off cultivating his Lot to work at the Orphan-Houfe 427

Eyles, Mr. Surgeon to the Regiment, kill'd in a Duel by Enfign *Tolfon* 403

Eyre, Mr. fent by General *Oglethorpe* to the *Cherokee Indians* 146. Returns to *Savannah,* his Conduct relating to the *Indians* 206. Goes to the South 210. Goes again to the *Cherokee* Nation 265. Brings a large Body of them to the Siege of *Augustine* 338, 342, 344

F.

FAllowfield fworn in fecond Bailiff at *Savannah* 159. An Account of his Conduct 236. Vifited by the Club of Malecontents 351. His Conduct relating to a Schooner feiz'd 241, 245, 248. His Plantation on the *Isle of Hope,* an Account of it 443

Fennel, Capt. his Relation of the Pofture of Affairs at *Havannah* 78. Arms a Sloop to go to *Jamaica* 176

Fofter, *Elisha,* a Tything-man, his Conduct in relation to Capt. *Davis* 126, 222. Goes a privateering with Capt. *Davis* 236

Freeholders, the Appearance of them at *Savannah* 81. Seventy of them deliver in their Claims of Lots to the Court 463. Seventy others deliver in their Claims 476

French, Col. *Bull*'s Account of their Defigns

INDEX.

J.

INDEX.

J.

K.

INDEX.

L.

M.

INDEX.

INDEX.

O.

P.

INDEX.

INDEX.

INDEX.

T.

INDEX.

T.

U.

INDEX.

INDEX.

F I N I S.